The Study of P...
A Source Book — Volume 1:
Perspectives

THE STUDY OF PRIMARY EDUCATION SOURCE BOOKS

The four volumes in this series are:

Volume 1   Perspectives
               Compiled by Colin Conner with Brenda Lofthouse
Volume 2   The Curriculum
               Compiled by Brenda Lofthouse
Volume 3   School Organization and Management
               Compiled by Geoff Southworth with Brenda Lofthouse
Volume 4   Classroom and Teaching Studies
               Compiled by Marion Dadds with Brenda Lofthouse

The complete contents for each volume are included at the end of this book.

The Study of Primary Education
A Source Book — Volume 1:
Perspectives

Second edition compiled by

Colin Conner

with

Brenda Lofthouse

(*First edition compiled by*
Colin Richards
with
Rosemary Clayfield
and
Brenda Lofthouse)

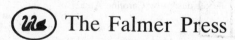 The Falmer Press

(A member of the Taylor & Francis Group)
London · New York · Philadelphia

UK   The Falmer Press, Rankine Road, Basingstoke, Hampshire, RG24 0PR

USA   The Falmer Press, Taylor & Francis Inc., 1900 Frost Road, Suite 101, Bristol, PA 19007

First published 1990

British Library Cataloguing in Publication Data
The study of primary education. — 2nd ed. *Compiled by Colin Conner with Brenda Lofthouse.*
Vol. 1, Perspectives.
1. Great Britain. Primary education
I. Conner, Colin II. Lofthouse, Brenda
372.941

ISBN 1-85000-734-9
ISBN 1-85000-779-9 pbk

Library of Congress Cataloging in Publication Data
The Study of primary education: a source book — Volume 1: Perspectives / compiled by Colin Conner with Brenda Lofthouse. — 2nd edn.

    Includes bibliographical references.
    Contents: Vol. 1. Perspectives — v. 2. The curriculum — v. 3. School organization and management — v. 4. Classroom and teaching studies.
    ISBN 1-85000-734-9 (v. 1) — ISBN 1-85000-779-9 (pbk.: v. 1)
    1. Education, Elementary. 2. Education, Elementary — Great Britain. I. Conner, Colin. II. Lofthouse, Brenda.
LB1555.S887 1990
372—dc20

                      90-33099
                      CIP

Jacket design by Caroline Archer

Typeset in 10/12 pt Times
by Graphicraft Typesetters Ltd., Hong Kong
Burgess Science Press,
Basingstoke

Contents

Contents

Contents

Contents

Contents

General Introduction

The nature of primary school teaching is difficult to appreciate for those who have no experience of it, except as a pupil. From a child's view, it seems straightforward enough. In reality, the task of the teacher is a complex and demanding one, requiring a wide range of skills and personal qualities, as well as extensive knowledge. The four volumes of these source books have been compiled to help in the professional development of primary school teachers, but the nature of the help they can give needs to be appreciated by potential readers.

In the report, *Postgraduate Certificate in Education Courses for Teachers in Primary and Middle Schools: A Further Consultative Report* (1982), the Universities Council for the Education of Teachers spelt out five elements in the professional 'equipment' of teachers of younger children: (1) techniques; (2) curricular knowledge; (3) professional knowledge; (4) personal and interpersonal skills or qualities; and (5) constructive revaluation. The compilers of these source books acknowledge the importance of all five elements but do not believe that any book or series of books can do justice to all of them. The source books focus on two: they contribute both to primary teachers' professional knowledge and to the development of their ability to re-evaluate their own experience and the enterprise of primary education itself. They do this by introducing readers to extracts from 'official' publications and from academic material which put primary education in context and which introduce readers to many of the important theoretical, yet professional, issues that need to be considered by practitioners. Most of the extracts focus directly on primary education or on primary-aged children; this was a major criterion used in selecting material for inclusion in the source books. The four volumes are not intended to provide a complete course of study; they need to be supplemented, where possible, by students' general reading in educational and professional studies: psychology, sociology, history, philosophy, curriculum studies and management studies. However, though not intended as a substitute for students' reading of a wide range of original material, the source books acknowledge the constraints of time and of availability of such material, under which students have to study.

The four books are intended to be used by students taking BEd or PGCE courses and by teachers in service, taking diploma or higher degree courses in primary education. The material extracted can be used by tutors as a focus for seminars or as reading to back up lectures, and by students as a source for essays or as a starting point for further reading. The books are not intended to be read straight through from cover to cover but can be used selectively and flexibly at various stages in the course. For convenience, the extracts have been organized into a number of sections.

Volume 1 comprises extracts which examine primary education from historical, ideological, philosophical, sociological and psychological perspectives. Volume 2 deals with curriculum studies, Volume 3 with school organization and management and Volume 4 with teaching and classroom studies. Because of limitations of space, primary education has been confined to the education of children aged 5 to 11, though the compilers acknowledge that in doing so they may offend those teachers in nursery or middle schools who regard themselves, justifiably, as primary practitioners.

The contents of these four source books indicate the demands made on primary teachers in just two of the five elements outlined above. They also illustrate that the professional development of teachers is almost as complex and demanding a task as primary teaching itself.

The Compilers
Summer 1990

Compilers' Notes

In editing the material the compilers have:

1 provided their own title for each extract;
2 standardized the format of the references;
3 deleted all cross-references in the original text;
4 placed editorial insertions in square brackets within the extract itself.

Immediately beneath the heading of each extract, the source of the material is given in detail. The page numbers in the detailed reference refer to each of the pages in the original text, from which passages making up the extract have been taken. For example, if the reference refers to pages 2, 2–3 and 3, then one of the passages making up the extract has been taken from page 2 of the original text, one passage has been taken from a piece beginning on page 2 and running on to page 3 and a third passage has been taken elsewhere on page 3.

In the editorial material introducing each section and each extract, all the page numbers in brackets within the text refer to other pages within the source book, so as to aid cross-referencing. Any quotation used in the editorial material, unless otherwise referenced, can be found in the text from which the extract has been taken.

Acknowledgments

The publishers are grateful to the following for permission to reproduce copyright material:

George Allen and Unwin for GRETTON, J. and JACKSON, M. (1976) *William Tyndale*; NEWSOME, J. and E. (1977) *Perspectives on School at Seven Years Old.*

Appleton-Century-Crofts for SKINNER, B.F. (1968) *The Technology of Teaching.*

The family of C. Schiller for SCHILLER, C. (1979) *In His Own Words*, in GRIFFEN-BEALE, C. (Ed.) A.C. Black.

The Editor and publishers of Bedford Way Papers, 25, for JACOBSEN, B. (1985) *Does Educational Psychology Contribute to the Solution of Educational Problems?*

Blackwell for EASEN, P. (1987) *Developing Real Problem Solving in the Primary Classroom*; and FISHER, R. (1987) 'Problem solving in primary schools' in FISHER, R. (Ed.) *Problem Solving in Primary Schools.*

The Editor and publishers of the *British Journal of Educational Psychology*, Monograph, 2, for DESFORGES, C. (1985) 'Matching tasks to children's attainment', in DESFORGES, C. and BENNETT, N. (1985) *Recent Advances in Classroom Research.*

Cambridge Institute of Education for CONNER, C. (1988) *Learning Styles and Classroom Practice.*

The Editor and publishers of the *Cambridge Journal of Education*, 17, for FRASER, A. (1987) 'A child structured learning context'.

The Editor and publishers of the *Cambridge Journal of Education Newsletter*, No. 11, for CONNER, C. (1988) 'Topic work: Where are we now?'.

Cambridge University Press for MARSHALL, S. (1963) *An Experiment in Education.*

Critical Quarterly Society for Cox, C. and DYSON, A. (1968) 'Fight for education'; Cox, C. and DYSON, A. (1969) *Black Paper Three.*

Acknowledgements

J.M. Dent and Sons Ltd. for Cox, C. and Boyson, R. (1975) *Black Paper 1975*.

The Editor and publishers of *Education 3–13* for Froome, S. (1974) 'Back on the right track', 2, 1; Presland, J. (1978) 'Behaviour modification: Theory and Practice', 6, 1; Wilson, P. (1974) 'Plowden aims', 2, 1.

Falmer Press/The Open University Press for Dale, R. (1981) 'Control, accountability and William Tyndale', in Dale, R. *et al.* (1981) *Politics, Patriarchy and Practice*, Vol. 2.

Fontana Paperbacks for Donaldson, M. (1978) *Children's Minds*; Rubin, Z. (1980) *Children's Friendships*, William Collins.

Granada Publishing for Scheffer, H. (1968) 'Identification', in Lunzer, E. and Morris, J., *Development in Human Learning*.

Harper and Row for Patterson, C.H. (1977) *Foundations for a Theory of Instruction and Educational Psychology*; Claxton, G. (1984) *Live and Learn: An Introduction to the Psychology of Growth and Change in Everyday Life*.

Heinemann for Edwards, A. (1976) *Language in Culture and Class*; Floud, J., Halsey, A. and Martin, F. (1956) *Social Class and Education Opportunity*, Heinemann Educational Books.

The Controller of Her Majesty's Stationery Office for extracts from Board of Education (1926) *The Education of the Adolescent*; Board of Education (1931) *Report of the Consultative Committee on the Primary School*; Board of Education (1933) *Report of the Consultative Committee on Infant and Nursery Schools*; Board of Education (1937) *A Handbook of Suggestions for Teachers*; Education Act (1944); Central Advisory Committee (1967) *Children and Their Primary Schools*; *Education in Schools: A Consultative Document* (1977); *Primary Education in England: A Survey by HM Inspectors of Schools* (1978); *Mathematics 5–11: A Handbook of Suggestions* (1979); Bolton, E.J. (1985) '*Assessment Techniques and Approaches: An Overview, in Better Schools, Evaluation and Appraisal*; The Third Report of the Education, Science and Arts Committee of the House of Commons (1986) *Achievement in Primary Schools, 1*; Des (1987) *The National Curriculum: A Consultation Document*.

Holt, Rinehart and Winston for Ausube, D. *et al.* (1978) *Educational Psychology: A Cognitive View*, 2nd ed.

Houghton-Miffin for Yamamoto, K. (1972) *The Child and His Image*.

The Editor and publishers of the Institute of Economic Affairs Education Unit for Sexton, S. (1987) *Our Schools: A Radical Policy*.

The Editor and publishers of the *Journal of Curriculum Studies*, 12, 1, for Richards, C. (1980) 'Demythologising primary education'.

Longman for Davie, R. *et al.* (1972) *From Birth to Seven*, Longman Group Limited.

The Editor and publishers of the *National Association for the Teaching of*

English, 21, 3, for BRITTON, J. (1987) 'Vygotsky's contribution to pedagogical theory'.

NFER for GOODACRE, E. (1968) *Teachers and Their Pupils' Home Backgrounds*, NFER-Nelson.

The Editor and publishers of the *New Era*, sq, 3, for ADIBE, N. (1978) 'The many implications of Piaget's Work for Education'.

Penguin Books Ltd. for MIDWINTER, E. (1972) *Priority Education*.

Martin Robinson for BANTOCK, G. (1980) *Dilemmas of the Curriculum*.

Routledge and Kegan Paul for BERNSTEIN, B. (1971) *Class Codes and Control*, Vol. 1; BERNSTEIN, B. (1975) *Class, Codes and Control*, Vol. 3, Towards a Theory of Educational Transmission, 2nd ed.; BLYTH, W.A.L. (1965) *English Primary Education*; BOYLE, D. (1983) 'The myth of Piaget's contribution to education', in MODGIL, S. and MODGIL, C. (Eds) *Jean Piaget: An Interdisciplinary critique*; DEARDEN, R. (1968) *The Philosophy of Primary Education*; DEARDEN, R. (1969) *The Aims of Primary Education*, from PETERS, R. (Ed.) *Perspectives on Plowden*; DEARDEN, R. (1976) *Problems in Primary Education*; EDWARDS, D. and MERCER, N., *Common Knowledge*; GALTON, M. *et al.* (1980) *Inside the Primary Classroom*; NASH, R. (1973) *Classrooms Observed*; PETERS, R. (1969) *A Recognisable Philosophy of Education*, from PETERS, R. (Ed.) *Perspectives on Plowden*; ROBINSON, P. (1981) *Perspectives on the Sociology of Education*; SHARP, R. and GREEN, R. (1975) *Education and Social Control*; WHITE, J. (1982) *The Aims of Education Restated*; WILSON, P. (1971) *Interest and Discipline in Education*.

Ward Lock for ISAACS, N. (1961) *The Growth and Understanding in the Young Child*, Ward Lock Educational.

Wiley for KING, R. (1978) *All Things Bright and Beautiful?* John Wiley and Sons.

Writers and Readers for KITWOOD, T. and MACEY, M. (1977) *Mind that Child*, Writers and Readers Publishing Cooperative Society.

1   Primary Education: Historical Perspectives

Introduction

For most of those who teach in them and for all those who learn in them, the place of primary schools within the educational system and within society more generally is rarely, if ever, seriously questioned. Teachers view them as the institutional expression of the state's concern to educate the young up to the age of 11; children see them as part of the 'natural' order of things. Yet primary, as opposed to elementary, education and schools to foster this kind of education are comparatively recent developments within the educational system of England and Wales. As a stage of education, primary education was formally established by the 1944 Education Act (pp. 34–6), though it had been government policy since 1928 to establish schools specifically for children of this age-group. During its short history, primary education has had to contend with a number of formidable problems in its attempts to create a distinct identity, as the second paper in this section documents. These included the legacy of the elementary school tradition with its relatively narrow, instrumental emphasis on the three Rs; the selective role assigned to primary schools and symbolized by the '11+' examination; the vast expansion followed by spectacular contraction in the number of children of primary school age; and the inability of the sector to attract resources on a scale comparable to secondary and higher education. Despite these difficulties it has established itself as a distinct, and in some ways distinctive, sector, though with very considerable internal variations in 'philosophy' and practice, as the papers in the second section of the reader reveal.

The material in this section has been chosen to illustrate developments and landmarks within primary education, not within elementary education (in relation to which there is a more extensive historical literature). For a short overall view of the 'pre-history' of primary education, readers are referred to Blyth's (1965) essay, 'Three traditions in English primary education' (in *English Primary Education*, Vol. 2, Routledge and Kegan Paul), from which the first extract in this section is taken. The second extract, Simon's essay on the 'Evolution of the primary school', is an important analysis of the development of primary education since it was first proposed as a separate stage in education by the Hadow Report of 1926 (pp. 22–3). Many of the remaining extracts are from government publications documenting the establishment of, and the official thinking behind, these new institutions. Prominent among these documents were the Hadow Reports of 1931 and 1933 (pp. 24–7 and 28–9) which did much to shape the development of primary education immediately before and after the Second World War, and the Plowden Report of 1967 (pp. 37–9) which provided more up-to-date 'footnotes' to Hadow, almost forty years on. This section also contains three extracts from the Black Papers outlining the kind of criticisms levelled against primary schools post-Plowden, and two pieces from official publications attempting a more balanced appraisal of the strengths and weaknesses of primary education. Simon's essay makes brief reference to the notorious William Tyndale 'affair' which helped fuel the public disquiet; some of the main issues associated with that cause célèbre are discussed by Gretton and Jackson (pp. 45–50). This is followed by a brief synopsis of changes which have characterized primary schools up until the 1978 Primary Survey.

The Parliamentary Select Committee report on *Achievement in Primary Schools* (HMSO, 1986) introduces a perspective on primary education nearly twenty years after Plowden, and the article by Eric Bolton, Her Majesty's Chief Inspector, introduces some critical commentary on the evaluation of primary education. The section concludes with a synopsis of the arguments offered to support the implementation of a National Curriculum.

Three Traditions in English Primary Education

(From Blyth, W., 1965, *English Primary Education*, Vol. 2, London, Routledge and Kegan Paul, pp. 20, 20–1, 30, 34–5, 35, 40–1, 41, 42, 43.)

This first extract has been included for two main reasons. Firstly, it serves to remind readers that primary education was not created from nothing by either the 1944 Education Act or the Hadow Reports of 1926, 1931 and 1933. Schools catering for children of primary school age had a long history, though state provision for this age group dates back only to the nineteenth century. As Blyth argues, primary schools grew 'mainly, if tardily' out of elementary schools, though other formative influences are distinguished in his analysis. Secondly, the extract indicates that competing views of primary education (such as those featured in the next section) have a history and are not simply the result of contemporary or near-contemporary circumstances and thinking. The author's historical analysis neatly complements the ideological analysis presented later in this book. A particularly valuable feature is the delineation of the 'preparatory' tradition — a tradition neglected elsewhere in this reader and in most contemporary discussion of primary education.

English society was not built round its schools. Whatever may have been true of newer nations such as the United States, whose social evolution has been mainly confined to the age of widespread education, in England social development has in general been concurrent with, or prior to, educational development. Consequently, primary education has taken institutional shape within English society, and it has done so in three interacting but distinguishable traditions. These bear some comparison with the developments in other Western European countries, but also display features peculiar to England. The first two of these traditions are much older than the third. They may be termed respectively *elementary* and *preparatory*. The third tradition is comparatively recent in origin but differs from the other two in that primary education is regarded as something for its own sake, a common right of all children in the Midlands of childhood. This will be referred to as the *developmental* tradition....

[The author begins by considering the elementary tradition.]

... Occasionally, one still hears the term 'elementary' used as though it were currently valid, often by those who never frequented elementary schools when it was in fact valid. Legally, it was intentionally drummed out by the Education Act, 1944, and its passing was acclaimed most joyfully by those who had been most closely associated with it. It had to go, if there was to be any true primary education in the modern sense. One can — we did — have both elementary schools and secondary schools, but one cannot have both elementary schools and primary schools. For elementary schools are a whole educational process in themselves and one which is by definition limited and by implication inferior; a low plateau, rather than the foothills of a complete education.

Yet English primary education grew mainly, if tardily, out of English elementary education with its characteristic emphasis on the basic skills, and in some ways it still bears the marks of its ancestry. . . .
[Alan Blyth goes on to discuss the development of the elementary tradition beginning with the song schools of the middle ages, through the elementary schools of the sixteenth century, and the 'whole complex of dame schools, parochial schools and private schools' of the seventeenth and eighteenth centuries, to the widespread provision of elementary schools in the nineteenth century.]
. . . The term 'elementary' is legally defunct but it still has a social meaning. The term 'preparatory' was never legally established; but it too, has been invested by tradition with a very precise and important meaning which is still current and influential. In one sense indeed it is nearer to the developmental than to the elementary tradition, for it does at least take some account of sequence rather than of social status as a principle of differentiation. But at the same time it implies in name what 'junior elementary' often implied in fact, that the education of younger children is mainly to be conceived in terms of preparation for the later stages of education rather than as a stage in its own right. In practice, the preparatory tradition has struck an uneasy compromise between the two meanings emphasising both the developmental and the strictly preparatory function. . . .
[He sketches the history of the preparatory tradition and suggests that its growth in the nineteenth century was related to two major developments in secondary education: the reform and growth of the public boarding schools for boys, and the revival and extension of day grammar schools both for boys and for girls. By the early twentieth century. . .]
. . . the preparatory tradition had become embedded in the upper and middle sections of English society while a few lower-middle and occasionally even prosperous working-class families also adhered to it. Whatever its diversity, it had one element in common, namely the assumption that post-preparatory education (if that phrase may be pardoned) was a normal expectation of childhood within higher socio-economic groups and that the education of younger children up to the age of ten in the preparatory departments of the girls' grammar schools, eleven in the private schools, or (exceeding the Midlands range) twelve or thirteen in the boys' preparatory schools, should be geared to what was to follow. For prep-school boys indeed, the next phase in the life cycle was often regarded as its zenith, with regrettable results. For girls, with the battle for equality still before them, the status of educated adulthood, married or not, probably exercised a greater appeal. But for them all, there was the incentive to look at least one step ahead with a justified expectation of educational and other advantage. In the preparatory tradition, real education was beginning at just the same

age as, in the elementary tradition, full-time education was assumed to be ending.

The twentieth century has seen a complex interaction between these two traditions but this has in its turn been overshadowed by the impact on both of the third, or developmental, approach. . . .

Alongside the two existing traditions, there has emerged in England a third which is bound neither by the limitations of an education felt or intended to be cheap and inferior, nor by the demands imposed by its own sequel. This may be referred to as the *developmental* tradition, because its principles are based on those of child development. Its origins cannot be sought earlier than the eighteenth century, for that was when education itself began to acquire some form of autonomy. On the whole, the developmental tradition has worked its way into the matrix of English social life from the periphery as is customary in many instances of social change. Indeed, much of its motivation has come from overseas, but it has been built into English institutions through a long period of individual endeavour, culminating in activity sponsored more directly from the centre. . . .

[A number of formative influences on this tradition are traced during the nineteenth and the early twentieth centuries. The author distinguishes five factors which gave impetus to the developmental tradition during the first half of this century.]

. . . The first of these was the growth of psychology which was becoming established as part of the general intellectual climate of the age. It was related both to the over-confident extension of mental testing, itself largely conducted within the elementary schools, but also to the new horizons in hormic and developmental psychology. At the same time, there developed a further facet of the teachings of Dewey, namely his emphasis on the curricular importance of collective preparation for change, and on liberation from the traditional thought-patterns which could be regarded as undemocratic whether in the home, the school or society at large. Third, and linked with the previous came the great wave of emancipation that characterised the years after 1918. Children were to be given the chance to be themselves at any age and in concert with their peers of both sexes. This trend, often associated with experimental schools, emphasised the positive support which the developmental tradition gave to co-education. A fourth factor which probably influenced the changing conception of primary education was the growth of what is now rather loosely described as the 'Welfare State'. The fifth factor is an extension of a process already mentioned. The rapid growth of the concept of 'secondary education for all', officially enunciated for the Labour Party by Tawney (1923) and soon afterwards to some extent by all parties led to a concurrent definition of primary education as the preceding stage. In one sense, it was thus 'preparatory'. . . .

[Schools catering for children of junior age became the battleground for a number of forces, especially those of child development and those of the 'scholarship' examination. The developmental tradition was given a great boost when ...] the Consultative Committee of the Board of Education prepared the report on *The Primary School* (1931). It was a consistent and radical-flavoured document which took its stand squarely on the developmental tradition and recognised the significance of the changes which were taking place. It paid due, though not excessive, regard to the philosophy of Dewey and his followers ... it espoused and reinforced unhesitatingly the nascent belief that children aged seven to eleven should be educated in a social institution with an autonomous quality of its own. Thus it firmly annexed the education of children throughout the Midlands years to the developmental rather than the elementary or preparatory tradition. This Report was followed two years later by its counterpart on *Infant and Nursery Schools*, but this, though equally forthright, was less of an innovation because it dealt with the heartland of the developmental tradition rather than its advancing frontier.

From this point onwards, the basis of a separate developmental tradition in primary education has been incontrovertibly laid.

[Writing at about the time when the Plowden Committee was set up (1964–5), the author concludes:]

... Recent developments have thus shown that the developmental tradition continues to gain ground, not only because of changes within the schools but also on account of social change in English society itself. Meanwhile, it must be remembered that the preparatory tradition continues to flourish modified only in part, with a clientèle that is numerically insignificant but socially preponderant, while the divisions within the teaching force, which cannot yet be confidently termed a profession, still run socially deep. The elementary tradition, too, lurks in many corners of the public educational system and is perpetuated by many instances of social inertia. Thus the developmental tradition is still far from unchallenged and the common primary school, for both sexes and all abilities and classes, is in practice a chimera. Any study of contemporary primary education which overlooked the continuing influences of the older traditions would present an over-simplified and distorted picture. On the other hand, any study which belittled the real and in a quite genuine sense revolutionary quality of the developmental tradition would ignore one of the greatest potentialities for wholesome growth which exists in English society today.

Reference

TAWNEY, R. (1923) *Secondary Education for All: A Policy for Labour*, London, Allen and Unwin.

The Evolution of the Primary School

(From Galton, M., Simon, B. and Croll, P., 1980, *Inside the Primary Classroom*, London, Routledge and Kegan Paul, pp. 29–42.)

The chapter which forms this extract clearly and succinctly puts contemporary primary education in context by providing an outline of its development in four stages, and by drawing attention to the forces, legislation and events which have shaped its character. It traces the roots of primary education in the elementary school, acknowledges the longstanding provision of separate infant schools or departments in some areas, and documents how primary schools arose out of a concern for the needs of *older* children. It discusses a number of important influences on the primary school:

1 the weight of the elementary school tradition with its concern for literacy, numeracy, conformity and obedience;
2 the scholarship examination, later to be called the 11+ examination, for which the primary school prepared so many of its pupils;
3 the views of psychologists such as Burt which justified streaming and selection at 11;
4 the perspectives of Froebel, Montessori and the New Education Fellowship which permeated training colleges and promoted a liberal romantic view of primary education; and
5 the abolition of selection at eleven in many local education authorities leading to a liberalization of primary education.

The chapter clearly demonstrates its thesis that 'primary education, very much the poor relation in the educational system, has been in a state of almost continuous transition throughout its short history, the result both of changes at the secondary level and of changing approaches to the education of young children'. With its overview, this extract forms a good introduction to each of the remaining extracts in this section of the reader.

Although several million children are now educated in separate primary schools of one kind or another, these have a comparatively recent and certainly a short history. This form of schooling was first accepted as official policy only some fifty years ago, in 1928. It then took some forty years to implement. Not until the mid-1960s were *all* children between the ages of five and eleven educated in separate 'primary' schools. No sooner was this achieved than new changes were brought about by new thinking and legislation. The Education Act of 1964 made possible the establishment of 'middle' schools covering the ages of nine to thirteen. To complicate matters further, only three years later, the Central Advisory Councils for Education for both England and Wales recommended that 'middle' schools for children aged eight to twelve should be the norm. Both these options have been taken up by a number of local authorities, with the approval of the Department of Education and Science, largely to facilitate comprehensive secondary reorganization.

'Primary' education today, therefore, in spite of its relatively recent establishment, is already again in a state of flux. What had become the norm (infant schools or departments for children aged five to seven followed by a junior school to eleven) has already been phased out in some parts of the country, to be replaced by one of two alternative systems, (i) 'first', sometimes called 'lower', schools for children aged five to nine, followed by 'middle' (nine to thirteen) and 'upper' schools (thirteen to eighteen), or (ii) first schools for children aged five to eight, followed by 'middle' (eight to twelve) and upper schools for the twelve to eighteens (or sometimes twelve to sixteen and sixteen to eighteen). These three systems now exist in parallel in different parts of the country.... It is essential, if we are to place existing schools and their practices in context, to gain some understanding of their development, of the forces that have shaped their character and procedures. Only historical analysis can throw light on the changing forms of primary education, explicate the reasons for the emergence of this particular institutional form, and illuminate its evolution both in terms of practice and of theory....

Origin of the Junior School (1870–1926)

The concept that education below eleven should be defined as 'primary', and that above as 'post-primary' (or 'secondary') first appeared in an official document in the Report of the Consultative Committee to the Board of Education, known after its chairman, as the 'Hadow Report' (Hadow, 1926). The proposal was adopted as national policy in 1928. Even at that stage, however, the discussion was largely conceptual. Only with the Education Act of 1944 was a public system of education finally brought into being in England and Wales which established, in statutory terms at least, the reality of two stages of education, primary and secondary. It is in this sense that the 'primary' school in this country has a short history, and, as we have seen, the concept of 'primary' education is already somewhat confused only some thirty to forty years later.

Before 1944 the great majority of children of the present primary age range (five to eleven) were in *elementary* schools; they were educated together with older children in 'all-age' schools within the elementary system. This system was established, specifically and deliberately, for one section of society only — that is, for the working class. The original objectives of universal, compulsory education, established by 1880, were then still defined in terms of the 'standard' system brought in by 'payment by results' in 1862, though this system began to be modified after 1870. Payment by results focused the teacher's attention very specifically on the three R's; the objective was the achievement of an elementary level of literacy and numeracy by the working-class population. Clearly there were other objectives as well, though not so overtly defined; specifically those which might be described as social-disciplinary, the achievement of which was sought through what is now referred to as the 'hidden curriculum' rather than through the content of instruction (acceptance of the teacher's authority, of the need for punctuality, obedience, conformity, and so on). It is worth noting that the system of payment by results was modified in the 1880s to put greater emphasis on this latter aspect, as compared with the three R's.

The elementary system, in its origins and indeed up to the mid-1920s, did not include any special provision for younger children below the age of eleven, with the exception of infant schools and departments covering the age range five to seven in some areas. These, which constituted a unique feature of the English educational system, were connected with the early start of compulsory education. At the age of five it was, in 1870, and is still, below the compulsory age in other advanced industrial countries (in France, Germany, Sweden, the age is six, in the USSR it is seven). This early age of entry was partly a product of the establishment, from 1870 and even earlier, as an accepted and essential part of the system of infant schools and departments catering for children below the age of six or seven and including many children aged three and four.

This tradition is normally said to owe its origin to Robert Owen's famous 'infant school' at New Lanark in the early 1820s and the subsequent development of such schools by Wilderspin and others in the 1820s to 1840s. But, by the 1860s and 1870s the main objective in separating out the infants, it appears, was to ensure that the teaching of the older children should not be unduly disturbed by what Matthew Arnold (and others) referred to as the 'babies'. Originally the infant school or department passed on its children to the elementary school at six, since the first 'standard' examination (standard I), brought in in 1862 under payment by results, was designed for children aged six to seven, but the code of regulations issued in 1871 created an infant stage below standard I for the five to seven age range. Thus the age of seven became the age of transfer from the infant school (or department) to the elementary school as a whole (Whitbread, 1972, p. 41). In the evolution of the concept of the junior school, the separate existence of infant schools or departments, defining the age of entry, is clearly important. However it must not be assumed that infant schools or departments were ubiquitous; in 1930 they accounted for approximately half the children aged five to seven, the rest were still in all-age elementary schools catering for children aged five (and below) to fourteen.

If the existence of infant schools and departments cut off the younger children, developments in the education system, particularly around and after the turn of the century, began to demarcate an upper limit of eleven or twelve, or at least to indicate that such a demarcation might, given the conditions, become a practical possibility. There were a number of reasons for this, all relating to the growth of new forms of 'secondary' schools following the 1902 Education Act. The scholarship and free place system, established in 1907 (but existing earlier), created a link between the elementary and secondary systems by which the latter recruited pupils from the elementary schools at around the age of ten to twelve. The same was the case with the new selective 'central' schools within the elementary system, established in London, Manchester and elsewhere from about 1910. So the age of around eleven was becoming accepted as the age of transfer to secondary and other schools already before the First World War. An impetus was given to this by the Education Act of 1918 which stated that special provision should be made for 'the older or more intelligent children' in elementary schools by means of central schools, extended courses, and the like, and by the actions taken (or proposed) by local authorities under the Act in the early 1920s. This set the scene for the proposals of the Hadow Report in 1926 for the division of the elementary school system into two stages, junior and senior, with a break at eleven for all. Here was the real origin of the junior school, or of the division between primary and post-primary education.

It is worth nothing at this point that the motivation for this fundamental change did not arise from any serious consideration of the needs and character of children aged seven to eleven (or five to eleven). It arose solely from a consideration of the needs of the older (senior) children; and indeed it is symptomatic that the crucial report on which action was taken, setting up separate junior or primary schools, was entitled *The Education of the Adolescent* (1926). The origins and significance of this report have been analysed elsewhere (Simon, 1974) so will not be gone into here; particularly since the establishment of the junior school as a separate institution was very much a by-product of the report, and little of any significance is said there on the topic. However, it is worth noting that, although in some of the large urban areas junior departments (so called) of all-age schools had already been established as a consequence of the developments mentioned above, by the mid-1920s, when the Consultative Committee reported, only some 6 per cent of children aged seven to eleven were in such departments. All the rest, the great bulk of the children in those age groups, were still organized as they had been since 1870, in all-age schools catering for children aged five or seven to fourteen. These normally were organized as separate boys' and girls' departments, usually with a mixed infants' school as the base. In large urban schools of the kind built by the School Boards following the Education Act of 1870, the infants' school was on the ground floor, the boys' and girls' departments on the floors above. In rural areas there would usually be a separate infants' class with one, two or more other classes according to the size of the school taking children up to fourteen.

Developments Following the Hadow Report

This, then, marks the beginning of the separate junior school as national policy; emerging, as it were, unforeseen and as a by-product, from the womb of the elementary system, and bearing, at least in its origin, all the marks of that system in terms of cheapness, economy, large classes, obsolete, ancient and inadequate buildings, and so on. With reorganization after 1928 (when the Hadow Report's recommendations were accepted by the government) the usual practice was to provide new buildings, where possible, for the older pupils in the new senior elementary schools, since these needed facilities for specialist teaching, for the first time including laboratories, craft rooms, gymnasia, art rooms and so on. So reorganization went ahead, though very unevenly in different parts of the country. Over-all, 48 per cent of children aged seven to eleven were in separate junior schools (or departments) by 1938.

Only in 1931 was attention focused specifically for the first time on 'The Primary School' with the publication of a report by the Consultative Committee with that title. Yet even here it is interesting to note the terms of the reference to that Committee. This was simply 'to enquire and report as to the courses of study suitable for children (other than children in infants departments) up to the age of eleven in *elementary schools* with special reference to the needs of children in rural areas' (our italics).

Reference has already been made to the original, narrow objectives embodied in the elementary school tradition; the strictly instrumental approach relating to literacy and numeracy and to its social disciplinary aspects. All this is well known and is explicable in terms of the original social function of this school system. Nevertheless, what might be called peripheral, or external theoretical influences were beginning to make some impact on the system from the turn of the century, or even before. There was, first, the kindergarten movement, based on Froebel's theory and practice, which began to penetrate the schools from the 1890s, involving the concepts of 'natural development', 'spontaneity', and so on; even if contemporary analysis, for instance, an investigation carried through by a group of women HMIs in 1905 (Board of Education, 1905), indicated that Froebel's system was applied in an extremely mechanistic manner; that is, was adapted to Board school drill practice, so losing its educative significance. Nevertheless the ideas were there, and the movement institutionalized with the foundation of the Froebel Institute and other colleges for the training of teachers on Froebelian principles, often financed by wealthy philanthropists interested in transforming middle-class educational practice for young children.

This was followed, after the turn of the century, by the considerable impact made by Dr Maria Montessori, with her emphasis on structured learning, sense training and individualization. Both influences were more strongly felt in the infant schools than in other sections of the elementary system (their main impact was probably felt in middle-class private schools). Perhaps more immediately relevant to the maintained school system was the work of Margaret McMillan, with her emphasis on improving hygienic conditions, overcoming children's physical defects, and providing an 'appropriate' environment for young children. This work and that of her sister, Rachel, was certainly influential in bringing new concepts concerning activity and creativity again largely to the infant school but nevertheless affecting teachers and others in the elementary school system as a whole. Finally, given this brief survey, the year 1911 saw the publication of *What Is and What Might Be* by Edmond Holmes, ex-Chief Inspector of Elementary Schools; the first striking manifesto of the 'progressives' in its total condemnation of the arid drill methods of the contemporary elementary school, and its espousal of the enlightened, all-sided, humanist approach of the model village school-teacher Egeria (who is said actually to have existed). The publication of this book marks the start of the 'new' education; ideas to be crystallized and institutionalized with the foundation of the New Education Fellowship shortly after the First World War (Selleck, 1972).

In the immediate post-war period ideas of this kind were strongly represented in theoretical discussion on the education of young children; and partially implemented in the practice of those schools which turned towards group work and individualization. This was a central feature of the so-called Sub Dalton Plan embodying some, at least, of John Dewey's ideas which, paradoxically, although emanating from the USA, was implemented to a far greater extent in British primary schools (Kimmins and Rennie, 1932, pp. 82–4). Another potent new influence from the early 1930s was Susan Isaacs, whose two books, on the intellectual and social development of young children, were published at this stage (Isaacs, 1930, 1933).

It was these aspects that were stressed in the Consultative Committee's report on *The Primary School* (1931). This emphasized the need for a completely new approach to primary education which, it was argued, was now made possible with the break at eleven. To give a sense of this report it is best to quote directly from the section on the curriculum for the primary stage of education (pp. 139–40). The report stresses the need 'to supply the pupils with what is essential to their healthy growth, physical, intellectual and moral', adding the much-quoted view that 'the curriculum of the primary school is to be thought of in terms of activity and experience, rather than of knowledge to be acquired and facts to be stored'. The importance of physical training, including training in 'good carriage and graceful movement' is emphasized, as is the fundamental importance of language training, with 'systematic training in oral expression'. Aesthetic sensibility must be cultivated through drawing, craft work and music, together with the development of manual skills. The traditional practice of dividing the matter of primary instruction into separate 'subjects', taught in distinct lessons 'should be re-considered' — central topics may be a useful alternative. Although the report emphasizes that provision should be made 'for an adequate amount of "drill" in reading, writing and arithmetic', over-all emphasis clearly reflects the new approaches; especially in the broader aims and objectives now conceived as relevant to primary education.

The 1931 report, though favourably received, made little impact at the time. Of course, very few separate 'junior' schools, as such, had by then been brought into being, while as M.L. Jacks put it, 'the conditions necessary for its implementation were almost wholly lacking' (Ross, 1960, p. 33). In 1932, for instance, well over 50 per cent of children of primary school age were in classes with over forty pupils. However this report, in general, certainly reflected the outlook of the 'new', child-centred, 'progressive' approach to education even if, as we shall see, it strongly recommended the introduction of streaming into the new junior schools. R.J.W. Selleck argues, in *English Primary Education and the Progressives, 1914 to 1939*, that the approach of the 'new' educationalists, somewhat watered down from its wilder manifestations in the early 1920s, had, by 1939, become the official orthodoxy; propagated in training colleges, Board of Education in-service courses, by local authority inspectors, and the like. How far it affected actual *practice* in the schools is, however, another matter.

The Selective Function of the Junior School

The primary school, though now envisaged in the sense outlined above, was, however, subject to sharply contradictory influences. While the 1931 report developed the idea of universal popular education of a new, broader, child-centred, activity type, the actual emergence of the junior school on a mass scale, which only took place *after* the Second World War, coincided precisely with the crystallization of the school system as primarily a sorting, classifying, selective mechanism; a function in which the junior school played a central role and one which reached its height, in this form, as late as the mid-1950s, just at the time when 'Hadow reorganization' was rapidly being completed throughout the country. The 1931 report, basing itself on the psychology of individual differences, and fully accepting the advice of psychometrists who at that time asserted the *absolute* determination of 'intelligence' by hereditary or genetic factors (Cyril Burt and Percy Nunn were both co-opted on the drafting committee) strongly advocated the necessity of streaming as the basic form of internal school organization for all primary schools large enough to form parallel classes in each age group. New schools, where possible, were to be designed on the basis of a 'treble track' system.

With the completion of reorganization following the Second World War, and the greatly increased competition for grammar school places which the 1944 Act, in spite of providing 'secondary education for all', did nothing to alleviate, streaming spread, in Brian Jackson's words 'with barely credible rapidity throughout the country' (Jackson, 1964, p. 150). Since the selection examination consisted normally of 'objective' tests in the three R's plus 'Intelligence', this inevitably provided the main objective for primary school education *as a whole* (*all* children were now entered for this examination, whatever their stream or educational level; this was regarded as essential to allow 'equality of opportunity'). So, in spite of the call for freedom and quite new approaches in the 1931 report, and in spite of a move in this direction in the late 1940s and some modification of practice in different parts of the country, in general the old elementary school syndrome which that report had regarded as quite out-moded, inevitably persisted, if in a somewhat modernized guise. The basic class teaching approach, with the main emphasis on numeracy and literacy, continued in the new junior schools after the Second World War; in fact the tradition derived from 1870 was still dominant. The continued existence of large classes through the late 1940s and 1950s reinforced this method of school organization with its related pedagogy.

From its inception, the junior school has always had a dual role in the sense that before the Second World War a few of its pupils (about 10 per cent) were selected for the secondary school, while the majority remained in the elementary system either in the same school (where it was 'all-age') or in the senior school. This remained the case in the new dispensation following the 1944 Education Act, the senior schools being re-named 'secondary modern'. The tripartite system then established (including secondary technical schools) gave enhanced importance to the 11-plus examination, and reinforced the system of streaming which had success in this examination (in terms of gaining places in grammar schools) as one of its objectives.

It may be thought that the concepts underlying the 'child-centred' approach, and those underlying streaming are contradictory, yet both were accepted by the Consultative Committee in the report on *The Primary School* (1931) (as in other reports in the inter-war years). However this is not necessarily the case. Child-centred approaches, particularly Froebelian, were based fundamentally on the notion that the child's inborn characteristics must be allowed to flower; that the school's function is, in Froebel's words, 'to make the inner outer' (Bowen, 1903, p. 98). Hence the emphasis on natural, spontaneous development. The school's role is to provide optimum conditions for such development. This ties in closely with the views of the dominant school of psychology in the inter-war years (psychometry) whose main tenet, as mentioned above, was that the child's most important mental characteristic, defined as 'Intelligence' (seen as a measure of intellectual potential) was *wholly* fixed and inborn, and was not subject to change as a result of educational or any other experiences. What was necessary was to provide an education appropriate to the child's inborn, and measurable, intelligence level. Thus Susan Isaacs, an influential proponent of 'activity methods', as they were called, strongly insisted on the necessity for differentiation of young children through streaming based on 'Intelligence'

(Isaacs, 1932). It was, therefore, possible to reconcile child-centred approaches with hierarchic organization (streaming) within the junior school. Nevertheless it is evident that a tension developed between the two approaches in the years following the Second World War, the selective function of the junior school imposing clear restraints on the teachers, whose outlook was inevitably affected by the need to get good results in the 11-plus examination, in the interests both of the pupils and of the school.

It is difficult now to reconstruct the intense pressure on schools and teachers that built up in the 1940s and 1950s relating to the selection examination; the league tables that parents drew up for local schools, the telephoning round to find out who had done well and the sense of failure that some teachers experienced when their pupils won fewer places than others, or than expected; not to speak of the effects on the children. This was the reality that teachers had to face, arising from the context of the junior school within the tripartite (or selective) system; and this clearly was a dominant influence relating both to teachers' objectives and, therefore, to the teacher's style and forms of organization within the classroom.... Once again the fate of the junior school and its educational role depended on developments at the upper levels.

Comprehensive Reorganization: The Abolition of the 11-plus

But, with the transition to comprehensive secondary education, this dependence showed itself in an opposite sense. Comprehensive reorganization can be said to have got under way, in terms of entire local authority systems, from the mid-1960s, when the junior schools — or those in reorganized areas — found themselves to a large extent freed from the direct pressures and constraints just mentioned.

The abolition of the 11-plus, which was the concomitant of this reorganization (and to a large extent its motive force) now quite suddenly, and somewhat unexpectedly, created a new situation, and, in a real sense, the schools found new options open. Ironically, as we have seen, this transformation brought with it the demise of the seven to eleven junior schools as *national* policy although this system still predominates in the country as a whole alongside the new forms of age grouping defined earlier.

One striking feature of recent developments is the rapidity of change the schools have experienced. This may link with the contradiction between theory and practice which clearly developed after 1931; between the theory of the 'progressives' as crystallized in the 1931 report, and the actual practice of the junior schools as this persisted under the mounting constraints of the 11-plus. During this period, the focus of 'progressive' developments in practice was the infant school, which, although certainly affected by the increasingly competitive nature of the 11-plus (it was not uncommon to introduce streaming for six-year-olds), was relatively free to develop auton-

17

omously forms of organization and activities which were held to be educationally appropriate for five- to seven-year-olds. Practice here was certainly affected from the mid-1930s by the highly 'progressive' report of the Consultative Committee on *Infant and Nursery Schools*, published in 1933, clearly influenced by the work of Susan Isaacs, as also by the ideas of Froebel, Montessori and Dewey. There is evidence that 'progressive' infant school practices spread into the lower forms (and streams) of junior schools following the Second World War, particularly during the 1950s and especially in certain specific local authority areas. It is perhaps symptomatic that when Lilien Weber came from New York to study advanced school practice in England in the mid-1960s it was to the infant school that she devoted her attention. There is very little on junior schools in her book subsequently published under the title *The English Infant School and Informal Education* (Weber, 1971).

But the ideas of 'progressive' educators, using this term in its broadest (and most positive) sense, suffered a continuous frustration as regards *practice* in the junior school both before and after the Second World War, even if pioneering books like M.V. Daniels's *Activity in the Junior School* did appear (and were influential) in the late 1940s when activity methods spread quite widely and had a certain vogue. A kind of backlog of progressive ideas and practices built up almost since 1911 (Holmes) (reinforced by war-time evacuation experiences, when teachers were driven back on to their own resources and began to act both more autonomously and more flexibly than before), was liberated in those areas where the 11-plus was early abolished or profoundly modified. These were particularly Leicestershire, the West Riding of Yorkshire, Oxfordshire, Bristol and London. Here were the nests of the new breakout. It was in these areas, also, that the system of streaming, which reinforced the methodology of class teaching, was most rapidly discarded. The swing from streaming in the junior schools in these and other areas, which started very slowly in the mid-1950s, meeting strong opposition, suddenly took off with extraordinary rapidity in the mid- to late 1960s, gaining influential support from the Plowden Report of 1967.

The 1960s

Educational developments in the 1960s were so rapid, all-embracing, and, in retrospect, perhaps surprising, that it is worth spending a little time on that decade, particularly because some of the problems facing primary education today clearly have their roots in this period and the apparent subsequent reaction from ideas and practices then regarded as positive. The 1960s saw not only the swing to comprehensive secondary education — one important condition for freeing the primary schools from earlier constraints — they also saw the acceptance *in toto* of the targets for a massive expansion of higher education as proposed in the Robbins Report, *Higher Education*

(Robbins, 1963), and of the perspectives outlined (if somewhat ambiguously) in the Newsom Report, *Half Our Future* (Newsom, 1963). Of major importance to the subject of this book was the publication of the Plowden Report, *Children and Their Primary Schools* (1967), which, if also ambiguous in parts (particularly as concerns the curriculum), clearly and definitely espoused child-centred approaches in general, the concept of 'informal' education, flexibility of internal organization and non-streaming in a general humanist approach — stressing particularly the uniqueness of each individual and the paramount need for individualization of the teaching ... learning process. There is little doubt that, when it appeared, the Plowden Report effectively crystallized a growing consensus as to the ideal nature of primary education; it built on, but took further, concepts initially propagated in the Consultative Committee's reports on *The Primary School* (1931) and *Infant and Nursery Schools* (1933).

But there were other factors affecting school practice at that time. One of these was the development of what is called the 'permissive society', and particularly the tendency to place fewer restraints on children and young people by parents and those in authority generally; combined on the other hand with a new consciousness on the part of young people as to their role in society, no doubt the result of higher earning powers in conditions of full employment, relative affluence, and so increased independence and autonomy. While it is difficult to evaluate such a tendency, there is little doubt that this affected pupil behaviour and attitudes in schools — perhaps even those of young children in primary schools. But there were other factors operating as well. Over this period there was a strong tendency, not only for local authorities specifically to encourage innovation and change in primary schools, but also for the head teachers themselves to allow a high degree of autonomy in classroom practice to class teachers; a result, perhaps, not only of the increased tendency towards the questioning of authority but also of the increasing professionalization of the primary school teacher, linked to the extension of training to three years in 1963. All this enhanced the variation of practice in the classroom. Schools tended no longer to operate as a single unit with common objectives using similar methods throughout the school; instead, different approaches could be found, and were tolerated, in different classrooms within the same school (Taylor, 1974).

In addition, the 1960s saw a decline in the inspectorial role both of HMIs and, in particular perhaps, of local authority inspectors who traditionally (especially in urban areas with their School Board traditions of administration) kept the primary schools on a tight rein. The former almost entirely ceased to carry out full inspections; in the case of local inspectors the tendency was to take on an advisory rather than an inspectorial function with the diminution of authority that this implies. This does not necessarily mean a decline in influence, since an effective adviser may have very considerable impact on the schools, and, through organizing activities such as the annual Leicestershire Teachers Primary Residential Workshops, profoundly affect school practice. Nevertheless, under this system, such influence has been exerted rather through the free concurrence of heads and teachers than through reliance on the authority of inspectors.

Finally, the 1960s saw the erection of new schools on the open plan principle, or the modification of old buildings on these lines. This created a new situation which inevitably affected classroom organization and methodology.

The Situation Today

It is in the light of these factors, many of them generally regarded at the time as educationally positive, that contemporary attitudes to and criticisms of the schools need to be evaluated. Here it is relevant to refer to the general disenchantment with education as a palliative of society's ills, which first found expression in the USA following the supposed (and some hold premature) evaluation of the Headstart programmes as a failure. This view, embodied in the Coleman (1966) and Jencks (1972) reports coincided with the beginning of a world economic recession (late 1960s), providing a rationale for economic cutbacks in education not only in England but in most advanced western industrial countries. If schools 'make no difference', why support them? The economic climate that developed also provided the context for the views presented in the series of Black Papers ... [of which] the first, published in 1969, specifically focused on new developments in the *primary* schools as a main cause not only of student unrest in the universities but of other unwelcome tendencies or phenomena (Cox and Dyson, 1969). It is in this context also that, in 1975, the events surrounding the Tyndale school dispute unfolded in London (concerning the implementation of an extreme version of 'progressive' methods in a primary school), followed in May 1976 by the massive publicity given by the media to Bennett's study (1976) represented as a condemnation of so-called 'informal' methods in the primary school. All this formed the background to Prime Minister Callaghan's speech (autumn 1976) warning against certain current tendencies in education, and the events which have followed: 'The Great Debate', DES and HMI initiatives relating to the curriculum, the establishment of the Assessment of Performance Unit, the beginning of mass testing by local authorities, and so on. The climate in which schools now function has certainly changed, affecting directly their mode of operation and perhaps also their objectives....

Summary

It appears that the history of the primary school may be divided into four phases. First, its pre-history up to 1928, when the junior school as such had no independent existence, though embryonic forms were embodied within the elementary school system including infant schools and departments. Practices, approaches, attitudes and buildings derived from this phase are still to be found. Second, the period from 1928 to 1944 when junior schools, as such, began to come into being within the system of *elementary* education, and when a specific theoretical approach to primary education began to be formulated and receive official support (for short 'progressive', or 'child-centred'). Third, from 1944 to about 1970, a period which saw the universal provision of primary schooling (in its various forms) covering the age range five to eleven; a period when the specific theoretical approach developed earlier began to be implemented on a reasonably wide scale, culminating in the Plowden Report. Fourth, the present period, from about 1970 or shortly after to today and projecting into the future; a period marked by economic difficulties, controversy over means and ends, new restraints on the teacher, and by the demise of 'primary schooling' in the sense previously established with the development of new organizational (or institutional) forms. One thing seems clear; primary education, very much the poor relation in the educational system, has been in a state of almost continuous transition throughout its short history, the result both of changes at the secondary level and of changing approaches to the education of young children. Evaluation of contemporary practice must take this into account.

References

BENNETT, N. (1976) *Teaching Styles and Pupil Progress*, Open Books.
BOARD OF EDUCATION (1905) *Reports on Children under Fives Years of Age in Public Elementary Schools, by Women Inspectors*, London, HMSO, Cd 2726.
BOWEN, H. (1903) *Froebel and Education by Self Activity*, Heinemann.
Central Advisory Council for Education (England) (1976) *Children and Their Primary Schools*, London, HMSO.
COLEMAN, J. (1966) *Equality of Educational Opportunity*, US Department of Health, Education and Welfare.
COX, C. and DYSON, A. (Eds) (1969) *Fight for Education: A Black Paper*, Critical Quarterly Society.
HADOW REPORT (1926) *The Education of the Adolescent*, Report of the Consultative Committee, London, HMSO.
HADOW REPORT (1931) *Report of the Consultative Committee on the Primary School*, London, HMSO.
ISAACS, S. (1930) *Intellectual Growth in Young Children*, London, Routledge and Kegan Paul.
ISAACS, S. (1932) *The Children We Teach: Seven to Eleven Years*, University of London Press.
ISAACS, S. (1933) *Social Development in Young Children: A Study of Beginnings*, London, Routledge and Kegan Paul.
JACKSON, B. (1964) *Streaming: An Education System in Miniature*, London, Routledge and Kegan Paul.
JENCKS, C. (1972) *Inequality: A Reassessment of the Effects of Family and Schooling in America*, Basic Books.

KIMMINS, C. and RENNIE, B. (1932) *The Triumph of the Dalton Plan*, Nicholson and Watson.
NEWSOM REPORT (1963) *Half Our Future*, Report of the Central Advisory Council for Education (England), London, HMSO.
ROBBINS REPORT (1963) *Higher Education*, Report of the Committee on Higher Education, London, HMSO.
ROSS, A. (1960) *The Education of Childhood*, Harrap.
SELLECK, R. (1972) *English Primary Education and the Progressives 1914–1939*, London, Routledge and Kegan Paul.
SIMON, B. (1974) *The Politics of Education Reform 1920–1940*, Lawrence and Wishart.
TAYLOR, P. *et al.*, (1974) *Purpose, Power and Constraint in the Primary School Curriculum*, Macmillan.
WEBER, L. (1971) *The English Infant School and Informal Education*, Prentice-Hall.
WHITBREAD, N. (1972) *The Evolution of the Nursery-Infant School: A History of Infant and Nursery Education in Britain, 1800–1970*, London, Routledge and Kegan Paul.

A Proposal to Establish Primary and Post-Primary Education

(From The Hadow Report, 1926, *The Education of the Adolescent*, Report of the Consultative Committee, London, HMSO pp. xix, 70–2, 139.)

This short piece summarizes the Hadow Committee's conclusions for the reorganization of elementary education into two successive stages: primary education and post-primary education. The reorganization was proposed, not mainly for the benefit of primary-aged children, but in order to cater more appropriately for the 'tide' of adolescence. Eleven was chosen as the age marking the end of primary and the beginning of post-primary education. The last part of the extract discusses the kind of examination to be given children of 11 to 'discover in each case the type [of school] most suitable to a child's abilities and interests'. This '11+' examination was to have a dominating, and largely restrictive, influence on the upper primary curriculum for many decades post-Hadow, and still exercises such an influence in some parts of the country.

There is a tide which begins to rise in the veins of youth at the age of eleven or twelve. It is called by the name of adolescence. If that tide can be taken at the flood, and a new voyage begun in the strength and along the flow of its current, we think that it will 'move on the fortune.' We therefore propose that all children should be transferred, at the age of eleven or twelve, from the junior or primary school either to schools of the type now called secondary, or to schools (whether selective or non-selective) of the type which is now called central, or to senior and separate departments of existing elementary schools. . . .

The first main conclusion which we have reached is concerned with the successive stages in education and with the relations which should exist between them. It is as follows: *Primary education should be regarded as ending at about the age of* 11+. *At that age a second stage, which for the moment may be given the colourless name 'post-primary', should begin; and this stage which, for many pupils would end at* 16+, *for some at* 18 *or* 19, *but for the majority at* 14+ *or* 15+, *should be envisaged so far as possible as a single whole, within which there will be a variety in the types of education supplied, but which will be marked by the common characteristic that its aim is to provide for the needs of children who are entering and passing through the stage of adolescence.*

Such a conception of the relations between primary and post-primary education obviously presents some points of contrast with the arrangement which has hitherto obtained in England, under which, until recent years, approximately 90 per cent of children have received elementary education up to the age of 13 or 14, and a small minority have been transferred to secondary education, or to that given in central schools, at about the age of 11;... It appears, however, to correspond to the views held by a large and influential section of educational opinion, and it has already received partial recognition both in administrative action taken by the Board and in a recent resolution on educational policy of the House of Commons. There was, indeed, something like unanimity among our witnesses as to the desirability of treating the age of 11 to 12 as the beginning of a new phase in education, presenting distinctive problems of its own, and requiring a fresh departure in educational methods and organisation in order to solve them.... *While we think all children should enter some type of post-primary school at the age of 11+, it will be necessary to discover in each case the type most suitable to a child's abilities and interests, and for this purpose a written examination should be held, and also, wherever possible, an oral examination. A written psychological test might also be specially employed in dealing with border line cases, or where a discrepancy between the result of the written examination and the teacher's estimate of proficiency has been observed. Where Local Education Authorities so determine, a preliminary examination might be held in order to discover candidates who should be encouraged to go forward to the free place examination proper.*

Arrangements for organising and conducting examinations for admission to schools of different types should be left to the Local Education Authorities.

Primary Education: A New Vision

(From The Hadow Report, 1931, *Report of the Consultative Committee on the Primary School*, London, HMSO, pp. 133, xv–xvi, xviii–xix, xxviii–xxix, 92–3.)

This extract and the report from which it is taken provide a classic statement embodying a conception of primary education which has served as an educational ideal for over half a century. The Hadow Report of 1931 provided a rationale for the primary stage of education, first proposed officially by the same Consultative Committee in its 1926 report (pp. 22–3). The Committee in its later report put forward a powerful vision of what primary education should be: a stage of education with 'its own standards of achievement and excellence' and with an aim of awakening children to 'the basic interests of civilized existence'. It envisaged an expanded role for the school: 'The schools whose first intention was to teach children how to read have ... been compelled to broaden their aims until it might now be said that they have to teach children how to live.' Its expressed concern was for all children: 'What a wise and good parent would desire for his own children, that a nation must desire for all children.' It stressed the importance of 'activity and experience', but not, on closer reading, at the expense of 'knowledge to be acquired and facts to be stored'. The whole report is a remarkably optimistic, forward-looking statement, all the more remarkable for being issued at a time of economic recession. Other reports or commentaries on primary education are but pale reflection (some might say 'distortions') of its vision.

In the evolution of educational theory and practice in England and Wales since the beginning of the last century the conception of the primary school for children between the ages of five and eleven, with a separate organisation, where possible, for those between the ages of seven and eleven, marks a new departure and brings with it new problems. To-day primary education is recognised as ending at about the age of eleven; secondary education of various types is that which follows; and the importance of considering the education of children in primary schools as something which must have a character of its own, arises from these facts ... clarification of the purpose of the primary school is the necessary pre-requisite of an improvement in its quality. It becomes possible to concentrate attention on the task of making provision for a relatively homogeneous group. If the successful development of secondary education depends on treating the years after eleven as a definite phase in child-life, with distinctive educational requirements and with problems of its own, the necessity for a similar realisation of the special province and role of primary education is not less imperative. The primary school is not a mere interlude between the infant school and the later stages of education, nor is its quality to be judged by its success in preparing children to proceed to the latter. It is continuous with both, because life is continuous, and it must be careful, accordingly, to preserve close contact with both. But just as each phase of life has its special characteristics, so the primary school has its special opportunities, problems, and difficulties; and these it must encounter by developing its own methods, perfecting its own technique and establishing more firmly its own standards of achievement and excellence. Its criterion must above all be the requirements of its pupils during the years when they are in its charge, not the exigencies of examinations or the demands of the schools and occupations which they will eventually enter. It will best serve their future by a single-minded devotion to their needs in the present, and the question which most concerns it is not what children should be — a point on which unanimity has hardly yet, perhaps, been reached — but what, in actual fact, children are. Its primary aim must be to aid children, while they are children, to be healthy and, so far as is possible, happy children, vigorous in body and lively in mind, in order that later, as with widening experience they grow towards maturity, the knowledge which life demands may more easily be mastered and the necessary accomplishments more readily acquired.... During the last forty years, and with increasing rapidity in the twelve years since 1918, the outlook of the primary school has been broadened and humanised. To-day it includes care, through the school medical service, for the physical welfare of children, offers larger, if still inadequate, opportunities for practical activity, and handles the curriculum, not only as consisting of lessons to be mastered, but as providing fields of new and interesting experience to be explored; it appeals less to passive obedience and more to the sympathy, social spirit and imagination of the children, relies less on mass instruction and more on the encouragement of individual and group work, and treats the school, in short, not as the antithesis of life, but as its complement and commentary.

What is needed now is not to devise any new system or method, but to broaden the area within which these tendencies are at work. It is not primarily a question of so planning the curriculum as to convey a minimum standard of knowledge, indispensable though knowledge is, and necessary as is the disciplined application by which alone knowledge can be acquired. The essential point is that any curriculum, if it is not to be purely arbitrary and artificial, must make use of certain elements of experience, because they are part of the common life of mankind. The aim of the school is to introduce its pupils to such experiences in an orderly and intelligent manner, so as to develop their innate powers and to awaken them to the basic interests of civilised existence. If the school succeeds in achieving that aim, knowledge will be acquired in the process, not, indeed, without effort, but by an effort whose value will be enhanced by the fact that its purpose and significance can be appreciated, at least in part, by the children themselves.... Few features in the history of the last thirty years are more striking or more inspiring than the improvement in the health, the manners, the level of intellectual attainment, the vitality and happiness of the rising generation. In that improvement the schools have played no unimportant part. The primary school is on the way to become what it should be, the common school of the whole population, so excellent and so generally esteemed that all parents will desire their children to attend it. It is in the light of that ideal that we should wish our report to be read. We do not pretend to have made startling discoveries or to have enunciated novel truths. The root of the matter is, after all, simple. What a wise and good parent would desire for his own children, that a nation must desire for all children ... the special task of the schools which are concerned with the later years of primary education will be to provide for the educational needs of childhood, just as it is the function of the nursery and infant schools to deal with the needs of infancy, and of the post-primary schools to deal with the needs of adolescence. In framing the curriculum for the primary school, we must necessarily build upon the foundations laid in the infant school and must keep in view the importance of continuity with the work of the secondary school, but our main care must be to supply children between the ages of seven and eleven with what is essential to their healthy growth — physical, intellectual, and moral — during that particular stage of their development. The principle which is here implied will be challenged by no one who has grasped the idea that life is a process of growth in which there are successive stages, each with its own specific character and needs. It can, however, hardly be denied that there are places in our educational system where the curriculum is distorted and the teaching warped from its proper character by the supposed need of meeting the requirements of a later educational stage. So long as this is the case, it must remain important to emphasise the principle that no good can come from teaching children things that have no immediate value for them, however highly their potential or prospective value may be estimated. To put the point in a more concrete way, we must recognise the uselessness and the danger of seeking to inculcate what Professor A.N. Whitehead calls inert ideas — that is, ideas which at the time when they are imparted have no bearing upon a child's natural activities of body or mind and do nothing to illuminate or guide his experience.

There are doubtless several reasons why a principle so obviously sane should in practice be so often neglected. Perhaps the reason most relevant to our inquiry is that in the earliest days of popular education children went to school to learn specific things which could not well be taught at home — reading, writing and cyphering. The real business of life was picked up by a child in unregulated play, in casual intercourse with contemporaries and elders, and by a gradual apprenticeship to the discipline of the house, the farm, the workshop. But as industrialisation has transformed the bases of social life and an organisation — at once vast in its scope and minute in its efficiency — has gripped the life of the people, discipline associated with the old forms of industrial training has become increasingly difficult outside the walls of the school. The schools whose first intention was to teach children how to read have thus been compelled to broaden their aims until it might now be said that they have to teach children how to live. This profound change in purpose has been accepted with a certain unconscious reluctance, and a consequent slowness of adaptation. The schools, feeling that what they can do best is the old familiar business of imparting knowledge, have reached a high level of technique in that part of their functions, but have not clearly grasped its proper relation to the whole. In short, while there is plenty of teaching which is good in the abstract, there is too little which helps children directly to strengthen and enlarge their instinctive hold on the conditions of life by enriching, illuminating and giving point to their growing experience.

Applying these considerations to the problem before us, we see that the curriculum is to be thought of in terms of activity and experience rather than of knowledge to be acquired and facts to be stored. Its aim should be to develop in a child the fundamental human powers and to awaken him to the fundamental interests of civilised life so far as these powers and interests lie within the compass of childhood, to encourage him to attain gradually to that control and orderly management of his energies, impulses and emotions, which is the essence of moral and intellectual discipline, to help him to discover the idea of duty and to ensue it, and to open out his imagination and his sympathies in such a way that he may be prepared to understand and to follow in later years the highest examples of excellence in life and conduct. . . .

Infant Education: The Orthodox View Repeated

(From The Hadow Report, 1933, *Report of the Consultative Committee on Infant and Nursery Schools*, London, HMSO, pp. 121–2, 122–3.)

This is an extract from a third report issued by the Consultative Committee of the Board of Education. The text is taken from the Committee's discussion of the infant school, described in Simon's essay as 'a unique feature of the English educational system' (p. 10). Liberal romanticism has always flourished in infant education to a greater extent than elsewhere; its influence can be clearly discerned in the text: 'It is the *special* function of the infant school to provide for the educational *needs* of the years of transition that separate babyhood from childhood.' 'Our main concern must be to supply children between the ages of five and seven plus with what is essential for their *healthy growth*.' 'It is through opportunities for further *experience* and *experiment* that *growth* will be best be fostered in the infant school.' The 1933 Report did much to confirm liberal romanticism as the accepted orthodoxy of English infant education.

At the age of five the child enters the primary school. In this country it has been the custom to deal with the earlier years (five to seven *plus*) in separate schools or divisions and since these are part of the primary school, it follows that the fundamental principle governing the curriculum which we enunciated in chapter VII (pages 91 to 106) of our *Report on the Primary School* applies broadly to the infant school also. *It is the special function of the infant school to provide for the educational needs of the years of transition that separate babyhood from childhood.* Our main concern must be to supply children between the ages of five and seven *plus* with what is essential for their healthy growth, physical, intellectual, spiritual and moral, during this particular stage of development. This does not mean that this stage is to be, or indeed can be dealt with in isolation from what has preceded it or from what is to follow it. It is essential to keep in mind the importance of continuity with the work of the later years of the primary stage, but no one who has grasped the idea that life is a process of growth in which there are successive stages, each with its own specific character and needs, will dispute the conclusion that the best preparation for a later stage is to base the training during the particular stage on the immediate needs of that stage. In the words of our previous Report (page 92), 'no good can come from teaching children things that have no immediate value for them, however highly their potential or prospective value may be estimated.'

We therefore adopt as the guiding principle determining the training and teaching of the infant school the same principle that we laid down for the primary school as a whole: *'the curriculum is to be thought of in terms of activity and experience rather than of knowledge to be acquired and facts to be stored.'* ...

This general principle requires the whole span of the primary stage for its full development and its application to the infant school will be more pervasive than direct. It would be entirely inappropriate for instance to attempt to translate it into any rigid or logically ordered curriculum for the infant school. Indeed to apply the term 'curriculum' at all to the training and teaching carried on before the age of seven *plus* is dangerous as suggesting a systematic procedure which is opposed to the unordered way in which the child has hitherto developed his powers. The child, even if he has unhappily missed the advantages of a good home, or a good nursery school or class, has already learnt to use his native powers over a wide field of activities and interests. He has acquired mastery of the simpler muscular movements and has begun to coordinate them. He has learnt to speak, and begun to build up a working vocabulary by which to express his needs. He has a general, and in some directions an intimate knowledge of his surroundings from which he has gained simple ideas about many things. All this he has acquired through personal experience and experiment in the natural course of growth, but always without plan or ulterior motive. It is through opportunities for further experience and experiment that growth will best be fostered in the infant school.

This does not mean that the school has to stand aside and leave the child to follow the wind's way all the time. In recent years, both in this country and in America, there has been a tendency to exaggerate the childishness of the child, and to deprecate any procedure, especially in the training of the mind, which will interfere with it. The free urge of the child is not sufficient to secure his full development; the best way of doing things is not always that which occurs to the unaided mind. The school, in providing opportunities for new experiences must deal with the child as a growing person and not merely as a child. It is hardly yet realised that after infancy is over intellectual growth is in many respects quantitative, rather than qualitative, and shows itself not by the sudden appearance of the power to carry out a particular intellectual function, but by a gradual extension of the time during which that function is carried out continuously. The healthy child attaches no value to his childishness; all his instincts prompt him to savour the experiences of those older than himself, and the school which would confine him entirely to childish things because it thinks them most appropriate to his years, does him a grave disservice. In the provision of opportunities for further experience and experiment the school must make a delicate compromise between the immediate powers and needs of the child and his future needs as a potential adult.

A Rationale for Infant and Junior Education

(From Board of Education, 1937, *Handbook of Suggestions for Teachers*, London, HMSO, pp. 98–9, 100–3.)

This extract, comprising two passages from the 1937 *Handbook of Suggestions*, summarizes the rationale for infant and junior school education which was part of 'official' thinking immediately prior to the Second World War and which was a major influence on the development of primary education following the 1944 Education Act (pp. 34–6). The passage on the infant school has a confident buoyant tone; the one on the junior school is rather more tentative, though still optimistic and forward-looking. The extract neatly embodies many of the tensions (some would say 'contradictions') which have characterized primary education (especially at the junior stage) since its inception: the tensions between what children are interested in and what adults judge to be of 'permanent value', between education for the here-and-now and 'preparation for the years beyond', between 'freedom' and 'discipline', and between teachers taking advantage of children's 'dominant interests' and 'planning a systematic course of activity' for their pupils. The attempted resolution of such tensions (or contradictions) has had, and continues to have, both positive and negative consequences; it has contributed to both the fascination and the frustration involved in educating children in primary schools.

An Infant School that is animated by the principles indicated in this chapter will be a place where life has all the freshness and vividness of early childhood, and where activities are pursued in a spirit of lively adventure. It will have provided the children with many new interests; and it will have given them in a measure suited to their age and maturity both the freedom and the discipline, through which their awakening sense of group membership may best be developed. Its product should be a child who, in comparison with the child of five, is self-possessed, responsible, independent, and capable of devoting himself to a straightforward task with a remarkable intensity of purpose and a high regard for the proper way of performing it.

Similarities and Differences between Children in Their Development

So far as the simple physical and social habits are concerned development is largely a matter of age and training and should not differ greatly as between one child and another at the end of the school course; but where activities are concerned which are not matters of routine, there will be marked variation in achievement. Hence it is undesirable in this field to lay down any fixed standard which all Infants may be expected to reach. Where conditions are normal, however, it is probable that the great majority of the children will have acquired considerable facility in speech, and in reading, writing, and number....

Differences in attainment, and indeed in most other respects, are natural and inevitable among children at the end of their course in the Infant School, but what has been said in this chapter will show that behind these differences lies a common training with a common purpose. Expressed briefly, this purpose is to give the children experiences that will help them both now and later to adjust themselves to life in a civilised community.

1 The Junior School as a New Form of Organisation. The Junior School, which is the final stage of primary education, is intended for children between the ages of 7 and 11, though in practice both the lower and the upper age-levels are found to vary considerably. It did not come into being because children of this particular age-range were known to have special needs and to present special problems. It arose through the successive splitting off of the Infant and the Senior School from the original type of Public Elementary school for children of all ages. As yet the Junior School is young, its traditions are still in the making, and its full potentialities unrealised, but already it has shown a surprising vitality and has opened up new vistas of educational progress that promise well for its future. Separation from the other types of school has given an impetus to the study of the characteristics of children between the ages of seven and eleven, but it has also brought difficulties inseparable from introducing yet another division into what after all is a single process of continuous organic growth. The transfer from stage to stage almost inevitably entails a temporary check in progress and only by the closest co-operation between Infant, Junior, and Senior Schools can the loss be reduced to a minimum.

2 The Junior Stage No Longer Regarded as One of Mere Passive Preparation. For a long time the work of Standards I to IV, the counterpart of the modern Junior School, was based upon the idea that the period of childhood which they covered was pre-eminently a time for a narrow and rigorous treatment of the 'Three Rs'. It was a common belief that the rote-memory of the child was then at its best, and his nature so plastic as to retain almost indelibly the impressions of any lesson learnt. Particularly did the notion prevail that the mind of the child at this age was a tool to be fashioned and sharpened for the more serious work of the later stages of education.

The danger in this view is, of course that the minds of children may be regarded merely as passive instruments in the hands of the teacher. But as Professor Whitehead has said, 'The mind is never passive.... You cannot postpone its life until you have sharpened it. Whatever interest attaches to your subject-matter must be evoked here and now; whatever powers you are strengthening in the pupil, must be exercised here and now.'

3 The Modern View: A Systematic Course Based on Children's Natural Interests. One of the main concerns of the Junior School will be to discover those activities of child life which promise the best combination of immediate interest and permanent value. The work of exploration demands close observation of the spontaneous behaviour of children and systematic study of their development. We must take note of the things which seem to them to be most significant in the life of the world about them, and find out in what sort of terms they explain to themselves the events that make up their life. We must study the growth of their language and familiarise ourselves with the words, phrases, and modes of expression, that pass into currency at this stage, and with the forms of literature that have the strongest attraction. We must discover their compelling motives and modes of activity and be able to say what things make the deepest appeal to their feelings. In all these things the Junior School child differs in greater or lesser degree from younger and older children, and only upon an understanding of his particular qualities and immediate needs can his education be rightly conducted.

But to take advantage of dominant interests as they arise does not mean that the course which the school provides should be wholly opportunist or unorganised. Inherent in each stage of growth are the resources of the earlier stages and the potentialities of the later ones, and it would be folly to ignore at any moment either the experiences which the child has hitherto had or the qualities which the school aims at developing. The school cannot evade the duty of planning a systematic course of activity for its pupils; nor can it escape its responsibility to the public for maintaining proper standards of achievement in the fundamental subjects.

II The Aim of the Junior School

4 A Full and Active Life Not Dominated by External Standards. There is every reason why the aim of the Junior School should be set out in terms of the nature of its pupils rather than exclusively in terms of subjects and standards of achievement. It would, indeed, be anomalous if on the one hand Infant School teachers were to be encouraged to plan a life of free activity for little children, and on the other hand the teachers of Senior School children were to be asked to arrange courses of work suited to the varying capacities and interests of their pupils, while at the same time the Junior School child had still to do nothing but follow the traditional track with an imposed curriculum and an external standard of achievement. If it is wrong in the Infant and Senior Schools to ignore the capacities and interests of children it must be equally wrong in the Junior School. But it by no means follows that children should decide entirely for themselves exactly what and how much they should do or learn, irrespective of the requirements of the society in which they find themselves. The course of instruction for children which will appear reasonable to most teachers will be one which can be followed with due regard both for the welfare of the child and for that of the community of which he is a member.

It is not to be expected that Junior School teachers will be able to free themselves at short notice from the external standards to which they have so long been accustomed. Indeed, it may be some time before they can win the same measure of freedom as is commonly conceded to their colleagues in other departments. Already, however, many Junior Schools have profited by adopting the more generous ideas set out in the Hadow report on *The Primary School*, and the movement thus started will no doubt gather momentum as the years go by.

It will be the aim, then, of the Junior School to provide an education which is suited to the nature of children between the ages of seven and eleven as well as to give a satisfactory form of preparation for the years beyond.

The Formal Establishment of Primary Education
(From the Education Act, 1944, extracts from Parts I, II and IV.)

The 1944 Education Act formally established primary education as the first of 'three progressive stages' into which the statutory system of public education in England and Wales was to be organized. This organization still remains, albeit with some minor modifications, such as those resulting from the creation of middle schools which straddle the primary and secondary stages. Under the 1944 Act, the Minister of Education was made responsible for the education of the people of England and Wales, and the local education authorities were made responsible, 'under his control and direction', for providing 'efficient education' throughout the three stages of primary education, secondary education, and further education. The extract also includes the clauses on the act of worship and religious instruction and the clause outlining the duty of each parent to 'cause' his child 'to receive efficient full-time education suitable to his age, ability and aptitude, either by regular attendance at school or otherwise'.

THE EDUCATION ACT · 1944

Part I

I. It shall be lawful for His Majesty to appoint a Minister (hereinafter referred to as 'the Minister') whose duty it shall be to promote the education of the people of England and Wales and the progressive development of institutions devoted to that purpose, and to secure the effective execution by local authorities, under his control and direction, of the national policy for providing a varied and comprehensive educational service in every area.

THE STATUTORY SYSTEM OF EDUCATION. LOCAL ADMINISTRATION

Part II.6

Subject to the provisions of Part I of the First Schedule to this Act, the local education authority for each county shall be the council of the county, and the local education authority for each county borough shall be the council of the county borough.

THE THREE STAGES OF THE SYSTEM

Part II.7

The statutory system of public education shall be organized in three progressive stages to be known as primary education, secondary education, and further education; and it shall be the duty of the local education authority for every area, so far as their powers extend, to contribute towards the spiritual, moral, mental, and physical development of the community by securing that efficient education throughout those stages shall be available to meet the needs of the population of their area.

Part II.25

(1) Subject to the provision of this section, the school day in every county school and in every voluntary school shall begin with collective worship on the part of all pupils in attendance at the school, and the arrangements made therefore shall provide for a single act of worship attended by all such pupils unless, in the opinion of the local education authority or, in the case of a voluntary school, of the managers or governors thereof, the school premises are such as to make it impracticable to assemble them for that purpose.

(2) Subject to the provisions of this section, religious instruction shall be given in every county school and in every voluntary school.

(3) It shall not be required, as a condition of any pupil attending any county school or any voluntary school, that he shall attend or abstain from attending any Sunday school or any place of religious worship.

(4) If the parent of any pupil in attendance at any county school or any voluntary school requests that he be wholly or partly excused from attendance at religious worship in the school, or from attendance at religious instruction in the school, or from attendance at both religious worship and religious instruction in the school, then, until the request is withdrawn, the pupil shall be excused from such attendance accordingly.

Part II.35

In this Act the expression 'compulsory school age' means any age between five years and fifteen years, and accordingly a person shall be deemed to be over compulsory school age as soon as he has attained the age of fifteen years:

Provided that as soon as the Minister is satisfied that it has become practicable to raise to sixteen the upper limit of the compulsory school age, he shall lay before Parliament the draft of an Order in Council directing that the foregoing provisions of this section shall have effect as if for references therein to the age of fifteen years there were substituted references to the age of sixteen years. . . .

Part II.36

It shall be the duty of the parent of every child of compulsory school age to cause him to receive efficient full-time education suitable to his age, ability, and aptitude, either by regular attendance at school or otherwise.

Part II.68

If the Minister is satisfied, either on complaint by any person or otherwise, that any local education authority or the managers or governors of any county or voluntary school have acted or are proposing to act unreasonably with respect to the exercise of any power conferred or the performance of any duty imposed by or under this Act, he may, notwithstanding any enactment rendering the exercise of the power or the performance of the duty contingent upon the opinion of the authority or of the managers or governors, give such directions as to the exercise of the power or the performance of the duty as appear to him to be expedient.

Part IV.76

In the exercise and performance of all powers and duties conferred and imposed on them by this Act the Minister and local education authorities shall have regard to the general principle that, so far as is compatible with the provision of efficient instruction and training and the avoidance of unreasonable public expenditure, pupils are to be educated in accordance with the wishes of their parents.

A Report of Progress

(From Central Advisory Council for Education (England), 1967, *Children and Their Primary Schools*, Vol. 1, London, HMSO, pp. 460–1, 463.)

As a landmark in the development of English primary education, *Children and Their Primary Schools* (the Plowden Report) features in several places in this volume. Pages 89–90 discuss the 'recognisable philosophy of education' with which the report has been associated; pages 206–10 refer to the importance the report attached to the home and, in particular, to parental attitudes, and pages 211–13 feature its proposals for educational priority areas. Here, there is a brief extract from the report's concluding chapter, the first section of which attempts a review of developments since the Second World War. The report is emphatic about the degree of progress which has been achieved: 'Our review is a report of progress and a spur to more ... in the report we have for the most part described English primary education at its best. That in our belief is very good indeed. Only rarely is it very bad. The average is good.' Though making passing reference to the 'moral dismal corners of primary education', the report is optimistic and confident — so much so that a questionable assertion is paraded as unchallengeable truth: ' "Finding out" has proved to be better for children than "being told".' The publication of the Plowden Report represented the high water mark in the fortunes of primary education post-Hadow. Neither before nor since have primary schools and, in particular, primary teachers received so much support and approval for their policies and practices.

1229. Our terms of reference, 'primary education in all its aspects and the transition to secondary education' were wide ranging. Our interpretation has been correspondingly wide. We conceived it as our duty to see the primary school not only in its strictly educational context but also as a part of society and of the economy. . . .

Since the war there has been a great increase in secondary education and in further and higher education. These developments were necessary if we were to hold our own with other advanced industrial countries. We are certainly not leading an advance party. This progress, however, has been in part at the expense of primary education. We think that a higher priority in the total educational budget ought now to be given to primary education. It is desirable in its own right: nobody ought to be satisfied with the conditions under which many of the four million primary school children are educated. It is also desirable in the interests of secondary and further education. A good deal of the money spent on older children will be wasted if more is not spent on them during their primary school years. Yet not everything costs money. Some of our recommendations call mainly for changes of attitude, understanding and knowledge in individual teachers. . . . We found that the Hadow reports understated rather than over estimated the differences between children. They are too great for children to be tidily assigned to streams or types of schools. Children are unequal in their endowment and in their rates of development. Their achievements are the result of the interaction of nature and of nurture. We conclude that the Hadow emphasis on the individual was right though we would wish to take it further. Whatever form of organisation is adopted, teachers will have to adapt their methods to individuals within a class or school. Only in this way can the needs of gifted and slow learning children and all those between the extremes be met.

1233. The appraisal we have made of the curriculum, and of the methods which have proved to be the most fruitful, confirm many or most of the suggestions that our predecessors made. Their insights have been justified and refined by experience. 'Finding out' has proved to be better for children than 'being told'. Children's capacity to create in words, pictorially and through many other forms of expression, is astonishing. The third of the three R's is no longer mere mechanical arithmetic, French has made its way into the primary school, nature study is becoming science. There has been dramatic and continuing advance in standards of reading. The gloomy forebodings of the decline of knowledge which would follow progressive methods have been discredited. Our review is a report of progress and a spur to more.

1234. This may sound complacent. We are not. The more dismal corners of primary education produce plenty of evidence of parochialism, lack of understanding of the needs of children and of the differing homes from which they come, lack of continued training of teachers and lack of opportunities for professional contact. Had we ignored these facts, we should have ignored what is well known to teachers and, increasingly, to parents. If all or most teachers are to approach the standards of the best, far more effort must be put into their in-service training.

There may be a good school without good buildings, though this is no excuse for the deplorable conditions in which many children are educated. There cannot be a good school without good teachers. Even one or two can leaven a whole staff. But there are staffs without leaven. We set these facts down here lest we should be accused of wilful ignorance because in the Report we have for the most part described English primary education at its best. That in our belief is very good indeed. Only rarely is it very bad. The average is good. . . .

The favourable judgment we have formed of English primary education as a whole, and the confidence with which we have made far reaching recommendations for its development reflect the devoted and perceptive service of the vast majority of the 140,000 primary school teachers. Most of what is best in English schools has come straight from individual teachers. We could wish no child a happier fate than to encounter as many do, a good teacher.

Progress Refuted: The Black Papers

(From Cox, C. and Dyson, A. (Eds), 1970, *Black Paper Three*, Critical Quarterly Society, p. 8; Cox, C. and Dyson, A. (Eds), 1969, *Fight for Education*, Critical Quarterly Society, pp. 5–6; Cox, C. and Dyson, A. (Eds), 1969, *Fight for Education*, Critical Quarterly Society, pp. 48–50.)

The accolade given primary education by the Plowden Report (pp. 38–9) was swiftly followed by virulent criticisms from those described in the second section of the source book as 'educational conservatives' (pp. 95–105). Through a series of 'Black Papers', the first of which was published in 1969, they attacked what they saw as 'permissive education' in primary schools and in comprehensive secondary schools. These three extracts capture the vehemence and insidiousness of their criticisms.

The first extract provides a simplistic but powerful caricature of what progressivism (or liberal romanticism) implies, that is, 'the belief that children must find out everything for themselves, must never be told, never be made to do anything, that they are naturally good, must be free of all constraints of authority.' Progressive education, and with it primary education, are then implicated in 'the growth of anarchy' and in 'the worst features of the pop and drug world'. The direct association of primary education with the 'roots of anarchy' is asserted in the second extract, published in 1969 at the climax of student unrest which had included the affair of Hornsey College of Art where the art students had taken control of their own education for several months. The 'revolution' in primary education (note the political overtones in the word) is directly linked with student protest and unrest. The third extract has been included partly as an example of the hearsay evidence on which many Black Paper assertions were based. It was written by a secondary school headteacher whose knowledge of primary schools was gleaned from some of his 'friends in junior schools'. Here again, changes in primary education are held partly responsible for changes in the wider society, such as the growth in the numbers of mentally-disturbed people, the increase in crime and the trend towards greater truancy at the secondary school stage. Although the absurdity of the most extreme Black Paper criticisms could easily be demonstrated, and although the validity of many of their less extreme assertions could be questioned, the Papers did have a considerable influence on political and public opinion. Why was this? Could it be that there was *some* substance in the disquiet so vociferously expressed by these writers?

[Basic Progressive Fallacies]

Just as the comprehensive factions are now split between traditionalists and non-streamers, so 'progressive' educationists are split in their attitudes to child-learning. Intelligent progressives rightly believe in the value of discovery methods, creative activity, new techniques of learning. So do we, when these methods are applied with common sense. But intelligent concern for new methods shades off quickly into the belief that children must find out everything for themselves, must never be told, never be made to do anything, that they are naturally good, must be free of all constraints of authority. Parents know how often the teachers in a progressive school do not properly understand the sophisticated techniques of 'progressivism,' and slip into easy acceptance of this permissive ethos. A teacher is an authority, a person specially trained to develop the potentiality of his pupils and in the disciplines of study. It is his duty to pass on skills and wisdom to children, and to ensure that they are trained in civilised manners and ways of thought. If he abdicates these reponsibilities he is guilty of the most serious neglect. This training must include helping children to evaluate the teacher's own opinions critically, to look objectively at all dogmas. But the duty of parents and teachers is *to direct*, not to remain passive and uncommitted to high standards of behaviour and learning.

The results of permissive education can be seen all round us, in the growth of anarchy. For if adults withdraw and allow children to find their own 'true' personality, the result is a vacuum into which all the worst features of the pop and drug world can enter.

[The Roots of Anarchy]

What are the roots of anarchy? In a recent article in the *Evening Standard* (15th October 1968) Timothy Raison suggested that a common malaise runs right through our present education; the roots of student unrest are to be found as early as the primary school:

> Nevertheless, the art students often embody the innocence, the passionate belief that if you would only leave people alone their best would come out, that is the attractive element in true, non-violent anarchism.... And this romantic view is widespread, not merely among art students, but many others who are likely to be marching....
>
> I sometimes wonder whether this philosophy — which I am sure many of the protest marchers feel, however inarticulately — does not owe at least something to the revolution in our primary schools.
>
> Influenced by a variety of psychologists from Freud to Piaget, as well as by educational pioneers from Froebel onwards, these schools have increasingly swung away from the notion (which characterises secondary education) that education exists to fit certain sorts of people for certain sorts of jobs, qualifications and economic roles, to the idea that people should develop in their own way at their own pace.

Competition has given way to self-expression. And now this has worked its way up to the student generation. They don't want to be chivvied through exams on to a career ladder: they want to be (what they conceive to be) themselves: and if the system stands in the way of this, marching about Vietnam in some indefinable way enables them to make a protest against the system and in favour of something better. At times one can imagine them, like infants' school children on television singing: 'There is a happy land, far far away'....

[Some of My Friends in Junior Schools Tell Me....]

No one would wish to return to the days when junior school children were rigidly confined to their rows of desks and learnt long lists of largely unrelated facts. But what is happening now? The restrictions of the old 11+ have almost disappeared, but the resulting freedom has been used in a multiplicity of ways. The children moving on to secondary schools present a bewildering problem even among the brightest groups.

Some at eleven can write fluently and imaginatively paying due attention to paragraphing, punctuation and spelling with none of their enthusiasm dampened. Others, of comparable intelligence, write illegibly, have no idea of arrangement of work and are thoroughly frustrated. Unfortunately the numbers in the latter category increase year by year.

These observations lead one to study methods in junior schools to try to see what is the effect not only on their progress mentally, but on their attitude and behaviour.

According to some present day psychologists, all teaching of young children must be child-centred: the teaching must grow from the child's interests and not be limited by any time-table divisions. Freedom of expression is all important and the method of conveying it is relatively unimportant. So far so good, but at what point should the child learn that correctness and accuracy have their place? All may be well at the junior school stage, but the freedom of the look and say method of reading, of the outpouring of ideas without arrangement or plan has disastrous results at a later stage. For instance, when learning a foreign language, one incorrect letter may well alter the whole meaning of a sentence.

Some of my friends in junior schools tell me that marking and correcting is a thing of the past as it may bring a sense of failure to a child. So one sees mistakes becoming firmly implanted in the child's mind. Many schools arrange projects for their children and some begin through this to learn the excitement of independent research and the joy of exploring in the library. Others undertake the work but do little more than copy passages from the encyclopaedia and stick cut out pictures in their books.

It is interesting to find that the children who, by the age of eleven, have mastered the skills of the three R's have gained a freedom which enables them to extend their horizons without the frustrations felt by those who at this stage realise the limitations imposed on them by the lack of disciplined thought.

To go back a stage further: at nursery level, the matron of a baby's home is told by the visiting inspector that her nursery is too tidy because she trains her under fives to put away their toys at the end of each day. In a nursery class another inspector says it is wrong to forbid children to take home toys which do not belong to them.

All these children are growing up in a welfare state where it appears to them that everything in school is free; it is a world where they follow their own inclinations and where things are not right or wrong but merely a matter of opinion and where there are virtually no rules.

Does this produce a happy, well-balanced child? Statistics show the opposite to be true. Never before have there been so many people mentally disturbed, and the official criminal statistics, issued by the Home Office, show that the greatest number of indictable offences recorded for males occurs in the 14 and under 17 age group, 3,242 per 100,000 of the population in that age group.

Attitudes and behaviour in the country as a whole, of course, exert great pressure on your young people, but the schools must take a share of the blame. At the very heart of the problem is the need for self-discipline, for freedom within certain defined limits, for the security resulting from a realisation of cause and effect, from having certain decisions imposed and being able to enjoy the peace and security that comes from an ordered life.

The world is a noisy, chaotic and restless place, yet in schools we see the same lack of quiet encouraged. It is putting a great strain on young children to leave them constantly to make decisions with rarely any time in the day when they are quiet and listening. This feeling was expressed in a delightfully naive manner by a little 11 year old, beginning life in an ordered secondary school, who said she liked her new school because discipline was allowed.

A child who has always followed his own inclination finds it hard to sit down and learn his French and Latin verbs or his tables and yet, this knowledge acquired, he has the freedom to make rapid progress towards the exciting discoveries awaiting him at a more advanced stage. How comforting it is to know that, whatever distress there may be among the nations, two and two still make four.

The child who has been free to wander in his junior school much as he pleases, fails to see at a later stage, why he should not wander further afield. Many children who come before juvenile courts have committed their offences during school hours, although the truancy is rarely known at the school. The boy has been present for registration and then has disappeared.

The lack of restraint at junior school level does not have such serious results as when the children are older. There are few restrictions and adolescents are nearly all to some extent rebellious, but they find there are no brick walls available against which they can bang their heads, so they vent their pent-up feelings on railway carriages and on rival youth groups. How much better it is for them to find an outlet for their feelings by breaking some school rule which will not do much harm to anyone! Does not the child-centred training produce the selfish and self-centred adolescent who cares little for any one but himself?

Many of my colleagues who are working in secondary schools would agree that the children who are the most well-balanced and who make the steadiest progress, are those who come from the junior schools where the children have had plenty of opportunity for independent, free study, but who have learnt the importance of listening and concentrating and who have found the satisfaction which comes from doing something, at whatever standard, really well.

The William Tyndale Affair: A Cause Célèbre

(From Gretton, J. and Jackson, M., 1976, *William Tyndale: Collapse of a School or a System?*, Allen and Unwin, pp. 5, 121–6.)

Following the publication of the first Black Papers at the end of the sixties, criticisms of state education continued to grow, fuelled by the writings and public statements of 'educational conservatives', by disquiet over reading standards and the teaching of English, and by growing political disillusionment with the effects of public expenditure on education. In the mid-seventies criticism of primary education reached a peak, partly as a result of the notorious William Tyndale affair. William Tyndale was a junior school in north London where in 1974 some of the staff, especially Messrs Ellis, Haddow and Austin, introduced radical changes, associated with an extreme form of liberal romanticism (though it needs to be said that many adherents of liberal romanticism did not wish to associate themselves with some of the changes introduced or with the manner of their introduction). The result was a violent dispute within the staff of the junior school, and between a segment of the staff and the school managers, which then involved leading local government politicians, the local inspectorate and, eventually, in 1975–6, a public inquiry conducted by Robin Auld QC into the teaching, organization and management of the junior school and its neighbouring infant school.

The affair was important in bringing out into the open and to the forefront of discussion a number of major educational problems requiring clarification and resolution. These issues included the control of the school curriculum, the responsibilities of local education authorities, the accountability of teachers, and the assessment of effectiveness in education. These problems have been the subject of much discussion and considerable action since 1976, as other papers in this source book and its accompanying volume testify. No attempt is made here to do justice to the complexity of the William Tyndale affair, especially to the differing interpretations of both events within the school and their wider significance. This extract provides *one* summary interpretation, written by two educational journalists. For other interpretations, readers are referred to Ellis, T. *et al.* (1976) *William Tyndale: The Teachers' Story*, Readers and Writers Publishing Cooperative; Dale, R. (1981) 'Control, accountability and William Tyndale', in Dale, R. (Ed.) *Politics, Patriarchy and Practice*, Lewes, Falmer Press, pp. 209–219; and Auld, R. (1976) *William Tyndale Junior and Infant Schools Public Inquiry*, London, ILEA.

In the autumn of 1973 William Tyndale was an ordinary enough junior school in a rundown area of north London; within just two years the school had fallen apart and striking teachers, angry parents and helpless politicians were confronting one another through the headlines of the national press and the current affairs programmes of television. It took a further year, which must have seemed to many of those directly concerned to have lasted as long as the previous two, for the inquiry to be completed and its report published and, in a further blaze of publicity, for the leading politicians and the more active of the school's managers to resign while the headteacher and five of his colleagues prepared to face disciplinary proceedings. . . .

The main ingredients of William Tyndale could be found all over the country: a staff with strong radical convictions, a weak headteacher, a dithering inspectorate, worried parents and a local education authority that did not know what it wanted of its primary schools. The mixture was common enough, but previously it had not been thought of as dangerously explosive. The *Zeitgeist*, however, had changed. Gone were the heady, spendthrift days of the 1960s when education and all the social services boomed, and books like Anthony Crosland's *The Future of Socialism* (actually published in 1956) could paint a rosy picture of a future full of beautiful people all happily caring for one another. In their place was the pessimism of the seventies, with their rapidly deteriorating cities and their visions of permanent economic decline inducing a desire to hang on to what was known and tangible, however irrational that might be. ('Catch a falling £ and put it in your pocket, Save it for a rainy day.') Combined with the fact that people's expectations of the welfare state had outrun their willingness to pay the consequent taxes, this meant, in education, a decline in the power of the teacher (the labour market was no longer running in his favour) and a concern for minimum standards. At its best, this could mean a concern for minimum standards for all children; at worst, it tended to be more selfishly inspired.

Attainment. Mr Ellis, Mr Haddow and Mr Austin, if not all their followers, had a fairly clear idea of what they expected schools to do. Schools, for them, had a profound effect on children; the point was how to use that effect ... their main preoccupation was with the (largely false) dilemma of whether they, and schools, should be agents of social change or agents of social control. They wanted change and that was a perfectly respectable position. That sort of thinking had not only inspired much of the Plowden Report on primary education, it had been responsible for the millions of pounds invested in Western-type education in the newly independent countries of the Third World. Thousands of teachers, too, who were not necessarily as extreme in their methods, were concerned that schools should exist to serve not just the average and above average, but also, and perhaps especially, the below average. Interestingly, by the time they came to give evidence at the inquiry, both Mr Ellis and Mr Haddow had adopted the position which has come to be associated with Christopher Jenks, following the publication in 1974 of his book *Inequality* — namely, that as agents of social change, schools and education were non-starters. However many resources were poured into them, schools just did not make that much difference to the life chances of the disadvantaged children. Whatever the rights and wrongs of that controversy, few people, whether parents, teachers or educationists, have ever behaved as though schools did not affect society. Most people, though, being naturally conservative, wanted them to buttress the society they knew rather than change it into something they did not; if change was to come, they wanted it brought about by mature minds which had been educated to be critical while at school — a very different proposition from the radical one.

Another view was that schools existed not to change society, but to prepare for change. The world was changing very much faster than in previous generations, and it was a reasonable prediction that the rate of change would go on accelerating. Technology that was taught in schools today would be out of date tomorrow, and would in any case be too much for any one individual to master. The world of tomorrow was bound to be a world of group activity and co-operative projects and it was important that children be prepared for a world of continuous adaptation. All questions of social reform apart, co-operative informal teaching methods would be more suitable for that purpose than formal, traditional ones.

Either of these approaches — changing society or preparing society for change — was bound to make exceptionally heavy demands on the teachers. The great innovators in education were all exceptionally gifted pedagogues. At William Tyndale, there were a few good teachers but that was not enough, even if it had been supplemented by the diligence and enthusiasm which many teachers show, on which to build the ambitious programme the staff had in mind. Teacher training, too often thought of as a panacea, could make little difference, as colleges of education were limited both by the quality of the students they received (Mr Ellis was one of the very few graduates in primary teaching) and by the intrinsic difficulty of teaching people how to teach. All they could do was to provide their students with a minimum of further education, a few good ideas for progressive teaching and one or two basic techniques of classroom control which it was hoped would act as a safety net.

What was left, then, as an aim of primary education? Once the 11-plus had gone, there was no measure of achievement at all, however unsatisfactory. Children moved on up into secondary schools when they were 11 or 12, whether or not they had learnt how to read or write; there was no question of keeping anyone back. The notion, popular among parents, that children should be taught the 'basics' while at primary school was the only hint of a minimum standard. Even that, though, if it were to be formalised, would require some form of attainment testing, and since the abolition of the 11-plus it had become impossible for educationists to reach agreement among themselves on a value-free objective test — or even on the merits of testing at all.

Assessment. It is difficult to talk of assessing the performance of teachers when there is no agreement on what teachers are supposed to be doing. In the absence of any agreed criteria all that is possible is for professional experts to go into a school, look at what the teachers were doing, talk to the teachers themselves about it, and then make their own assessment. That is what a full inspection was all about. But there was no basis on which one school could be compared with another — except the subjective impressions of the inspectors, a group of men or women whose sole qualification for the job was that they had once been good teachers. Moreover, the touchiness of many teachers and their unions, concerned with their status as qualified professionals and therefore not subject to outside control ... contributed to the general unwillingness of the inspectors to force their opinions down anybody's throat.

Another factor at work here was what one might term the unacceptable face of authority. Research evidence suggests that both parents and children like teachers to be tough, authoritarian figures but, like social workers, teachers had come increasingly to think of themselves — and be thought of by others — as one of the 'caring professions'. That meant, in this context, that they did not make 'judgments' about their 'clients', whether they were incontinent old men, dangerous juvenile delinquents or backward school-children; all they did was make the non-moral assessments that were necessary for them to do their job. But what was true for their clients had also become true for themselves. Together with the fashion for participation and democratic decision making in everything (and not just politics), that meant that it had become virtually impossible for anybody who had a position of responsibility in the hierarchy to say: you are doing your job badly — do it better or get out. Soft-centred liberals should remember that more revolutions have failed through inefficiency than for any other single cause.

Inspectors, therefore, preferred the role of adviser. In fact, rather than see themselves as the shock troops who could be sent in at the slightest hint of trouble, they preferred the image of staff officers, helping, advising, prodding the troops in the front line, but rarely taking the field themselves. They saw themselves rather as a teaching elite; knowing that there were not enough of them to go round every school, they tried to spread their qualities as wide as possible by working at one remove through the classroom teachers. There was certainly a case for that, just as there was a case for fewer, better-trained teachers and more untrained (and less expensive) teacher aides.

But if inspectors abandoned their role of assessors, who was to make judgments about how well or badly teachers might be doing their job? The teachers themselves? The ILEA inspectorate, at least, would like to evolve some formula for teacher self-assessment. Curiously, however, that is something teachers themselves have not pressed for. Despite their oft-repeated concern for their professional status, they have been strangely unpreoccupied with some of the things that would give meaning to that status, such as control of the qualifications for entry into the profession, or the sort of freedom from the judgment of outsiders that is enjoyed by doctors and lawyers. Both these professions have some sort of council which hears and judges claims of professional misconduct. The teachers have never pressed for a general teaching council along the same lines.

Indeed, one of the points to emerge most strongly from any discussion of the issues raised by William Tyndale was the ambiguous nature of teachers' claims to professional status. Certainly, there were ways in which teachers could justifiably claim that they adopted a professional attitude to their work, but the fact that in other respects society was not prepared to grant them that status was symptomatic of something very important. A doctor's clinical judgment is just that: a judgment of fact and diagnosis about clinical matters. A teacher's judgments are made about values, and very fundamental ones at that. Those sort of judgments were thought to be too important to be left to teachers alone.

Accountability. But by the same token as the story of William Tyndale amply illustrated, nobody else was willing to take on the responsibility for the judgments — and performance — of teachers. If nothing was done about it, sooner or later market forces would begin to take a hand, as in a sense they did at William Tyndale when parents began to vote with their feet by taking their children away. There were already pressures, by those involved in educational politics on the extreme left as well as the extreme right, for this sort of parental assessment to be institutionalised — say, through a voucher system, under which parents would be given an educational ticket for each of their children which they could cash at the school of their choice. Schools would then be competing with one another for clients, just as they do already in the private sector. But that would have several disadvantages, the major one of which is common to all solutions that involve the undifferentiated voice of parents or the community. Everybody has been to school, but nobody has ever learnt anything about education there. If it was wrong, as it surely was, to leave teachers free to exercise their uncontrolled will on children, then it was also wrong to leave decisions about the type of education children should receive to parents. . . .

That left some sort of representative community control — which of course had been the thinking behind the institution of managers and governors in the first place. However, . . . under that system managers left a lot to be desired, in terms of both their appointment and their competence. One solution might have been for them to be directly elected at the same time as local councillors. But however they might be appointed, they had to know something about education and educational issues so that, if teachers or the headteacher wanted to introduce new policies into the school, they would have to justify them to the managers — but to managers who would be reasonably well informed.

All these issues we have mentioned — the powers and responsibilities of local authorities, the control of the curriculum, the criteria for assessing a school's efficiency, the aims of primary education, the need for testing, the role of the inspectorate, the function of managers and the professionalism and accountability of teachers — are proper subjects for consideration by the Secretary of State for Education. Only he can see that the lessons of

William Tyndale are, where appropriate, applied nationally and only he is in a position to assess the implications for bodies such as the Schools Council. But above all, only the Secretary of State can take an overview of the issue which underlies every other: the proper balance to be struck between politicians and the community on the one hand, and teachers and the other professionals on the other. After William Tyndale, the Secretary of State can no longer pretend, as he and his predecessors have so often tended to do, that it is all happening somewhere else.

Public Debate and Official Response

(From Department of Education and Science, 1977, *Education in Schools: A Consultative Document*, London, HMSO, pp. 2–3, 8–9.)

Criticism of the state educational system led to James Callaghan's Ruskin College speech in the autumn of 1976 and to the resulting 'Great Debate', discussed in paragraph 1.5 of this extract. The extract is taken from the 'Green Paper' of 1977, published by the Department of Education and Science at the end of the 'Debate'. The first of the two passages reproduced here attempts a balanced appraisal of the criticisms made about the educational system in general. It acknowledges that 'there is legitimate ground for criticism and concern' but refutes the major claim of critics: 'It is simply untrue that there has been a general decline in educational standards.' The second passage discusses primary education and argues that 'child-centred' developments have been influential but only partially successful in the schools. It provides a heavily qualified endorsement of developments in primary education. In particular, liberal romanticism is believed to have been successful only 'in the right hands'. The Department stresses the centrality of numeracy and literacy and the importance of progression within the curriculum, of continuity between schools and of consistency across schools 'in kind if not in detail'. The 1977 Green Paper was the first Departmental criticism of the effects of developments in primary education, since these were set in train by the Hadow Report of 1931 (pp. 25–30). The period since 1977 has seen considerable efforts being made by the Department, through the Inspectorate, to help schools 'restore the rigour without damaging the real benefits of the child-centred developments'.

Introduction

1.1   In his speech at Ruskin College, Oxford on 18 October 1976 the Prime Minister called for a public debate on education. The debate was not to be confined to those professionally concerned with education, but was to give full opportunity for employers and trades unions, and parents, as well as teachers and administrators, to make their views known.

1.2   The speech was made against a background of strongly critical comment in the Press and elsewhere on education and educational standards. Children's standards of performance in their school work were said to have declined. The curriculum, it was argued, paid too little attention to the basic skills of reading, writing, and arithmetic, and was overloaded with fringe subjects. Teachers lacked adequate professional skills, and did not know how to discipline children or to instil in them concern for hard work or good manners. Underlying all this was the feeling that the educational system was out of touch with the fundamental need for Britain to survive economically in a highly competitive world through the efficiency of its industry and commerce.

1.3   Some of these criticisms are fair. There is a wide gap between the world of education and the world of work. Boys and girls are not sufficiently aware of the importance of industry to our society, and they are not taught much about it. In some schools the curriculum has been overloaded, so that the basic skills of literacy and numeracy, the building blocks of education, have been neglected. A small minority of schools has simply failed to provide an adequate education by modern standards. More frequently, schools have been over-ambitious, introducing modern languages without sufficient staff to meet the needs of a much wider range of pupils, or embarking on new methods of teaching mathematics without making sure the teachers understood what they were teaching, or whether it was appropriate to the pupils' capacities or the needs of their future employers.

1.4   Other criticisms are misplaced. It is simply untrue that there has been a general decline in educational standards. Critics who argue on these lines often make false comparisons, for instance with some non-existent educational Golden Age, or matching today's school leavers against those of a generation ago without allowing for the fact that a far larger proportion of boys and girls now stay on into the sixth form. Recent studies have shown clearly that today's schoolchildren read better than those of thirty years ago. Far more children, over a wider range of ability, study a modern language or science than did a generation ago. Many more take, and pass, public examinations. Many more go on to full-time higher education.

1.5   The picture, then, is far from clear. Much has been achieved: but there is legitimate ground for criticism and concern. Education, like any other public service, is answerable to the society which it serves and which pays for it, so these criticisms must be given a fair hearing. In response to the Prime Minister's initiative the Ministers concerned held a series of meetings with national organisations representing a wide range of people having a special interest in education. These meetings set the scene for a series of regional conferences held in the opening months of this year with invitations issued to local authorities in each region, to teachers, employers, trades unions, the churches, parents and students. In this setting many valuable ideas were put forward, both at the conferences themselves and in written documents. The conferences were followed by a further round of meetings with those consulted the previous autumn. This combination of meetings and conferences — in many ways a unique form of consultation for this country — identified a substantial measure of agreement on what needed to be done to improve our schools....

Primary Schools

2.1   Primary schools have been transformed in recent years by two things: a much wider curriculum than used to be considered sufficient for elementary education, and the rapid growth of the so-called 'child-centred' approach. The primary curriculum has been enriched by a feeling for colour, design and music, and by the introduction of simple scientific ideas. Children engage in work designed to increase their control over themselves physically and mentally, to capture their imagination and to widen their knowledge and understanding of the world about them. The child-centred approach takes advantage of the child's individual stage of development and of his or her interests: it complements the wider curriculum by harnessing the natural enthusiasm of young children for learning things by their own efforts instead of merely being fed with information. In the right hands, this approach has produced confident, happy and relaxed children, without any sacrifice of the 3Rs or other accomplishments — indeed, with steady improvement in standards. Visitors have come from all over the world to see, and to admire, the English and Welsh 'primary school revolution'.

2.2   Unfortunately, however, the work has not always been in the hands of experienced and able teachers. While only a tiny minority of schools adopted the child-centred approach to the exclusion of other teaching methods, its influence has been widespread. It has proved to be a trap for some less able or less experienced teachers who applied the freer methods uncritically or failed to recognize that they require careful planning of the opportunities offered to children and systematic monitoring of the progress of individuals. While the majority of primary teachers, whatever approach they use, recognize the importance of performance in basic skills such as reading, spelling and arithmetic, some have failed to achieve satisfactory results in them. In some classes, or even some schools, the use of the child-centred approach has deteriorated into lack of order and application.

2.3   The challenge now is to restore the rigour without damaging the real benefits of the child-centred developments. This does not imply any great change in the range of what is taught, but the following features, already recognized by the most effective schools, need to be accepted throughout the system:

  (i)   in all schools teachers need to be quite clear about the ways in which children make and show progress in the various aspects of their learning. They can then more easily choose the best approach for their pupils.
  (ii) Teachers should be able to identify with some precision the levels of achievement represented by a pupil's work. In parts of the curriculum such as arithmetic, it is relatively easy to organize a

series of targets for the pupils according to a logical sequence of difficulty. In other parts of the curriculum where teachers are planning to develop their pupils' imagination and social awareness, it may not be possible to be so precise. Teachers can nonetheless plan a progression in these parts of the curriculum and so ensure that they make their proper contribution to the child's education.

(iii) Teachers in successive classes or schools need to agree about what is to be learned. They should as a matter of professional habit pass on clear information about work done and levels of achievement.

(iv) Even allowing for local and individual needs, children throughout England and Wales have many educational requirements in common. It is therefore reasonable to expect that children moving from a primary school in one part of the country to another elsewhere will find much that is familiar in kind if not in detail.

(v) There are some skills for which the primary schools have a central, and indeed over-riding, responsibility. Literacy and numeracy are the most important of these: no other curricular aims should deflect teachers from them. By definition they must form part of the core of learning, the protected area of the curriculum.

A Brief Professional Appraisal

(From Department of Education and Science, 1978, *Primary Education in England: A Survey by HM Inspectors of Schools*, London, HMSO, pp. vii–viii.)

This short piece is included as a complement to the paragraphs from the 1977 Green Paper (see pp. 51–4). It is reproduced from the foreword to the report of the national primary survey, which involved HM Inspectors of Schools in visiting a representative sample of English primary schools and in inspecting the work of over a thousand classes. The passage provides a very brief summary of the state of English primary education in the mid-seventies, as seen by the Inspectorate. It records the concern of primary teachers that children should be well-behaved, literate and numerate; it refers to 'encouraging results' in reading; but it also acknowledges that 'in some aspects of the work the results overall are sometimes disappointing'. The report to which it was a foreword presented a description and analysis of primary education based on professional observation and evaluation rather than on hearsay or on wishful thinking. Its significance is discussed in the next extract in this section; many of its most important passages are reproduced in Volume 2 of the source book.

This report is an account of some aspects of the work of 7, 9 and 11 year old children in 1,127 classes in 542 schools so chosen as to be representative of primary schools in England. It gives information about the organisation of schools, the range of work done by the children, and the extent to which the work is matched to their abilities. It also includes an analysis of the scores obtained by children in objective tests administered by the National Foundation for Educational Research.

It is based on the direct observation of children's work that HM Inspectors experienced in primary education. The suggestions for the further development of that work reflect what was already successfully practised in a substantial number of classes and schools. . . .

What emerges from the report is that teachers in primary schools work hard to make pupils well behaved, literate and numerate. They are concerned for individual children, and especially for those who find it difficult to learn. If the schools are considered as a whole, it is clear that children are introduced to a wide range of knowledge and skills.

The efforts of children and teachers have produced encouraging results in the reading test for 11 year olds, where objective comparisons can be made with the past; there is no comparable objective evidence of past standards in other parts of the curriculum. In some aspects of the work the results overall are sometimes disappointing. The reasons for this vary, and rarely stem from inattention or poor effort. In some cases, the evidence clearly suggests that difficulty arises because individual teachers are trying to cover too much unaided. Some fairly modest re-adjustment of teachers' roles would allow those with special interests and gifts to use them more widely, as is shown in some classes where particularly successful work is done.

'Demythologising' Primary Education

(From Richards, C., 1980, 'Demythologising primary education', *Journal of Curriculum Studies*, 12, 1, pp. 77–8.)

The HMI primary survey, featured in the previous extract, was the first publicly accessible, rigorous professional appraisal of developments in primary education since the changes set in train by the Hadow Report of 1931 (see pp. 25–8). As this extract argues, the survey did much to strip primary education of its myths, both favourable and unfavourable. The picture it painted was one of organizational rather than curricular or pedagogic change: a perspective very different from the views of either primary education's detractors or sympathizers. Many of the previous papers in this section dealt in visions, in prescriptions, or in criticisms (often based on very partial evidence). The survey provided much needed information to correct utopian or simplistic perspectives. It provided an agenda for professional discussion and renewal, based on closer knowledge of primary policy and practice.

When the history of English primary education in the twentieth century comes to be written, three dates are likely to be seen as particularly significant: 1931, when the notion of the 'primary school' received official recognition in the Hadow Report; 1967, when 'child-centred education' (however loosely defined) was accepted as the official orthodoxy of English primary education; and 1978, when the publication of *Primary Education in England: A Survey by HM Inspectors of Schools* provided the first publicly accessible, rigorous overall appraisal since Hadow. (The appraisal conducted by the Inspectors of the Plowden Committee in the 1960s did not, in my view, meet these criteria.) The survey published in 1978 counters very effectively the wild assertions and scare-mongering rife following Tyndale and Bennett in 1976, a year when the fortunes of primary education reached their nadir. However, it provides cold comfort for curriculum developers and for both the advocates and the critics of 'child-centred education'. To my mind, with the major exception of its very simplistic treatment of teaching approaches the survey does justice to many of the complexities, successes, shortcomings and subtleties of primary practice.

The survey's findings and recommendations do not rest on carefully conducted classroom observational research: it cannot be criticized by the canons of OSCAR, PROSE, STOS, ORACLE or whatever. It is an evaluation report in a very important but (for curriculum workers) much neglected tradition which has its own repertoire of techniques, its own standards of appraisal and its own code of professional conduct — a tradition stemming from the 'craft' of school inspection. However, the confidential, almost apostolic nature of the transmission of this craft (itself predating curriculum evaluation as we know it by almost a century) makes it impossible for outsiders to provide (in its own terms) methodological critiques of the national inspection reported in the survey. Perhaps publication of this and other recent DES appraisals of practice might encourage curriculum scholars interested in evaluation to explore more thoroughly the problems and issues raised by the evaluative aspects of inspection.

Most importantly, the survey underlines the centrality of the curriculum in primary education. Its concern for intellectual development through appropriately designed curricula represents a significant readjustment of emphasis compared with Plowden; though important, organization, pupil grouping, teaching approaches, staffing and resource allocation have for too long preoccupied decision-makers in primary schools and deflected them from the still more central tasks of deciding what particular skills, concepts, knowledge and attitudes primary children should acquire and of incorporating these into planned (and evaluated) teaching/learning sequences. The report focuses on these problems, draws up a valuable, though incomplete, agenda for professional discussion (which cannot be reviewed in detail here) and provides opportunities for work in curriculum studies to make a contribution to reviewing, refining and enhancing the rather impoverished primary curriculum.

Curriculum studies in the British tradition has been largely ameliorative in orientation, with the problems of secondary education being predominant among its concerns. In comparison, the primary curriculum has been relatively neglected, partly at least because those working in curriculum have appeared to accept the mythology of primary education current over the last decade or so. The survey does much to 'demythologize' primary education. Judging from the practices revealed in the survey, the 'quickening trend' towards 'child-centred education' detected by the Plowden Committee has not materialized on a substantial scale in top infant and junior classes; 'the primary school revolution' has not been tried and found wanting but never been tried at all except in a small number of schools; most primary school teachers have not responded in the 'open', flexible, imaginative way curriculum developers naïvely assumed they would. In particular, most proposals for curriculum change made in the 60s and early 70s have been based on assumptions about teaching, learning, knowledge and children which do not appear to inform the practice of the majority of teachers. The current curriculum is revealed as scarcely more than a revamped elementary school curriculum with the same major utilitarian emphases.

These findings raise a number of interesting questions. How and why did the myth of 'the primary school revolution' arise? How was it sustained for such a long period? In whose interests was it perpetuated? What part was played in this by the media (and those with ready access to the media) and by individuals like Christian Schiller who seems to have exercised an unpublicized but tremendous influence on many who later became important opinion-leaders? During the period 1960–1975 what was the nature of the 'political' interplay among various interest groups within primary education?

The major changes that the survey notes are organizational rather than curricular — in particular the remarkable spread of non-streaming and the introduction of vertical grouping in a substantial number of infant and junior classrooms. How did the non-streaming movement develop, by whom was it fostered and for what reasons? Were the practices associated with the supposed 'revolution' simply teachers' pragmatic, relatively superficial responses to the need to cope with unstreamed or vertically grouped classes? Has organizational rather than curricular or pedagogic change been the major distinguishing feature of primary education during the last 20 years?

In this way, the publication of the national survey raises many important issues for students of the primary curriculum, some concerned with the recent history of primary education, and others with future curriculum policy-making (though the latter need the perspective provided by the former). The survey should be read as both an educational and a political document — political in the sense that it reflects and influences the distribution and exercise of power over the primary curriculum. If it appears to read awkwardly at times, this is not usually because it is hiding a lack of substance behind convoluted, constipated civil-service prose. This is because it is deliberately conveying different messages at different levels to a variety of interest groups within and outside primary education. *Primary Education in England* is often very subtle and not always clear, but so is the process of primary education itself.

Achievement in Primary Schools

(From the Third Report of the Education, Science and Arts Committee of the House of Commons 1986, *Achievement in Primary Schools*, 1, London, HMSO, pp. xii–xxi.)

This extract endorses the view of primary education reflected in much of the previous historical discussion. It extends the debate by the emphasis it places upon recognizing the importance of primary education as laying the foundation of all future learning. The Committee were also realistic that the expectations they set were likely to require time for teachers to implement. Such time was clearly unavailable to primary teachers with their limited non-contact time. In the light of this, the Committee recommended the appointment of 15,000 additional primary teachers, not to reduce class sizes, but to create opportunities for teachers to work with each other, with individuals and small groups of children. Considerable reference is made throughout the report to the importance of the Plowden Report in establishing the basis for thinking about the education of primary-aged children, but the report moves the discussion on to consider the economic and social context within which primary schools operate.

1.1   Primary education is the foundation upon which the education system is built. A child's experience of primary school and the education he or she receives there has a substantial, and often crucial, effect both on future attitudes to education and on future achievement. Successful teachers of young children require a high degree of skill, keen perception of children's reactions and educational needs, and a clear comprehension of the underlying principles of what is being taught. Nursery and primary school teaching is not second best to teaching in other phases. In particular it calls for high organising ability to ensure that young children are working effectively and efficiently.

1.2   Your Committee makes this observation at the outset because we have obtained the firm impression during the course of our inquiry that the importance of primary education and of the skills required by the primary teacher are often undervalued. Many of our witnesses have supported our view. The recent emphasis upon the later years of education is only partly responsible. There is still, unfortunately, a tendency to regard primary teaching as 'second best', and to look upon primary education as a prelude to real education, and the differential resourcing of primary and secondary, to the disadvantage of the former, is but one aspect of this entrenched and misguided tradition. We hope that this Report can make some contribution to erasing this attitude once and for all. The comments we make below, some of which are critical, are made in the context of the high value we place upon education in the primary years and our high regard for the skills of good primary school teachers and our recognition of the complexity of their work.

1.4 The focal point for the inquiry was to identify those factors which encourage and those which inhibit a child's achievement at primary school. We also agreed to have regard to the following subjects (though not in any order of priority): (1) pre-school education and the links with primary school; (2) the effects of falling rolls; (3) the viability of small schools; (4) methods of teaching: including remedial teaching; (5) the curriculum: including the role of specialist teaching in providing that curriculum; (6) the role of parents; (7) the role of governors; (8) comparisons with primary education in other countries.

1.5 Apart from the HMI survey *Primary Education in England* of 1978 (which covered only the 7–11 age range), the last detailed study was the monumental report of the Central Advisory Council for England chaired by Lady Plowden, published in 1967 and based on almost four years' work. We did not attempt to emulate so comprehensive a review of the subject, but we deliberately decided to make our survey wide ranging. Primary education is not an area which can easily or sensibly be broken down into compartments. In a young child's life each part impinges upon and merges with all other parts and this unity embraces not only school but also life at home and in the community. It seemed to the Committee that any inquiry must focus on the nature and on the needs of children within society and consequently to have regard to the full range of their experience. In this respect, at least, our Report has something in common with the Plowden Report.

1.6 We also had another reason for deliberately choosing a broad approach. Education has seldom been more important for the nation's future than it is today, but seldom has it confronted greater pressures. These arise partly because of falling rolls, economic recession and the effects upon schools of public expenditure policies, partly as a result of rising public expectation of what both primary and secondary education can and should achieve and partly as a result of changes in technology, for example in mass communication and micro-computing. An assumption of the mid-1960s, reflected in the Plowden Report, was that full employment was here to stay. That now seems a world away. Parents are inevitably more concerned with the effectiveness of schools when the job prospects for any child without educational qualifications are poor than they were not so long ago when the problem was to persuade teenagers to stay on at school rather than to go straight into employment. Rising public concern and expectation are inevitably reflected in the attitude and policy of central government which, also inevitably, sees the provision of a well educated and trained workforce as essential to improving the economy. It is no coincidence that the period of economic difficulty that set in with the oil crisis in the early 1970s has also seen an acceleration of the central government's search for greater influence over the curriculum and a higher performance from teachers. Over the same period violence within society has become a national concern and there has been an increase in recorded crime, including juvenile crime. Schools have been under attack from some quarters for being responsible for lowering national standards of public behaviour. They have also shared with other representatives of authority, such as the police, the experience of having their authority questioned by some sections of the public. All these pressures have affected morale. Schools have become less certain of their objectives and teachers of their role. The examination in detail of one sector of the education system has enabled us to reflect upon a number of the major issues affecting education today.

1.7 Moreover, we have been only too well aware that our inquiry has taken place against the background of what has probably been the most damaging dispute ever to have taken place in the education system. Relations between the Government and many sections of the teaching profession have recently been worse than they have ever been. It would be a fruitless exercise and would only exacerbate the differences if we attempted to apportion blame. What is certain is that raising the quality of education, which is a central theme of the Government's policy, and an aim of all the major political parties, is going to be extremely difficult unless wounds are healed and the morale of the teaching profession improved. Nothing is going to alter the reality that the nation is dependent on the existing teaching force and those who will enter it for improving standards of achievement in education. There is no alternative labour force with magical properties of engendering national rejuvenation which is suddenly going to replace them. Nor, whatever the perceived basis for the alleged 'crisis in education' are dramatic political gestures or cosmetic or presentational changes going to alter the realities of the situation. Any education system is a complex structure. It cannot be changed overnight. In this report we have heeded the advice of an experienced educationalist given to us early in our inquiry 'there is no instant solution to any educational problem: you set a solution into motion today and you will probably realise it in fifteen or twenty years time....' We have therefore taken the long view, but we recognise that much of the progress we wish to see and towards which our recommendations are directed will not be achieved or will be delayed unless those responsible for education — central government, local education authorities, and teachers — are all pulling in the same direction.

Part 1

II Education, Achievement and Values

2.1 The starting point of the Plowden Report was the child and it constantly measured its recommendations against the needs of the individual child at the appropriate age and stage. This reference point is a good one provided the broad needs of society and the longer term needs of children are taken into account as well. In practice virtually all children now have to spend at least 11 years in school. Every child and his or her parents have a right to expect that during that time the education system will enable that child to develop as an individual, obtain a range of skills appropriate to adult needs, and exploit his or her natural abilities. For both children and parents the system will be judged more often than not on the basis of whether it provides the skills and qualifications needed for employment. This is as true at the primary stage as it is at secondary. If one asks children of eight or nine what the purpose of school is one obtains a variety of answers, but quite frequent among them will be 'to get a job' or 'to get a better job'. This is right and proper, and parental concern is inevitable, particularly when unemployment is high and, for the unskilled, looks like remaining so. Government and industry are bound to share this concern when the economic wellbeing of a modern industrial country depends so considerably on the ingenuity and skills of its work force.

2.2 But education is about a good deal more than this. As the Secretary of the Catholic Education Council put it: 'surely one of the purposes of education is to uplift'. The national economy is important, but ultimately a society stands or falls by its social cohesion and by shared moral values. Education, perhaps particularly primary education has a crucial role to play in promoting and safeguarding that cohesion and these values. Schools have the difficult task of being part of the community and at the same time standing for what is best in it as well as giving its children a glimpse of what is most valuable in our civilisation, aesthetically, morally, and spiritually. Such aspirations are not beyond the primary school: many already possess this ethos, whether they fully realise it or not.

2.3 Since the essential foundations of education are moral and spiritual as well as intellectual and physical its aims must be correspondingly broad. We consider in some detail later on in this Report the foundations and the content of the primary curriculum. But, like several of our witnesses, we are attracted, at least as a starting point, to the definition of the aims of education contained in the Warnock Report summarised by Lady Warnock in her brief guide as follows: 'first, to increase a child's knowledge of the world he lives in and his imaginative understanding, both of the possibilities of that world and of his own responsibilities in it; and, secondly to give him as much independence and self sufficiency as he is capable of, by teaching him those things he must know in order to find work and to manage and control his own life'. Although intended as a definition to be used in the context of children with special educational needs it is a valid definition to use in respect of all children. One is tempted to add other items: appreciation of cultural and aesthetic values; the development of natural or acquired abilities; the acquisition of skills, the development of a concept of moral and civic duty but these are, perhaps, only elaborations of the original definition.

2.4   We believe that 'achievement' needs to be assessed in the context of such a broad based definition of education and that such a definition is perhaps particularly relevant at the primary stage when children learn for the first time to live and work together and when beliefs and attitudes are acquired which can last a lifetime. The development of the 'whole child' is not to be despised or lost sight of though the acquisition of skills is an important part of the process. 'Education' encompasses and far exceeds 'training'.

2.5   'Achievement' relates to all these aspects of education. It also relates to each individual child. Each child brings different attributes to a school and different advantages and disadvantages. Each child has a potential for different levels of achievement in different areas. There is consistent and long standing evidence to show that children of families in the Registrar General's social class categories IV and V do less well on average in the education system than those from other social classes, as do children from families affected by poor housing and low family income. Emotional disturbance, which can derive from home background, and language difficulties are also significant factors. Notwithstanding what appear to be significant disadvantages some such children are high achievers. But for a proportion of children from some backgrounds it is a significant achievement if they succeed in keeping up with the average standards of other children; or emerge from the educational system as good and useful citizens.

2.6   Achievement is therefore relative to a variety of factors and consequently difficult to measure. This does not mean that we should not attempt to do so. To do this we need first to define it. Although made in a context of secondary education the analysis of achievement contained in the Hargreaves report is relevant to the primary stage as well. Hargreaves divided achievement into four components or 'aspects' which we might paraphrase as follows:

'Aspect 1': academic attainment as measured by examinations of the traditional kind 'it involves most of all the capacity to express oneself in a written form. It requires the capacity to retain propositional knowledge, to select from such knowledge appropriately in response to a specified request and to do so quickly without reference to possible sources of information. The capacity to memorise and to organise material is particularly important.

'Aspect 2': the capacity to apply knowledge rather than knowledge itself: with the practical rather than the theoretical; with the oral rather than the written. Problem solving and investigational skills are more important than the retention of knowledge.

'Aspect 3': is concerned with personal and social skills; the capacity to communicate with others in face-to-face relationships; the ability to co-operate with others in the interests of the group as well as of the individual; initiative, self-reliance and the ability to work alone without close super-vision; and the skills of leadership.

'Aspect 4': involves motivation and commitment; the willingness to accept failure without destructive consequences; the readiness to persevere; the self-confidence to learn in spite of the difficulty of the task. This aspect may be seen both as a prerequisite to the other three aspects of achievement and as an achievement in its own right.

2.9   What happens in schools is only part of education. Children begin to acquire knowledge and skills from the moment they are born and during the early years parents are normally the child's main educators. Schools have become increasingly aware in recent years that the attitude of parents to what their children do in school and the extent to which they reinforce what is done, continue to play a very significant part in the child's achievement throughout the primary stage and beyond. It is commonsense to suppose that if a parent supports the objectives of the school, and demonstrates to the child by example the value of what the school is teaching then that child will achieve more. Commonsense is supported by a growing body of re-search evidence. The youngest children will tend to be most influenced by the behaviour and attitudes of the family circle (and perhaps more by the community generally) than by school. Both education and achievement will be served if ways of life at school and at home are not needlessly at variance. On occasion, however, the school will need to stand by its values.

2.10   Establishing those values is not easy. In a thoughtful memorandum the Methodist Church reminded us of the changes that have taken place in society in the past few years and which schools are expected to take in their stride. There has, for example, been a decline in Christian belief and church attendance. Teachers are expected to uphold standards and values which much of society has long since abandoned. Other witnesses also reminded us of significant cultural changes that have taken place. Very many schools contain children from a number of different ethnic backgrounds and even where all children are from the ethnic majority, schools need to take account of cultural diversity and the multi-faith society in which we live. Sexual equality is an issue which has gained considerably in importance and which concerns primary as well as secondary schools. We visited schools where a large percentage of children's parents (or at least, children's fathers) were unemployed, and others in communities where there had recently been bitter industrial conflict. If a school gets too far out of touch with the society which it serves, if it becomes for some of its parents and children part of an 'alien culture' unrelated to their own then it will fail to recognise and respond to the needs of its children. More so now than in the past there are wide differences in society on a large number of moral and social issues. The dilemma of schools in providing effective moral and social education in such circumstances is most acute at secondary level, but exists at primary level too. Yet despite the difficulties, we believe that each school would gain from establishing a clear sense of the values which it cherishes and wishes to defend and to foster and keep to them though with tolerance and with sensitivity.

III   Some Issues in Primary Education

3.1 Expectations of what schools should achieve and what children can achieve are rising. To quote Professor Philip Taylor of Birmingham University again 'since the beginning of the century we have ... leapt an enormous distance with primary school teachers and primary school children, and rightly so. I think we can make another leap forward'. We agree. But this will only be done if we first make a realistic assessment of the difficulties to be overcome and the constraints upon future progress. We also need to take some account of how the existing varieties and complex structure of primary education came to be, and to look more closely at the changing demands of society. In making this assessment we have found it useful to use the Report of the Central Advisory Council on Primary Education, the 'Plowden Report', as a reference point. It has been of fundamental importance to many of the educational developments over the last 20 years and many of its conclusions and recommendations continue to be relevant.

References

CENTRAL ADVISORY COUNCIL FOR EDUCATION (England) (1967) *Children and Their Primary Schools*, London, HMSO.

COMMITTEE OF ENQUIRY INTO THE EDUCATION OF HANDICAPPED CHILDREN AND YOUNG PEOPLE (1978) *Special Educational Needs*, London, HMSO.

ILEA (1984) *Improving Secondary Schools*, London, ILEA.

Primary Education: Evaluation and Assessment

(From Bolton, E.J., 1985, 'Assessment techniques and approaches: An overview', in *Better Schools: Evaluation and Appraisal*, London, HMSO, pp. 27–9, 30.)

Throughout the 1980s, economic reality considerably affected education and primary schools began to feel demands for criteria by which their effectiveness could be judged. The extract which follows, from Her Majesty's Chief Inspector of Schools, raises important questions about the extent to which the primary curriculum could be appraised and the learning achieved by children at the end of their primary education evaluated.

There is, I imagine, little disagreement with the general idea that the work of the education system should be subject to a range of assessments, evaluations and reviews. But every particular attempt to introduce or reform an assessment or evaluation procedure seems to give rise to prolonged, and sometimes bitter, debate and argument.

Public examinations are perhaps the most obvious example from the last twenty years. Some would of course argue for their total abolition, but even those who take that view would in general substitute some other way of assessing pupils' performance. Each proposal for change has rightly been subjected to critical scrutiny because there genuinely are dangers. We know from experience that examinations can be designed or used so that they limit pupils' development; so that they favour this or that section of society; so that they lead to rigidity in the system, preventing change and development; so that they exercise an undesirable and over-strong influence on what is taught. The current debates about the appraisal of the performance of teachers and the evaluation and assessment of whole schools reveal sharply divided views about the efficiency of proposed techniques, and rightly stress the complexity of the realities with which these techniques seek to deal. Yet judgements are frequently made about individual teachers and particular schools — judgements which often have a significant effect for the futures of those concerned, and few people can be satisfied that such judgements are usually soundly based. What is at issue is not whether judgements should or will be made — the question is how are they going to be made.

Indeed, a national education system costing over £13 billion, having as its central purpose the education of the people of England and Wales, that was not subject to review, evaluation and assessment is unthinkable. In one way or another, of course, a great deal of assessment and evaluation takes place all the time, nationally, at LEA level and in schools and classrooms. Some of this — public examinations for example — is carried out across the whole country. Whereas much of the rest is local (LEA screening programmes, for example), or confined to individual schools or even to particular parts of a school.

Whatever the real or perceived limitations of performance assessments of one kind of another, the fact is that in our school system those assessments that enable general messages to be discerned and comparisons to be made across all or large parts of it, are in exceedingly short supply. In some other European countries, which appear to have fewer tests and seem to make less use of external examinations, there is greater national or regional agreement about the curriculum and about the standards to be achieved by the full range of pupils. Within these frameworks the teachers are entrusted with the important tasks of assessment carried out at various stages of the pupils' educational careers. We do not have such frameworks favouring and facilitating assessment.

Much of the same lack of helpful and useful data about the performance of various parts of the system exists at LEA level, although quite a number of authorities have developed systems for screening pupil performance. Although these screening programmes differ from authority to authority, in the main they deal with little more than reading, numeracy and verbal reasoning. In these screening programmes, most LEAs make use of one or other of the variously standardized tests available, none of which is free from controversy as to their reliability, relevance and usefulness in the situations in which they are used.

In schools much assessment is for specific purposes and it is thus not standardized in any way. Nonetheless, there is an understandable and perfectly respectable case for wishing to know how the performance of schools in similar and different circumstances compares. This is not only of interest and use to those outside the schools, such as the LEAs and parents, but it is, or should be, of great importance to the school itself. Any half-way-good school needs and wants to know how it is performing, and part of the answer to that question involves a comparison, however crude, with similar schools in similar circumstances as well as with schools of the same general type in different circumstances.

Perhaps more pressingly in need of consistent assessment and review inside schools is what has come to be called 'the value added factor': what has the teaching and learning in the school added to the pupils' competence, understanding, knowledge and skills? To assess the 'value added' calls for not only suitable instruments and techniques, but also some way of knowing where the pupils started from and where they got to if we are to judge whether the journey was worthwhile. To somewhat oversimplify this complex matter if may be helpful to view it as having two broad uses:

(a) as an input/output model;
(b) as a means of allowing for the effects that external social background factors have on performance.

At the levels of the individual teacher and school it is important to be able to gauge what has been achieved by the pupils in the light of some understanding of where they started from and of what they are capable, and to recognize that even relatively good performance may be poor for those pupils, and indicate poor teaching. This is generally important for all pupils in any type of school. But it is crucial in schools where, despite the best efforts of the teachers, the performance of the pupils as a group falls far short of what can be generally expected of the age range. However, while an assessment of the value added by schools may show that relatively low or poor performance is not a function of poor teaching, it is essential that sight is not lost of the fact that by national standards the performance is poor. Keeping both perspectives in a constructive balance lies at the heart of the difficult task that faces many teachers of maintaining high expectations of individual pupils, while knowing that affecting their pupils generally are realities external to the schools, inimical to educational success and only marginally influenced by good schools and effective teaching.

In seeking to be better informed about the performance of schools and progress towards desired ends there are differences of degree, emphasis and detail between what the Government, the LEAs, schools and individual teachers need to know. But generally in evaluating and appraising the performance of schools and teachers we are all, in one way or another, concerned with:

(i) the curriculum that is offered: its coverage, structure and relevance in terms of what is available to pupils generally as well as what each individual pupil receives;

(ii) the quality of teaching, and of other education processes and learning experiences provided for pupils across the whole curriculum and the whole period of their school education;

(iii) the standards achieved by pupils in relation to their abilities, aptitudes and circumstances across the whole curriculum and period of schooling.

While primary schools must satisfy themselves and others that their curricula are broad, balanced, relevant and that there is appropriate differentiation, it is by no means clear what kind of curricular model or models should form the basis for review and scrutiny at primary level. Similarly the question of what individual pupils receive is a different kind of question in relation to primary schools, where class teaching is the dominant mode of delivery. In addition, while external examinations in secondary schools may be agreed by all to be an insufficient measure of the range of pupil performance and school effectiveness, at least they provide some guidance and may be developed so as to do so more effectively. But there are no comparable or different instruments available for obtaining an overall picture of the achievements of primary-aged pupils.

It is difficult to identify sufficient common ground, or at least sufficient common language, to begin to discuss the primary curriculum nationally, let alone carry out the kind of scrutiny and development required to establish a primary curricular framework and agreed objectives. At every stage such a necessary debate is complicated by sharply polarized disagreements about process and content; teaching children and teaching subject matter; and the balance between generalist and specialist uses of primary teachers. Unlike the secondary phase, there is relatively little history of a sustained debate about, and scrutiny of, the curriculum in primary schools, and while LEAs are now moving, admittedly somewhat slowly, towards establishing curricula-led staffing in their secondary schools, there is very little evidence of any such notion of the primary curriculum developing to which the staffing of the schools could be linked. Yet, paradoxically, the successes of primary education in broadening provision since the 1950s to include music, art, physical science and craft, design and technology (CDT), as well as revealing the high standards that pupils of 10 and 11 can achieve in these and other areas of the curriculum, have added to the pressure for a clearer articulation of what in practice is meant by a broad, balanced and relevant curriculum for 5–11 year-old pupils. Since there is so much similarity of good practice in many primary schools, it looks as if much of the confusion and disagreement about the primary curriculum is essentially semantic. Unless clear formulations can be developed and agreed, and there is no question of forcing primary schools into a secondary curricular mould, it is hard to envisage a constructive approach being developed to the deployment of primary schoolteaching staff; to the initial and in-service education of primary teachers; and to the assessment of how primary schools perform.

There is even less clarity or agreement about the learning standards to be achieved by pupils at the end of the primary phase. As with the debate about the primary curriculum there is a substantial lobby in the primary world that eschews any attempt to establish broad-based notions of standards to be achieved. Some of that resistance stems from a fear about a 'return to the 11-plus' and the restrictions on teaching, learning and children's educational and personal development that went along with it. But the distrust of achievement objectives goes deeper than that. The setting of any external achievement objectives is seen by some as striking at the heart of child-centred primary education. Yet, despite those reservations, most if not all primary teachers have some notions about what they expect their pupils to achieve, not only in terms of individual needs, but as a necessary basis for successful progress through the education system and into the adult world: a preparation for what comes after. Also, most primary teachers would wish parents to understand how the development of the child, on which they are both engaged, relates to the requirements of the 'real world'. Experienced teachers are aware of how the performance of individuals and particular groups of pupils compares with that of similar pupils elsewhere, or those they taught previously. This being so, the challenge facing the primary phase is to articulate those learning objectives in terms of competencies and understandings to be mastered in ways that meet with broad agreement and do not cause damage to what is now commonly agreed to be effective primary practice across a broad and balanced curriculum.

Where then does this leave us in relation to the development of useful techniques, instruments and strategies for assessment and evaluation across the system? There is a lot of useful work under way, but a number of key issues remain and there are some difficulties to be resolved.

Towards a National Curriculum

(From DES, 1987, *The National Curriculum: A Consultation Document*, London, HMSO, pp. 1, 2–4, 6.)

This historical overview of primary education concludes with an extract which catalogues one of the most significant developments in English primary education in the last fifty years: i.e., proposals for a National Curriculum. Volume 2 of this series offers more detail of the responses and reactions to a National Curriculum for primary schools (Lofthouse, 1990).

1   The Government intends to introduce legislation this autumn to provide for a national curriculum in maintained schools in England and Wales. This document sets out the reasons for this decision, describes what the legislation will contain, and indicates what other steps the Secretaries of State for Education and Science and for Wales intend to take so that the national curriculum can begin to be introduced in schools as soon as possible.

The Need for a National Curriculum

4   Since Sir James Callaghan's speech as Prime Minister at Ruskin College in 1976, successive Secretaries of State have aimed to achieve agreement with their partners in the education service on policies for the school curriculum which will develop the potential of all pupils and equip them for the responsibilities of citizenship and for the challenges of employment in tomorrow's world. A substantial measure of agreement has already been achieved, and there is now widespread support for the aims of education which were set out clearly in the White Paper 'Better Schools' (Cmnd — 9469. 1985).

5   Many LEAs and schools have made important advances towards achieving a good curriculum for pupils aged 5–16, which offers progression, continuity and coherence between its different stages. There is much agreement too about the subjects which should be included in the secular curriculum for 5–16 year olds; and valuable progress has been made towards securing agreement about the objectives and content of particular subjects.

6   But progress has been variable, uncertain and often slow. Improvements have been made, some standards of attainment have risen. But some improvement is not enough. We must raise standards consistently, and at least as quickly as they are rising in competitor countries.

7   The Government now wishes to move ahead at a faster pace to ensure that this happens and to secure for all pupils in maintained schools a curriculum which equips them with the knowledge, skills and understanding that they need for adult life and employment. Some schools already offer such a curriculum, but not for all their pupils. Many schools offer something far less good. The Government does not find this acceptable. Nor do parents and others in the community. Pupils should be entitled to the same opportunities wherever they go to school, and standards of attainment must be raised throughout England and Wales.

8   A national curriculum backed by clear assessment arrangements will help to raise standards of attainment by:

(i)   ensuring that all pupils study a broad and balanced range of subjects throughout their compulsory schooling and do not drop too early studies which may stand them in good stead later, and which will help to develop their capacity to adapt and respond flexibly to a changing world;

(ii)   setting clear objectives for what children over the full range of ability should be able to achieve — which the pupils themselves and their teachers, supported by parents and others, can work towards with confidence. This will help schools to challenge each child to develop his or her potential. HM Inspectorate has consistently reported in its national surveys and in many reports on individual schools that a weakness far too frequently apparent in the present system is under-expectation by teachers of what their pupils can achieve. Far from deflating expectations, the national curriculum is intended to help teachers to set their expectations at a realistic but challenging level for each child, according to his or her ability;

(iii)   ensuring that all pupils, regardless of sex, ethnic origin and geographical location, have access to broadly the same good and relevant curriculum and programmes of study which include the key content, skills and processes which they need to learn and which ensure that the content and teaching of the various elements of the national curriculum bring out their relevance to and links with pupils' own experiences and their practical applications and continuing value to adult and working life;

(iv)   checking on progress towards those objectives and performance achieved at various stages, so that pupils can be stretched further when they are doing well and given more help when they are not.

9   In addition to thus raising standards, a national curriculum will:

(i)   secure that the curriculum offered in all maintained schools has sufficient in common to enable children to move from one area of the country to another with minimum disruption to their education. It will also help children's progression within and between primary and secondary education (and on to further and higher education) and will help to secure the continuity and coherence which is too often lacking in what they are taught;

(ii) enable schools to be more accountable for the education they offer to their pupils, individually and collectively. The governing body, headteacher and the teachers of every school will be better able to undertake the essential process of regular evaluation because they will be able to consider their school, taking account of its particular circumstances, against the local and national picture as a whole. It will help alert teachers to problems experienced by individual children so they can be given special attention. Parents will be able to judge their children's progress against agreed national targets for attainment and will also be able to judge the effectiveness of their school. LEAs will be better placed to assess the strengths and weaknesses of the schools they maintain by considering their performance in relation to each other, and to the country at large, taking due account of relevant socio-economic factors; and the Secretaries of State will be better able to undertake a similar process nationally. Employers too will have a better idea of what a school-leaver will have studied and learnt at school, irrespective of where he or she went to school.

10   The Government has concluded that these advantages and consistent improvement in standards can be guaranteed only within a national framework for the secular curriculum. To be effective, that must be backed by law — but law which provides a framework not a straitjacket. Legislation alone will not raise standards. The imaginative application of professional skills at all levels of the education service, within a statutory framework which sets clear objectives, *will* raise standards.

13   English, maths and science will form the core of the curriculum, and first priority will be given to these subjects. They and other foundation subjects are to be followed by all pupils during compulsory schooling. The Government has proposed that, in addition to English, maths and science, the foundation subjects should comprise a modern foreign language, technology, history, geography, art, music and physical education. The degree of definition in the requirements set out for each of these subjects will vary considerably, and will be greatest for the three core subjects.

14   It is not proposed that a modern foreign language should be included in the foundation subjects for primary school children. The majority of curriculum time at primary level should be devoted to the core subjects.

2   Primary Education: Contrasting Views

Introduction

At its simplest, primary education can be regarded as an administrative stage, set up as a result of the 1944 Education Act: 'The statutory system of public education shall be organized in three progressive stages to be known as primary education, secondary education and further education' (see pp. 35–6). Even that seemingly straightforward view has its problems forty years on. Should pre-school education be regarded as part of primary education or separate from it? Are middle schools of all types included, or only some variants, or none?

Primary education, however, is much more than an administrative entity. It is something experienced by millions of children over a number of years and conveyed through the intentions and actions of many thousands of teachers. It is not at all easy to characterize faithfully, but very easy to simplify, as extracts from the Black Papers (see pp. 40–4) illustrate. Primary education comprises beliefs and practices thought appropriate for children in a particular age-range (variously defined, but for our purposes the 5–11 age-group). Primary education does not refer to a clearly specified set of beliefs and associated practices held by *all* teachers and influencing *all* primary-aged children, but to a dynamic variety of competing views as to what the enterprise is all about and how it might be conducted. Though seldom stated explicitly and often taken for granted, these differing views influence the patterns of relationships established between teacher and children, the form of the curriculum undertaken, and the way schools or classes are organized. Except in an administrative sense, there is no single entity called primary education, but a set of competing beliefs (or ideologies) and their associated practices. This section of the book seeks to introduce readers to the most important of these competing ideologies. (For a general introductory perspective on ideologies see Skilbeck, M., 1976, *Ideologies and Values*, E203 Curriculum Design and Development, Open University Press.)

Educational ideologies comprise different clusters of beliefs, values, principles, sentiments and understandings; they attempt to give meaning, and direction to the complex and diverse practical enterprise of teaching. They employ their own combinations of ideas and metaphors which give their adherents sense of what is 'right' for children in schools. Most have their 'gurus', their 'sacred books' and their 'texts'. At least three writers have attempted to examine primary education from this general perspective, though the first of these did not use the term 'ideology' as such. Twenty years ago Blyth (1965) distinguished three 'traditions' (elementary, preparatory and developmental) in the development of English primary education; extracts from his analysis appear as the first paper in section 1 of the reader. More recently, Golby (1982) has examined three 'traditions' in the primary field — the *progressive, elementary* and *technological* traditions (see the last paper in this section). These writers provide alternative frameworks to the one employed here to characterize contrasting views of primary education. Here, four main ideologies are identified (Richards, 1979, 1982):

1 *liberal romanticism* — which starts from, and constantly refers back to, the individual child when developing educational principles. Compared with other ideologies it advocates a more equal partnership of teacher and taught, with teachers learning 'alongside' children, and it offers children a relatively high degree of choice in the type, content and duration of activities;

2 *educational conservatism* — which stresses the importance of continuity with the past and views the curriculum as a repository of worthwhile activities and values into which learners need to be initiated in an orderly systematic way;

3 *liberal pragmatism* — which argues that schools need to be equally responsive to the demands of the wider society as to the 'needs' of the individual. School is seen as providing a set of learning experiences, largely but not entirely structured and directed by the teacher, but respecting, to some degree, both the individuality of the child and the importance of continuity with the past;

4 *social democracy* — which views education as one means towards realizing social justice. School is seen as an agency concerned, not so much with enhancing the individuality of each child, but with helping to create social beings who can work cooperatively to bring about change both in the immediate environment and in society generally.

With the exception of the last extract, the extracts forming this section have been chosen to illustrate each of these ideologies. They demonstrate clearly that primary education is far from being a simple uncontentious matter.

References

GOLBY, M. (1982) 'Microcomputers in the primary curriculum', in GARLAND, R. (Ed.) *Microcomputers and Children in the Primary School*, Lewes, Falmer Press.

RICHARDS, C. (1982) '*Primary Education 1974–80*', in RICHARDS, C. (Ed.) *New Directions in Primary Education*, Lewes, Falmer Press.

A   *Liberal Romanticism*

Basic Assumptions

(From Blyth, A. (Ed.) 1988, *Informal Primary Education Today: Essays and Studies*, Lewes, Falmer Press, Introduction pp. 1–5.)

One of the problems for students of primary education is the looseness of many of the terms used in educational literature. Terms such as 'child-centred', 'open' or 'informal', for example, have a range of meanings. Too often, authors do not clarify what they mean by particular terms in particular contexts. In the first extract in this section, Alan Blyth provides a thoughtful and critical appraisal of the major principles of 'liberal romanticism' or 'informal education' as he describes it. He identifies five aspects of informality which reflect how children learn and the role of the teacher in that process. Such beliefs are deeply held but, often, not made explicit by teachers subscribing to this view of primary education. They underlie the criteria for a 'good' school put forward in the second extract, the 'philosophy of education' discussed in the third, and the approach advocated in the fourth. This is followed by Jennifer Nias' discussion of teacher's accounts of primary education in action. The ideas expressed in these extracts are also endorsed by Armstrong's summary of Hawkin's 'Informed vision', which appears later in the text (pp. 166–72). For a critical analysis of the issues raised readers should consider Dearden's analysis of child-centred education (pp. 139–42) and Bonnett and Doddington's discussion of the contribution of philosophy to decision making in primary schools (pp. 173–80).

Today in 1987 public education is a matter for public debate. After more than a decade of ferment, education is now to be the subject of major legislation that will affect the entire structure and process of public schooling in England and Wales.

Within public education, primary education will receive its full share of scrutiny, as the legislative process begins to roll. This will be something almost unknown for half a century. Since the 1930s, and even more so since the widespread elimination of selection for secondary education, the political searchlight has been focussed elsewhere, while primary education, and especially nursery-infant education, has been left to develop an optimistic autonomy of its own, behind what it has now become fashionable to describe as a screen of secrecy. But now, again, primary education has become problematic.

The debate about primary education will centre around several issues. The first of these is about the nature of primary education itself. Should it be based essentially on the needs and present interests of children, or should primacy be accorded to the acquisition of skills needed in secondary education and afterwards? Should it be essentially formal and traditional, or essentially informal and progressive? These are questions that the public, encouraged by the media and by some politicians, would like answered. Although each question permits of a continuum of answers from one extreme to the other, the ballot box, and the impending legislation, may give the impression that they can be answered in a simple, straightforward way.

The second issue arises directly from the first, and is exemplified by that impression. At one extreme are found those who believe, with Matthew Arnold (in an uncharacteristic moment), that primary education is a simple, easy matter that can be understood by any competent parent or employer or businessman or shop steward in a few weeks, though the grasp required by a Secretary of State might take a little longer. It is these who believe that a simple choice is possible on the first issue. At the other end of the continuum are the professionals, differing among themselves, but all in some measure experienced in the practice and study of primary education, who are obliged by the very nature of their commitment to engage in constructive criticism, rather than to endorse simple answers to simple questions such as 'Is informal primary education good or bad?'. The public reception of Neville Bennett's first major study of teaching styles (Bennett *et al.*, 1976) showed clearly how readily the two issues can become entangled. For the attempts made to use his carefully-designed research and carefully-qualified findings as ammunition in the first debate inevitably involved his study itself in the second. In its more extreme form, this second controversy is really about the nature of professional competence. The accumulated experience of all who have been concerned with primary education is now sometimes alleged to be nothing more than pseudo-expertise, an Emperor's-clothes facade for personal aggrandizement or political subversion and for an annexation of parental rights which is now to be countered by repossession through the agency of a resolute government. Of course there have been a handful of instances that have given substance to such allegations, but not such as to warrant an indictment of an entire profession whose responsible evolution is itself the best guarantee against perversion or excess. As with child health, so with child education, the basis for effectiveness is a genuine partnership between parents who must in some ways know their own children as nobody else can, and professionals with an expertise based on wider knowledge and experience. That is the stance that must, inevitably, be taken by teachers and others involved in primary education against the populist claims of today.

[Blyth goes on to suggest that the term 'informal' itself demands some scrutiny since it defies simple logical definition.]

It certainly should not be thought to imply flabbiness or aimlessness, as is sometimes believed. In practice, it is as likely to be opposed to 'traditional' as to 'formal'. It invokes much the same images of educational ideology and practice as are summoned up by 'progressive', 'child-centred' (the one shrewdly analyzed by Harold Entwistle, 1970), 'developmental' or even 'open'. Yet all of these adjectives are themselves rather cavalier ways of grouping together ideas which, in detail, display considerable discrepancies and even contradictions. In order to impart some additional structure as well as to extend a little the analysis of informal primary education, five aspects of informality are selected for particular attention.

The first of these aspects is informality in *pedagogy*. By this is meant an emphasis on educational play, and subsequently on experimentation, problem-solving, exploration, guided discovery, and data search, rather than on formal instruction. It implies the strenuous engagement of all children in these procedures.

A second aspect that sits easily alongside the first is informality in *curriculum*. Here, projects and topics and centres of interest take the place of separate subjects, though these procedures should not only foster a balanced development in skills, concepts, interests and attitudes across the curriculum, but should also lead progressively towards appreciation and understanding of different subjects as collective human achievements. In that process (and process is the essence of informal curriculum) relevant knowledge, though not necessarily uniform knowledge, in subjects is cumulatively acquired, all the more effectively because of its meaningful relationship to children's experience and interests in school and beyond.

The third kind of informality refers to *organization* and is closely linked with both the others. Informal organization involves a departure from a strict timetable (except for activities that must use facilities at specific times) and the introduction of such practices as team teaching, open-plan architecture, vertical grouping across age-categories, and flexibility in grouping and in the use of space. On a wider plane, it can involve the design of administrative structures and contexts within which informal pedagogy and curriculum can be most readily encouraged.

Informality also calls for its own means of *evaluation*. This applies both to the assessment of pupil progress and to the evaluation of the effectiveness of informal primary education itself. For both purposes it is inadequate to rely exclusively on means devised to suit more traditional practices. Informal pedagogy and curriculum require their own evaluation, by their own different, but no less demanding, criteria.

Finally, informality often implies a characteristic kind of *personal style*. An informal style is one that depends on friendliness rather than on status in a hierarchy, and is also one that attempts to promote democratic values through informality in dress and manner, thereby minimizing the social distance between teachers and children. First names and even nicknames are more likely to figure than the conventional Mrs Jones or Mr Smith (or the older Sir or Miss). Sometimes, informality in personal style also implies irreverence towards social institutions and customs regarded as incompatible with the purposes of informal education.

These five aspects of informality — pedagogy, curriculum, organization, evaluation, and personal style — are independent but related threads in the texture of primary education. The five aspects are not all essential to every example of informal primary education — indeed, it is unusual to find all five of them at once — yet they do cohere in a recognizable fashion in a description of informality in English primary education today.

There is a final adverb in the book's title: *today*. Primary education is undergoing rapid transitions — that is almost a truism — and so what is said today can have its full meaning only for today. By tomorrow, it will have grown tawdry and begun the transition that will metamorphose it first into an outdated reference on a reading list, and then, if it survives at all, into a source for the recent history of education. So perhaps it will still be of some interest, when the next millenium begins, to read again what some writers in England thought about informal primary education in the climacteric year 1987, when 1987 was still Today.

References

BENNETT, N. *et al.* (1976) *Teaching Styles and Pupil Progress*, London, Open Books.
ENTWISTLE, H. (1970) *Child-Centred Education*, London, Methuen.

Informal Primary Education in Action: Teachers' Accounts

(From Nias, D.J., 1988, 'Informal primary education in action; Teachers' accounts', in Blyth, A. (Ed.) *Informal Primary Education Today: Essays and Studies*, Lewes, Falmer Press, pp. 123–4, 142–5.)

In this extract, Jennifer Nias draws upon descriptions of their practice by six primary teachers. As she suggests, primary teachers rarely see one another in action and discuss their classroom methods and the assumptions underlying them even less frequently. Yet there is a surprising degree of similarity in their responses, which appear strongly committed to a liberal view of education. At the heart of their descriptions are two related beliefs, cornerstones of the liberal romantic view. Firstly, that knowledge is actively constructed by the learner rather than being passively received. By implication it is individual, both personally and uniquely. Secondly, the role of the teacher is seen as that of enabler and facilitator, the creator of the optimal conditions within which learning is to take place.

'But what *is* "informal education?"' they all replied, when I told them I had been asked to write this chapter. Their response confirmed my doubts. Could anyone, least of all one who now taught adults not children, present an accurate, up-to-date picture of 'informal education in action', when its putative practitioners — primary and middle school teachers — had no clear understanding of the term? So I changed the question and over a period of some months asked experienced teachers if they could describe 'formal teaching'. With hesitations and qualifications most of them could: 'to teach formally' was to show, tell, instruct, direct, with a view to controlling what their pupils learnt; it was often, but not always, directed at a large group of children, with the intention that they should all learn the same things at the same time; it therefore involved teacher control of social interaction as well as learning (for example, to restrict pupil-initiated talking and movement); it was often associated with testing or some other form of assessment of a learning outcome or product against externally derived criteria. A 'good' formal teacher could command the attention of learners, present information or instructions clearly and reinforce correct learning swiftly and encouragingly. There was also general agreement that 'formal teaching' was logically independent of numbers of pupils; it described a set of assumptions about the nature of knowledge, of learning (and therefore of teaching) which could be brought to bear upon one pupil or many.

All of the teachers to whom I spoke felt that they used 'formal teaching' at some time, often when dealing with curriculum areas (such as spelling or computational skills) for which there were accepted 'right answers'. Almost all of them felt that it was a useful component of their repertoire of teaching skills and was sometimes a highly effective way of ensuring that children acquired a particular skill or piece of information. However, many said they used it more often than they wanted to, as a control device, as an expedient to help them cope with large pupil numbers and inadequate resources or because they felt compelled to concentrate on their classes' attainment of pre-defined learning outcomes.

But a fair degree of consensus about the nature of 'formal teaching' did not help them to define 'informal teaching'. I therefore approached six experienced teachers of children from 6 to 12 years old, working in very different types of primary or middle school in various parts of England, and asked them if they could let me have a brief description of a situation in which they felt they had not been teaching formally. They did not know one another and all they had in common was that, in one context or another, I knew them all. Five wrote their accounts; one gave hers orally.

To my surprise there was substantial agreement within these teachers' accounts, despite the personal differences between them, the variety of contexts in which they taught and the ages of their pupils. Their descriptions suggest that they hold similar views about the conditions under which children learn, the classroom relationships which make these conditions possible, the role of the teacher and the nature of the curriculum.

It is commonplace that teachers seldom see one another in action, and discuss their classroom methods and the assumptions underlying them even less frequently. Yet the accounts given by these six experienced teachers have much in common despite their different education, training and career history, and the varying contexts in which they were teaching. There might be several reasons for this, for example, a conscious or unconscious desire to supply me with responses of which they thought I would approve; shared socialization into a common professional culture; similar influences during training which, though in different institutions, took place for five out of the six between the mid-1960s and mid-1970s.

It is also possible, however, that they had a common view of education, forged from their own experience of working with children in situations which did not require them to instruct, direct or dominate. Their accounts suggest that as experienced practitioners they were guided by educational principles relating to learning, teaching and the context in which both take place which were the same irrespective of the school and the pupils in which and with whom they were working. These principles themselves may be rooted in a set of beliefs about the nature of knowledge and how it is acquired, but since I asked the teachers to describe their practice, not to examine the philosophical origins of it, without further information my analysis must be speculative. Notwithstanding, at the heart of their descriptions seem to lie two related beliefs — that knowledge is actively constructed by each learner rather than being passively received or stored and that it is therefore in two senses individual, being both personal and unique. It follows from these beliefs that the function of the teacher is to encourage each learner to engage actively with the material to be learned. This in turn requires that learners have the will to become and remain involved in constructing their own knowledge — that they are, in short, motivated to learn. So, much teaching becomes a matter of arranging the optimal conditions under which each learner can, in the often-quoted words of the Plowden Report, become 'the agent of his own learning'. The teachers' work is likely to include directing learners to material which will engage their attention and be within their capacity, helping them to set themselves appropriate goals, assisting them to talk purposefully about and monitor their progress towards these ends and organizing the context, direction, pace and scope of their endeavours. In such a situation the organization of time, space, resources and attention must be flexible, learners should be free to seek help, guidance and stimulation from many sources. Moreover, since in schools one teacher has the task of simultaneously helping many pupils to construct their own learning, it is imperative that the latter learn to help one another as well as themselves; in the crowded, dense conditions of the classroom, learning must be co-operative as well as autonomous.

Whether or not this summary expresses the epistemological beliefs of these teachers, they certainly wanted their pupils to assume responsibility for and take control of their own learning. To these ends they tried to ensure that classroom activities were perceived by their pupils as having meaning, purpose and value (whether or not the impetus came initially from the learner or the teacher). In particular, they therefore sought to involve them in direct experiences, from which they could draw and to which they could impart their own meanings, and in practical activities, by means of which they could act upon, interpret, transform and make sense of their experiences. In these senses, as Rowland (1984) persuasively argues, they encouraged their children's classroom learning to resemble their play.

However the resemblance does not stop there. Like play, the learning in these classrooms was both individualistic and collaborative. Self-directed and self-controlled learning is, by definition, egocentric; it serves personal ends and is achieved by the expenditure of individual effort and resources. While accepting and to some extent encouraging these characteristics of individualized learning, these teachers also encouraged interaction. They arranged for children to work with partners and in groups and to have access to other adults. Wherever possible they also participated in the children's activities themselves, as co-learners, by presenting alternative viewpoints and new ideas and as critics of the emerging end products. Implicit in these arrangements is the idea that the development of autonomous learning depends upon discussion; the self can best develop through challenge from and with the support of others.

There is a further similarity between self-directed classroom learning and children's play; neither are constrained by adults' ways of organizing knowledge. These teachers encouraged their pupils to draw upon all the curriculum areas with which they came in contact. Their learning ranged widely, guided by their felt need for specific information and skills and not by their teachers' desire that they should attain specific learning outcomes. Yet, because they were learning in a collaborative context, they were open to suggestions and intervention from their teachers who permeated the curriculum with opportunities to learn, practise and apply both the basic skills of numeracy and literacy and more complex cognitive skills such as classification, comparison, conjecture and the making and testing of generalizations. In short, what the children learnt was the outcome of interaction and negotiation between their own interests and the guidance of their teachers.

Negotiations of this kind could only go on, however, in an atmosphere of mutual trust. Teachers wanted to know their pupils very well and to have a relaxed, informal relationship with them not only because it created a pleasant working atmosphere for all of them, but also because it was through that relationship that they could, as it were, enter into their pupils' play and influence their learning. In other words, teaching went on by means of, rather than simply as a consequence of, the open communication which existed between teachers and pupils. Their relationship enabled learning to be negotiated rather than imposed, but was at the same time the tool by which this was accomplished.

Now it is not easy for teachers to sanction, let alone encourage, playlike activities in their classrooms. They are expected to discipline the children in their care and are accountable for their learning. Moreover, an essential part of 'being' a teacher is to feel in control of the classroom (Nias, 1988). Yet, paradoxically, it was confidence in that control that enabled these teachers to behave as they did; it is only those who are secure in their power that can afford to give it away. So, 'good relationships' with pupils served a second purpose. By helping teachers to relax and 'be themselves' they facilitated the transfer of control over learning to pupils themselves. To put it another way, for teachers to feel 'in control' may be a necessary condition for the development of autonomous learning among children.

References

NIAS, D.J. (1988) *On Becoming and Being a Teacher*, London, Methuen.
ROWLAND, S. (1984) *The Enquiring Classroom*, Lewes, Falmer Press.

Criteria of a Good Primary School

(From 'What are the criteria of a good junior school?', Junior School Sub-Panel, Ministry of Education, May 1946, reprinted in Griffin-Beale, C. (Ed.), 1979, *Christian Schiller — in His Own Words*, London, A. and C. Black, pp. 1–2.)

As the text indicates, this paper was originally concerned with the junior school, an institution only recently established when the paper was first written. It is included here because it applies equally well to the primary school or, with the possible omission of the last point, to the infant or first school. The document was written by Christian Schiller, the first Staff Inspector of Junior Education, and a very powerful, though almost unacknowledged influence, on the development of post-war primary education. Concisely and clearly, it embodies many of the ideas and metaphors associated with liberal romanticism. It refers to stages of development, to phases of growth, and to children's powers of expression. It emphasizes the importance of language, observation, movement and the arts — all themes later elaborated by theorists and practitioners of like persuasion. It talks of children's happiness, self-confidence, interests and 'that pecular absorption which comes when activities exactly meet children's immediate needs' (see p. 167). It is a beautifully written and deceptively simple distillation of a very powerful view of primary education — a view which was to have a great influence on the Central Advisory Council for Education, the Plowden Committee, when it produced its report, *Children and Their Primary Schools*, published in 1967.

What Are the Criteria of a Good Junior School?
Junior School Sub-Panel, Ministry of Education

These notes try to suggest an outline to one answer to this question. But even the outline of an answer can only be drawn in words, and in this case in words which describe new ideas. New ideas should be spread out and all their meanings noted before being packed in a phrase, and this is a task which we might well undertake. But it will take time. Meanwhile it may be useful to launch out hopefully into language and see where we can get. What we might look for first in a junior school is its purpose; what it is attempting to do. In a good junior school we might expect to find:

● that the school conceives of primary education, not as a preparation for something to follow, but as a fulfilment of a stage of development;

● that the school seeks to achieve this fulfilment, not by securing certain standards of attainment, but by providing in abundance such experience and activities as will enable all the children to develop to the full at each phase of growth.

Next we might look to see in what ways this purpose is being carried out. In a good junior school we might expect to find:

- that the children are expressing their powers in language, in movement, in music, in painting, and in making things — that is to say, as artists;
- that the children are developing their powers in language, in observation, in counting, and in the use of the body — that is to say, as workmen;
- that the children are learning to live together to the best advantage.

Then we might look to see how effective is the organization of the experience and activities provided. In a good junior school we might expect to find:

- that all the children in every class, from the very slow or backward to the very bright and forward, can be usefully occupied within the range of experience and activities normally provided;
- that the children's need for movement and for rest determine the arrangement of experience and activities, and how much the children get out of an experience or activity determines the amount of time given to it;
- that the children's experience and activities take full advantage of all the facilities available, and especially outdoors.

Lastly, we might look to see how far the school's purpose has been accomplished by noting what the children are and what they can do. In a good junior school we might expect to find:

- that the children are happy, self-confident, and are able to live agreeably with others;
- that the children are not only interested, but show that peculiar absorption which comes when activities exactly meet their immediate needs;
- that the children can talk freely and with understanding about the town or country around their home, and about what it contains;
- that the children's power of self-expression in at least one of the arts has developed sufficiently to satisfy their power of criticism;
- that in the oldest class there are only odd children who cannot read, write or count a little; and that in this class there are many children who can read fluently and with understanding, write quickly and legibly, and calculate easily by the four rules with numbers, and simple measures, up to 100 in size.

'A Recognisable Philosophy of Education'
(From Central Advisory Council for Education (England), 1967, *Children and Their Primary Schools*, Vol. 1, London, HMSO, pp. 187–8.)

Liberal romanticism received official endorsement in the report issued by the Central Advisory Council for Education (England) under the chairmanship of Lady Plowden. Thereafter, it became the orthodoxy of English primary education for almost a decade, at least as perceived by many policy-makers, commentators and educationists. The three paragraphs reproduced here capture the essence of that 'recognisable philosophy of education' which the Plowden Committee believed, mistakenly as it turned out, to be 'a general and quickening trend'. In particular, paragraph 505 is a memorable encapsulation of the liberal romantic view, standing along with paragraph 75 of the Hadow Report of 1931 (see p. 28) as the embodiment of a view of primary education which many have found very inspiring and many others have found sententious, sentimental and verging on the anti-intellectual. These paragraphs are superb examples of educational rhetoric, unsurpassed in style by the rhetoric of Plowden's opponents, as scrutiny of other papers in this source book will reveal. For a critique of this ideology, see the paper by Peters (pp. 146–51).

504.   If these methods were applied to all primary schools it would be apparent that the trend of their practices and outlook corresponds to a recognisable philosophy of education, and to a view of society, which may be summarised as follows.

505.   A school is not merely a teaching shop, it [transmits] values and attitudes. It is a community in which children learn to live first and foremost as children and not as future adults. In family life children learn to live with people of all ages. The school sets out deliberately to devise the right environment for children, to allow them to be themselves and to develop in the way and at the pace appropriate to them. It tries to equalise opportunities and to compensate for handicaps. It lays special stress on individual discovery, on first hand experience and on opportunities for creative work. It insists that knowledge does not fall into neatly separate compartments and that work and play are not opposite but complementary. A child brought up in such an atmosphere at all stages of his education has some hope of becoming a balanced and mature adult and of being able to live in, to contribute to, and to look critically at the society of which he forms a part. Not all primary schools correspond to this picture, but it does represent a general and quickening trend.

506.   Some people, while conceding that children are happier under the modern regime and perhaps more versatile, question whether they are being

fitted to grapple with the world which they will enter when they leave school. This view is worth examining because it is quite widely held, but we think it rests on a misconception. It isolates the long term objective, that of living in and serving society, and regards education as being at all stages recognisably and specfically a preparation for this. It fails to understand that the best preparation for being a happy and useful man or woman is to live fully as a child. Finally, it assumes, quite wrongly, that the older virtues, as they are usually called, of neatness, accuracy, care and perseverance, and the sheer knowledge which is an essential of being educated, will decline. These are genuine virtues and an education which does not foster them is faulty.

507. Society is right to expect that importance will be attached to these virtues in all schools. Children need them and need knowledge, if they are to gain satisfaction from their education. What we repudiate is the view that they were automatically fostered by the old kind of elementary education. Patently they were not, for enormous numbers of the products of that education do not possess them. Still more we repudiate the fear that the modern primary approach leads to their neglect. On the contrary it can, and, when properly understood, does lay a much firmer foundation for their development and it is more in the interests of the children. But those interests are complex. Children need to be themselves, to live with other children and with grown ups, to learn from their environment, to enjoy the present, to get ready for the future, to create and to love, to learn to face adversity, to behave responsibly, in a word, to be human beings. Decisions about the influences and situations that ought to be contrived to these ends must be left to individual schools, teachers and parents. What must be ensured is that the decisions taken in schools spring from the best available knowledge and are not simply dictated by habit or convention.

Teaching Through the Arts

(From Marshall, S., 1963, *An Experiment in Education*, Cambridge, Cambridge University Press, pp. 170–3, 106–8.)

An educational ideology such as liberal romanticism is not a tightly argued creed codified in words and ritualized in practice. It admits of a variety of interpretations. English primary education has witnessed a number of variants of liberal romanticism, in some cases associated with geographical regions such as Oxfordshire or Leicestershire or the former West Riding of Yorkshire, and in some cases associated with individuals such as Robin Tanner or Sybil Marshall. This fifth extract is from the latter's aptly named 'experiment' in education and describes an approach through art, a theme underlying other variants, but idiosyncratically and powerfully rendered by Marshall in her village school in the fifties. The extract is in two parts. Part I describes her 'symphonic method' around which she based so much of her work and from which her children produced such 'vital, vigorous, felt English' and superb art work. Though concerned with art teaching in particular, Part II addresses a more general and perplexing question for the liberal romantic: What is the role of the teacher? How, in Plowden's words, is the teacher 'to select an environment which will encourage curiosity, to focus attention on inquiries which will lead to useful discovery, to collaborate with children, to lead from behind' (para. 875). How, in particular, is the teacher to assess children's work? [The extract begins with Marshall considering how her approach to education through art evolved, that is:]

... From a starting point which was nothing but an intuition that 'art' (meaning drawing) was a good thing, to the realisation that it was an education in itself; to the widening of the field by using art as a means towards a better, fresher view of the social subjects, history, geography, nature study; to the comprehension of its astounding significance in encouraging vital, vigorous, *felt* English, in direct contact with life being lived and to be lived. To bring the wheel full circle, one more turn was necessary. Education must have an end in view, for it is not an end in itself. The end can only be the knowledge of what it means really to live, and the wisdom to accept and make the most of what life offers each individual person. Such knowledge and such wisdom cannot be found within the limits of one's own age, ability and aptitude, nor by heredity, environment, nor instruction. It cannot even be bounded by time itself, for it would be an impercipient spirit who could not 'place' his own inevitable suffering a little better for having read and heard The Book of Job, *King Lear* or Mozart's G Minor Symphony, and an even poorer one who could not be uplifted by some work of art which for him had special significance.

To believe in their own potentiality for creativity was for the children the first half of their journey towards being educated beings. The other half could be completed only when they could see their own lives surrounded, sustained, and indeed explained by the general experience of all humanity. This part of the journey will take them all the rest of their lives, but to know this is the greatest wisdom they can learn at school. To be able to approach the classic works of art without fear, and with pleasure, interest, understanding and love is to be able to tap the inexhaustible well of past human experience. It was a tentative search for the path leading to the second half of the journey, for a track of some kind that they could in future follow to the world of strength and delight they could find in the arts, that made me recognise the opening when yet another lucky chance delivered the chart right into my hands.

John had been a pupil of the school since he was four, but now he was seven, and about to be transferred to a preparatory school in Cambridge. On the evening of the day he left us, his mother rang me on the telephone, saying that John would like to give a school a present, and could come down to deliver it. Naturally, I was pleased with this mark of appreciation, and as these parents were of the very nicest kind and could be relied upon to choose wisely, I anticipated something in the nature of some really good books for the school library, or something similar. But when John and his mother arrived, I was overwhelmed. The gift was a Pye 'Black Box' record-player!

School had already closed for the Easter holiday, so I kept the precious thing in my house until we opened again for the summer term. On the first morning back I carried it round to school and presented it to the astonished class. After the first dumbfounded moment — I remember only one other like it, when surprise and delight robbed everybody of speech; that was when I announced to them that we had been given the prize for the best co-operative frieze in the 1957 *Sunday Pictorial* Exhibition — the first child to find a voice said, 'Play us something on it'.

I had no suitable records in school, so I dashed round the corner to my house and began to turn over records in frantic haste to find one I thought the children might enjoy. The first one to come to hand was Beethoven's Pastoral Symphony. I rushed back to school and set the disc spinning — no prayers, no register, no dinner money collection, no formal beginning to the day or the term; just twenty-six children, one adult, and Beethoven. At the end of the second movement, Derek said ecstatically 'Isn't it SMASHING!' I felt that it was indeed an extra-special moment, for while they had listened I had found the answer to the problem I had been trying to work out. We were going to base our whole term's work on 'The Pastoral', and see what came of it. The work in the last section of this book is the result.

It was only the first term of several that work was pushed off from some chosen work of art. I called my new method, in fun, 'the symphonic method', but the more I thought about it, the more I realised how apt a title I had hit upon. In this method the separate subjects are analogous to the different sections of an orchestra, playing in concert for full effect every now and then, but in between these moments, first one and then the other taking up the theme. This theme occurs and recurs, but the entire symphony is not one endless repetition of the melody. Though all the work is in some way related to the theme, it is not tied to it nor limited by it, as it is in the so-called 'project method'; nor does it employ one group of instruments only, as in the 'centre of interest' method. My objection to both those otherwise good ideas has been that the various subjects have been made to fit into the chosen theme, whether they would or not, or else neglected entirely because they were too far away to be tied to it, however clumsily. The 'symphonic method' allows for second subjects, bridge passages, variations, differences of tempo and indeed, wholly separate movements; yet the term's work, like a symphony, is only completely satisfactory as an entire whole.

This method is obviously not for everybody, any more than a violin is every musician's instrument; there are many who could get a better tune out of a mouth organ than they ever could out of a violin, and if they know that, they will be wise to leave the violin alone. But have they ever tried anything but a mouth organ? Until they have, they must not be too sure. Then again, for all I know, the sciences, in the hands of an expert teacher, might produce the same amount of interest and the same fresh English. Because I am by nature incapable, it seems, of working up much enthusiasm in myself about scientific matters, I doubt my own ability to teach through the sciences — but I think it could be done, and I expect the results in mathematics by that method would parallel the results I claim for English in my own method through the arts. The real secret of any method is the teacher's devotion and enthusiasm; one string and Paganini makes better music than a bored orchestra and a befuddled conductor. So, if anybody at all in the educational world has enjoyed this description of my experiments enough to start experimenting on his own behalf, I shall be well paid.

[What Is the Role of the Teacher?]

The new conception of child art simply takes into account that children are not solely adults in the making, but creatures in their own right, as tadpoles differ from mature frogs, or caterpillars from butterflies. They have their own set of emotions, abilities, and techniques. What is expected of them is child-like, not pre-adult work. All that is asked is that they should do what comes naturally to them, within the bounds of reason and common sense.

This never has meant that 'just anything' will do in art, any more than a set of figures printed upside down and back-to-front would be called a sum and accepted as such for very long, in the arithmetic lesson, though many children write their number symbols the wrong way round at first. In the early stages of number, as long as they understand the threeness of three, so to speak, the printing of the symbol backwards is of small moment, but the teacher usually tries her hardest to persuade a child that there is a right way round before he leaves the infant school. Similarly, in art, the figure with the arms coming out directly from the side of the head would be completely acceptable from a four-year-old, because of the moment of vision behind the attempt to portray a man: but to allow a normal child of eleven to draw a man like this on the grounds that it was 'child art' would be a piece of conscious naïveté that would turn the stomach of a sincere artist or teacher. So while we do not now impose adult standards, we work towards them as the child grows towards adulthood, which really means that all children go on developing naturally, and that the development should show in the work they produce.

It is therefore absolutely imperative for any teacher that he possess criteria of his own, and that because they can trust his judgement, his pupils can learn to form their own. He must have standards, and they must be high. In applying them he is bound to be critical, and fails in his duty if he is not. The teacher who smiles encouragingly at every unrecognisable daub and tells the perpetrator that it is good, just to encourage him, must expect nothing better, for as Dr Johnson so rightly said, he who praises everybody praises nobody. In fact, this teacher may often expect worse, especially from an intelligent class, for I would not put it beyond any boy I had in my recent class, under such influence, to put his tongue into his cheek and try deliberately to see just how far he could go. Most children instinctively mistrust this kind of fulsome flattery, and know, as country people say of a frozen potato, that it is 'oversweet to be wholesome'.

Nor are children averse to candid criticism provided that it is honest, fair and constructive. Moreover, they are the very best critics of each other's work, and once trained well, of their own. The boy or girl who always says 'I don't like mine' is the most dangerous, for he is usually courting flattery from his teacher and his fellows: but the child who will stand before his own picture now and then and say 'I think mine is the best' has proved his confidence in himself not only as an artist, but as an unbiased critic.

In being critical, however, the teacher must not avoid Scylla only to fall a victim to Charybdis. However good the children are, they will not produce adult work. Their work will be essentially child-like, and to assess this work anyone is up against a very real difficulty. For though he was a child himself once, though he may have made a serious study of child psychology and development, though he may have spent years at work among children, the fact is inescapable that he is an adult now. His memories of childhood are remembered with an adult memory, his knowledge of children is an adult's knowledge, and his conception of what is child-like is adult, too. The absolutely impossible thing for most people is too see anything as a child sees it, unclouded by maturity, and not through the mirror of assimilated experience. So in being critical he must beware of judging by what *he thinks* a child should do, or what a child should like; the criterion is what the child does do, and what he likes.

B *Educational Conservatism*

Black Paper Basics

(From Cox, C. and Boyson, R. (Eds) 1975, *Black Paper* 75, Dent, p. 1.)

Educational conservatism found its most vocal expression in the polemical set of Black Papers issued from 1969 onwards. Initially, these were dismissed very easily by those in schools and higher education, but later they had to be taken very seriously indeed as their criticisms struck raw nerves in both politicians and parents. Educational conservatism represented a reaction to the so-called 'libertarianism', believed by Black Paper writers to have characterized education in the sixties. Black Paper slogans included 'Back to the basics', 'The preservation of standards', and 'The importance of structure'. As this first extract shows, liberal romantic (as well as social democratic) notions of 'freedom', 'equality of opportunity', and 'non-competitive ethos' were violently attacked and, reinterpreted, were used as weapons against the purveyors of 'left-wing radicalism' in the schools. Primary education was singled out as a major cause of student unrest and other unwelcome tendencies and phenomena both within education and the wider society. Though some of the ten points do not apply directly to primary education, 'Black Paper Basics' is reproduced in full here; it represents educational conservatism at its most assertive and strident. The ten points advanced are regarded by their authors as self-evident; there is no invitation to discussion, only pressure to concur. The emotional appeal of such confident assertions to anxious politicians, parents and teachers cannot be disputed; their intellectual validity is much more open to question.

Black Paper Basics

Ten Points

1 Children are not naturally good. They need firm, tactful discipline from parents and teachers with clear standards. Too much freedom for children breeds selfishness, vandalism and personal unhappiness.

2 If the non-competitive ethos of progressive education is allowed to dominate our schools, we shall produce a generation unable to maintain our standards of living when opposed by fierce rivalry from overseas competitors.

3 It is the quality of teachers which matters, rather than their numbers or their equipment. We have sacrificed quality for numbers, and the result has been a lowering of standards. We need high-

quality, higher-paid teachers in the classroom, not as counsellors or administrators.

4　Schools are for schooling, not social engineering.

5　The best way to help children in deprived areas is to teach them to be literate and numerate, and to develop all their potential abilities.

6　Every normal child should be able to read by the age of seven. This can be achieved by the hard work of teachers who use a structured approach.

7　Without selection the clever working-class child in a deprived area stands little chance of a real academic education.

8　External examinations are essential for schools, colleges, poly-technics and universities. Without such checks, standards decline. Working-class children suffer when applying for jobs if they cannot bring forward proof of their worth achieved in authoritative examinations.

9　Freedom of speech must be preserved in universities. Institutions which cannot maintain proper standards of open debate should be closed.

10　You can have equality or equality of opportunity; you cannot have both. Equality will mean the holding back (or the new deprivation) of the brighter children.

Putting Primary Education Back on the Right Track

(From Froome, S., 1974, 'Back on the right track', *Education 3–13*, 2, 1, pp. 13–16.)

Educational conservatism has spoken with voices other than the shrill tones of the more extreme Black Paper writers. It has found intellectual justification in some of the work of Bantock, part of whose critique of progressivism is reproduced later in the reader (pp. 162–65). Here, it finds relatively moderate expression in the views of Stuart Froome, former primary head and member of the Bullock Committee. In this extract he offers a reasoned critique of post-war developments in primary education and makes his own suggestions for getting education back on the *right* track. By seeking to portray children and schools 'as they really are', he attacks some of the assumptions outlined by Blyth (pp. 79–82) earlier in this book (p. 000). His concern for 'more systematic and structured methods of schooling', the importance he attaches to the acquisition of knowledge by primary children, and his unwillingness to allow children too much freedom in what or how they learn, are representative of the views of a substantial proportion of primary teachers, many more than the advocates or detractors of liberal romanticism or educational conservatism may care to admit.

When Edmund Burke, the eighteenth century political thinker remarked that one sure symptom of an ill-conducted state was the propensity of the people to resort to theories, he was not thinking about education, but this cogent observation might well be applied to the situation in which we find ourselves today. Since the last war there has been a greater expansion of education in terms of money and manpower than had ever before been contemplated, and at the moment the cost of education exceeds what is spent on national defence. It would, however, be foolishly complacent to claim that the vast expenditure on schooling of all kinds has significantly improved standards of achievement in what used to be called the basic subjects of the curriculum. Indeed, during the past five years there have been significant murmurs of discontent from a number of quarters about the many school-leavers who cannot spell, write accurately or cipher satisfactorily, while the public at large is beginning to think that a return to more systematic and structured methods of schooling is long overdue.

After the passing of the Butler Act in 1944, which laid it down that every child must be educated in accordance with his age, aptitude and ability, the public was generally agreeable to vast sums of money being spent to achieve this highly desirable end. As Professor Parkinson would have warned however, increased expenditure on a project does not necessarily result in increased efficiency or productivity, and it is certain that the appointment of too many cooks is quite likely to water-down the nutritional strength of the educational broth.

With the dissatisfaction expressed with reading standards in a number of surveys made, after the war and the general willingness to spend money to improve education came a spate of untried theories, nostrums, stunts and gimmicks which were only notable for their transience and impracticability. It was claimed that many of these innovatory ideas were based on the child-centred philosophy of John Dewey, who it was said had advocated the abandonment of the traditional scholastic approach to education and the replacement of it by a method of teaching in which the child was the sole agent of his own learning. Dewey had certainly criticized the formal, didactic, 'chalk and talk' mode of teaching because of its 'passivity of attitude, its mechanical massing of children, its uniformity of curriculum and method.' While it must be admitted that there were some valid grounds for such criticism, it was extremely doubtful if the ordinary run-of-the-mill teacher would ever be capable of organizing his approach to pupils on any but the most formal, traditional lines. Certainly with the huge classes and cramped accommodation of the post-war era, it was quite unrealistic to attempt to put Dewey's child-centred notions into practice.

However, the limitations of the average school establishment did not in any way deter the theoretical educationists from promulgating the Dewey dogmas and urging on the schools educational methods which were remarkable more for their plausible attractiveness than for their soundness and practicability. For myself, I was in no way convinced by the champions of informal child-centred schooling, because I did not think such methods were appropriate for schools and children as they really are, not as they exist in the minds of dilettante advisers who seldom have to carry out in practice the theories which they so strenuously advocate.

I have moreover, always felt that there was a wide gulf between the theoretical advice offered to teacher-students by college of education lecturers and educational advisers and the practicalities of classroom procedure. Having begun my teaching career as a student-teacher at the age of seventeen, I had largely learnt how to cope with the problems of class control and the complications of organizing a programme of work with overlarge classes before I entered upon my college training. I had thus served a useful practical apprenticeship, and with this behind me I could absorb educational theory and psychology with a certain critical appraisal. I confess however, that I never felt that what was regarded in colleges of education as ideal teaching methodology, could ever be equated with the humdrum pedestrian practices which of necessity were the mainspring of the teacher's daily round. It was fascinating to read Rousseau, William James and Dewey and to feel that what they said might have some relevance in an ideal classroom situation and with small groups of amenable children, but I knew that real-life schools had classes of fifty or sixty and that the children were in the main unwilling participators in the educational struggle. After college training, to return to the schools was to begin a further period of disillusionment with current educational thinking, and since that time it has appeared to me that the purpose of most advice proferred by both county and Her Majesty's Inspectors has been not to improve the amount of quality of learning to be assimilated by the child, but both to water ... down the content of knowledge and at the same time to prolong the period over which children are to be taught. This process of dilution appears to me to have been deliberate, but it was done so gradually and insidiously that those who suffered under it were hardly conscious of the changes taking place.

First of all there came an attack on what was called rote-learning. It was alleged that to commit to memory the facts of such subjects as history or geography was rather an unworthy accomplishment, and in any case what was the point of remembering and repeating facts like a parrot when they could be so easily discovered in a reference book? Having made the retention of information sound rather disreputable it was an obvious sequitur to suggest that the learning of multiplication and other tables was equally obnoxious because a table-book or ready-reckoner could provide all that was necessary to be reasonably successful at elementary arithmetic.

At the same time as this general condemnation of rote-learning was being thrust upon the schools as official policy, came the universal move towards 'look-and-say' as the most efficient method of teaching children to read. Because practised readers do not need to spell-out the sounds of letters but are able to recognize whole words at a glance, it was naively claimed that little children starting to read would be capable of the same skill, and would in fact learn to read altogether by this means. This putting the result at the beginning, which Professor Jacques Barzun has described as a 'preposterism', is in my view wholly responsible for the parlous state of reading in the schools of this country. I recently visited a large ILEA comprehensive school where the Head of the Remedial Department which employs no less than five teachers, informed me that of the school's yearly intake of 240 children aged eleven, no less than one-third had reading ages of eight or below, while the average reading age of the entire intake was 9.3 years as against their actual average age of 11.6. This number of retarded readers moreover was increasing year by year and was attributable in the Head of Department's opinion partly to 'look-and-say' and partly to the lack of teacher pressure in the contributing infant and junior schools.

What an indictment of current reading methods is revealed in these gloomy statistics! Indeed, 'look-and-say' which seeks to replace the tedium of repetitive drill in letter-sounds by something akin to pure guess-work is in the view of many teachers, largely responsible for the decline which has been revealed in the two latest surveys of children's reading ability. Reading is certainly the basis of writing and so it was inevitable that with the slowing-down of this skill should come a decline in the art of children's written expression. This was contributed to, by persistent advice from inspectors to teachers not to worry children unduly with writing-form, spelling, punctuation and grammatical sentence-construction. These so-called 'pedestrian and mechanical aspects of writing' were regarded as impediments to the fluent flow of ideas which children were bursting to communicate. It is of course not surprising that while older and more experienced practitioners were sceptical of this free-writing notion, the new laissez-faire approach to written expression was welcomed by younger teachers because there was now a legitimate excuse to avoid the tedious labour of marking and correcting the unimpeded upsurge of creativity which flowed unrestrainedly from so many juvenile pens. It is moreover also not surprising that after a decade or two of uncorrected creative writing, it is now common to find newly-qualified teachers who cannot spell, punctuate or write their sentences according to the rules of syntax. It would seem that their ability to communicate accurately has been stultified by the exuberance of their own creativity, and those who have shamefully advised them against excessive care in composition might well ponder the opinion of Dr Johnson on this subject. That which is written without much effort, is likely to be read without much pleasure.

Effort however, is a word to be avoided in modern educational parlance. Even though a distinct decline in the basic subjects has been apparent to many older teachers and even to the public at large, no steps have been taken to halt the downward slide, or to tighten-up the slackness which inevitably accompanies excessive freedom in educational practice. On the contrary. The Plowden Report endorses unreservedly what is called freedom and flexibility of curriculum whereby teaching on a subject base is replaced by topic-teaching and the integrated day.

Now the idea of topic-learning through which a child or group adopts some theme or subject of current interest such as air-travel or water-pollution and by consulting reference-books and making general enquiries is able to use reading, written-expression art and modelling as aids to investigation, seems at first sight an altogether admirable alternative to the dull routine of following subjects on a conventional time-table. However, like all such attractive innovatory practices, topic-learning can, and does in many instances, degenerate into mindless copying of information from books on to pages in 'project-folders' and interspersing these plagiarized extracts with cuttings from newspapers and magazines. In a recent HMI's report on reading for information in a number of schools in connection with project and topic work, it was stated that it was much less successfully practised than might have been expected, and extensive and selective consultation of reference books and sources appeared rare. More usually, the child just sought an encyclopedia or single-reference book and copied down what he found there, while often, questioning showed that this was done without any any real understanding of its meaning.

It would be manifestly unfair to condemn all modern innovatory practices in school because of the misapplication of them in some cases. However, it is the fact that most such innovations are foisted on to a long-suffering body of teachers without any real evidence of their usefulness, that has prompted my suspicion of such unproven methods, for I do at least know from personal experience that working from a subject timetable with stipulated schemes of work, and using a straightforward didactic approach did ensure that attainable stages of schooling were reached at certain stated intervals. Could such a claim be seriously made by the advocates of topic-learning, the integrated curriculum and the open classroom?

Now while I freely admit that scholastic method is in need of periodic critical assessment, reform and redirection if it is not to become ossified and out of touch with contemporary thought and social change, I believe that the hostile reaction against the somewhat rigid and narrow conception of schooling as typified in some of the old elementaries, has been emotional rather than intellectual, and those who urged teachers to follow Dewey's child-centred theories, conveniently forgot that in emphasizing the need for children's freedom of activity and experience, he also stressed the necessity for systematic training, accuracy and plain hard work. 'Play should not be fooling,' he said, 'the only way to prevent this consequence is to make regard for results enter into even the freest play activity.'

I have spent longer than I had intended on attempting to trace how the pattern and methods of British education have altered substantially during the past three or four decades, and how in consequence standards in the basic subjects of the curriculum have deteriorated. Such a critical review however, would have little point unless some suggestions were offered on how past errors can be rectified, and the mischievously misdirected educational train be put firmly, 'back on the right track'.

First, we must clearly define what it is we want our children to learn during that vital 3 to 13 period of their schooling. It would I think be generally agreed that reading should come at the top of the list of priorities, and it should be mastered with the aid of early phonics as soon as possible (three is not too early for some) without any regard for that chimerical notion 'reading readiness', which in my view was specifically invented to excuse an unnecessary prolongation of the reading process. After reading, whose function it is to enable the child to garner information and to be instructed as well as entertained, come speech and writing for articulacy, and number for computation. With the mastery of these basic skills children can express, research and solve, for with this competence comes a self-reliance which is necessary for true discovery.

Secondly, there is a need for a structured programme, where teacher, the expert, will build step-by-step understanding. The acquisition of knowledge is much too important to be left to the spontaneous whims and fancies of little children. It must be laid down in a systematic sequential pattern easily understood by teacher and taught, so that both participants can observe and measure the progress which is being made, while school inspectors should regard it as part of their task to ensure that viable schemes of work do exist.

Thirdly, because of the brevity of school life, every minute must be utilized fully, and that means the use of teacher demonstration followed by much general practice of skills to improve both group and individual standards. To avoid monotony, children can do individual assignments on choice, or specified tasks, but they must be able to follow instructions, work to plan and must always complete their chosen projects.

Fourthly, it must be recognized that learning is a difficult process involving much conscious effort and memorization. Without this there can be no progress. It is not a jolly, pleasant game and so Dewey's activity and experience are not enough to bring it to a successful conclusion. Consequently, there must be stated aims, a timetable, an observable overall framework and a corpus of knowledge in every discipline to be transmitted from the teacher to the class. Informality of procedure is time-wasting and inefficient, and although some group-work is necessary to let children learn the value of co-operation, thus becoming aware of their fellows' strengths, the teacher must at all times be in charge. He cannot abdicate. Periodic testing of accomplishment, although today unfashionable, is also necessary not only for the teacher's benefit but so that pupils and parents can see the progress being made. Moreover, there should be recurrent national surveys of children's attainment which could best be carried out under the guidance of the Schools Council.

Fifthly and finally, I think it is time to dispel the romantic illusion that schooling must always be a joyful, agreeable and largely entertaining experience in which the child is always self-motivated. We may not desire a return to the rigid imposed discipline of the past when the schoolmaster was, in Goldsmith's words, 'a man severe, and stern to view'. On the other hand, the teacher's recent public image has become badly tarnished by association with methods which are more noteworthy for their sloppy informality than for their effectiveness. If we wish to refurbish this image it is necessary to disassociate the teaching profession from that popular anti-intellectualism which derides verbal learning, deplores structure, system and sequential scholastic attainment, seeks to abolish standards and examinations and above all desires to make the teacher a bosom pal of the pupil.

Goldsmith's schoolmaster may have been a somewhat forbidding character, but he was at least loved and respected for his wide knowledge and integrity. He is certainly preferable to the current Joyce Grenfellian caricature of the genial child-minder who, with toothy inane smile and sentimental posturing, waits hopefully in the background for her little charges to read, write and computate in their own good time. We should remember that firmness and sympathy are not incompatible qualities in a teacher, a fact which Goldsmith noted in his poem: *Yet he was kind, or if severe in aught, the love he bore to learning was in fault.*

Our Schools: A Radical Policy

(From Sexton, S., 1987, *Our Schools: A Radical Policy*, Institute of Economic Affairs Education Unit, pp. 4–6.)

Educational conservatism considerably influenced government opinion in the 1980s and many of the ideas advocated by the proponents of such news were incorporated into the 1988 Education Act. A more extreme perspective of educational conservatism came from the Institute of Economic Affairs, particularly its director, Stuart Sexton, who argued that the only way to improve quality and choice in education and to improve schools was to change the way they are managed and funded.

1 Nothing short of radical measures are needed to improve the State maintained system of education, and to placate its growing critics, the parents, employers and the children themselves.

A package of radical measures is needed for implementation now, or at least immediately after the next general election. The radical proposals offered in this paper constitute an election manifesto for schools for any party with the courage and foresight to adopt it and to implement it. Let us have no more grand announcements, no more 'policies in principle'; let us get down to the 'nitty-gritty', to specific proposals which should and could be implemented. These proposals assume far less control, by both the Department of Education and Science and the local education authorities. The proposals are therefore bound to offend an enormous vested interest, namely that great army of civil servants, both local and central, now concerned with the running of education. Many of those civil servants, however well meaning and well intentioned, will be offended by proposals which shift power away from them. They have come to assume that they, collectively, are better placed to run education than almost anyone else, and that their wisdom is greater than that of anyone else, and most particularly greater than that of the parents.

This in-built resistance to change of the present system should not be underestimated. Really radical proposals will be objected to as being 'technically impossible', or 'impracticable', and alternative 'radical options' will be offered by the present establishment. Such alternatives will not of course be radical at all, but will seek to buy peace and maintain the *status quo*.

The burden of this paper is better education for all children through the exercise of genuine parental choice, harnessing 'parent power', and leading ultimately to the only true parent power, parent *purchasing* power.

2 There is widespread dissatisfaction with the present State maintained schools. Many are good, some excellent, but the popular perception is:

- poor standards of the 3 Rs;
- poor standards of discipline and behaviour;
- poor academic standards generally, for the most intelligent, the average and below average ability children;
- insufficient attention to practical and vocational subjects;
- too much party politics in the running of schools and of education generally;
- not enough money spent, especially shortages of books and equipment.

3 The fact that we now spend more in real terms per child per year on schooling in this country than ever before in our history, when said, is met with derision by the parents. They just do not believe it. Their experience 'on the ground', 'with their own children', points in exactly the opposite direction. They observe a gross shortage of text books. In most schools the old idea of one text book per subject per child for the exclusive use of that child for the school year (handed back at the end of the year of course for the next year group) was dropped in many schools years ago. It is said that there is no way such could now be afforded, although for some subjects, the 'educationalists' have justified such absence of books as being an 'educational virtue', saying that a book per child is not necessary anyway. Parents observe lack of modern equipment in schools, except where they, the parents, have paid for it directly. They observe poor maintenance in schools, often neglect going back twenty or more years.

They observe the current levels of teachers' pay, and whilst they are angry at teachers' 'industrial action', and their unwillingness to agree to sensible contracts and sensible differentials, most parents nevertheless sympathize with the teachers on their levels of pay, and believe that teachers should be paid more, have no idea where the extra money might come from, but blame the government all the same. That said, all the evidence suggests that the latest 'imposed' pay rise will be regarded by most parents as fair and adequate.

4 In summary, therefore, the current education service seems to be:

- offering poor academic standards;
- offering poor standards of discipline and behaviour;
- inadequate in its response to modern technology and the needs of tomorrow's jobs;
- staffed by disgruntled teachers who are poorly paid;
- under-funded, whether from an inadequate total sum of money, or (as is in fact the case) from the inefficient use of the already large sum spent, is not relevant to the parent, money is not getting through to the chalk face;
- providing poor and inefficient management of schools.

5   In response to such dissatisfaction, the current debate on ways of solving the problem can be summed up in three, very different, policies.

1   One approach is to centralize education under direct Government control.

2   The second approach is to maintain the present mix of powers and responsibilities between central and local government, but to 'do it better', including more spending.

3   The third approach is the reverse of the first, namely to decentralize the system, not just from central to local government, but from local government to the schools themselves, with the ultimate target being schools (whoever owns them) responsible for their own management, being their own cost centres, and being in a position to respond directly and positively to the demands of their customers, namely the parents and their children.

C   *Liberal Pragmatism*

The Importance of Planning, Organization and Assessment

(From DES, 1979, *Mathematics 5–11*, London, HMSO, pp. 7–11.)

Judging from the surveys reported by Ashton (1975, *The Aims of Primary Education*, Macmillan), Bennett (1976, *Teaching Styles and Pupil Progress*, Open Books) and Taylor (1974, *Purpose, Power and Constraint in the Primary School Curriculum*, Macmillan), liberal pragmatism may well be the most widely held of the four ideologies outlined in this section of the reader, but paradoxically it is the most difficult to characterize and to exemplify clearly and concisely through extracts. At the primary stage advocates of liberal pragmatism advocate a broad curricular grounding for all children, in part preparatory for secondary education, but a grounding which takes account of the fact that children learn through both first- and second-hand experience, which uses children's knowledge and interests as starting points and contributions to ongoing work, but which shapes and refines children's experience along teacher-directed lines. Liberal pragmatism is characterized by a concern for planning and policy-making, for 'systematic progression and continuity', and for evaluation and assessment of children's learning. The ideology finds intellectual justification in the work of writers such as Dearden (pp. 156–61) and Richards (Volume 2), and underlies many of the recent HMI statements on primary education, such as (1980) *A View of the Curriculum* (London, HMSO, Volume 2) and (1978) *Primary Education in England* (London, HMSO). Neither of the latter contains a short passage which neatly exemplifies the ideology. Here, an extract from the HMI book, *Mathematics 5–11*, is reproduced. The concerns it voices about primary mathematics are very much the concerns that liberal pragmatism has for each area of the curriculum.

The primary teacher today is faced with a considerable task, brought about by the changes which have taken place in the teaching of mathematics. These have involved new content, new terms, new concepts and what many regard as a new approach to the teaching of the subject (although this approach has a very long history).

Today, the child is encouraged to make enquiries, investigate, discover and record; learning is not looked upon only as something imposed from without. It is recognized that it is through his own activity that the child is able to form the new concepts which will in turn be the basis of further mathematical ideas and thinking. These early experiences provide the foundation on which future learning is built.

The school which concentrates single-mindedly upon arithmetical skill alone is neglecting the whole range of important logical, geometrical, graphical and statistical ideas which children can meet before the age of 12. The school which stresses 'modern' topics and practical work for its own sake at the expense of consolidating number skills, systematic thought and learning, is equally guilty of neglecting its charges. The challenge is to encourage children to develop their mathematical education along a broad front of experience while ensuring systematic progression and continuity.

The primary teacher, confronted with the task of providing a wide experience for her children, can be bewildered by the wealth of apparatus, material and equipment which are now available. *She must be capable of informed choice, bearing in mind the needs of her individual class within the school.* Planning is vital; and it cannot be achieved by teachers in isolation. Infant and junior teachers need to plan together within the school and between schools.

Although most schools have a scheme of work for mathematics, in many schools this needs to be revised, what is perhaps a greater problem is that large numbers of teachers experience difficulty in translating the scheme into an effective mathematics programme.

Within some primary schools today, teachers are endeavouring to work for some of the time in such a way that subject barriers are not emphasized. Many 'integrated' studies, resulting from this way of working, lend themselves admirably to the introduction of mathematics. This mode of working requires understanding of the mathematical potential of a wide variety of situations, and this in turn demands more mathematical knowledge than many teachers possess. As a result, the opportunities for developing mathematics from an integrated topic are too often underdeveloped. The thematic approach is unlikely to motivate all the mathematics which most children need to cover within the age range 5–11 years; it is necessary to provide adequate time for mathematics, to cover a scheme of work systematically, and to include sufficient regular revision of those skills which have been identified as necessary for further progress.

Organization

The school or classroom organization can be critical in determining the effectiveness of mathematical learning. Any decision on organization needs to take into account the aims and objectives decided by the school or by teachers themselves.

It is essential for the teacher to intervene appropriately and give support and help, not only in the later stages of mathematical learning but also in structured 'play'; otherwise these activities are not fully utilized and can easily become meaningless and result in time wasting and a lack of progression. An activity which does not have the teacher's attention can seem to be less important to the children. In addition, if the only work which draws the teacher's attention is that written in a book, it is quite natural that children should desire to work in this way however inappropriate it may be, in order to attract the teacher's approval. There are occasions, particularly with the younger children when the teacher needs to recognize that participating with the children in the activities she arranges might sometimes be the best use of mathematical time.

When the activities of a class are well organized children are able to work with much less direct supervision and teacher support. This allows the teacher to work with smaller groups and individuals within groups. Class organization which allows children the opportunity to exercise an informed choice need not override the wish of the teacher to withdraw a group of children in order to teach them. Indeed, professional time can easily be wasted if on one day a teacher finds that she needs to introduce or teach the same skill eight times with eight individuals separately. In general, it is the extremes in classroom organization which militate most acutely against the effective learning of the subject.

Forms of organization which require children and their teacher to change their activity after a set period of time inhibit sustained work in mathematics. This is particularly true if the child has been working constructively with material or apparatus and needs an extension of time to complete his task before the equipment is packed away or used again for something else. A child will often work with deep concentration and effort on a task which has interested him, and to ask him to move off quickly on to some other area of experience can be unwise. If it is decided to impose timetabling restrictions these should be interpreted flexibly, bearing in mind the needs of the individual child. Over-fragmentation of the child's day should be avoided.

A further cause for concern is the quality of mathematical education which is available to those children who are able in the subject. Too often, schools present an insufficient challenge to the more able or highly gifted. In primary schools the problem is as important as at the secondary stage.

The efficacy of an organization for mathematics can be judged by the following criteria.

Does the organization provide opportunities for:

    (i)   direct teaching of individuals, groups of various sizes and the whole class;

    (ii)   practical work with appropriate material in a range of situations;

    (iii) children to use mathematics across the curriculum and to see the relevance of mathematics in the different areas of study which mathematics pervades;

    (iv) discussion and consolidation of mathematical ideas with individuals, groups and the class;

    (v)   project work or studies;

    (vi) effective remedial work for a variety of ability levels;

    (vii) extended experiences for the more able pupils;

(viii) children to reflect on their experience and the kind of thinking they are engaged in, so that they are aware that the activities in which they are involved are mathematical;

(ix) children to learn relevant work skills:

recording and clear presentation, including an understanding of why this is important;

the use of reference books;

the use of measuring instruments.

Assessment

If teaching is to be successful, it is essential that the teacher should assess what is happening. *Assessment, evaluation, diagnosis* and *prescription* are all important and should feature in the planning of work in school, in a particular class or for groups or individuals. These forms of assessment are essential if children are to learn mathematics effectively and to make progress that is in accord with their ages and abilities. . . .

As a first step, the school should decide the purpose of its assessment procedures. The aim may be to grade children in order to assist transition to the next stage of education, and in this case there is little choice. A uniform scheme devised by the LEA would seem almost essential. Where the school has discretion, assessment may be part of a philosophy which embodies a belief in the stimulus of competition, or its purpose may primarily be diagnostic (seeking to reveal the learning problems of individual children), or it may be part of a more general strategy seeking to modify the future teaching planned for a group of children in the light of the collective progress made. All of these objectives imply different types of tests and appropriate record-keeping procedures.

It is necessary to evaluate what both individuals and groups are learning; the results may or may not reflect what the teacher believes she has taught. These procedures demand great courage and professionalism. A teacher should not feel a failure if, on occasion, what has been taught has not been learnt, providing that assessment is continually being carried out. Following the evaluation of the work done by pupils, it may be necessary for the teacher to diagnose the difficulties of a group of children or of a single child within a group. When a difficulty has been identified a prescription which gives specific help should follow, if success is to be achieved.

It is all too easy to restrict assessment to those aspects of mathematics teaching which are most easily tested. Efforts should be made to broaden assessment procedures to include as many as possible of the initially planned objectives of the course.

It is essential to know the ability of the child to apply skill and knowledge to problems associated with the world in which he lives. The teacher needs to know the child's attitudes towards mathematics, his perseverance, creativity (elaboration, fluency, flexibility and originality), his understanding, visualization and psychomotor skills. At the present time, skills which are described as mathematical are applied across the curriculum. It is necessary to assess this — to assess the ability to generalize, to classify and to identify and select the essentials which determine the solution of a practical problem.

Formal examinations, based on syllabus content, frequently limit the teaching of mathematics to that which is to be tested. Objective tests, although they give a wide coverage and facilitate rapid marking, seldom reflect good methods of teaching or satisfactory levels of learning. In addition, the existing tests in no way assess mathematical creativity.

Oral questioning is an important method of checking particularly for some areas of the curriculum and for some pupils. Certain aspects of the work can be reliably tested particularly well in this way (for example, rapid recall of number facts). For other work, judgement based on this type of testing, unless very carefully prepared, can be unreliable. Oral questioning is usually very time consuming.

There are certain long established standardized tests. The use of a well validated test will not of itself be helpful unless the teacher takes the trouble to learn the purpose of the test, studies the appropriate method of administration, and appreciates the limitations. Some teachers prefer to plan their own assessment tests, believing that such tests can be more closely related to the teaching objectives. Where this is the practice, an attempt should be made to learn something of the expertise laboriously acquired by professional testers over many years, and to apply it appropriately.

It is also necessary for schools and for teachers to evaluate the teaching methods and materials they use. This involves the careful scrutiny of materials, schemes of work, test-books, work-cards, equipment and apparatus, to see if they are providing what is required.

Assessment might be regarded as a procedure which challenges the teacher to define aims and objectives more clearly, and subsequently leads to more effective teaching and learning. It allows the teacher to check if the aims have been achieved and the objectives reached. Most learning experiences need to be planned, and it is at the planning stage that the fullest assessment (evaluation, diagnosis and prescription) is important if the experiences are going to meet the real needs of the children. For this there are no standardized tests, and the teachers involved must rely on their professional judgement. This judgement can often be sharpened by collaborative work within the school or at a teachers' centre.

Finally, no methods of assessment are sacrosanct. From time to time, the methods themselves require reappraisal in order to decide whether or not the purposes they are intended to serve are being achieved.

Topic Work: Where Are We Now?

(From Conner, C., 1988, 'Topic work: Where are we now?', *Cambridge Journal of Education Newsletter*, No. 11, pp. 4–5.)

Another example of liberal pragmatism is reflected in changing views about topic work in the primary school. It was once the bastion of 'child-centred' practice, endorsing the liberal-romantic tradition described earlier (pp. 79–94), where the Plowden report (1967) described it as being:

> . . . designed to make good use of the interest and curiosity of children, to minimize the notion of subject matter being rigidly compartmentalized and to allow the teacher to adopt a consultative, guiding, stimulating role rather than a purely didactic one. (Paragraph 540)

Topic work became the focus of criticism following various surveys by HMI. For example, in the 1978 Primary survey evidence suggested that copying was widespread in topic work, and Maxwell (1977) in his review of Scottish Junior schools found that:

> . . . frequently the interested and able pupils read widely on a topic while the poorest readers did little other than copy statements or cut out pictures.

Similarly, the 1982 HMI survey of first schools revealed that the copying kept children busy and that they produced work of a reasonable standard but that:

> . . . it did not promote real progress in language development, or reveal what the children had remembered or understood.

Criticisms of this kind have caused many primary teachers to reflect on their topic work practice and to consider more careful and appropriate planning strategies. The article by Conner which follows captures the dilemma for many primary teachers of attempting to hold on to cherished liberal principles, whilst recognizing pragmatically that many of the criticisms of topic work were justified.

References

CENTRAL ADVISORY COUNCIL FOR EDUCATION (England) (1967) *Children and Their Primary Schools*, (The Plowden Report), London, HMSO.

DEPARTMENT OF EDUCATION AND SCIENCE (1978) *Primary Education in England — A Survey by HM Inspectors of Schools*, London, HMSO.

DEPARTMENT OF EDUCATION AND SCIENCE (1982) *Education 5–9: An Illustrative Survey of 80 First Schools in England*, London, HMSO.

MAXWELL, J. (1977) *Reading Progress from 8 to 15*, Slough, NFER.

One of the first courses I was asked to take responsibility for when I arrived at the Institute in September 1985 was a DES Regional Course on Topic and

Thematic Work which was due to run during 1986. In close consultation with group leaders and advisers representing local authorities in the region, we put together a package of activities, the central intention of which was to offer course members the opportunity to reflect critically upon their own practice and at the same time learn from the practice of others. As you can imagine, the initial impetus for the course derived from the increasing demand for accountability within and outside the education system, exemplified by comments such as the following from Eric Bolton, the Chief HMI (in the proceedings of a Conference on Evaluation and Assessment published by HMSO in 1985):

> We lack broad agreement about how to describe and scrutinise the primary curriculum. The absence of clarity and agreement about what children should be capable of at various stages of their primary education leads to a distinct lack of information about standards of pupil achievement in individual primary schools and a consequent difficulty of establishing any standards of achievement as a basis for an assessment of performance.

Comments of this kind when directed at topic work have called increasingly for more structure. For example in a recent *Times Educational Supplement* article (13.5.88), it was suggested that:

> today's topic work should be tighter and considerably more purposeful than the kind of activity which gave project work a bad name in the sixties.

During the DES course, however, concern was expressed about the changes that were occurring and that there was 'a danger of throwing the baby out with the bathwater'.

As the course progressed, an important question began to emerge from the keynote presentations and as a result of the small group discussions amongst course members: 'Where was the child in all the recent deliberations about topic work.'

Also, it was felt that many of the original justifications for topic work were either being forgotten or ignored. The roots of topic work can be traced back to the writings of Rousseau and Dewey and were given practical demonstration through the work of W.H. Kilpatrick in the United States. The suggested benefits were seen in terms of children taking responsibility for their own learning, with increased motivation, by undertaking studies which were interesting, relevant, cross-curricular and drawing upon first hand experience. The teacher was to be seen as an enabler and facilitator rather than the director of children's learning. All of these justifications were applauded in the Hadow Report, later endorsed by the Plowden Committee, and advocated by HMI in many of their recent reports.

Things have moved on since 1986, however, particularly with the 1988 Act and the impending introduction of the National Curriculum. More than ever there needs to be a clearly thought-out rationale and justification for our topic activities. Paragraph 14 of the consultation document on the National Curriculum (HMSO, 1987) states that 'the majority of curriculum time at primary level should be devoted to the core subjects'.

We are assured that this does not mean a return to subject specific teaching, but subjects still predominate. Kenneth Baker, in his presentation to the North of England conference in November 1987 commented, for example:

> Integrated studies are, I recognize, of particular importance for primary schools. Let me say clearly that we are not trying to suppress project work or eliminate themes. I do, I assure you, understand the importance of teaching traditional subjects across the curriculum in varied and imaginative ways.

He went on to warn us, however, that:

> schools should remember that integrated work makes great demands on the teacher and, to be effective, needs to be organized with clear direction and attainment targets. Without those it often lacks all sense of purpose and direction. (*Times Educational Supplement*, 25.9.87)

Yet despite these 'confirmatory and supportive' comments topic work is not without its critics in the higher echelons of Her Majesty's Inspectorate. Eric Bolton presenting evidence on the curriculum of the ILEA commented, with reference to primary schools:

> The main area of weakness is in topic work. In common with this type of work in the country at large, teachers leave too much to chance in their planning and are unclear about their objectives and the opportunities for learning that need to be exploited. As a result the work is often over-prescribed, undemanding and lacking in rigour.

This view is apparently supported by evidence from a recent 'dipstick' survey of primary schools by HMI, where topic work was seen as extremely patchy. There were good examples of practice in evidence but many schemes lack a coherent framework and attention needs to be given to continuity, progression and record keeping.

In a recent article Alan Blyth (1987), former Professor of Education at the University of Liverpool and a strong supporter of primary education, suggests that one factor contributing to the mixed reaction towards topic work derives from the lack of precision with which this area of the primary curriculum can be defined. One only has to look at the 'topic work' literature, to find reference to 'themes', 'topics', 'centres of interest', integrated studies, basic studies, general studies, environmental studies etc., all of which are addressing similar skills, concepts, processes and areas of knowledge.

Blyth advocates the adoption of the term 'Primary Humanities', since this description 'enjoys more currency in secondary education . . . so that its embodiment in primary education denotes a recognition of continuity without subject rigidity', and he goes on to suggest that we are in need of a clearer definition because 'in the primary curriculum the whole humanities range is now distinctly vulnerable'.

The lack of clarity is also endorsed by Robin Alexander (1985), who suggests that primary teachers are disinclined to define their teaching in terms of other people's curriculum labels and that topic work probably more than any other aspect of the primary curriculum 'falls victim to this and suffers from the inability of teachers to communicate their ideas and understanding to each other, let alone the general public'.

Yet for many primary teachers topic work is a central feature of the organization and structure of their work with children. They see it as a way of working that is challenging and rewarding for themselves and their pupils, allowing children to explore and relate their knowledge to the wider world and to examine their skills and understanding within a relevant context.

Marion Dadds discussing the findings of the recent SCDC project, 'Developing Pupils' Thinking through Topic Work', suggested that 'topic work was not only alive and well, but in some classrooms, thoroughly dyed into the fabric of teachers' and children's lives'.

In fact, a variety of studies (The Oracle Project, 1979, and SCDC, 1985) have demonstrated that *on average* something like 17 per cent of curriculum time is given over to topic work, such that, 'thematic studies, the equivalent of topic work, is given almost as much time as maths, the *prima donna* of the primary curriculum'.

Similarly, from the perspective of children, topic work has a high priority. Tony Yendoll, when questioning children about their curriculum experience found that when the formal curriculum does receive comment it is usually about some aspect of the day's activity which has been concerned with the topic, project, theme or centre of interest which the children are currently investigating. The basics (or core subjects in Mr Baker's term), are seldom mentioned (Yendoll, 1988). When one investigates the varied views of children and teachers about the processes and purposes of topic work, however, considerable differences emerge. Sarah Tann (1987) describes them as follows:

> for children Topic Work is knowledge orientated (its purpose is 'to find out things'), and resources are increasingly book based, whilst for teachers the goals for Topic Work are process orientated ('to learn how to learn') and resources are intended to be mixed and varied. The children perceive the context of topic work as being an individual enterprise, but they would like to work in groups, whilst teachers regard it as a group experience — though this appears to

mean seated in groups rather than collaborative group work. Finally the children tend to view the process of doing Topic Work to be one of looking things up in books, writing it all down for the teacher to mark ... whilst the teachers tend to view it as a process of developing general study skills, and presenting the findings in an individually pleasing format.

A review of the literature which discusses topic work identifies a variety of weaknesses, probably the most serious of which is the distinct lack of procedures for evaluation and monitoring and recording children's progress (Kerry and Eggleston, 1988). In this context Alan Blyth (1987) argues that it has become increasingly necessary:

to consider not only the place of humanities in the primary curriculum, but also the means by which an effective policy of pupil assessment can be derived, for on those means the defence of the place of humanities in the primary curriculum may increasingly depend.

Elizabeth Clough (1988) offers some interesting examples which look at ways in which we might evaluate the use of visits, visual materials, progress in learning, and dramatic activities. Evaluation is also a theme taken up in the most recent publication on this area, by Kerry and Eggleston (1988), which draws together the experiences of the SCDC project described earlier. They concluded that effective topic work depended upon:

1 A clear and agreed policy.
2 The development of structures which draw upon teachers' strengths and interests and which make planned use of the school's environment.
3 Where attention is given in planning, to the purposes of the topic, what content, skills and concepts were the pupils to be introduced to, how did these relate to previous and future experience?
4 That critical reflection on topic work activities was essential, both in terms of the effectiveness of teaching strategies and the evaluation of children's learning.

It is certainly worth the effort to reflect critically on our present practice, because of the satisfaction that teachers and children gain from their topic work experience. A recent document published in the Isle of Wight offers the perfect justification for working through topics by drawing upon 'HMI speak'.

Breadth, balance, relevance and differentiation; these are the Government's familiar watchwords for the curriculum, and they provide a useful checklist for curriculum review, and the planning of new initiatives within schools. Nowhere are they more effectively exemplified than in the topic work tradition of primary education which ensures:

Breadth — through the range of curriculum areas which may be covered in the topic, and the connections drawn between them.

Balance — through the selection of topics with different curriculum emphasis and the adjustments which may be made within the topic.

Relevance — through learning from direct experience, and seeing the practical application of skills and knowledge.

Differentiation — through the opportunity for work within the topic to be finely tuned to the capacity of the individual, whilst still contributing to the whole.

At the same time, the immediacy of the topic work approach provides motivation and excitement in learning, and the diversity of learning approaches develops skills, including elusive ones such as use of reference material, independent learning and teamwork. Finally, topic work affords unrivalled opportunities for the creativity of the individual teacher, and for curriculum-led links with the wider community. In short, it is a bulwark against the mechanistic and abstract approach which can so quickly extinguish the natural enthusiasm and inquisitiveness of children. (*Topic Work How and Why?* Isle of Wight, 1988)

Finally, as Ted Wragg commented in an article in the *Times Educational Supplement* (12.2.88):

If you think about the world of the 21st century which awaits children currently in school it is clear that they will need to be flexible, imaginative, capable of using leisure wisely, able to work individually or in a team, as well as track down information for themselves in a society increasingly drowned in knowledge. The combination of basic-skills teaching and imaginative project and topic work common in many primary schools have been a unique preparation for the future.

It is up to us to see that this remains the case.

Bibliography

ALEXANDER, R. (1985) *Primary Teaching*, Holt, Rinehart and Winston.

BLYTH, A. (1987) 'Towards assessment in primary humanities', *Journal of Education Policy*, Vol. 2, No. 4, pp. 353–360.

CLOUGH, E. (1988) 'Evaluation of learning in topic work: Some implications for INSET', in CONNER, C. (Ed.) (1988) *Topic and Thematic Work in the Primary and Middle Years*.

DADDS, M. (1988) 'Whose learning is it anyway? Concerns about continuity and control in topic work', in CONNER, C. (Ed.) (1988) *op cit.*

GALTON, M., SIMON, B. and CROLL, P. (1980) *Inside the Primary Classroom*, Routledge and Kegan Paul.

ISLE OF WIGHT TEACHERS' CENTRE (1988) *Topic Work How and Why?*

KERRY, T. and EGGLESTON, J. (1988) *Topic Work in the Primary School*, Routledge and Kegan Paul.

SCDC (1985) *Developing Pupils' Thinking through Topic Work*, Longmans.

TANN, S. (1987) 'Topic work: a mismatch of perceptions', *Reading*, Vol. 21, No. 1, pp. 62–70.

YENDOLL, T. (1988) 'Project Work — its roots and ancestry', in CONNER, C. (Ed.) (1988) *Topic and Thematic Work in the Primary and Middle Years*, Cambridge, Cambridge Institute of Education.

D Social Democracy

The Community School and Community Education

(From Midwinter, E., 1972, *Priority Education*, Harmondsworth, Penguin, pp. 19–20, 22–5.)

Unlike the writing of the educational conservatives, where the political underpinning is implicit though easy to detect, social democratic views of primary education have an explicit political stance. They are concerned with the promotion of social justice and with the role of the school as an essential (though by no means the only essential) agency in the creation of a fairer society. In the words of the last sentence in this extract, social democracy as an educational ideology seeks 'to make the state's educational system more truthfully the people's system and to deploy it more beneficially as a support and as a keystone for grassroots democracy and community involvement.' Social democracy was powerfully represented by certain members of the Plowden Committee and was reflected in the report's recommendations on educational priority areas and on the importance of home-school-community links (see pp. 206–10, 211–13). With some influential individuals in primary education such as Schiller (pp. 87–8) social democracy seems to have co-existed along with liberal romanticism. As an ideology, social democracy was particularly influential in schools associated with the Educational Priority Area action research projects (see pp. 214–19) set up after the publication of Plowden and in inner-city areas such as Coventry. One of its leading spokesmen has been Eric Midwinter. In this extract he develops his ideas of social education, community education, and community development, all aimed at 'self-renewal and community revitalization' in the disadvantaged areas of inner cities. [He begins by suggesting that there is an alternative to the kind of education usually offered children in disadvantaged areas:]

The alternative might be to offer the majority of children a social education; one that might give them the social competences to examine the depressing reality of their world, in the hope that they might learn to repair or change it in ways agreeable and pleasing to them. Through a close investigation of their social environment, the children might be that much readier to understand their own needs with more clarity. From that standpoint, they might come to invent ways and means of satisfying those needs. This is the opposite of persuading children to resign themselves stoically to their lot. This is an attempt to make them think and act boldly and inventively about their lot. What it does not do is pretend the lot is necessarily a happy one. One hopes to replace resignation and negative rebelliousness with a positive reformist attitude.

Such an open-ended investigation of the social environment (not just, let it be noted, the *local* environment: for example: television and advertis-

ing are non-local forces in the children's environment) might be the foundation of the EPA Community School. There would be an attempt to tap the
potential and the experience of the city child in his own right, with rather
less of that escapism with which teachers have superficially attempted to
polish the urban child. It has been as though they wanted to paint a
quick-dry cultural gloss on to the pupil. The social environmentally-based
curriculum is psychologically more accurate. It begins with the child's experience and works purposefully *outwards*. So much teaching of the urban
child has, in the past, postulated new experiences without lifelines from the
old.

Such a radical re-think of the EPA syllabus would, of course, require
many changes in the structure of the school and of teaching and it would
imply a much more exciting and intimate relation of the school to its
catchment area. It means long looks at the school's situation vis-à-vis many
social institutions, the most prominent of these being, naturally enough, the
home. But the other social and economic amenities around the school must
also be introduced into and related to the exercise, so that the school might
become the hub of a thriving, socially-based educational process, rather
than the exclusive and sometimes withdrawn agency of education.

[This kind of social education requires a particular kind of school, a
community school, if it is to flourish and help equip future citizens with the
means to respond creatively to the challenge of disadvantage.]

The Community School, then, emphasizes the differences rather than
the similarities of schools precisely because it attempts to relate fluently and
productively with the ethos, character and values of the community it
serves. This is what makes it a relevant school. By establishing school-
community interconnections, it constructs a stable basis upon which a three-
cornered partnership of parent, teacher and child might harmoniously
operate. The Community School ventures out into the community. The
Community School welcomes in the community. Ideally, the barriers
would collapse completely and the borders become indistinguishably blurred. Physically, one might foresee a time when, architecturally, the school,
along with all other social agencies, might be subsumed into the community.
The shopping precinct prampark might run into the nursery unit; the school
clinic and the civil group surgery might be one; and the children might eat
their school dinner in what is also the local café and snack-bar.

Gone would be the seclusion of the traditional English school, with
children drawn in and instructed behind closed doors and high walls. The
Community School requires a highly socialized format because it has a social
rather than an academic aim. Its long-term purpose is to equip the critical
parent, worker, consumer and citizen of the next generation, in the hope
that that generation might respond creatively to the challenge of deprivation. It is an attempt to break the poverty cycle, in which deprived parents
have bred deprived children in deprived situations to become, in turn, the
deprived parents of deprived children. It is an attempt to replace the ad hoc

sporadic governmental palliatives with a fullrun policy of self-renewal and community revitalization.

As such, it turns the traditional school approach on its head. The school has always been a relatively uninfluential agency for social change. It is an affirming mechanism. It is not going to Eton or to St Pancras RC Primary in Braddersfield that transforms you into an overemployed cabinet minister or an unemployed cabinet maker; it is being born into that particular avenue of life in which Eton or St Pancras stands and which you experience as you pass down the avenue. This is the lesson of the home and school researchers. It is home and neighbourhood that is important; the school merely accepts and confirms.

Willy nilly, schools have tended to defend the status quo, and there are countless social and professional pressures upon teachers to continue this hundreds-year-old convention. But, in our deprived urban districts, it is the status quo that is wrong. The Community needs to be changed and thus the Community School has to be involved in changing and not in standing still. Teachers will have to become social prosecutors rather than social defenders, if the school is, in effect, to shift itself massively and become a positive influence on social change.

It is immediately obvious that the school cannot operate alone, and here one meets one of the first golden rules of the Community School; namely, one cannot have community education without community development and one cannot have community development without community education. It would be, on the one hand, frustrating to turn out a sane, critical, well-balanced product, eager for the participatory democracy fray, only to find that participatory democracy — in the workplace, on the streets, over local issues, in the shops and so on — was absent. It would, on the other hand, be wasteful to create a grassroots community organism, if the people had not been given the opportunity to develop the essential social skills for its most fruitful usage. The planner, paying his lipservice to consultation, knocks on the door and asks the client what sort of home or environment he would like. The answer should properly be: 'I was never educated to hear that question; I was never educated to articulate an answer; if you'd like me to tell you about Who Flung, the little Chinese boy, a day in the life of Egbert, the little Anglo-Saxon boy or the story of Tobias, the little boy who knew St Paul, come round in the morning and we'll give it a whirl'.

Community education should provide an important servicing agency for community development ensuring that, if all the elements — law and order, housing, welfare, transport, social and utility services — are drawn into a unified communal enterprise, its patrons would be well-versed in how to cope with the operation. Children in school should be, in A.H. Halsey's compelling phrase, 'eager apprentices for community life'. Community education for the socially disadvantaged should be part of the gamut of community development for the socially disadvantaged. Perhaps, indeed, it should be first among equals. It is increasingly apparent that, of itself, education cannot compensate for the malpractices and injustices of society. It can contribute, but it can only contribute profitably in a propitious community clime.

The community module is no stranger to political science. Aristotle anticipated one for us. It has respectable medieval and nineteenth century antecedents. Now it is the task of the community developer to modify the ideal of autarchy to twentieth century conditions and, assuredly, education has a significant role to play. The community educationist is at once more long-sighted and more pessimistic than the compensatory educationist. He looks far beyond the short-term blandishments of an improved reading age to the sunny vision of a highly skilled citizenry recreating high quality civic life in our cities. In so doing he notes, at base, that education cannot go it alone — he is not, then, optimistic about the school as a kind of Lone Ranger solving all educational and thereby social problems, with the silver bullets of language programmes and numeracy drives. To hack at a fearful metaphor, this particular Lone Ranger would need a number of Tontoes to be guarding the flanks of all the other social factors in civic life.

Of course, it is a spiral process. It is not a question of solving problems independently. Community education does not have to be perfected, it need only be well under way, to provoke articulate and valid pressures for reform through an improved utilization of existing possibilities; as reforms in other spheres are accomplished, the confidence in and investment in community education could grow, and so on. For example, a more socially aware community could use the existing channels of social welfare benefits or the existing avenues of political protest with increased skill. This, in turn, might bring about alterations in welfare administration or an acquaintance with political techniques (such as school management) and both could visibly affect the everyday life of the Community School.

There is a circular argument surrounding the promulgation of democracy. Can the individual be trusted to exercise democratic power fully or must he be content with his quintennial excursion to the polling station; if he be given sovereign power, will the efficiency and productivity of our society be undermined because of his lack of know-how and his insufficiency or responsibility? We tend to keep democracy at arm's length or, rather, at ballot-box length. It seems we cannot afford the risk of popular as opposed to constitutional democracy; naturally, the only way to discover the truth of the argument is to give it a try, but we flinch from this. In terms of the schools, there are many ready to argue that we should leave well alone and tamper but gently with a reasonably effective system which produces a modicum of scientists, doctors, engineers and clergymen. Parents, it is still argued, would be in the way and would not be expert enough to join in a total discussion about their own children's future.

Here is the crux. It is the age-old state versus individual dilemma. But the state is an aggregate of individuals. As for the state education system, it is a remarkable illustration of the point, for — as community developers have been quick to observe — it is the highest common multiple of community development. Everyone has been to school; many have children at school; education should and could be a lifelong process; everyone lives near to and recognizes the school as an ongoing social agency; rate-payers and taxpayers both fork out mightily for it. It is the goal of community education to make the state's educational system more truthfully the people's system and to deploy it more beneficially as a support and as a keystone for grassroots democracy and community involvement.

Education for Life

(From Kitwood, T. and Macey, M., 1977, *Mind that Child!*, Writers and Readers Publishing Cooperative, pp. 41–8.)

The booklet from which the extract is taken attempts to explain the issues underlying the debate over standards in primary education which took place as a result of the Black Papers (pp. 40–4), the William Tyndale Affair (pp. 45–50, 236–45), and the publication of Bennett's research, *Teaching Styles and Pupil Progress* (Volume 3). The authors argue that the issues go well beyond the question of how children should be taught in primary classrooms, and involve the kind of society we want to create. They characterize our present society as unjust and believe that schooling is a major means through which this unjust society reproduces itself. They argue that the focus of education needs to shift away from individual competition and narrowly conceived 'standards' towards an emphasis on cooperation, social responsibility, caring, creativity and joyfulness. Their social democratic stance is evident in the final paragraph: 'The message we have inherited is outmoded and unjust. "To the many — education for drudgery; to the few — education for power". This must now be replaced by a different message, the one to which so many of the positive changes in our schools have been pointing. "To all of society — education for life".'

The claims of this booklet thus far can be summed up in seven simple points. First, while primary schools must maintain high standards of literacy and numeracy, these are not the only things that matter. Second, it is unrealistic and unhelpful to force a division between 'traditional' and 'progressive', as rival styles of education. Third, the debate about standards is part of a much larger issue, from which it cannot be separated. Fourth, our judgement must take into account the long-term educational history of Britain, looking both back into the past and forward into the future. Fifth, the research which has been cited by those who cry out for a return to the old ways is unsound, even by its own standards. Sixth, the debate, including the research, has generally been carried out on a false basis, because it has forgotten the most important element — people. Seventh, education must be seen not as a factory for producing exam passes, but as a means for enabling people to live more fully human lives.

Now the argument must be pressed further. We must face the vital question of the broader purpose of education in relation to society, both now and in the future. For it is not just an individual matter; education and society affect one another constantly, and sometimes in powerful ways. Here, perhaps, the controversy over standards has reached its highest level of confusion. Probably we all realise, if dimly, that Britain is still a society with great inequalities, inherited from the past. This is true on an individual level, but also for whole social groups. If we compare, say, the life-prospects of solicitors with those of unskilled labourers in the chemical industry, the point is immediately clear. There are vast differences between the various sectors of society, extending over virtually every aspects of life — and death. The statistics, which are well documented, tell their own story. A person's chances of surviving at birth, of receiving adequate and timely medical care, of moving easily through the educational system, of remaining employed, of avoiding insanity (or being well cared for when insane), of having a pension, of living to a ripe old age, are all related to social class. This is not simply a matter of income, status, power, or wealth, though these are included. Fundamentally, the quality of life is at stake.

It is, of course, the job a person does which mainly determines lifestyle. It is the education which mainly determines the job. And it is the social background (in other words, the lifestyle of the parents) which mainly determines the education. Of course there are exceptions, the success-stories which seem to reassure us that our society provides the means of advancement to everyone. These, however, are conspicuously rare. The main fact is that we have a social system which inexorably seems to reproduce itself. Education is one of the main means by which it does so.

People sometimes talk as if Britain were gradually becoming a classless society. This is largely a fiction, as the statistics make very plain. It is easy to draw false conclusions here, on the basis of casual impressions. Indeed, it is very difficult for anyone to gain a balanced picture of the whole of society, because we all tend to gather among people of our own kind; our friends are generally like ourselves. Unless we make a very deliberate effort to find out the truth, other parts of the social system remain hidden from us. Of course some of the centres of power and wealth in that system have shifted to some extent. There is, however, little indication that we have gone very far towards creating a society with genuinely human prospects for all.

Teachers, probably more than most, are aware of the divisions and inequalities which surround us. They know that education provides the main tickets to success, and therefore what power and responsibility are in their hands. They may well feel that the main way they can help their pupils on to a 'better' life is by getting them through exams: for some this is the main expression of their caring. If they can convince themselves that they have gone some way towards providing equality of opportunity to school children, they can feel slightly more comfortable when faced with the disheartening reality of a social system which is a society only in name.

There is a fatal flaw, though, in this way of thinking, if everyone were to adopt it. The number of privileged jobs in any country is strictly limited; schools have no direct effect on the structure of opportunity. Suppose, then, we could wave a magic wand and turn all today's academic failures into tomorrow's successes, what would be the result? Society would not change so as to create privileged positions for all who had then achieved the necessary qualifications. Universities, colleges and employers would simply raise or alter their bases of selection, so that there would again be the right number of people to fill the posts. The rest would still be the failures, at a higher educational level.

The realistic conclusion, then, is this. As long as we live in a country where access to advantage is via educational qualifications, education as a means to that end can only benefit the few, never the many. Under this arrangement schools are bound to confer the label of failure on the majority of children, in the process of enabling a few to succeed. It seems likely that the loss of zest for living and learning which occurs in many during their 11 or so years at school is partly the result of this fact. Children from all social backgrounds show great promise at 5 or 6 years old. Somewhere, en route to adulthood, their potential becomes lost or deeply hidden. Many of those who are on the way to acquiring the 'failure' label are psychologically 'camping' at school, accepting it sullenly or with defiance, truanting when they can or dare, and waiting day by day for the farce to end.

This might appear a depressing and inevitable picture, but it need not necessarily be so. We ought always to remember that social structures are man-made, not God-given: they *are* amenable to change. To bring this about on a large scale will require understanding, persistence and moral courage.

One radical change of attitude is required. We should look on the future, not from the narrow vantage-point of personal gain, but considering society as a whole. This is difficult for parents, because naturally they want the best possible foundation for life for their children. It is often hard for teachers, too, who are eager that their own pupils should get as much as they can from the opportunities education provides. But this, by itself, is shallow thinking. On the present system, if one child is an educational success, four others will be failures; if the children in one class do well, the price will be that others have done badly. The same system that makes some, breaks others.

In the long run, however, the successes and the failures will have to live side by side. Judging by the last hundred years, and the state of the country at present, this is not a satisfying or harmonious form of social existence. If we perpetuate it for our children, strife will certainly continue, and democracy itself may well collapse.

So it is essential that we change our view of education, and see it as serving a larger and more human purpose. It must be something for every person, a means towards the unfolding of the abilities which they undoubtedly have. Education is not just about 'standards', as narrowly conceived. It is about the natural world, about human relationships, about social responsibility, about culture, about responding to the wonder of being alive. Of course, amongst this, both literacy and numeracy are important. But it would be sadly mistaken to see them as merely part of the technique for gaining personal advantage, or as tools of the trade in a complex technological society. Institutions exist for people, and not the other way round.

So our schools must not be allowed to be no more than heartless academic factories, turning out people dominated by self-interest, as has so often happened in the past. This is why we have stressed the need to see the current debate in a broad context — and this includes an historical one. For the controversy about falling standards seems to be taking us in the direction of a system which contains remarkable similarities to the very early days of 'universal' education. When the notion of education for one's station on life was replaced by some notion of equality of opportunity, the way to achieve this was seen as being via a national core curriculum (the 3 R's) and by nationally implemented testing procedures. Under this system, school classes were 'inspected' to ensure that the children had 'attained' to a certain level — and if they hadn't their teachers were deemed to be failures.

Now, at first glance, this does not seem to be a totally unreasonable situation. But a moment's thought tells us, as it told eminent educationalists of the day, that the consequences of such a system are purely mechanical learning on the part of the children, and purely mechanical (rote or drill techniques) on the part of the teachers. Little 'real' learning takes place in this kind of situation, although it was, and is, relatively easy to train children to pass tests in a 'parrot-type' fashion. Yet this is the kind of farcical situation to which the Black Paper writers would have us return; this is the kind of situation to which certain politicians would have us return. But now they do this by reference to 'scientific' research, and in the name of equality and objectivity.

And the real tragedy is that the present educational system contains many promising signs. Some of our schools are becoming centres of community, serving not only children, but people of all ages. Library facilities are being used more. There is an increased demand among young and old for education which is not geared to exams and qualifications. There is greater parental and community involvement with schools than there ever has been in the past. There are some indications of increased social and political concern, and of a greater sense of caring among young people. It is quite false to claim that these work against high academic standards. There is now, throughout the country, a higher level of education than there has been at any other period.

Putting it another way, it is the dominant conception of human worth — at present accepted by many of the 'failures' as well as the 'successes' — which must be altered. In our traditions we lay stress on individual competition and put people into rank orders. We implicitly teach that possessing much and consuming more are the outstanding human achievements. Now is the time for the focus of our education to be placed elsewhere: on co-operating with others, being creative, caring, joyful, making the most of the conditions of life. Of course we need people to carry forward our industrial and commercial effort, but industry and commerce need humanity too.

And the point that must be stressed again is that none of this implies a lowering of standards in any sense at all; if anything it implies a much higher

— though broader — conception of standards. But the widespread belief in our society that we can, and should, rank people according to their performance on so-called 'objective' tests tends to mitigate against this broader conception of standards, talent and general human worth. Here we would make two points. The first is that our ability to measure intelligence, 'talent' and even attainment, is far more limited than some people would have us believe. The second is quite simply that even if we had perfected the techniques required to measure such aspects of persons, would we really wish for a society dominated by the 'able' as measured only by such tests? Would we really want all our decisions to be made by people who scored highly on so-called intelligence tests, with no reference to qualities of personality, humanity and so on?

The relevance of this to our education system in general, and to the heated debate about standards lies in the fact that testing and measurement seem to be accepted as being the 'right' and 'proper' way of going about things. Our secondary education sector, in general, is dominated by exams which make reference to the concept of intelligence. Now it seems that our primary sector is to be 'brought back into line' — it was apparently straying too far away from routine testing as a means of assessing children's ability and attainment. The threat of a reactionary, retrograde movement is a very real one. The recommendations of the Black Paper writers for national testing at prescribed stages have been accepted. One of the editors of these publications has received 'formal' recognition at Central Political Party level; and the education system is characterised by increasing bureaucracy at all levels and in all forms. The wheel appears to have turned full-circle. The only 'basic' difference between the modern call for maintaining standards by regular testing, and that same call nearly 100 years ago, is that we now have bigger and better tests. But what *kind*? Tests to process people more accurately and efficiently?

The world is changing, whether we like that fact or not. It is time for us to take responsibility for change, and turn it to the social good. There can be little doubt that during the next decade hours of work will become shorter and retirement will generally be younger. There will be less work for society to share around. If we hold onto the conception of education which is built into our history it means that large parts of life are going to be very empty for many people. The message we have inherited is outmoded and unjust. 'To the many — education for drudgery; to the few — education for power.' This must now be replaced by a different message, the one to which so many of the positive changes in our schools have been pointing. 'To all of society — education for life.'

Educational Priority Areas

(From Central Advisory Council for Education (England), 1967, *Children and their Primary Schools*, London, HMSO, pp. 50–53, 59.)

In reflecting upon taxonomies of primary education, Cunningham (1988) suggests that Richard's classification of the four contrasting views of primary education discussed in this section places the Plowden report very much within the liberal romantic tradition, yet he argues that:

> the Plowden Report could also be said to have embraced aspects of the 'social democratic' view, i.e. — 'School as a means of realizing social justice'. There is something of a natural continuity between these now, though the latter also represented a challenge to 'liberal romanticism' arising from the changing social circumstances in which the primary curriculum was delivered in the later 1960s. (p. 3)

The extract from the Plowden report (1967) which follows emphasises the 'social democratic' principles which underpin the report. The research project on Educational Priority areas undertaken by Halsey (and included as pages of this publication) suggested that despite difficulties of definition, EPAs were socially and administratively viable and a means of applying principles of positive discrimination.

Reference

Cunningham, P. (1988) *Curriculum Change in the Primary School Since 1945*, Lewes, Falmer Press.

132. In a neighbourhood where the jobs people do and the status they hold owe little to their education it is natural for children as they grow older to regard school as a brief prelude to work rather than an avenue to future opportunities. Some of these neighbourhoods have for generations been starved of new schools, new houses and new investment of every kind. Everyone knows this; but for year after year priority has been given to the new towns and new suburbs, because if new schools do not keep pace with the new houses some children will be unable to go to school at all. The continually rising proportion of children staying on at school beyond the minimum age has led some authorities to build secondary schools and postpone the rebuilding of older primary schools. Not surprisingly, many teachers are unwilling to work in a neighbourhood where the schools are old, where housing of the sort they want is unobtainable, and where education does not attain the standards they expect for their own children. From some neighbourhoods, urban and rural, there has been a continuing outflow

of the more successful young people. The loss of their enterprise and skill makes things worse for those left behind. Thus the vicious circle may turn from generation to generation and the schools play a central part in the process, both causing and suffering cumulative deprivation.

133.   We have ourselves seen schools caught in such vicious circles and read accounts of many more. They are quite untypical of schools in the rest of the country. We noted the grim approaches; incessant traffic noise in narrow streets; parked vehicles hemming in the pavement; rubbish dumps on waste land nearby; the absence of green playing spaces on or near the school sites; tiny play grounds; gaunt looking buildings; often poor decorative conditions inside; narrow passages; dark rooms; unheated and camped cloakrooms; unroofed outside lavatories; tiny staff rooms; inadequate storage space with consequent restriction on teaching materials and therefore methods; in-adequate space for movement and P.E.; meals in classrooms; art on desks; music only to the discomfort of others in an echoing building; non-soundproof partitions between classes; lack of smaller rooms for group work; lack of spare room for tuition of small groups; insufficient display space; attractive books kept unseen in cupboards for lack of space to lay them out; no privacy for parents waiting to see the head; sometimes the head and his secretary sharing the same room; and, sometimes all around, the ingrained grime of generations.

The Educational Needs of Deprived Areas

136.   What these deprived areas need most are perfectly normal, good primary schools alive with experience from which children of all kinds can benefit. What we say elsewhere about primary school work generally applies equally to these difficult areas. The best schools already there show that it is absurd to say, as one used to hear, 'it may be all very well in a nice suburb, but it won't work here'. But, of course, there are special and additional demands on teachers who work in deprived areas with deprived children. They meet special challenges. Teachers must be constantly aware that ideas, values and relationships within the school may conflict with those of the home, and that the world assumed by teachers and school books may be unreal to the children. There will have to be constant communication be-tween parents and the schools if the aims of the schools are to be fully understood. The child from a really impoverished background may well have had a normal, satisfactory emotional life. What he often lacks is the opportunity to develop intellectual interests. This shows in his poor com-mand of language. It is not, however, with vocabulary that teaching can begin. The primary school must first supply experiences and establish rela-tionships which enable children to discriminate, to reason and to express themselves. Placing such children in the right stance for further learning is a very skilled operation. But those who have done remedial work will be

aware of the astonishing rapidity of the progress which can be achieved, particularly in extending vocabulary, once children's curiosity is released. The thrust to learn seems to be latent in every child, at least within a very wide range of normality. But however good the opportunities, some children may not be able to take advantage of them. Failure may have taken away from them their urge to learn.

Educational Assumptions and Policies

140.   Our study of these problems compelled us to consider the process of economic and social development and the contribution made to it by the schools. Industrial development in many respects is the motor of social progress. We recognise that there are limits to the resources that can be mobilised for education and the primary schools. But it does not necessarily follow, as many have assumed, that the fruits of economic growth, together with the present pattern of public services, will in time give every child increasing opportunities of contributing to the nation's progress. It does not follow that education, because its development depends in the long run on the growth of the economy, must therefore follow in its wake, rather than contribute to the promotion of growth. Nor does it follow that a 'fair' or 'efficient' distribution of educational resources is one that provides a reasonably equal supply of teachers, classrooms, and other essentials to each school child in each area. Nor does it follow that the government's responsibility for promoting progress within the limits permitted by these resources must be confined to encouraging development in the most capable areas, spreading word of their progress to others, and pressing on the rearguard of the laggard or less fortunate whenever opportunity permits. Though many of these assumptions are already being questioned or abandoned, our own proposals are unlikely to convince those who still accept them, and we must, therefore, challenge each in turn.

146.   Our argument thus far can be briefly summarised. As things are at the moment there is no reason why the educational handicaps of the most deprived children should disappear. Although standards will rise, inequalities will persist and the potential of many children will never be realised. The range of achievement amongst English children is wide, and the standards attained by the most and the least successful begin to diverge very early. Steps should be taken to improve the educational chances and the attainments of the least well placed, and to bring them up to the levels that prevail generally. This will call for a new distribution of educational resources.

154.   All authorities would be asked to consider which of their schools should qualify, to rank them according to criteria such as those we have listed, and to submit supporting data. Advice would also be available from H.M. Inspectors of Schools. In this way the Department of Education and

Science would have full information both about the social and the educational needs of the schools and areas. Many of the criteria would be closely correlated. With experience the data required could be simplified so as to ease administration; but meanwhile, a wide variety of criteria should be employed. The schools near the bottom of the resulting rankings would be entitled to priority. We envisage a formal procedure enabling the Secretary of State for Education and Science to designate particular schools or groups of schools as priority schools or areas. Those so designated would qualify for the favourable treatment described later in this chapter. Local education authorities would submit regular reports on these schools to the Secretary of State for the purpose of determining what progress was being made, how long their designation should continue, which aspects of the programme were proving most effective, and what further steps should be taken.

E   An Alternative Perspective

The 'Progressive', 'Elementary' and 'Technological' Traditions

(From Golby, M., 1982, 'Microcomputers and the primary curriculum', in Garland, R. (Ed.) *Microcomputers and Children in the Primary School*, Lewes, Falmer Press, pp. 206–7, 208.)

This short extract provides a rather different ideological perspective from that presented in the rest of this section. Golby distinguishes three traditions in primary education:

1   an elementary tradition concerned with the inculcation of essential knowledge into passive pupils;
2   a progressive tradition celebrating self-expression, individual autonomy and personal growth, but lacking an adequate theory of knowledge to help it define the primary curriculum; and
3   a technological tradition stressing utilitarian values associated with the pursuit of science and technology.

His brief characterization of the progressive tradition is particularly interesting.

It may be of value to distinguish three broadly separate 'traditions' ... which are still discernible in the primary field. They are discernible ... both in the practice and in the discourse about primary education. Two of the traditions represent the familiar antithesis of elementary and progressive ideologies while the third, which I shall call the technological tradition, is a relatively new arrival....

We could perhaps deal with the first two traditions summarily. The elementary tradition takes as its guiding metaphor the inculcation of essential knowledge into passive pupils. Most of us learned to reject or at least become highly sceptical of this utilitarian tradition in our early training but many of us returned to it in various modified forms later in our careers. I suggest that this tradition is by no means dead and the modern primary curriculum is still heavily underlain by a 'drills and frills' approach. The nineteenth century elementary curriculum lives in many schools' division of the curriculum into the 'basics', consisting of the three 'R's and the 'extras', consisting in an uncertain melange of literary, aesthetic, humanistic and now scientific ingredients.... The elementary tradition expressed a political will to 'gentle the masses' through the controlling power of a curriculum which would be limited in scope. This curriculum is an education (though today's philosophy might deny it the title of education at all, and substitute socialization or training as the appropriate concepts) for subservience. The elementary curriculum survives, despite the abolition of the 'eleven plus', in the deeper structure of many schools by emphasizing certain conforming performances rather than the expansive qualities of questioning and imagination.

The progressive tradition has very largely gained its identity not through the coherent expression of new rationales but through its romantic opposition to the elementary tradition. Thus, instead of stressing control, subservience and conformity, it celebrates self-expression, individual autonomy and personal growth. None of these formulae have, in my opinion, been adequately defended in philosophical terms. The tone of progressive teaching has always been enthusiastic and evangelical. The contents of the curriculum have always been poorly defined and this for the simple reason that content is not to the fore in this line of thinking. Indeed, it is the weakness of the progressive tradition that it has no adequate theory of knowledge to help it define the curriculum above the rhetorical level. Accusations of incoherence in *practice*, however, seem to me to be less well substantiated than those against the theory of progressive education. In practice, progressive educators know very well how to bring to bear all manner of subject matter in the interests of individual children as they individually grow and develop. There is, I believe, a practical logic composed of a blend of fundamental opposition to the values of elementary education with a perception of children not as empty vessels but, rather, as centres of consciousness and potentialities beyond what we can preconceive. It is also possible, I believe, to assert that progressive ideas have a romantic and rural texture much in contrast with the practical and urban fabric of the elementary tradition.

These contrasts are vastly over-simplified. This should go without saying but needs repetition here as I am about to offer a third, also over-simplified, opinion. There exists, I believe, a more recent tradition which may be broadly labelled technological. This tradition has emerged most noticeably in the years since 1976 when education has come under a closer political scrutiny. What I have in mind here is the recent emphasis since the Great Debate on the utilitarian values associated particularly with the pursuit of science.... The technological tradition I perceive has its most tangible emphasis in the continuing and developing concern of HMIs, for example in their Primary and Secondary working papers and surveys. In both of these endeavours the place of science and in the secondary field of Craft, Design and Technology is taken for granted as an aspect of the 'core curriculum'. The debate about the core curriculum has not as yet penetrated beyond the level of such atavistic assumptions as the above concerning science and we have to look into still relatively unknown theoretical literature for a clear defence of the position of Science, Craft, Design and Technology in the 'protected core' of the curriculum. Perhaps most obviously this new technological tradition comes into view in the Primary survey where the conclusion is drawn that improvements in science teaching in primary schools are greatly to be desired. Yet no rationale for the inclusion of science, a subject of very low visibility historically in the primary curriculum, is to be found in the survey itself. While we should not expect of the kind of research which the survey was an accompanying philosophical statement on the rationale for the 'whole curriculum', we could hope to see the issues raised somewhere. And the literature, both from official quarters and from the research community seems to me deficient in this major respect. I assert then, that I perceive a new tradition, building on old assumptions, making inroads into the primary curriculum. 'Hard science' — and, perhaps, especially, 'science that works' or technology — is making a claim; a claim I do not reject or concede here but merely hold up for inspection. It is no part of my task here to take up a side in this as yet unformed debate but rather to point out that the primary curriculum, though it has seen the rather successful innovation of *Science 5–13*, has traditionally not found space for the sort of utilitarian emphasis on technical skills that may be implied in the crudest form of this new technological imperialism over our curricular thinking.

3 Primary Education: Philosophical Perspectives

Introduction

The Philosophy of education has developed into a distinctive branch of study in Britain during the last twenty years. It has established itself as a foundation discipline in the study of education with its own distinctive group of theorists, a developing tradition of enquiry, and a considerable number of publications, including the *Journal of Philosophy of Education*. For a review of its development, readers are referred to an article by Dearden (1982), and, for an overview of the current state of play in the discipline, to a collection of papers edited by Barrow (1982).

According to Hirst (1982), 'three distinctive features' have characterized the kind of philosophy of education which first developed in England in the 1960s. Philosophy of education has used the techniques of conceptual analysis to examine major terms used in educational discussion (for example, 'education', 'teaching', 'growth', and 'creativity') so as to explore the complexities in their meanings. This has led to greater clarity in the meanings of educational beliefs and principles employing such terms. Secondly, philosophy has examined the justifications offered for educational principles (such as those associated with 'liberal romanticism' or 'educational conservatism'). This work 'has sharpened up an awareness of the value-judgements often implicit in educational doctrines and of the philosophical beliefs about the nature of knowledge, mind and moral values that were being presupposed' by adherents of such doctrines or ideologies. Thirdly, philosophy of education has helped in the development of more adequate educational theory by contributing more justifiable philosophical beliefs, based on contemporary work in the general field of philosophy.

These 'three distinctive features' are useful in characterizing the philosophical material related to primary education, which is featured in this section of the source book. The first two extracts illustrate the work done on the analysis of important concepts. Much of this work has focused on concepts applicable to education generally, but some attention has been given to concepts of particular significance in primary education. Dearden, for example, has analyzed concepts such as 'needs' (pp. 139–42), 'growth' and 'play', while Wilson has examined the concept of 'interest' and its connection with 'education' (pp. 143–5). The next four extracts illustrate the contribution made by philosophers to the critical examination of educational ideologies or doctrines. In particular, philosophers have examined the justifications offered for 'child-centred' education; it is regrettable that the same degree of attention has not been accorded the ideologies of 'liberal pragmatism' or 'social democracy'. The remaining two extracts reveal how philosophers can contribute to the development of more adequate theories of primary education.

The extracts in this section exemplify some of the points made by Dearden (1982) in his discussion of the potential contribution of philosophy to study and debate in education:

It should make any necessary distinctions to clarify meaning, explore conceptual possibilities and try to identify what is necessary and what is contingent. It should expose question-begging, misleading claims and inconsistency. It should draw implications, show the full extent of someone's commitments, reveal absurd consequences, highlight by parallel arguments, draw attention to unnoticed alternatives and test assumptions. It should probe the validity of justifications, draw attention to areas of undeserved neglect, redress serious imbalances and assemble pertinent reminders.

Further, philosophy of education should expose narrow conceptions, probe presuppositions and reveal hidden connections, or expose spurious unity. It should clarify ideas and articulate imaginative new conceptions. It should re-describe to bring into focus, show how certain notions will or will not do the work expected of them, show how one thing prevents the recognition of another, identify misplaced emphases or misdirected attention and set things in a wider illuminating context.

References

BARROW, R. (Ed.) (1982) 'Philosophy and education', *Educational Analysis*, 4, 1.
DEARDEN, R. (1982) 'Philosophy of education, 1952–82', *British Journal of Educational Studies*, 30, 1, pp. 57–71.
HIRST, P. (1982) 'Philosophy of education: The significance of the sixties', *Educational Analysis*, 4, 1, pp. 5–10.

Children's Needs

(From Dearden, R., 1968, *The Philosophy of Primary Education: An Introduction*, London, Routledge and Kegan Paul, pp. 14–18.)

Of all contemporary English philosophers of education, Dearden has contributed most to clarifying thinking in the area of primary education. In his book, (1968) *The Philosophy of Primary Education* (Routledge and Kegan Paul), he analyzed a number of very important concepts (including 'interests', 'play' and 'experience'), and he put forward a carefully argued theory to underpin the primary school curriculum. Here he analyzes the concept of 'need', as exemplified in the phrases 'The needs of children are ...' or 'In the primary school children need...'. He argues that needs-statements do not simply describe what children lack but go beyond that to imply that what children lack is in some ways desirable or valuable. He maintains that 'one has to look behind statements of need to the values that are guiding them, for it is here that the issue substantially lies.' This explains why proponents of any educational ideology can argue their case by reference to children's 'needs' and why the nature of these 'needs' differs crucially from ideology to ideology.

Statements of 'need' abound in educational writing. One of the most recent examples relevant to primary education is to be found in *Primary Education in Scotland* (HMSO, 1965), the first chapter of which is not, as one might reasonably have expected it to be, devoted to setting out aims, but rather gives a statement of the 'needs of the child', which are apparently five in number. Furthermore, this statement of needs concludes a chapter the character of which is almost purely psychological, so that one is led to suppose that if one wants to know what children need, then it is to psychology that one ought appropriately to turn. Empirical research will show the way, or so it is implied.

There are, however, two serious defects in any attempt to by-pass a discussion of aims by furnishing statements of need instead. The first of these defects relates to the logical impossibility of passing from statements of psychological fact to value-based judgements about what one ought to do. The second defect concerns some hidden assumptions behind thinking, as indeed is often thought, that an education which starts from the 'needs of the child' will solve the problem of motivation. Each of these defects merits some further elaboration, though for a more fully developed discussion, with due qualifications added, one would have to look elsewhere (see Komisar, 1961, or Dearden, 1966).

The first defect, then, concerns the attractiveness of the apparently empirical, or observationally based, character of statements of need. And indeed, on the face of it at least, needs-statements are simply empirical. If someone says that teachers need a salary increase of three hundred pounds per year, or that students need at least two advanced levels to enter university, or that owners of dogs need a licence, is it not simply a matter of fact that this is so? If one had occasion actually to make a categorical assertion of the form '*x* needs *y*', would it not simply be a matter of fact that *x* had not already got *y*, and furthermore that getting *y* would indeed achieve whatever results were regarded as desirable of achievement. Surely these would be matters of fact, and some appropriate method of fact-finding, whether ordinary observation or sophisticated research, would be not just relevant but absolutely indispensable. The catch, however, lies in the implication of there being a condition desirable of achievement; for this brings to light the *valuational* basis of needs-statements, and the necessary subservience of the empirical data to such values.

Teachers *need* an increase of three hundred pounds only if it is a good thing to have one's salary so advanced. Students *need* two advanced levels only if going to university is regarded as something desirable, or worthwhile. Owners of dogs *need* a licence only because the law backs with an obligation the desirability of having one. Simply that someone does not actually have something, or that he would have to have it *if* he wanted to do something else, does not establish a need. Teachers do not have classes of seventy children, but no-one will therefore detect a *need* here. Yet if we thought mass instruction a good thing, as it was thought to be in one phase of the elementary school tradition, then we might well say that classes of seventy were needed. Confronted with statements of need, then, it is appropriate to inquire into the valuational basis of such statements. What values are being assumed here? What is being assumed to be desirable? And to see this is to see through the merely apparent empirical character of needs-statements. It is also to see that psychology, or indeed any other empirical science, logically must fail at some point as a sufficient warrant for asserting something to be needed.

Of course, often there is wide and proper agreement as to what is valuable, or desirable, or obligatory, and against a background of such consensus it is the researcher who has the important points to make. Thus when Bowlby claimed to have found, and let us assume for the sake of discussion that it really was there to be found, that maternal deprivation in early childhood caused an 'affectionless' character to be formed, then he was warranted in asserting the need of maternal care in childhood, for we all agree that being an 'affectionless' character is *undesirable*.

But we do not always agree over what is desirable. The child-centred reformers did not agree with the architects of the elementary tradition over what was desirable. In such circumstances, it is simply begging the question to talk about needs, or to pretend that there is nothing at issue that cannot be settled by empirical research. One has to look behind statements of need to the values that are guiding them, for it is here that the issue substantially lies. Defenders of the elementary school tradition could, with perfect propriety, talk of the 'needs of the child'. On their view, the needs of the child would be to pay attention and to listen, to do as he was told and then wait for further instructions, to show obedience and respect towards adults in authority, and so on. What was *desirable* was that the proclivities of a bad nature should be curbed and re-directed, that future responsibilities should be prepared for, and that certain social attitudes should be inculcated.

A further illustration of this same important point about the valuational basis of needs-statements is provided by a consideration of educational books which are imported from other cultures or societies significantly different from our own. For here one may find needs-statements the warrant for which is culture-relative, and which are therefore invalid when exported, in spite of all their research support. P.T. Young mentions 'the need to maintain one's status within one's group, the need to win pre-eminence, the need to save one's face, the need to avenge an affront ...' (Young, 1943, p. 150), which nicely illustrate this point. In connection with cultural relativity, however, mention might be made of Maslow's useful distinction between 'basic' or 'deficit' needs and 'growth' needs (Maslow, 1955). 'Deficit' needs are those without which we become 'mentally ill', such as safety, love and respect, and which are therefore needed by anyone. Much more relative, however, both to cultures and to individuals within cultures, are 'growth' needs. By these Maslow means, for example, the need to be a good artist, carpenter or scientist. . . .

The second of the defects earlier mentioned related to the assumption that an education which starts from the 'needs of the child' will solve the problem of motivation. But the trouble here lies with the equation of what a person *needs* with what he *wants*, for the motivational problem is only in some degree solved when the relevant item comes to be wanted. From the judgement that '*x* needs *y*' it by no means follows that '*x* wants *y*'. John may need Latin to enter university though he loathes the subject. The patient may need to convalesce for a month though what he wants is to return to work immediately. And certainly such an optimistic conclusion was unwarranted in the elementary school, where it was not even expected that children would want what they were judged to need.

Child-centred theorists, however, are sometimes apt to take wanting as a *criterion* of needing. If a child in an infant classroom wants to play with sand, *ergo* he needs to. Sometimes perhaps indeed he does: if, for example, he would in that way work out some phantasy or emotional problem which it is desirable that he should work out. But even here, to say that he needs to play with the sand is to say more than simply that he wants to. It is to sanction his desire as being an urgent or important one that *ought* to be satisfied, and plainly not all wants come into that category. Taken as an unrestricted generalization, the statement that what children need is what they actually want would be as near as makes no difference to saying that we should start from children's *interests*. Such a shift in the argument is at least to be desired for giving up talk about a curriculum based on children's needs, for as Komisar has pointed out, every curriculum is a needs-curriculum (Komisar, 1961). No-one dreams of including in the curriculum anything that is not needed, and hence no criterion of choice is or could be furnished by resort to bare statements of 'need'. As has already been argued, the heart of the matter lies in the prior notions of what is valuable or desirable. It is here that a criterion of choice must be found.

References

DEARDEN, R. (1966) '"Needs" in education', *British Journal of Educational Studies*, 14, 3, pp. 5–17.

KOMISAR, P. (1961) '"Need" and the needs-curriculum', in SMITH, B. and ENNIS, R. (Eds), *Language and Concepts in Education*, Rand McNally.

MASLOW, A. (1955) 'Deficiency motivation and growth motivation', in JONES, M. (Ed.), *Nebraska Symposium on Motivation*, University of Nebraska Press.

SCOTTISH EDUCATION DEPARTMENT (1965) *Primary Education in Scotland*, HMSO.

YOUNG, P. (1943) *Emotions in Man and Animal*, Wiley.

Interests and Education

(From Wilson, P., 1971, *Interest and Discipline in Education*, London, Routledge and Kegan Paul, pp. 66–8, 68–9.)

The book from which this extract has been taken was described by Peters in 1971 as 'one of the first attempts at a precise and well-argued defence of a point of view associated with "progressive" education'. This description remains true well over a decade later. In the interim, little has been done in England to put liberal romanticism on a sound philosophical footing (though see pp. 166–72). In the book, Wilson explored the meanings of 'interest' and 'discipline' in a variety of contexts and attempted to tease out the connection between such concepts and that of 'education'. He was careful not to imply that 'education' and 'schooling' were co-extensive: 'Although most of what takes place in schools could be called "schooling", only some of it (and not necessarily any of it) is "educative".' In this extract he argues for a very tight connection between 'education' and 'whatever is of intrinsic value', such that a person's education 'can only proceed through the pursuit of his interests, since it is these and only these which for him are of intrinsic value'. On this view, an individual's education, 'whether in or out of "school", consists in whatever helps him to develop [his] capacity for valuing and [his] inclination to pursue what is valued'. In the light of his analyses of 'education' and 'interest', Wilson indicates in general terms what he believes the educative function of the teacher to be.

Interests and Education. What I am advocating here has often been called 'child-centred education', but a teacher who stands back and just *allows* children to pursue whatever interests come into their heads is practising, as I have argued elsewhere (Wilson, 1969), a travesty of 'child-centredness'. The feature of the concept of education which 'child-centred' educators were concerned to stress was its connection with the development of whatever is of intrinsic value, and thus, in the case of children just as much as in the case of adults, its connection with the notion of 'interest'. The point of calling education 'child-centred' lies in emphasizing that even when the person who is being educated is a child, and even, therefore, when his interests often seem 'childish' or silly or undesirable from the point of view of his adult teachers, nevertheless his *education* can only proceed through the pursuit of his interests, since it is these and only these which for him are of intrinsic value. However ridiculous a child's interests may seem, there is nothing else in terms of which he can become *more* 'educated'. He can be 'schooled' to adopt adult values, but only at the expense of leaving his own in their present childish and uneducated state.

A person's interests, dispositional and occurrent, represent his capacity (such as it is) to find intrinsic value in the circumstance of living, and his inclination to pursue or seek such value in terms of feeling and understanding and of activity which seems appropriate to its practical point. Such a person's 'education', I believe, whether in or out of 'school', consists in whatever helps him to develop this capacity for valuing and this inclination to pursue what is valued. Thus, whatever enables him to appreciate and understand his interest more fully, and to pursue it more actively and effectively, is 'educative'. But this does not mean that teachers, even when they are thinking about 'educating' children rather than just about 'schooling' them, should give assistance in the pursuit of anything and everything which catches the interest of a particular child. Still less does it mean that they should stand aside, or merely 'follow' the child down 'divergent paths'. There is a difference between helping a child to follow an interest for himself, and abandoning him to get on with it *by* himself. A merely tolerated child is apt to wonder in the end what his teacher is doing at school at all, if all that he ever hears from that teacher is 'Yes, Billy. On you get with it, then.' Ultimately Billy will be bound to start asking what *teacher* is 'getting on with'. Meanwhile, the interest which he had been casting around for ways of pursuing 'appropriately', founders for lack of help.

There is a constant risk involved in pursuing an interest, since no one can ever say in advance exactly how it is going to turn out. In it, one is not trying to approximate to a *norm* of action, or in other words to do what the majority of people might agree that one 'needs' to do. It is not a matter of trying to conform to *proven* or *consensual* standards or norms of value. It is more like trying to find out more about what it is which gives value to norms, or like *seeking* a measure of value against which to *evaluate* norms. In principle, this is a risky business. There might turn out to be precious little value in the direction in which we have taken it to lie. Or, in gaining what is of value in an interest, we might lose other values which previously we had achieved in other directions, or jeopardize the future achievement of further values in store. Just as each new understanding which we gain restructures our entire conceptual grasp of the world in which we live, so each new value which we find or seek, in pursuing an interest, brings about a shift — and sometimes a radical shift — in our entire current *scale* of values. Such changes, although pursued for their interest, are by no means always in *our* interest, let alone in the interest of anyone else. The inherent uncertainty of life's outcomes is what makes possible its interest. It also makes unavoidable its risk. Children, therefore, and perhaps especially children educationally speaking, need constantly the kind of confidence to proceed which comes from receiving effective help. This effective help is the educative function of teachers, and it *includes* the weighing of each risk against its possible gains.

By contrast, then, with the kind of manipulative changing of behaviour which I described [earlier in the book], 'teaching' of an *educative* kind consists in helping children to structure their experience and activity in ways which enable them to see more of its intrinsic point and value ...

... What I am trying to suggest ..., is that children benefit 'educationally' by *learning* how to pursue their interests both more effectively and in an increasingly selective and discriminating way, and that 'educative teaching', therefore, is whatever intentionally serves to bring about this end. '"Ought",' as philosophers would say, 'implies "can"' (e.g. Henderson, 1966; 1969), but not everything which *can* be done *ought* to be done. It would be unintelligible to say that a person 'ought' to be interested in *anything*, unless from time to time he were inclined already to see intrinsic value in *something*. But this means only that a sense of the intrinsic value of *some* thing or things in life cannot be induced in people solely by manipulating the external conditions in which they live. It does *not* mean that anything and everything which a particular person values is *bound* to prove valuable or to be most worth pursuing here and now.

A child's interests are already selective. Through them he begins to discriminate intelligible and possibly valuable features of the world. Trying to pursue an interest means always, then, trying to see those features more and more clearly, and in doing so, *trying out* (as it were) their possible value. The child's *educational* need is to be sustained and helped through these trials, so that his interests neither become fixed in some stereotyped form through his inability to see how to develop them further, nor remain at the fleeting level which, by themselves, his own unaided efforts might achieve. But neither on educational nor on any other grounds does the child 'need' to pursue *all* his interests. Indeed, it is only on educational grounds that he 'needs' to pursue *any* of them. There is room, then, for other grounds such as prudence, practicality and morality to be considered, when the selection is being made as to which of his interests should be pursued in school.

If *only* these 'other grounds', however, are being considered both by children and by teachers, then school becomes a place where no education can possibly be going on at all. If one were *always* to be prudent, it would be unwise *ever* to pursue an interest for its own sake, because of the *unavoidable* risks involved. A school staffed by teachers who are never more than prudent becomes, therefore, a sort of value-dump of supposedly good things whose *intrinsic* value is the one feature of them which no one can ever afford to consider. The prudent children, meanwhile, become artists in stategies for *concealing* their interests from adults whom they know, from bitter experience, will merely make use of those interests for well-intentioned but unintelligible purposes of their own. The child's own culture or sense of values, such as it is, is the price which he is required to pay, in such schools, for the acquisition of adult norms. There is no other reason for his going to school, in that case, than that he must.

References

HENDERSON, G. (1966) '"Ought" implies "can"', *Philosophy*, 41.
HENDERSON, G. (1969) 'Moral pragmatism', *Philosophy*, 44.
WILSON, P. (1969) 'Child-centred education', *Proceedings of the Philosophy of Education Society of Great Britain*, 3.

A Critique of Plowden's 'Recognisable Philosophy of Education'

(From Peters, R.S. (Ed.) 1969, *Perspectives on Plowden*, London, Routledge and Kegan Paul, pp. 3–4, 4, 5, 6, 6–7, 7–8, 10, 11–12, 12, 13, 13, 14, 14, 15, 15–16, 16, 20.)

In their report, the Plowden Committee stated that teachers 'should bring to bear on their day-to-day problems astringent intellectual scrutiny'. Two years after their comments were published, their own report was subject to such 'astringent intellectual scrutiny' by a group of educationists from the London Institute of Education, led by Professor Peters. Peters provided a hard-hitting critique of the 'half-truths' underlying Plowden's 'recognisable philosophy of education' summarized in paragraph 505 (reproduced on p. 89 of this source book.) Here, he examines some of the principles enshrined in the report, including the importance attached to development and self-direction, the approval given to the non-compartmentalization 'of knowledge, and the image of the teacher. He finds many of the report's notions 'suspect', in particular its neglect of the 'inescapably social character of thought and language, of processes of transmission, and of motivation'.

[Plowden's] 'recognisable educational philosophy' proliferates in important half-truths that are paraded as educational panaceas. It is necessary, therefore, to separate out its various components and to attempt to place them in a more adequate perspective. They are as follows:

(a)   That the child has a 'nature' which will 'develop' if the appropriate environment is provided. What will he develop into? Presumably a 'mature adult' who can 'be himself' and be critical of his society.

(b)   Self-direction is very important in this development. 'The child is the agent of his own learning' (Para. 529). 'Sensitivity and observation are called for rather than intervention from the teacher' (Para. 527). Children have an intense interest in the world around them together with powers of concentration which will ensure learning if they are provided with materials for which they are 'ready' (Paras. 533, 534).

(c)   Knowledge cannot be divided into separate compartments. Self-chosen activity within an 'integrated curriculum' is desirable.

(d)   The teacher must be a guide, an arranger of the environment, rather than an instructor. . . .

A Constructive Critique

Development. What is to be made of the notion that children have a 'nature' or that the individual has a 'self' which will emerge if the right environment is provided? This raises, of course, a host of old questions about what is innate and acquired; but it also raises equally crucial questions about the concept of 'development'. . . .

How is such development to be conceived? In most books on child-development 'development' is divided into physical, intellectual, social, moral and emotional aspects, as if social and moral development were devoid of 'intellect', as if morality and the use of the intellect were free from passion, and as if emotional development was separable from thought and social awareness. This indefensible type of classification should surely be scrapped and replaced by a more logical division into forms of thought and awareness, each of which has its affective aspect. This would include scientific, mathematical, moral, historical, inter-personal, aesthetic, and religious forms of awareness; proper attention should also be paid to the developmental aspects of various forms of skills — 'basic' and linguistic ones included.

What is urgently needed is a new approach to child-development in which the logical aspects of these forms of awareness and the values inherent in them were more closely related to facts about the learning process of young children. . . .

But even if one tidied up these various aspects of 'development' how would this help to determine the emphasis of education? Is a man more 'developed' if he is highly trained scientifically but aesthetically insensitive or if he is aesthetically sophisticated but a scientific ignoramus? Is a man more developed who is 'well-rounded' but with a thorough knowledge of nothing, than one who is a brilliant mathematician and musician but ignorant of most other things? Was Lenin more 'developed' than Gandhi? . . .

There was a time, of course, when forms of awareness were comparatively undifferentiated and when the religious one, in the form of various brands of Christianity, provided some kind of unifying ideal of man against which a man's development could be roughly measured. But those times have passed. We now live in a pluralistic type of society without any such unifying ideal, and as educators we must come to terms with this. Those who stress the importance of individual self-realization as an educational aim are, perhaps unwittingly, lending their support to a pluralist conception of the good life. . . .

But what tends to be forgotten by those who identify themselves with this type of ideology is what Dewey called the 'shared experience' which such individual development presupposes. On the one hand there are high-level moral principles such as toleration, respect for persons, fairness, and consideration of people's interests which underpin democratic institutions and which provide the interpersonal framework within which individuals can be encouraged to pursue a variety of interests that are thought to be worth-while. Without some such consensus, into which children must be initiated, the pluralist pursuit of value would be impossible. On the other hand all the different options open to individuals are inescapably social in character. No individual can embark on science, singing or tool-making without being introduced to a vast body of knowledge and skill that has gradually been accumulated, and in most of them he will share a form of life with others who are also engaged on them. Furthermore when we encourage children to be themselves we surely take for granted a vast array of activities and forms of awareness that we think *worthwhile* within which we encourage children to find the ones to which they are particularly suited. As teachers we must make value judgments when we think of any sort of curriculum; for we do not offer blowing up live frogs with bicycle pumps or bingo as possible options. Talk of 'development', like talk of children's 'needs', is too often a way of dressing up our value-judgments in semi-scientific clothes....

Self-Direction. Obviously enough the stress on self-direction and self-chosen activities is closely connected with the ideal of individual self-development. But it incorporates additional doctrines, one proclaiming a value judgment, the other relating to theories of learning. I will briefly consider each of them in turn.

(i) *Autonomy as a moral principle.* On the one hand a powerful plea is being made for the value of individual autonomy, for the importance attached in a democratic society to individual choice, independence of mind, and to more recondite virtues such as creativeness and originality. I need not expatiate on the importance of this in a pluralist society. But three types of comment are in place. Firstly this, like any other value, must surely be asserted not absolutely but with an 'other things being equal' clause....

Secondly too little is known about how such autonomy independence, and 'creativeness', is developed. It may well be that a very *bad* way of developing this is to give children too many opportunities for uninformed 'choices' too young. One thing, however, is obvious enough — that the notion of 'autonomy' makes very little *sense* unless a child first has a grasp from the inside of what following rules means and has taken rules into himself between which he has to choose. Similarly general talk of 'creativeness' is cant; for there is no such general faculty. One can be creative in science without being a creative cook. And to be 'creative' in any sphere presupposes some mastery of the skills and body of knowledge appropriate to it. As Whitehead wisely put it, the stage of 'generalization' or autonomy comes after the stage of precision. The implication of all these points is that it is essential for children to be initiated into skills and bodies of knowledge which are part of our public heritage, before they can sensibly strike out on their own.

Thirdly, if we accept that there are many ways in which an individual can strike out on his own in a pluralist type of society, and if we think that children should be encouraged to stand on their own feet and find their own way, then we must think seriously about equipping them to do this effectively. This means not only taking them a certain distance in the various options so that they may have experience on the basis of which they may choose; it also means paying special attention to activities such as literature, history, and social studies which are an aid to them in this sort of choice....

(ii) *'Discovery' methods*. The doctrine of self-direction relates, on the other hand, to a theory of learning. It suggests that children learn things better if their activities are self-chosen and approximate to 'discovery'. This claim is based almost entirely on teacher's hunches not on objective evidence ... *too much* emphasis on self-chosen activities may lead to a certain type of promiscuity amongst children against which Liam Hudson recently warned us in his stimulating book called *Contrary Imaginations* (Hudson, 1966, p. 49). What has happened in this case is a further example of what has happened too often in psychology — a method for learning some things has become puffed up into *the* method for learning almost anything....

Non-Compartmentalization of Knowledge. The committee, predictably enough, made its obeisance to the fashionable view that knowledge cannot be split up into distinct slabs and that the curriculum should therefore be undifferentiated though, interestingly enough, little attention is paid to this conviction when in Chapter 17 'Aspects of the Curriculum' were set out in a traditional way with few suggestions for 'integration. Again there are important truths in this view, but the various issues need to be disentangled. Firstly though it is perfectly true that many problems require a combination of forms of knowledge for their solution it does not follow from this that distinctions between forms of knowledge are arbitrary. It took acute thinkers such as Hume and Kant a considerable time to establish that mathematics is different from empirical science in important respects.... Surely one of the great achievements of our civilization is to have gradually separated out and got cleared about the types of concepts and truth-criteria involved in different forms of thought....'

Secondly, in these discussions about the curriculum, forms of knowledge are often confused with school subjects which may or may not correspond to pure forms of knowledge. Mathematics and science obviously do; classics and geography obviously do not, and educational theory is, of course, one of the biggest bastards of them all. Whether forms of thought should be taught separately or linked together in some kind of 'topic' or 'project' approach is a matter which cannot be settled without empirical investigation into how successful the various alternatives are in relation to agreed criteria....

Too often, so it seems to me, reformers pass from the undeniable truth that the present 'subject-centred' curriculum is often boring to the conclusion that it should be abandoned and a topic centred one substituted for it. They do not consider sufficiently seriously the less radical suggestion that the more traditional type of curriculum could be both more imaginatively and more realistically interpreted. As with the emphasis on 'discovery' methods one can detect in all this a yearning for some overall recipe for teaching. My contention is that no such overall recipe is possible. What is needed is a down-to-earth, clear-headed, experimental approach which takes due account not only of general criteria but of the differences in what is taught and the children to whom it is taught.

The Role of the Teacher. The image of the teacher presented in the Plowden Report is of a child-grower who stands back and manipulates the environment so that children will proceed from discovery to discovery when they are 'ready'. There is so much wrong with this image that one scarcely knows where to begin in criticizing it. Most of what is wrong with it can be summed up by saying that it systematically ignores the inescapably social character of thought and language, of processes of transmission, and of motivation. The notion that children can peel concepts off the world without sensitization to selected aspects of it incorporated in a public language, that most of their interests are self-originated rather than caught from others, that children become 'ready' by some kind of internal ripening without imitation, identification, and instruction — all such notions are highly suspect....

The derogatory impression created by the statement 'The school is not a teaching shop' is again characteristic of this one-sided approach to teaching. For what is teaching? There is masses about learning in the Plowden Report, but almost nothing about teaching. Yet teaching can take the form of instruction, and explanation, of asking leading questions, of demonstrating by example, of correcting attempts at mastery, and so on. It can be done with a whole class, with small groups, and with individuals....

The moral of all this is not, of course, that we should throw overboard all that has been learnt from 'progressive' methods and revert to archaic systems of undiluted mass instruction. It is rather that we should do all in our power to help teachers to develop a critical, empirical, adaptable attitude to methods of teaching and encourage them to learn to think on their feet and experiment with different ways of teaching different types of subjects to different types of children. If only this critical, experimental attitude to teaching could be more encouraged we might soon cease to turn out teachers who thought that if they can only keep talking — or stop talking — then children are necessarily learning something, or teachers who practice something approximating to a free day without keeping a careful check on what in fact each child has learnt. Better still, we might turn out no teachers for whom 'teaching' has become a dirty word.

Reference

HUDSON, L. (1966) *Contrary Imaginations,* London, Methuen.

Plowden's 'Facts' about Children:
A 'Child-Centred' Critique

(From Wilson, P., 1974, 'Plowden aims', *Education 3–13*, 2, 1, pp. 52, 54–5.)

The principles underlying the Plowden Report were attacked by some critics for being too 'child-centred' and for neglecting the importance of teaching as a way of initiating the young into public forms of knowledge (pp. 117–22). Here, one of the report's sympathizers criticizes it for not being consistently 'child-centred'. Wilson accepts the overall aim of the report — to place the child in the centre of the educational process — but criticizes the document for failing to work out the implications of this central aim, owing to its reliance on so-called experts (psychologists and sociologists) who provide misleading 'facts' about children's nurture, nature and education. He attacks passages in the report which, he argues, assume that education is a manipulative process conducted on passive children. He argues that the child's nature cannot be regarded simply as the product of the interaction between nature and nurture but that it depends crucially on the view the child himself takes about his life and the way it might develop. In line with the thinking in his book (pp. 113–16) Wilson maintains that education should aim to help the child develop his capacity to pursue 'possibilities of value' leading to personal development and transformation.

In spite of pooh-poohing the value of overall educational aims, the Report's own overall educational aim is stated right at the beginning and, in various more specific reformulations, again and again all the way through. There's nothing trite, perfunctory or apologetic about it. Teachers have not dismissed it but have responded to it, perhaps recognising in it the central concern of the deliberative aspects of their own best practice, or the core in other words of the known and valued ends which as educators they are already continually trying to reach.

This statement of overall aims is as follows: 'Underlying all educational questions is the nature of the child himself . . .' (p. 1). 'At the heart of the educational process lies the child. No (educational) advances . . . have their desired effect unless they are in harmony with the nature of the child, unless they are fundamentally acceptable to him . . .' (p. 7).

What is unfortunate, and what has led (I believe) to the bulk of the criticism by philosophers and others of the Report is that instead of trying to work out the implications of this central aim, by reflecting and deliberating further on the best *educational* practices which they could find, the reporters for some extraordinary reason turned aside at this point and consulted 'experts' — not *educational* experts (i.e., not those whom they considered most expert in the practice of placing the child at the heart of the educational process), but experts at everything under the sun *but* education, and principally of course experts in psychology and (to a lesser extent) in sociology....

Fundamentally, I believe, the error of the Report lies in its reliance upon non-educational experts. It has ... presented us with a picture of 'the facts' about children on an analogy with facts about the nature of merely physical processes such as skeletal growth in babies or the nutrition and 'training' of plants or the neurological development of brain cells, which in turn are thought of on a further analogy with the invariably law-following motions of inanimate objects such as stones rolling downhill or waves rippling inevitably towards some shore.

We thus emerge from our reading of the Report with a picture of children as passive objects. We see them as no more than 'products' of the interreaction of their 'nature' and their environment or 'nurture'. Children become no more than links in a causal chain. What they themselves happen to think, feel and do about their nature, their environment and their education can make as little intelligible difference to their behaviour, on this view, as a stone's 'thoughts' about itself or about the law of gravity could make to its rolling downhill. Of themselves, children such as these cannot be imagined as capable of doing anything educationally significant, any more than by 'taking thought' they could add inches to their physical stature. Their education, on this view, must depend entirely (like the movement of a stone) on the manipulation of their environment by external agencies for ever beyond their control or influence (and principally, of course, by external agencies such as teachers, parents and others with whom they come into the most immediate environmental contact).

Just as we may dislodge a stone to get it moving, or shine light into the pupil of the eye to make it contract, or put compost around a row of vegetables to get the best development of their best natures (or the highest possible development which is 'in harmony with' their natures), so education is therefore conceived of in the Report as a manipulative process which 'motivates', 'stimulates' and 'nourishes' objects which may be moved about, grown and developed in desirable directions, but whose *own* views and values can never be taken seriously into account any more than could those of stones, cabbages, or the pupil of someone's eye: 'There is a strong association between the circumstances which affect the nutritional conditions underlying progress in physical development and those other conditions which nourish, as it were, intellectual and emotional growth,' (p. 15). Exactly! and whether the children are left to forage about for sustenance or to suck up their educational chemicals and nutrients for themselves ('learning by discovery'), or on the other hand are supported by teachers of good character (as plants by string and strong stakes), or given compensatory doses of 'enrichment' like ailing chrysanthemums, or instructed individually in ways designed to meet special deficits or 'needs', the educational position of the child remains the same: he is an object or organism to be manipulated, or as the Report puts it: 'The child's physique, personality, and capacity to learn develop as a result of continuous interaction between his environmental [*sic*] and genetical inheritance. Unlike the genetic factors, the environmental factors are, or ought to be, largely within our control . . . (p. 26) but never to any extent within his! At no time, then, can the child's own thoughts and feelings about his education be seriously considered. How *could* they be? One might as well ask a chrysanthemum if it wants to win the prize for which you are growing it, or a young police-dog what it thinks of the laws which you are training it to help enforce.

If children were like chrysanthemums and so on, this theory of education might be useful — although, even then, we'd still have to decide what goals we were cultivating the children for (other than for the question-begging end of a 'good' or 'adaptable' adult life). But children, in fact, are more like persons than like plants, insects, animals, machines, or inanimate objects, and 'the facts' about persons and their development cannot be verified or given attested universal description in the way that 'the facts' about plants and so on can.

Not only their educational development but, really, anything at all about persons (their health, for example, or whether they have to have certain physical characteristics such as two arms and legs in order to qualify as persons) exists as a 'fact' only in a conjectural and provisional sort of way, since it always depends in part upon the views of those persons themselves. In particular, however, the 'facts' of a person's educational development are especially and distinctively provisional, since our theories about people's educable 'natures' are interdependent with our theories about the sorts of valuable life which people *might* live and the sorts of valuable person whom possibly they *might* become. With chrysanthemums, the interreaction of their nature and their environment governs the 'facts' of their development entirely. With children and other persons or person-like beings, however, their own view *of* their nature and nurture is itself a factor in what they may become. In other words, their view of how they *might* develop or what they *might* become or prove to be, is itself an uncontrollable constituent *in* their development and its outcomes.

It is this interpenetration of fact and value in the 'nature' of persons and of their education, by contrast with the nature and motions of plants, stones and so on, which makes the Report's error a basic one. When I want 'the facts' about a person or about what I should do for his education. I must consult his opinion as well as my own or anyone else's, since 'the facts' both of his life and of his education will depend, at least in part, upon the view which that person himself is forming *of* his life and of his education. A person's 'nature' is thus provisional, open to agreement and disagreement, open to thought and feeling — open to education. Education is not something which we should regard as being determined, then, by a person's nature, nor by his environment, nor by the 'interaction' of the two. Indeed, we should not, I believe, regard it as determined, fixed, settled, by anything at all. Whatever a person might valuably become, may be an educational aim for him. Our own educational aim for him, in turn, should be to keep those possibilities of value as open as we can, not to close them off prematurely by making particular children conform to merely statistical 'facts' about children in general. By following non-educational experts in leading us to believe that 'the facts' about children's nature and nurture are as fixed and therefore as theoretically discoverable (through research, etc.) as the facts about the repair and maintenance of machines, the trajectories of falling stones, the maturation and sensitisation of bones and brain cells, or the domestication and control of animals and plants, the Report makes inconceivable the personal developments and transformations in which the value of education lies.

What is so unfortunate about this is that it was with persons, not with statistical regularities, that the Report began and with which (in its child-centred spirit as least) I believe that it was concerned. 'At the heart of primary education lies the child', not universal child-nature. The child is always a person. It is because he *is* a person, from the start, that we can hope to educate him, rather than just to push him around like a machine with a row of buttons, fill him up like a digestive tract, train him up against a wall like a plant, or domesticate him like an animal to our house-rules, however 'universal' we conceived those rules to be.

'Child-Centred' Education: A Critique

(From Dearden R., 1976, *Problems in Primary Education*, London, Routledge and Kegan Paul, pp. 53–9.)

In the first half of the chapter from which this passage has been extracted, Dearden outlined what he saw as the 'broad principles of the child-centred tradition'. Such principles included the importance of respect for the child as a person in his own right, the acknowledgement of each child's unique individuality, the necessity for an imaginative and sympathetic insight into the world of each child, and the need for the teacher to structure the educational environment to provide the child with much freedom of choice, chance to pursue interests and many opportunities for discovery and self-expression. In this passage, he provides a constructive, not unsympathetic, critique of such principles, indicating to what degree he believes them to be justified and to what degree deficient. He believes that fundamentally, the deficiency of 'child-centredness' lies 'in what it neglects rather than in what it celebrates', especially 'its failure, or perhaps refusal, to come to terms with the need for adult authority' — a view shared by Peters in his critique reproduced earlier in this section (pp. 146–51).

'Strong on methods, but weak on aims', is a judgment that has often been expressed on child-centred educational theory. But it may be questioned whether it is possible at all to be strong on methods if one is weak on aims. How could a sequence of activities be regarded as the expression of a method at all if there were no aims, no end-in-view? Is blowing a whistle a good method? Well of course, it all depends on the circumstances and what you are aiming at in those circumstances. Is it to get a train started, or a game stopped, attention in a playground, the boiling of the water advertised, the rescue team directed, or extra help in making the arrest? Blowing a whistle may be a good method of doing all of those things, but we cannot judge that until we know the aim. So if child-centred educational theory is strong on methods it can hardly be weak on aims. Perhaps all that was meant by this epigram was that child-centred teachers can easily get children going on activities, without any motivational problems. But simply to achieve that, without any closer specification of which activities, could be an achievement of little educational value. By all accounts, bedlam is a state of considerable activity.

Then what are the characteristic child-centred aims? Aims there must be, even if they are left implicit and unstated, because choices and decisions constantly have to be made. Materials and equipment have to be selected and ordered, an environment has to be chosen and constructed, and decisions have to be made about the questions one asks and the possible lines of development one sees. In all of these lie value-judgments implying a set of aims. And the characteristic child-centred aims, ... are relational rather than prescriptive of content to be learned. They specify the various desirable ways in which the child should be related to what he does and learns, rather than the content of the learning. What he learns is thought to be of less importance than that he should develop good attitudes in learning it. These relational aims can be conveniently grouped under three main headings: (i) intrinsic interest (eagerness, curiosity, learning to learn, absorption, etc.); (ii) self-expression (expressing one's own individuality, being oneself, etc.); (iii) autonomy (making independent judgments, choosing with confidence, self-direction, learning by discovery, etc.). But such relational, or attitudinal, aims leave undeclared the directions in which they will be pursued. As Edmond Holmes resoundingly declared 'let the end of the process of growth be what it may; our business is to grow'. But Hitler grew.

In practice, many child-centred teachers are no doubt more sensible than the pure doctrine might lead one to expect, but to a degree many teachers are also misled by the doctrine (as we can see from several of the firsthand reports in the series of booklets *British Primary Schools To-day*, prepared under the aegis of the Schools Council). Often the necessary value-judgments are there in practice, though disguised in the horticultural language of nourishing or feeding and of not stunting or forcing. But again, plants can be trained to go in different directions, some better than others. Yet one does not really want to depreciate child-centred values as such. To quote from the Plowden Report in a way which reverses the direction of its own concession: 'these are genuine virtues and an education which does not further them is faulty' (para. 506). The relational aims mentioned above are very important. The deficiency of child-centredness, however, is surely to be found in what it neglects rather than in what it celebrates.

Two things especially it neglects, both of them to do with the selection of the content of what is to be learned. First of all, it neglects the importance of achieving a certain balance of spread of activities over a period of time, not necessarily daily, or perhaps even weekly, but within a manageable period over which the teacher can keep steadily in view where the educational process is going. Of course, ideas of all-roundness are often found in child-centred literature. But it is, as we should expect, the all-round child rather than the all-round curriculum which is in mind. The five- or six-sided child is to benefit from an all-round development: emotionally, physically, socially, morally, spiritually and (always last nowadays) intellectually. But what of the kind of all-roundness traditionally celebrated in the concept of a liberal education? That implies an initiation, to whatever degree time and individual ability allow, into a selection of the main forms of knowledge or understanding which have historically developed.

It is none the less true for sounding platitudinous to say that a child has a culture to inherit as well as a self to express. And a selection from that culture made according to the best judgment available ought surely to complement child-centred 'relational' aims. We might even say that the latter can be realized only through the former. In practice, if one scratches a child-centred teacher one usually uncovers the traditional subject curriculum. The Plowden Report in fact proceeded from its child-centred principles to a chapter on the curriculum which was mainly divided into ten very traditional sections. But this does not necessarily mean that virtue triumphs in the end, since the traditional subject curriculum is not necessarily the best conception of a modern liberal education.

The second neglected perspective on content is that of future usefulness, whether for the later stages of education itself or by way of 'preparation for life'. Plowden may say that 'children should live first and foremost as children and not as future adults', but children unavoidably are future adults. It is undoubtedly a great educational and human gain when children are respected as persons in their own right, and childhood is seen as part of life and not just as a preparation for life. But the suggestion here is not that schools should be just a preparation for later life; it is only that that is one important aspect of it. Children still need basic skills if they are to take full advantage of their subsequent education, and it is no service to them, let alone to the wider society in which they will live, if they are unemployable or incapable of social co-operation.

Historically, child-centred theories have usually been wedded to a belief in the natural goodness of children. This is an obscure doctrine, but to the extent that clear sense can be given to it, then it is false. In the first place, it is a fallacy though a popular one to infer from the fact that if some characteristic is natural that it is therefore good. What is natural might also be good, but it cannot follow simply from its being natural that therefore it is good. In reality, much that seems to be natural (spontaneous and untaught) would normally be judged to be bad, such as spite, selfishness, aggressiveness, boastfulness and jealousy. These tendencies take their turn along with sympathy, generosity, kindness and other more amiable characteristics. It may have been necessary historically for crude ideas of original sin to be corrected by the contradictory doctrine of natural goodness, but the truth seems to lie somewhere between the two.

Again, the epistemological status of the doctrine is unclear. Is it an empirical generalization? When pressed with apparent counter-examples, a determined advocate of the doctrine, such as A.S. Neill, will retreat until even the foetal environment is blamed for bad tendencies. The fault, he clearly thinks, must be found in some environment or other, and not in the intrinsic nature of the child. The problem of the status of the doctrine is further complicated by the fact that nature is often only too obviously read into the child from whatever unconscious assumptions prevail at the time. Thus Rousseau found it entirely natural for Sophy, destined to be Emile's wife, to have an authoritarian upbringing, to be dependent on the good opinion of others, and to be taught a dogmatic religion. 'Nature', here, is made to bear a face which no women's liberationist would recognize as her own. In contemporary versions, 'nature' is perhaps more apt to look like someone's highly-reflective and articulate niece at play in some middle-class back garden. But whatever the truth of the matter may be, it is evident enough that by school age, even nursery school age, nature has taken on many socially determined characters, some of which are remarkably recalcitrant to any change initiated by the teacher. Language and interests, or their absence, are prominent examples. True or false, 'natural goodness' seems to be an eminently dispensable doctrine.

The relativity of conceptions of 'nature' is sometimes matched by the relativity of the child-centred observer's special insights into the inner world of childhood. The problem of how we can know other minds is a long-standing one in philosophy, though most would agree that we do have such knowledge, however difficult it may be to give an adequate account of its possibility. And it would also be widely agreed that different people have very different degrees of insight into others' minds and experience. There is a world of difference between the one extreme of the person so full of prejudices and self-preoccupations that others appear before him as little more than physical presences, and the other extreme of the person who can immediately read intentions and respond to feelings on the slightest cues and indications. And, since in general ability follows interest, a teacher of child-centred sympathies might be expected to have developed greater perceptiveness and sympathy in this respect. There is no evident reason to doubt that this is often so. But, equally, there is no reason to doubt that many a traditional teacher has, through experience, gained considerable insight into children. But here a caution needs to be sounded. Error is also possible, and is likely to be more frequent if we have a preconceived doctrine as to the nature of the child. For this may lead us to read into children's activities a significance which either is not there at all or else which ought to be set against other features which the doctrine leads one altogether to fail to notice. A reasonably objective and often very rewarding exercise is closely to watch a given child's activities over a period, then to ask the teacher what he thinks the child has been doing. In that teacher's situation, we should probably all be to some degree surprised by the discrepancy, but to the extent that it is doctrinally induced it is not inevitable. Respect for children as persons is not incompatible with respect for truth. It may well be dependent on it.

A further respect in which child-centred views on the nature of children may be questionable concerns the idea of development. Frequently presupposed is an idea of development as an unfolding according to an inner principle. And in physical respects there may be much in this. There may also be much in it to the extent that the development of mind has physiological and especially neurological necessary conditions. It may even be, though doubts have been cast on it, that something very like Piaget's development through distinctive stages is unalterable in its order and not to be hastened in its evolution. But it does not follow from any of this, even if it is all true, that education must be an unfolding. Even Piagetian stages require experience for their emergence. And if we consider the acquisition of objective knowledge, as in mathematics, the sciences and history, then if the truth is to be known belief has to agree with reality and the external discipline of fact is unavoidable. Nor is it just that matters of fact are independent of what we think. The critical standards which have been historically developed in these disciplines also present themselves initially as external, as do moral standards, which would have no point if we did by nature all that morality requires. Getting everything from the child and always starting from an existing interest may therefore be frequently useful practical principles, but cannot be universally appropriate. But in relation to every aspect of children's natures and their development detailed observation, unprejudiced by general doctrinal prescriptions, is really what is most appropriate. That is not to say that we can ever observe without making assumptions, but we can at least be ready to observe on the assumption that we may be wrong in our particular expectations.

In many ways the principal deficiency of child-centred educational theory, where it is deficient, is its failure, or perhaps refusal, to come to terms with the need for adult authority. One is given the overwhelming impression that though teachers may be formally in authority, they should not really exercise that authority in any overt or noticeable way. All can be accomplished in the way of discipline by utilizing the child's own strong interests and purposes, or by appealing to the rules imminent in the playing of a game or the accomplishment of a purpose. And if the reality should stubbornly turn out to be otherwise, then the child concerned is plainly not ready for whatever it is. Doubtless there are instances, education being a highly complex and varied enterprise, where this is indeed so. Nevertheless, justice is still not done to the need for authority, the more so the younger the children.

The fact is that what children do, or do not do, affects their later lives. So too do the experiences which they now have, or miss, involve consequences for their futures. Dewey amongst the traditional child-centred theorists was perhaps the most aware of this. He even tried to extract a value criterion from it. But a child's life now and later is all part of a single life. It is all his life, even though he may now be conscious of nothing beyond to-day or even the present moment. Since he often does not know of his own future, and of the consequences for it of what he does now, he cannot form a judgment of his best interests on any adequate basis. Even his interest in becoming autonomous is subject to this deficiency.

On the frankly paternalistic ground of being in his best interests, it therefore falls to adults who have a special knowledge of him, and a natural or professional care for him, to try to discover those interests and secure their satisfaction on his behalf. Parents and teachers therefore rightly exercise a certain directive influence over him for his good, though to the extent that autonomy is one of his interests then that authority should set itself as one of its tasks its own demise in the face of growing powers of self-direction. This authority is, of course, dependent for its justification on the relevant adult being able and willing to discover the child's best interests, or at least to do so better than can the child himself. Mistakes will no doubt be made, and in the transition period the child will in fact sometimes know better, all of which makes a responsible task that much more difficult. But so far as schooling is concerned, it seems clear that throughout the primary stage general judgments of interest will still have to be made by the teacher and the headteacher. The curriculum cannot simply follow felt interests, but should be liberal in its balance and scope, and it must to some extent prepare for life. Again, true knowledge of fact and the acquisition of the critical standards involved in the discovery of fact are external disciplines which will not always be in perfect harmony with mood and interest. The best accommodation between these sometimes conflicting interests must be judged by the teacher.

Teaching well is a difficult art if only because it requires balancing conflicting claims in order to find the best course in a great variety of circumstances. The individual has claims but he is also part of a group containing others who have equally valid claims on the teacher's limited time. Present interests are sometimes at variance with future needs, of which needs the child himself may even be unaware. Then the tension between the claims of different parts of his own life becomes the tension between the child's freedom and the adult's authority. Eagerness and confidence are sometimes misplaced or misdirected in the light of critical standards and objective fact, so that self-esteem and respect for truth may be in conflict. It is a one-sided simplification in such conflicts to resolve them all by the expedient of always 'starting from the child', just as much as it is an illusion that teaching can ever be an entirely conflict-free, happy and harmonious affair. As well as having a sensitive and sympathetic insight into the world of childhood experience, a teacher also needs determination and a will directed towards the future. It is not too harsh to say that fascinated spectatorial absorption in children and their world sometimes usurps the role of teacher. An essential and valuable source of insight then becomes the object of a form of self-indulgence.

Principles Governing the Content of Education: A Critique of Progressivism

(From Bantock, G., 1980, *Dilemmas of the Curriculum,* Martin Robertson, pp. 42–6.)

The author of the passage below is a leading intellectual proponent of 'educational conservatism' which views the 'business' of education as the transmission of culture, and the curriculum as the repository of worthwile activities and values into which the young have to be initiated (p. 77). Bantock uses his extensive knowledge of the history of educational ideas to contrast the underlying principles of 'traditional, "liberalizing" education' and those of progressivism (or liberal romanticism). He argues that whereas the former was informed by conceptions of excellence, the latter is guided by the immediately useful or the temporarily relevant. He asserts that in 'the modern British primary school in its more progressive guise', temporary interest and immediate need are guiding principles and too easily foster 'a magpie curriculum of bits and pieces, unrelated and ephemeral. In the interests of a temporary relevance a more permanent and deeper comprehension is often sacrificed'. He concludes that principles which favour the exploitation of the immediate and the everyday in order to provide stimulation and interest may be more appropriate with younger children but that 'even at this stage, such principles governing the content of education should be treated with some caution as at best limited guides'. The importance Bantock attaches to confronting the young with the achievements of others in the past and to getting them inside the concepts and developments of various subject fields finds echoes in the arguments of Peters and Dearden reproduced elsewhere in this section (pp. 146–51 and 156–61).

There is one general point of great importance, concerning the whole orientation of the traditional education vis-à-vis the progressive [education].

As I have made clear earlier, the enterprise of traditional 'liberalizing' education was informed by conceptions of excellence, by the search for perfection, for the Idea in its highest form. Whether the aim is to produce the Philosopher-King (Plato), the Orator (Quintilian), the humanist Courtier (Castiglione) or the Autonomous Mind (initiated by Locke) — all, incidentally, intended to take an *active* part in affairs — in each case it is a notion of the Ideal type which exercises the controlling influence over the content of their education. It would be absurd to deny that a philosopher is a lover of truth and reality; or that his nature, as we have described it, is allied to perfection' (Plato). 'The Orator whom we are educating is the perfect orator, who can only be a good man' (Quintilian). 'I would like our game this evening to be this: that one of us should be chosen and given the task of depicting in words a perfect courtier' (Castiglione); and the tradition was carried on into the nineteenth century by Herbart, Arnold, Cardinal Newman and others. It is this 'vision of greatness' — in Whitehead's phrase

— which has informed the determination of curriculum in the past; and, as the social role aimed at has been conceived of in its perfection, so the contributory activities, whether mental or physical, have been conceived of in their own specific perfections. Hence the frequent emphasis on 'imitation' — of the best models; and any 'usefulness' was to be informed by an antecedent liberalization. The autonomy of mind was, in fact, an autonomy from daily exigencies. In these ways, the accidental events of everyday life would be encountered by a mind already prepared to assess such accidents by reference to 'philosophic' principle and contextual significance, by a mind initiated into the circle of knowledge.

But the principle behind the progressive view of the curriculum is essentially that of the accidental; Rousseau wishes for an education that will be immediately useful — 'Life is the trade I would teach him' (1943, p. 9) — and the motivating force is provided by the incidents of daily existence: the activities of the gardener, a conjurer at a fair, a note from Emile's parents, an attempt to gather the cherries from the tree in the garden. Clearly Rousseau is still sustained by the Christian-humanist ethic — 'life' for him would not have included the activities of a Fagin — but his approach involved little ordered attempt to convey the structures of knowledge in a coherent fashion that fastened attention on the primary importance of mastering disciplines and their essential natures. And the same is true of the modern British primary school in its more progressive guise — as it is becoming of many middle and comprehensive schools. Temporary *interest* and immediate *need* are the guiding principles implicit in the attempt to 'psychologize' learning; hence the emphasis on motivation and endogenous development too easily fosters a magpie curriculum of bits and pieces, unrelated and ephemeral. In the interests of a temporary *relevance* a more permanent and deeper comprehension is often sacrificed.

Let us, with this indictment in mind, consider the current fashion for the interdisciplinary. Subject divisions are often dismissed as 'artificial', largely on the grounds that everyday living constantly involves the crossing and recrossing of subject boundaries and 'life as real as the home or the playground' is the object of our endeavour. But, of course, our 'living' is only interdisciplinary, as it were, in our moments of inattention and of imperfect consciousness. As soon as we focus our attention, seek to transcend the often mindless play of our daily existence, we enter an essentially specialized would. That building is a certain shape — what is the meaning of that shape, of the way the space has been deployed? Only a knowledge of architecture in its central concern with mass, space and line can provide the answer. A study of 'Our Town' (a popular subject) involves historical, economic, geographical features (among others) that, to take on significance beyond the most superficial, imply some degree of inwardness with the concepts and developments of the various subject fields involved; otherwise all that occurs is a meaningless copying from books and authorities (a not infrequent manifestation, it can be said), in undifferentiated enthusiasm.

The error implicit in an exclusive diet of this sort of thing lies in its haphazardness — and its subjectivity. It is to see the world as an appendage of self, without a meaning to be sought or guessed at apart from the meaning temporarily assigned in relation to one's immediate interests; it marks a failure to appreciate the integrity of the other, of what lies outside the self. All action, of course, is personal action and depends in the last resort on the responsibility of the self. But that self, to be wisely formed, must display some humility before the achievements of other selves, which is what is implied by a culture, and which it is the business of education to transmit. The danger of an education based totally on imitation is, of course, atrophy; the danger of an education based on novelty, the 'dominance of the foreground' as Santayana puts it, and immediacy is instability and parochialism, with the eccentricities, and worse, that accompany these conditions.

As a child, I was brought up in a way that would currently seem barbaric — with an almost exclusive emphasis on rote learning. Between the ages of five and ten, I learnt chunks of the Bible, gobbets of Shakespeare, fifty spelling words a week, the names of the kings and queens of England and the chief battles, the names of county towns, chief manufacturers, capes, bays, isthmuses, rivers — sometimes in blank incomprehension. (Never tell a child what he cannot understand, advised Rousseau; cf. 1943, p. 76). I have forgotten much of this — but I have not forgotten the lesson it implied: that the world, physical and cultural, existed as an entity apart from myself and that if I wished to learn about it I must come to terms with its existence. The famous remark in the Primary School Report of 1931 perpetuates a false dichotomy: 'the curriculum is to be thought of in terms of activity and experience rather than of knowledge to be acquired and facts to be stored.' Knowledge, as I have tried to indicate above, is an essential part of experience: mind is selective and left to itself only focuses meaningfully on what it already knows about.

I am far from saying that occasional projects of an interdisciplinary nature should not be undertaken; but it should be realized that even their value as stimuli is limited to an essentially restricted attraction unless the ephemeral configurations of daily existence are informed by a deeper understanding of the parts that are brought into temporary contiguity in the project — and that have been studied as 'subjects'. For 'subjects' are precisely ways in which the incoherence of everyday experience is made meaningful, broken down into its constituent elements and illumined by study in depth. Such study is not to be dismissed as artificial but is an essential element in that very comprehension of the foreground the progressives wish to promote.

Furthermore, it is a psychological error to think that even young children are attracted only by the immediate — the assumption being that their world is bound in by the scope of their sense experiences and their present, and often temporary, 'interests'. In contradistinction to Rousseau's analysis of La Fontaine's fable of the 'Fox and the Crow', with its emphasis on the scientific inaccuracy of the elements of the fable, Coleridge urged the need for the remote and the imaginative:

> For from my early reading of fairy tales and genii, etc. etc. my mind had been habituated to *the Vast*, and I never regarded *my senses* in any way as the criteria of my belief. I regulated all my creeds by my conceptions, not by my *sight*, even at that age ... I have known some who have been *rationally* educated, as it is styled. They were marked by a microscopic acuteness, but when they looked at great things, all became a blank and they saw nothing, and denied (very illogically) that anything could be seen ... [Coleridge, 1933, p. 532]

Even very young children appreciate some amplification of their surroundings. The theory behind a recent set of readers for young children, Leila Berg's *Nippers*, is that children appreciate the familiar and are at home among the actualities of language and sights assumed to belong to their everyday life. But many find it embarrassing to read out loud: 'Cor, don't it point', which represents a degeneration into a patronizing uncouthness, and are bored with the mundaneness. They much prefer the 'unreality' of Sheila McCullogh's charming imagination or Dr Seuss's *A Cat in the Hat*.

The argument in favour of the exploitation of the immediate and the everyday in the name of stimulation and interest would seem to be most compelling at the younger ages, when children are, arguably, in the terminology of Piaget, at the level of 'concrete operations' and need the stimulus of the actual. What I have tried to show is that, even at this age, such principles governing the content of education should be treated with some caution as, at best, limited guides — limited both in the way in which sense experience itself is a limited principle to guide curricular choice and also in the way in which this is meaningless unless it is enforced by comprehension of significance — and significance is not a characteristic of surface.

References

COLERIDGE, S.T. (1933) quoted in POTTER, S. (Ed.) *Select Poetry and Prose, Nonesuch Press.*
ROUSSEAU, J. (1943) *Emile,* trans. by B. FOXLEY, Everyman.

The Beginnings of a Reformulation of 'Progressive' Education

(From Armstrong, M., 1977, 'The Informed Vision: A programme for educational reconstruction', *Forum*, 9, 3, pp. 76–80.)

As the extracts in this section illustrate, 'progressive' education (or liberal romanticism) has been the subject of considerable philosophical criticism since the publication of the Plowden Report in 1967. Apart from the work of Wilson (pp. 143–5), little has been done in England to provide a closely argued philosophical basis for this educational ideology. Significantly perhaps, the beginnings of more adequate 'progressive' educational theorizing have been provided by an American philosopher of science, David Hawkins, who was himself greatly influenced by his contacts with English primary schools arising out of his development work on elementary school science in the 1960s. Some of the most important points in his (1974) book of essays, *The Informed Vision* (Agathon), are synthesized here by Armstrong and represent ideas for the reformulation of 'progressive' education along more justifiable philosophical and psychological lines.

Most of the themes that dominate *The Informed Vision* emerge in the title essay [the first essay in Hawkins' book]. For David Hawkins an informed human vision is the ultimate goal of education. Education is not, not first and foremost, a utility, a means of growth, of 'producing a population increasingly ready to embrace and further the new industrial technology which development requires'; nor is it primarily a means to economic or political power, either for individuals or for classes. It is, in its essence, a way of informing and enhancing the human vision, of sustaining a sense of involvement and of commitment within our world, of 'being at home in the world', a quality which also implies 'that we very well understand the opposite condition of non-involvement, the many moods of alienation'. The most important kind of estrangement in our own world, 'derives from the fact that the extraordinary technological and material evolution of the last century or two expresses a way of life and thought that has been genuinely available only to a minority among us. To the rest it is, in essence, an alien affair'. The consequence is twofold: the majority are deprived both of a proper sense of involvement and commitment in our world, and of access to the means of power which depend upon a knowledge they do not share, while the select and privileged minority who do possess the knowledge, divided as they are from the rest of society, are inevitably 'subject to all the corruptions of caste and status'. 'A world so deeply committed to science', and to other forms of symbolic knowledge, 'cannot survive with a vast majority of its population intellectually and aesthetically alienated from' these forms.

It is the purpose of the essays [in Hawkins' book] to describe and to defend 'a style of education that would permit correction, in our culture, of this basic defect'. Hawkins seeks an analogy for the style he has in mind in Colin Turnbull's account of education among the Pygmies in his book *The Forest People*. 'It is an education which begins in play suffused with enjoyment and evolves into an apprenticeship premised on commitment.' He acknowledges the vast difference between our needs and those of the Pygmies. 'What we must learn is in part more remote from the immediate environment, more abstructed and dependent on symbolic skills. And that is the challenge to our education; to recover for our world', a world of abstraction and symbol, 'the ways of learning that are concretely involving and aesthetically rewarding, that move from play toward apprenticeship in work'.

It is characteristic of any achievement of learning of this order that it possesses a quality of spontaneity which Hawkins, quoting John Dewey, defines as 'complete absorption in subject matter that is fresh, the freshness of which holds and sustains emotion'. Spontaneity of human expression 'is no mere display or outburst: it is a synthesized achievement compatible, as Dewey goes on to say, "with any amount of labour provided the results of that labour emerge in complete fusion with an emotion that is fresh"'. Among the conditions that foster and nourish such an achievement two are pre-eminent. One is the child's 'freedom for active involvement', for exploration and for choice; the other is the teacher's provisioning of an environment rich in exploratory potential. To reinforce 'the natural probings and explorings of children's is, as Dewey saw, 'the basis of all true education'. But that is only one side of the story. Content is no less important than method and 'absorption in subject matter requires a major effort of provisioning for that subject matter'. In its preoccupation with the child's freedom for active involvement 'progressive education' has sometimes neglected to show an equal, matching concern for provisioning 'the world of children's exploration with subject matter they could explore well, could penetrate deeply'.

Exploration with Explanation

Education, then, requires the freedom to explore 'the order and organisation of the world' through 'complete absorption in subject matter that is fresh' and in the company of teachers who have made ample provision for that subject matter. But the emphasis on exploration does not preclude the value or necessity of explanation. 'There comes a time for harvesting, gathering, organising, even programming, and here individual learners must be drawn together under a common discipline. In our schools, this time comes much too early. Or, better, it is too little preceded and followed by periods — long periods — of individualised and diversified work of a more exploratory and self-directed kind.... We must learn better to instruct children, when, after absorption in subject matter, they communicate by their behaviour those directions which they are prepared to find meaningful because they themselves have begun to define and seek them. And then there is the opposite transition, when formal instruction has brought children to new levels of understanding and interpretation; to open again the door to less directed probing and testing at these new levels — and thus to consolidate what has been learned, to use it for further learning.'

Of all the themes presented in [the] opening essay the foremost is that of autonomy. In essay after essay Hawkins insists that it is 'a fundamental aim of education to organise schools, classrooms and our own performance as teachers in order to help children acquire the capacity for significant choice' and that 'learning is really a process of choice'. 'If children are deprived of significant choice in their daily activities in school then the most important thing that education is concerned with is simply being by-passed.' Traditionally, autonomy has been viewed as one of the ends of education but not as part of its means, or at any rate not an essential part. It is from this mistake that much of the failure of traditional education derives. Thus 'it is often conceded that a superordinate aim of education should be the cultivation of competence in children to fashion well their own lives. But it is NOT supposed steadily that such competence is gained through exercise of it. It is supposed, rather, that self-organisation will appear magically AFTER years of schooling subordinated to a quite different principle, according to which children are DEPRIVED of autonomy. They are deprived in the interest of what is conceived to be an efficient imparting of information and guidance. During all this time, and in the interest of such efficiency, children are essentially deprived of any significant exercise of autonomy in choice, discrimination and judgment. They are coerced, however politely, into a frame of organisation intended to promote their acceptance of information and exercise in specific curricular topics, these being justified on the ground that they are necessary to competent adult functioning. This induced organisation is thought of as a kind of scaffolding to be torn down after the process is finished and the product certified as complete. But it is in fact a powerful moulding of character, and of a kind of character antagonistic to the superordinate aim which education professes to serve. The scaffolding gets built into the structures and cannot be removed'.

Already Advantaged

Hawkins suggests that the children who succeed under such a programme do so because they already possess a capacity for individual choice, acquired OUTSIDE of school. 'But children are very unequally endowed by previous condition and experience with this capacity for independent choice, which the schools do little to help them cultivate. No one can catalogue all the conditions of such relative success but it is a conspicuous statistical fact that the successful come commonly, though not universally, from a background which could be called the folk-culture of the already well-educated. The deeper conditions of academic success, which schools often unconsciously work against, are in fact supplied from another cultural source. But for vast numbers of children the mismatch between their own developing capacities and the experience available in shcool is so great that they are unable to avoid the induced pattern, with its constant accompaniment for them of failure and boredom, withdrawal, manipulation of rebellion.'

Alternative Learning Theory

To remedy this deep defect in 'standard educational practice' and theory we require a radically new theory of education, reflecting an alternative conception of learning and of knowing, 'the theory of a design which seeks to optimise the eolithic component in education, to optimise children's capacity to conduct their own learning and to become their own teachers.... The key proposition in this theory is that learning, in its most significant educational dimensions, it not something of a different kind from self-government, self-organisation, choice, but is a species of that very genus. Learning in an educationally important sense is an active process of self-organisation and reorganisation which takes place through the mediation of choice among significant alternatives available to the learner'. Hawkins opposes such a theory to classical Learning Theory, and, in an essay entitled 'Mind and Mechanism in Education' and again in the long philosophical essay which closes his collection, he discusses the relationship between the alternative conception of learning and knowing which he proposes and the philosophical and psychological theories of Kant and of Piaget. Tentative and schematic though it is, this discussion is of great importance in the development of an adequate theory of 'progressive' education. However I do not have space to discuss it further here. I would like, rather, to draw attention to some of the implications which Hawkins extracts from his conception of the primacy of autonomy in education, implications which are often ignored in traditional discussion of 'progressive' education.

'Progressive' thought has seemed on occasion to make a mystery of autonomy as if it were a quality of mind that was self-generating, self-sustaining and self-sufficient, an innate and inexplicable flowering of intellect and character. Nothing could be further from Hawkins' intention. The proper exercise of autonomy in learning is inseparable, he insists, from communication with others — adults, teachers, other children — and communion with things — the subject matter of their common concerns. 'No child, I wish to say, can gain competence and knowledge, or know himself as competent and as a knower save through communication with others involved with him in his enterprises. Without a Thou there is no I evolving.

Without an It there is no content for the context, no figure and no heat, but only an affair of mirrors confronting each other.' This triangular relationship, between teacher, pupil and task, he explores in one of the few essays in this collection that is already relatively well known in England, an essay entitled 'I, Thou and It'.

He begins his discussion by considering 'a kind of electronic analogy for what goes on in a child's mind. Think of circuits that have to be completed. Signals go out along one bundle of channels, something happens, and signals come back along another bundle of channels; and there's some kind of feedback involved. Children are not always able to sort out all of this feedback for themselves. The adult's function, in the child's learning is to provide a kind of external loop, to provide a selective feedback from the child's own choice and action. The child's involvement gets some response from an adult and this in turn is made available to the child. The child is learning about himself through his joint effects on the non-human AND the human world around him. The function of the teacher is to respond diagnostically and helpfully to a child's behaviour, to make what he considers to be an appropriate response, a response which the child needs to complete the process he's engaged in at a given moment'.

Intervention Strategy

'Progressive' teachers sometimes give the impression of forgetting 'the unique importance of the human role'. 'We tend to say "Oh well, if children just have a good, rich, manipulable and responsive environment, then everything will take care of itself...." But, of course, that's a dangerous illusion. It's true only in those periods — in good schools frequent periods — when children don't need the external loop. When they do need it and there's no-one around to contribute the adult resonance, then they're not always able to carry on the process of investigation, of inquiry and exploration, of learning, because they need help over a hump that they can't surmount through their own resources. If help isn't available the inquiry will taper off, and that particular episode, at least, will have failed to accomplish what it otherwise might have.'

Of all the many kinds of intervention a good teacher is required to make, the most important is the kind of intervention that encourages, or helps to sustain, a child's absorption in subject matter, in the various objects of children's and teachers' inquiries. It is here that we can see most clearly 'how the "It" enters into the pattern of mutual interest and exchange between the teacher and the child', and why it is that Hawkins attaches supreme importance to the interrelationship of teacher, pupil and task.

'The investment in the child's life that is made in this way, by the adult, the teacher in this case, is something that adds to and in a way transforms the interest the child develops spontaneously. If, as sometimes happens, a child gets particularly interested in a variation on a soap bubble theme that you've already given him, you can just happen to put nearby some other things that might not at first seem related to soap bubbles — some geometrical wire cubes, tetrahedra, helices, and wire with a soldering iron. The resulting soap films are almost bound to catch the fancy of many human beings, including children. What have they got? Well they've got a certain formal geometrical elegance, they've got colour; when you look at the films in the right kind of light you see all those marvellous interference colours. Such a trap is bristling with invitations and questions. Some children will sample it and walk on; but some will be hooked by it, will get very involved with it. Now, this kind of involvement is terribly important, I think. It's aesthetic, or it's mathematical or it's scientific. It's all of these potentially, and none of them exclusively. The teacher has made possible this relation between the child and "It" even if this is just by having "It" in the room; and for the child even this brings the teacher as a person, a Thou, into the picture. For the child this is not merely something which is fun to play with, which is exciting and colourful and has associations with many other sorts of things in his experience: it's also a basis for communication with the teacher on a new level and with a new dignity.

'Until the child is going on his own the teacher can't treat him as a person who is going on his own, cannot let him be mirrored there, where he may see himself as investigator or craftsman. Until he is an autonomous human being, who is thinking his own thoughts and making his own unique, individual kinds of self-expression out of them, there isn't anything for the teacher to respect, except a potentiality. So the first act in teaching, the first goal, necessary to all others, is to encourage this kind of engrossment. Then the child comes alive for the teacher as well as the teacher for the child. They have a common theme for discussion, they are involved together in the world.'

They have proved, as Hawkins puts it at the end of his essay, 'that we're in "It" together'.

Authority of Teachers

The I-Thou-It relationship is the indispensable complement to Hawkins' insistence on the primacy of autonomy in learning, and it is this feature of his work, above any other, that helps him to escape from many of the stereotypes that bedevil discussion of 'progressive' education. Thus his emphasis on adult intervention belies the common accusation that 'progressive' is synonymous with 'permissive'. Indeed Hawkins is at pains to point out that 'authority is one of the primary sources of learning. To be an authority in this sense (the sense of being one whose activities or contribution to your existence you value because it has proved itself to BE valuable), to be a teacher whom children honestly respect because you give them something which helps them on the way and which they know they couldn't get for themselves, is to be a teacher. If you are not that kind of authority, you are not a good teacher, you're not functioning properly as a teacher'.

Worth of Content

Similarly, his deep concern for subject matter, 'the order and organisation of the world' which children and teachers investigate together, makes nonsense of the presumption that 'progressive' education is inevitably weak on content or curriculum, on 'the public forms of experience' as Hirst and Peters have it. 'Adults involved in the world of man and nature bring that world with them to children, bounded and made safe to be sure, but not thereby losing its richness and promise of novelty. . . . Adults and children, like adults with each other, can associate well only in worthy interest and pursuits, only through a community of subject matter and engagement which extends BEYOND the circle of their intimacy. The attitude of deprecating subject matter, and of deprecating curriculum as a guide to the providing of worthy subject matter, reflects therefore the half-truth badly used.'

Even his insistence on the necessarily informal, unpredictable and incommensurable nature of education, of learning and teaching, is balanced by a recognition of the appropriate moment for formality, didacticism, rote-learning. 'One has to fight against the belief that because the central priority is self-directed learning there is never any value in instruction or didactic teaching. There are times when a group of children is very ready to be instructed about something, or to engage in a set task which might even be rote learning under certain circumstances. Their readiness to do this means that it has become for them a significant choice and it is therefore by no means violating the principle of choice to say there is room, and sometimes a significant amount of room, for quite formal instruction.'

There is, then, a salutary note of caution in many of the details of Hawkins' account of education, which helps to guard his argument against the misconceptions to which 'progressive' education is particularly prone. Yet, when all is said and done, this cannot, as indeed it should not, blunt or blur the radical and demanding nature of his vision.

Primary Teaching: What has Philosophy of Education to Offer?

(A contribution specially written for this volume by Bonnett, M. and Doddington, C., lecturers in the philosophy of education, Homerton College in Cambridge. An extended version of this article is to appear in one of the 1990 volumes of the *Cambridge Journal of Education*.)

In recent years, the educational disciplines have come under considerable scrutiny, with a demand for increased practical experience rather than theoretical discussion as an appropriate preparation for teaching. In this article, Bonnett and Doddington argue that philosophy of education still has a significant contribution to make in terms of ensuring that decisions made by teachers are based upon careful relection and analysis. Philosophy, they suggest, helps develop an awareness of issues and problems which may not seem immediately apparent. It provides varied ways of perceiving and interpreting educational situations. It provides a logical framework for analysis and interpretation and through encouraging systematic critical reflection it develops the capacity to articulate clearly and justify one's educational practice.

There is one thing that can be said about philosophy of education with a fair degree of certainty and present: it has a bad name amongst many practising teachers. This is a feature that it shares with education theory as a whole. Education theory is still frequently viewed as irrelevant to the harsh realities of day to day practice, and philosophy of education has often been experienced as arid and verbose to boot. In this article we hope to show that, properly viewed, philosophy of education has a distinct and vital contribution to make to the thinking and practice of primary teachers, and to their professional development.

Let us begin by making clear one point about the relationship between theory and practice which bears directly on the issue of the potential contribution of philosophy: education theory cannot produce any sure-fire recipes for success in practice. There are simply too many variables involved in the differing contexts in which teachers operate. Insofar as education theory makes any recommendations, then, they must be received as considerations for teachers to bear in mind rather than foolproof rules or techniques to be directly applied. No one can simply be told how to teach. This must always be a matter for the practical judgement of the person who is most familiar with the many facets of a particular teaching situation. Does this mean that philosophy of education has nothing to offer the practising teacher? Quite the contrary.

Philosophy is a form of critical reflection, indeed it is in a certain sense the form of critical reflection. It is an attitude of mind in which one wonders and questions rather than simply accepts things as given and unproblematic. In this frame of mind one wonders about the meaning of things, about the quality of our understanding or perception of a situation or event, and about the appropriateness of the criteria that we use in evaluating what we perceive. Philosophy as such, then, is often concerned to call into question both new ideas and ones that we normally take for granted (which is why it can be felt as initially confusing and undermining) – with the aspiration of eventually becoming clearer about them and evaluating their worth. It attempts to do this through sustained and systematic reflection on their cogency and coherence, and a sensitivity to sometimes subtle but significant distinctions in meaning. Philosophy is constantly in search of clarification of meaning and justification of purpose, and it is for this reason that it has sometimes been regarded as subversive by those in authority, and liberating by those under it. Philosophy of education is simply the application of this sustained questioning attitude to ideas and events that have some significant practical educational consequence. Let us try to illustrate what this might mean for the primary teacher by considering a specific situation.

Many primary teachers offer children opportunities for making choices within the classroom. One example of this might be allowing children to choose an area of interest to study within an overall class theme. Teachers often reason that this means children are able to select something that interests them with the result that, in general, motivation is higher. This may well be endorsed by experience in that one may find that the introduction of choice co-incides with increased enthusiasm on the part of the children, initially at least. Now a teacher might value that enthusiasm for many different reasons, but at a purely pragmatic level it can sometimes release him or her from the role of having to 'make things interesting'. Much effort can be directed at helping children to overcome reluctance or indifference and strategies that mean that there are fewer children dependent on the teacher for such stimulation and encouragement are an attractive proposition in a busy classroom. It is possible to argue therefore, that when children are motivated by choice, it is justified in part because the teacher gains more time and energy to direct elsewhere.

By taking a fictional example we hope to illustrate how philosophical reflection might influence/affect the kind of reasoning described above, and in turn strengthen curriculum development and the work of the teachers involved. Suppose two teachers have decided to combine their classes for project work so that they can share the planning of the theme of 'Day and Night' and experiment with sharing the teaching. Children are to be allowed to choose from a list of study areas as a way of mixing them into groups and motivating their learning. The teachers, perhaps, intend that all children will explore some common areas and that the options will cover observing, investigating, and recording, so as to draw primarily on maths and science activities. Initial suggestions for possible areas of choice includes one of examining aspects of 'light'. Now our teachers have agreed to collaborate because previous discussions about their work have indicated that they share broad agreement in terms of their overall approach to education, including the matter of offering choice to children whenever it is practicable. In trying to plan this new development, they decide to re-examine exactly why they believe offering choice is worthwhile — the intention being that clarification here will strengthen the collaborative decisions and judgments that will be made subsequently in their organization and teaching.

An initial suggestion that the choice being offered is valuable for the scope it provides in pursuing interests collapses under closer scrutiny since while selection from a limited number of options might mean that you can pursue an interest, clearly this will not always be the case. In reflecting critically upon the value of offering choice to children in their learning, our teachers perhaps come to realize in a more explicit way, that for choice to be worthwhile it has to be made thoughtfully so that it carries commitment or an initial personal investment in what has been selected. That is to say, that while choice may help to increase pupils' interest in their work, a more fundamental purpose is to raise the level of their sense of ownership and responsibility in their learning. This being so, the benefits in terms of teacher time and children's motivation are no longer perceived as the basic justification for allowing choice, and choosing can no longer itself be viewed as optional. The opportunity to choose is seen as worthwhile for all children, and for those children who do not automatically welcome choice it is clear that the teacher will have an important role to play in helping them to cope with it and grow through it.

Now this improvement in the ability to justify choice may appear rather minimal and of no great significance for teaching. After all the opportunity for choice already existed within each classroom and appeared to be working according to the teachers' original criteria of improving children's motivation. We would like to suggest, however, that what we have described illustrates an aspect of practice which did not appear problematic, but which, upon more careful reflection, provoked a change in perception which offered the possibility of far reaching consequences. For example, the practical implications for these teachers are already more complex than for the teacher who aims solely at easing problems of motivation through giving choice: a closer look at the range and the nature of the choices offered is required if they are to be significant and meaningful to each child. There will also be a realization that the value of choosing is not necessarily achieved by a once and for all decision, but may rest on being able to make a series of meaningful choices. It might now be felt necessary to consider how further choice might be built into each option offered within the class theme. Making reference to the National Curriculum Science programme of study relating to 'Using Light', our teachers could consider allowing groups of individuals to select objects and materials which might affect the way light travels in various ways. They may go further and consider encouraging children to create their own experiments in order to investigate the properties and behaviour of light. In this way the building in of choices and decisions into the children's work could enhance ownership, express the spirit of the first science profile component concerned with 'Exploring Science', and still achieve the appropriate levels of attainment in the child's substantive understanding of the uses of light. Indeed, providing the opportunity for children to take responsibility through these kinds of choices may well enable some of them to pursue their investigations and approach attainment targets above those that might have been predicted for them through pre-determined experiments.

If we might now take the example a little further, it could be that the sense of clarity and coherence offered by systematically analyzing ones practice and the assumptions that underlie it might encourage our teachers to reflect upon other related aspects of their teaching. In considering their normal approaches to record keeping for instance, they may now may feel there will be a need to assess children's involvement: their thoughts and feelings about the activities they have chosen. Maybe pupil self-evaluation, systematic observation, or individual discussion will need to supplement other forms of monitoring. Further general discussion might be necessary on how the teachers can sensitively support each child's learning without taking it over, so that their feeling of ownership of their work is not lost. In sum, with the principle of offering responsibility and ownership in mind, a host of practical and managerial implications might follow as to how choices are presented, selected, resourced, monitored and analyzed for achievements. Further, logical implications might also be thought through in a broader context of curriculum consistency. If responsibility and ownership is valued and stressed in one aspect of the curriculum, are there other times when adjustments should be made to the way things are done to further enhance the development of these desirable qualities? Are there times when the way the curriculum or learning is managed blatantly denies children a sense of ownership? Do alternative arrangements and situations contradict and therefore counteract what is being encouraged by giving children the chance to choose, or are there other equally or even more important aims that take priority at other times? To pursue such broader considerations which involve gradually identifying and justifying those basic values that one wishes to try to exhibit in ones teaching is to be well on the way to establishing a personal philosophy of education — something which can serve as a frame of reference in responding to a range of new challenges and changing circumstances. This is important because it facilitates a way of being open to new possibilities without being overwhelmed by them — whether it be at the 'micro' level of specific classroom occurrences, or the 'macro' level of large scale curriculum innovation.

At this point though, perhaps we should consider an obvious objection: 'Just how much time and energy have these fictional teachers got to spend on such philosophical reflection?' The point that we would like to make here is that no one outside the situation can say. The teachers themselves are the best judges of how far they can pursue their deliberations, together with the changes they imply. Their clearer sense of direction and understanding of the value of what they are attempting could well affect their priorities so that they may decide to pursue some changes but not others. Indeed, this ability to discriminate what ideas it might be worthwhile to pursue in a certain context is itself an aspect of using philosophical thinking. But suppose it is argued that too much reflection and questioning is itself simply a bad thing, immobilizing rather than empowering for a teacher? Our answer would be along the following lines: We have tried to show that in this context questioning is not an end in itself, and processes which enable teachers to come to, and express clearer understandings and assessments of worth and purpose, can give an increased confidence and sense of direction. This in turn can invigorate practice and its development as well as having a direct influence on the quality of educational experience provided for children. Clearly although our example refers to two teachers working together, it naturally follows that teachers can reap the benefits of such philosophical reflection in relation to their practice individually, or as groups in considering whole school policy.

It is clear from the foregoing that certain assumptions are being made about the role of the teacher. Philosophy of education only has a significant part to play in the job of teaching if we continue to uphold a role of the teacher which requires them to critically reflect upon their practice as autonomous professionals. That is to say, if we uphold the role of practitioners who in some significant degree a) are prepared to exercise their own informed judgement of what or how to teach in their own class or school, and; b) have some special responsibility towards, and contribution to make to, broader issues concerning the overall character of education. Insofar as their role is not reduced to that of mere operative or technician who make judgements on their performance purely in terms of detailed and clearly pre-specified criteria, teachers must operate out of their own understanding of ideas and situations, which they can therefore intelligently adapt to the constant subtle (and not so subtle!) changes in the classroom and school environment.

Now the question might be raised as to whether much of this room for professional discretion has not been seriously eroded by recent legislation associated with the National Curriculum. The final answer to this may well lie with teachers themselves in terms of the manner of their response and the determination with which they express and act upon their considered views as a group claiming professional status. But even within the framework of a more standardized, product-orientated education system, teachers have still to mediate such a curriculum in their own particular context, and continue to have wide discretion over the means by which they achieve whatever prescribed levels of attainment are laid down. Curriculum innovation can be imposed, or it can be initiated by teachers as a result of their own reflection on existing practice. In the former case particularly, large scale changes are notoriously difficult to implement because of mis-understandings about necessary preconditions for success and unanticipated ripple effects. It is hardly surprising, then, that surveys of the effectiveness of attempts at curriculum innovation over the years highlight one crucial factor: the quality of teacher involvement. Our argument is that changes associated with the National Curriculum will be managed with more grace and efficiency if the teacher who is ultimately responsible for mediating them is able critically to evaluate their worth and implications, in relation to their own teaching situation. The intention to improve education through a national curriculum will succeed or fail largely on the basis of how well teachers can respond in the exercising of their own judgments, and taking responsibility for the changes that may occur. It is the teachers who have to find the workable answers, and it is therefore the rigour and clarity of their thinking that really matters. Further, if the rhetoric is to be believed, they have an important role to fulfil in providing feedback which will enable the National Curriculum to evolve in desirable ways.

While much of this must remain at the level of speculation at the moment, one thing that remains unchanged is that at the heart of education is a relationship between human beings. There will always be aspects of human beings' behaviour and potential that cannot be pre-specified, quantified, and mechanized. This simple fact lies at the kernel of the teacher-pupil relationship, and for it we should be thankful. It may be that what cannot be objectively assessed will enjoy lower status in official eyes for a while, but at least it is not so easily targeted by those outside the community of the school and the families it serves. If, for the moment, less time can be ostensibly devoted to the less tangible but highly important aspects of a child's education, they can still be respected and nurtured where possible by independent minded teachers. And it remains perhaps their chief duty to do so. If so, we have another reason why the role of teaching will continue to benefit from philosophical reflection of the kind we have tried to describe.

So far, we have discussed some of the more specific contributions which we believe philosophical reflection can make to the practical decision-making of teachers. But our account of what such reflection has to offer would be seriously incomplete if we were not at least to mention one further aspect. Perhaps the most profound contribution that it can make is in the context of the personal development of teachers. It may be that this kind of concern is falling out of fashion in a time when emphasis is increasingly placed on quick, tangible — not to say objectively measurable — results. There are undoubtedly considerable pressures in the various fields of teacher training and education to aim at the development of clearly delineated and demonstrable competences as an indicator of value for money. But this cannot detract from the importance of a certain contemplative attitude towards our experiences through which we critically evaluate, imagine new possibilities, and seek to discern the deeper meaning of events. It is in this way that relatively subtle but long lasting and influential changes in attitudes, ways of perceiving children and situations, and our own role and personal potential for contributing to a child's education, can occur. At base, philosophy of education, in common with philosophy as a whole, is concerned with the development of persons in their ways of perceiving and valuing. Proper understanding of our situation is not simply a matter of having acquired knowledge in its various public forms, but is the process of attaching personal significance to that which in some sense we may already know. For example a technically perfect understanding of say some aspects of a theory of evolution, of child development, of the working of society, or of our planetary ecosystem, remains essentially hollow and unfulfilled until we begin to decide how it should affect our conception of our human situation and the course of our actions. That is to say we have in a sustained and consistent way, to work out our own attitude towards the content of what we may learn so that we come to feel how and why it matters in terms of our own existence and human existence in general. In this way our knowledge acquires a subjective weight — the significance of what we know is brought home to us. This is the essence of philosophical reflection and the premise of truly thoughtful action and practice.

We will conclude by drawing together what we have taken to be the main contributions that philosophy of education can make to the professional development of teachers, and the continuing evolution of 'good primary practice':

(a) It helps develop an awareness of issues and problems that are not necessarily manifest as such on the 'surface' — the problems (and therefore possible solutions) you might otherwise not know you've got, but which are nonetheless affecting the quality of ones teaching;

(b) It provides different ways of perceiving and understanding educational situations and claims, and can enable helpful reconceptualization of a task or situation;

(c) It helps to provide a logically coherent overarching framework of understanding in which particular issues and decisions are embedded;

(d) It is pre-eminently concerned with the development of the capacity to articulate clearly and justify to others one's views and practice (— something likely to be in increasing demand in the new age of professional accountability);

(e) Through encouraging explicitness, honesty, and **systematic** critical reflection (e.g., facing up to the consequences and implications of a claim, or an opinion, or kind of practice), it helps a teacher to develop his/her own position — an explicit and evolving personal 'philosophy' of education. As well giving a steady sense of direction and purpose in terms of which to initiate and respond to change, the subtle changes in attitudes, increasing sensitivity and sense of the significance of what we may know or learn that results, constitutes a fundamental aspect of the personal development of a teacher.

4   Primary Education:
       Sociological Perspectives

Introduction

The sociology of education is now a major branch of educational study. During the last thirty years, its theories, methodologies and areas of enquiry have been the subject of development and controversy (Banks, 1982). At no time during this period have primary schools been the main focus of its attention. Nevertheless, the foundations of a sociology of primary education have been laid through a variety of studies, extracts from some of which are reproduced in this section.

During the 1950s and 1960s, sociologists were interested in the ways in which the educational system was related to structural features of society such as social stratification, industrialization, and the division of labour. At that time education was viewed by policy-makers as a means of providing a literate and adaptable labour force and as a way of promoting social mobility for individuals from 'lower' socio-economic groups. There was particular sociological interest in documenting how far children from different social classes had access to selective education and in explaining how these class-related inequalities came about. The extracts from Floud, Halsey and Martin (pp. 193–6) and Davie, Butler and Goldstein (pp. 197–205) illustrate some of the class-related differences in educational attainment in primary schools and the 11+ examination, revealed by a large number of investigations. Attempts were made to search for the factors responsible for these differences and for the resulting inequalities of opportunity. The factors investigated included family size, briefly referred to in the extract from Floud, Halsey and Martin (pp. 193–6), socio-linguistic codes investigated by Bernstein and others (pp. 220–3), and parental aspirations, values and attitudes, which were the subject of many enquiries, including a major one sponsored by the Plowden Committee (pp. 206–10). Some sociologists such as A.H. Halsey were involved not just in documenting and explaining class-related inequalities, but in devising strategies to help alleviate them (pp. 214–9). As part of the general interest in the social and economic functions of education, some sociologists studied the patterns of social structure, methods of social control, and processes of social change in particular institutions, as illustrated by the first extract from Alan Blyth on the five social functions of primary schools (pp. 185–7).

Around the end of the 1960s, the structural-functional approach to the sociology of education was challenged by the interactionist perspective which stressed, not the constraints of social structures and functions, but the ways in which man was able to create and define his own social reality. In Banks' words, 'the central task of the sociology of education, therefore, was seen as an examination of the participants in the educational process through an exploration of their perceptions and assumptions as well as their interaction with each other. There was a change in method, most significantly, in the exchange of observation for the social survey, and a change in what were seen as problem areas'. The brief extract from Nash (pp. 255–7) illustrates the concern for the way in which participants build up identities and bodies of knowledge about educational reality through day-to-day interactions. Two new foci of attention emerged: the study of classroom interaction, as illustrated here by the work of King on infant education (pp. 258–62), and the study of curricula as socially organized knowledge 'processed' by schools — an area of enquiry aided by the theoretical work of Bernstein (pp. 227–31).

In addition to the other two sociologies of education, a third emerged in the 1970s. This neo-Marxist perspective viewed the educational system as an agency for the social and cultural reproduction of capitalist society, with teachers cast very largely as unwitting collaborators and with working-class pupils largely as unknowing victims. On this view, schools socialize the young by getting them to accept the way things are and by preventing them from considering alternative possibilities to the existing social order. Most of this neo-Marxist theorizing has been conducted at a highly abstract level, not often accompanied by detailed empirical work to test the arguments advocated.

In the late 1970s and early 1980s, however, a number of sociologists began to accept the classroom as a legitimate focus of study, drawing upon principles established in ethnography, where naturalistic methods are employed to investigate the perspectives of all involved in a particular social situation. Primary schools and primary classrooms offer a rich source of data for critical reflection. The studies by Sharp and Green (pp. 251–4), Nash (pp. 255–7), and Jackson (pp. 263–8) and Davies (pp. 269–74), are typical of such studies, which Ingleby (1986) has described as 'social constructionist'. This perspective he suggests, reflects a concern for representing human thought, perception and action through meaning created by the interaction of people in social settings, where language is of particular significance. Ingleby recognizes that 'social constructionism' is at present rather incoherent drawing upon various disciplines, in particular psychology as well as symbolic interactionism, phenomenology, analytic philosophy and some forms of Marxism and Structuralism.

As Pollard (1987) has commented:

> There are serious theoretical philosophical and methodological differences between these approaches which will probably always produce tensions but they share the conviction that human action is best understood as being meaningful and as a product of social contexts and social interactions. In doing so they, of course, cross the artificial disciplinary boundary between psychology and sociology which in itself provokes much debate.

The extracts in this section of the source book do not constitute a complete course in the sociology of primary education. They need to be supplemented by more extensive general reading, but they do illustrate the value of a sociological perspective, or more accurately a variety of perspectives, on primary education. For more detailed overviews on developments in the sociology of education, readers are referred to Banks, O. (1982) 'The sociology of education 1952–1982', *British Journal of Educational Studies*, 30, 1; and Robinson, P. (1981) *Perspectives on the Sociology of Education: An Introduction*, Chapters 1 and 2, London, Routledge and Kegan Paul. Also the recently published *British Journal of the Sociology of Education* contains articles of relevance to primary education. Andrew Pollard's study of *Children and Their Primary Schools* (Falmer Press, 1987) contains extracts from sociological and social-psychological research pertinent to primary schools. Finally, John Boyd's *Equality Issues in Primary Schools* (Paul Chapman Publishing, 1989) addresses important current sociological concerns and *The Family, School and Society* (Edited by Martin Woodhead and Andrea McGrath, Hodder and Stoughton, 1988) includes articles which place primary education in a sociological context.

References

INGLEBY, D. (1986) 'Development in social context', in RICHARDS, M. and LIGHT, P. (Eds) *Children of Social Worlds*, Cambridge, Polity Press.
POLLARD, A. (Ed.) (1987) *Children and Their Primary Schools*, Lewes, Falmer Press.

The Five Basic Roles of the Primary School

(From Blyth, W., 1965, *English Primary Education*, Vol. 1, London, Routledge and Kegan Paul, pp. 17, 17–18, 19, 20, 20–1.)

This extract has been taken from an analysis of primary schools as social institutions — an analysis written in the first half of the 1960s and informed by a structural-functional approach to the sociology of education. Through discussion of the primary school in terms of social structure, social function and control, and social change, Blyth placed it in relation to the education system and to the wider social structure. Here, he suggests that the primary school discharges four basic roles — instruction, socialization, classification and welfare — to which he adds a fifth, and less clear dimension, that is, the creation of a distinctive, semi-autonomous identity. In discussing the five roles, he draws on his analysis of traditions within primary education, which is featured elsewhere in the source book (pp. 5–8). Though the theoretical perspective adopted here is no longer fashionable, the sociological description offered provides a useful and still recognizable view of the primary school as an institution.

There are five basic roles which primary schools may be said to discharge in contemporary English society: to instruct; to socialize; to classify; to promote social welfare; and to develop autonomy for themselves. . . .

First: *instruction*. Whether one judges from the volume of controversy or from the nature of the formal structure of primary schools, there is no doubt about the importance attached to instruction, especially in the basic skills. Despite the impact of the developmental tradition, there is still general support for the view that primary schools instruct, and that the expansion of children's cognitive horizons is among their principal objectives. However, instruction is often broadly and generously defined, so that this role may at its best involve an exciting intellectual adventure and concurrently an extension of social learning.

The second role is that of *socialization*. This is more directly associated with the developmental tradition, and implies that primary schools are places where children learn to live together in such a way that they will continue to live, in later years, in a manner appropriate to a civilized community. This may also involve some instruction; but socialization is more than instruction, and it is doubtful whether social values can be acquired in any other way than through participation in collective living, even though the excellence of the social values may depend heavily on the quality of the social living and the influences with which it is surrounded, and the wisdom with which this environment is adjusted to the developing capacities and vision of the children. The actual patterns of socialization in primary schools vary according to the fundamental beliefs of the teachers and others who influence policy, but there can be little room for dispute about the importance of the socializing role itself.

Next in the series comes *classification*. In England today, one aspect of classification — that of selection for secondary education — is so prominent that the very existence of others is masked. But in fact, classification is a continuous and ubiquitous process in primary schools. Children come to be classified informally according to the aspects of the curriculum in which they do well or badly, and also according to their physical and social abilities and attainments. From all of these they may derive a general reputation which adheres to them as a stereotype, as tends to happen also in their peer-life outside school. For some of these classificatory processes official records are kept — of physique, for example, and of general and specific abilities and attainments, and of personality ratings — but others are informally but decisively committed to the children's own minds and those of their associates....

The fourth role is that of *welfare*.... In England,... the welfare role of primary schools has a statutory basis ... and indeed several observers (Mellor, 1950, p. 88; Gray, 1955) have pointed out that schools have become focal points of the Welfare State, just because almost the whole child population passes through them. This welfare function is derived in part from traditional religious and philanthropic concepts of social service, and in part from widely-accepted views about the functions and responsibilities of the modern State. In addition primary schools have a specific welfare role for, as Mays (1962) points out, they are nowadays the only true neighbourhood institutions....

Last in order of consideration comes the *autonomous* role, and it is the most difficult to define. It is closely associated with the developmental tradition; ultimately, it is the role which obliges each school to be itself. For this purpose it must draw on the collective experience and talents of its staff, and on the support of various elements in the community, but for the rest it grows spontaneously....

A school must do more than reflect the culture of part or even all of its pupils. It cannot even be content to reflect that culture in its idealized form. The only way in which it can realize its autonomous role is by cutting purposefully adrift from the culture-patterns associated with the various parts of its clientele and creating something new and worth-while in itself. Once this is achieved, it can lead to the establishment of a social climate in which the operation of the usual conventions and counter-conventions of society and of its subdivisions are minimized, so that individuality and initiative can develop within an accepted framework of stable and considerate behaviour. Feeling that theirs is a good and satisfying school, the children are then more favourably disposed towards it, more ready to go along with it in the implementation of its other roles, and incidentally thereby more tolerant towards others whose cultural background differs from their own. The effective implementation of the autonomous role involves the consummation of the other roles also.

References

GRAY, K. (1955) 'Social welfare and the teacher', *Social Welfare*, 9, 5, pp. 104–10.

MAYS, J. (1962) *Education and the Urban Child*, University of Liverpool Press.

MELLOR, E. (1950) *Education through Experience in the Infant School*, Blackwell.

Socialization into School

(From Newsom, J., Newsom, E. and Barnes, P., 1977, *Perspectives on School at Seven Years Old*, London, Allen and Unwin, pp. 41, 41–2, 42–3, 44, 44–5, 47–8.)

Socialization is one of the main roles or functions of the primary school according to Blyth's analysis summarized in the first extract of this section (pp. 185–7). The material reproduced below is written within the same structural-functional framework and examines how children's socialization into the school's structure, norms and values is achieved. According to the Newsoms, 'school is the contact which crystallizes the child's transformation into a social creature, which formalizes his experience of the peer group and of outside authority, and which presents a new set of demands which may be totally alien to the expectations of home but which are too powerful for the child to reject altogether'. The passage describes how infant children adjust to the dynamic social structure of the primary school (helped by the infant teacher as a key mediator of their experience), how they develop very considerable knowledge of how teachers, fellow pupils and schools operate, and how they acquire an evolving social status. The material for this analysis is derived from the Newsom's large-scale longitudinal study of child-rearing in Nottingham and complements the authors' parallel study of the home environment of 7-year-olds (Newsom, J. and E., 1976, *Seven Year Old in the Home Environment*, Allen and Unwin). For a contrasting interpretation of socialization into school, at least as far as lower working-class children are concerned, see the first extract by Bernstein later in this section (pp. 220–3), and that by Sharp and Green (pp. 251–4).

The teacher,... as well as being the key figure in the child's introduction to formal learning, also mediates his experience of the school world in which that process of learning takes place; and the school itself serves (for most children) as the earliest model of the complicated patterns of behaviour and social interaction which evolve in the institutional or organizational settings that will continue to be important to a greater or lesser extent as the child grows up.... It is part of the teacher's role not only to identify herself with the school, but to cause the child to do so too, usually via the transitional stage of himself identifying with her. If the child's relationship is only with the teacher and not with the school beyond her, she has failed to wean him from the purely personal bond of which the mother was the first model. Eventually the child must familiarize himself with the corporate entity of the school, come to feel that he belongs to it and it to him, and learn in his turn to initiate younger children into its customs and values. In becoming socialized in the school as social institution, children are carried onward by repeatedly experiencing the rhythms and rituals of the school day and the school week, as well as by innumerable encounters with other people who themselves have a known place in the pattern: children from their own class and their own year, children from the 'babies' class' or the 'top class', in-between children who are not 'the big ones' but yet are bigger than themselves, teachers who are soft and motherly from looking after the little ones, teachers who are bright and brisk from keeping nine-year-olds in order, the head and the deputy head, the school secretary, the dinner-ladies and the caretaker. Through such encounters, in which he may be either participant or observing bystander, the child begins to appraise his own position within the hierarchical age-graded structure of the school as a whole.

Probably no one person has full knowledge of all the customs, beliefs and practices which make up the social organization of a single primary school. In our daughters' school, for instance, it was only the lower junior girls who knew about the Green Lady behind the cupboard in the hall, and how she needed to be propitiated; and no doubt any group one could identify, among children and staff alike, would be found to have its own beliefs which contribute to the total social edifice. But even understandings which have the status of 'common knowledge' must be acquired gradually over time by any given child, by piecing together a thousand scraps of experience....

From all these diverse sources of information, then, children gradually absorb a rather different set of standards from those which have come to govern their behaviour in the intimate family environment. Because the seven-year-old is an extremely social animal, the child approaching this age will be very responsive to a philosophy of 'This is the way we all do it, so this is how it has to be'. Schools are thus enabled to guide and mould the behaviour of their children in hundreds of different and subtle ways, often without resort to any coercion other than the social pressure which is implicit in the example of the majority being willing to conform to group expectations. The compelling difference between home socialization and socialization to the school lies in *the degree of tolerance accorded to egocentricity*. At school, egocentricity must fairly quickly accept subordination to group needs. Obviously the pre-school child *is* developmentally more egocentric than the primary school child; but it is not just a question of age. Obviously, too, parents subscribe in general terms to the idea that one child cannot be allowed to dominate the whole group; it is their own conscious endeavour that one member of the family should not ride roughshod over the others. None the less, children of any age, including adolescents, do dominate their families egocentrically for brief or longer periods according to their special problems or needs or preoccupations of the moment; and it is perhaps the family's special function to put up with such episodes of domination because they are necessary to the child's development at the time and because no other institution in society will tolerate them.

In fact, although children of seven still respond to their teachers in a highly personal way, it is a mistake to suppose that the relationship between teacher and pupil is at all similar to that between parent and child. The teacher's role, however democratic or benign he or she may be, is deliberately formalized; and in the school environment all sorts of social forces are in operation to constrain the behaviour of both adults and children. Teachers themselves naturally assume — and are indeed accorded — a respect proper to their status within the institution, which is quite different from that which parents would nowadays expect from their own offspring at home. Related to this is another consideration: that teachers behave, and are expected by parents to behave, according to a code of professional conduct....

The development of group norms of acceptable school behaviour is a factor of considerable practical importance, since it is only this development which enables such a small number of adults to cope effectively and benignly with such large numbers of children. Many parents express deep admiration for the way teachers surmount what appears to be the almost impossible task of controlling such an enormous 'family', and it is clear that their admiration stems from this false comparison with their own parental role. Surely teachers must be almost superhuman if they can deal with thirty children single-handed! Imagine what it would be like if their own families were to be increased by a factor of ten! It is this mixture of awe and sympathy which can lead parents to ignore their children's complaints, feeling that they themselves could not do such a job and therefore have no right to criticize if something goes wrong. This is interesting, since not being able to do a job ourselves does not normally prevent our criticism of, say, an inefficient television repair or an inept comedian; and it does appear to be the sense of comparability, *coupled* with parental feelings of inadequacy, which produces this reaction....

What needs to be understood, however, is that the attempt to teach such a large group of children would indeed present an impossible task were it not that they are already, by the time they reach junior school age, in bond to a substantial network of group conventions. The average benign primary school is a complex social institution with a tightly knit and well-ordered social structure. The hierarchy is dominated at one level by older children whose own status is served by assisting in the socialization of the younger ones; and at another level by experienced adults who are deliberately accorded considerable power over the children in their charge. As in most social organizations, the participating members, whether higher or lower in the hierarchy, are constrained within a system of values and customs which govern when, where and how the participants are expected to behave towards each other. Some few of these customs will be made explicit as school rules or school information, to which the attention of children and parents will be deliberately drawn; but many more will be absorbed through the pores, as it were, as 'natural' and established usage — the accepted ways in which pupils and teachers do behave in school. The child imperceptibly comes to adopt and make his own a quite complicated notion of a dynamic social structure and his own evolving status within it, by a long accretion of incidental learning.

When we say that children adjust or 'settle down' to school, then, we may be in danger of missing the crucial point: that they are being subjected to a compelling socialization process, much of which offers persuasive rewards, but as a result of which they learn to accept their place as very junior members of an elaborate social hierarchy. This is by no means to say that the child simply learns passive conformity to rules and conventions: on the contrary, the power of the system lies in the fact that the child internalizes its values in a very active sense. . . .

Schools today, as parents often pointed out, offer much more freedom of choice than many of these parents themselves remember from their own early schooldays. The style of control has changed; the atmosphere is more child-centred and permissive. Harshness of punishment or threat of punishment is only rarely encountered. This does not, however, mean (as some parents supposed) that children can do whatever they like, or that teachers have given up any control over their pupils: only that teachers, like parents, have moved towards a democratic image, and have learned to use group forces, at least in the primary school, to maintain an illusion of democratic choice within a relatively unyielding framework. Within this framework, parents and teachers are at some pains to keep the child contented, and with goodwill and easy communication can often smooth the difficulties which the child encounters. However, problems of communication can arise, both between parents and teachers, and between parents and their own children: home and school *are* different worlds, and the two worlds foster myths about each other which may not be helpful to the child moving between them. Certain facts, beyond the myths, have to be lived with. Teachers have always been aware that some parents provide a frankly damaging environment for their children, and that these children will continue to be at risk however compensatory the education that may be devised for them. It is also true that some teachers are incompetent and that some are unsuitable for their profession and damaging to the children they teach: when this happens, both parents and children are likely to find that there is very little to be done to change the situation, other than to sweat it out as best they can. It is here that both communication for parents and democratic choice for children break down.

In this introduction to the parents' perspective on school, we have attempted first of all to present the school situation from a more objective perspective than parents are usually themselves able to take: they are, after all, usually too immediately concerned with the individual personalities involved and the actual activities being undertaken from day to day. We have tried to show how the child extends his horizons from home and family, to school, peers and less intimate authorities, and how his adaptation to the more formal social system takes place. In his first months in the infant school, the child's teacher will make considerable allowance for his individual quirks and foibles: less responsive than his mother to his egocentricity, she is still a tolerant, nurturant figure, to whom he can ascribe a mothering image and who can offer him a protective transition from home to school expectations. Loving his teacher uncritically, yet also compelled to share her with a greater number of peers than he has been used to, he learns two massive adaptations: he identifies with his teacher, and thence with the school world which she represents; and he is introduced to a discovery for which he is now intellectually ready — the discovery that group co-operation brings its own rewards in greater achievement and more complex and satisfying play. These crucial social lessons of the infant school, mediated chiefly by the teacher herself, allow him to become fully integrated with the peer group and with the school as social institution, and bring him under the powerful influence of both: and in this way he is enabled to wean himself from the protective nurturance of his teacher, and become an independent 'junior'. At this stage, while retaining a close and friendly relationship with his class teacher, he is also more able to look beyond her to other teachers with whom he enjoys more casual contact; and, detached from his personal dependency, he begins to show the emergence of 'us and them' loyalties in relation to peer group *vis-à-vis* teachers, turning more frequently towards other children as a source of comfort and support in meeting difficulties at school. Socialization takes on a new emphasis.

Social Class and Educational Opportunity

(From Floud, J., Halsey A. and Martin F., 1956, *Social Class and Educational Opportunity*, London, Heinemann, pp. 142–7.)

The major preoccupation of the few sociologists studying the English educational system in the 1950s was the relationship between social class and educational opportunity. Sociologists documented the access to selective secondary education (through the 11+ examination) by children from different social classes and attempted to provide explanations of what brought about these differences of access. The passage below comes from the conclusions of a major sociological study of the social distribution of access to grammar schools by boys in South-West Hertfordshire and in Middlesbrough. In their investigation the authors documented the marked differences in the chances which boys of different social classes had of obtaining grammar school places in both the areas studied. They concluded that although there was a close relationship between 'ability' (defined as 'measured intelligence' on IQ tests) and 'opportunity' (defined as access to grammar schools), 'the problem of inequality of educational opportunity' was 'not thereby disposed of', since material and cultural differences in the environment of children from different social classes affected their performance on tests and hence their access to selective secondary education through the 11+ examination. The social determinants of 'educability' in which the authors were interested became a major focus of sociological investigation at the end of the 1950s and the early 1960s, as illustrated by the work of Bernstein (pp. 220–3) and the 1964 National Survey conducted for the Plowden Committee (pp. 206–10). At that time there was general agreement with the concluding sentences of the study from which the passage below has been extracted:

> The problem of equality of educational opportunity is now more complicated than when it took the simple form of the need to secure free access to grammar schools on equal intellectual terms. With the expansion of educational opportunity and the reduction of gross economic handicaps to children's school performance the need arises to understand the optimum conditions for the integration of school and home environment at all social levels in such a way as to minimise the educational disadvantages of both and to turn their educational advantages to full account.

It is obvious that the number of working-class boys entering the grammar schools each year has been increasing fast, and that there are more in the schools today than ever before. Nevertheless, the probability that a working-class boy will get to a grammar school is not strikingly different from what it was before 1945, and there are still marked differences in the chances which boys of different social origins have of obtaining a place. Of those working-class boys who reached the age of 11 in the years 1931–41 rather less than 10 per cent entered selective secondary schools. In 1953 the proportion of working-class boys admitted to grammar schools was 12 per cent in Middlesbrough and 14 per cent in South West Hertfordshire. Thus, approximately one working-class boy in eight was admitted in Middlesbrough, as compared, for instance, with nearly one in three of the sons of clerks; and approximately one working-class boy in seven in South West Herfordshire, as compared with nearly one in two of the sons of clerks.

Our findings as to the social distribution of measured intelligence are closely consistent with those of earlier enquiries, and provide an adequate explanation of these differences. Virtually the full quota of boys with the requisite minimum IQ from every class was admitted to grammar schools and the distribution of opportunity stands today in closer relationship to that of ability (as measured by intelligence tests) than ever before. Yet the problem of inequality of educational opportunity is not thereby disposed of.

We have considered some of the material and cultural differences in the environment of the children who succeed, as distinct from those who do not succeed, in the selection examination for secondary education, and we have shown how the success of children varies with the distribution of these features of the environment even at the same social level. Since measured intelligence is so closely related to the results of the selection procedure our findings are relevant to the problem of the influence of environment on intelligence test scores. But this was not our direct concern, and the features of the environment we have selected for study cannot, of course, be regarded as social determinants of intelligence. Nevertheless, though they touch on less fundamental problems, certain conclusions do emerge concerning the part played by differences of environment in the social distribution of educational opportunity.

In the past, the problem of social waste in education could be seen in comparatively simple terms, for gross material factors overshadowed all others. Poverty caused ill-health and poor attendance; facilities for study could not be provided in slum homes, nor proper instruction given in over-crowded schools; grammar school places were refused by parents who could not afford to forgo adolescent earnings. But the influence on the distribution of educational opportunity of the material environment in which children live at home and are taught at school before the age of selection, is tending to diminish in importance in the face of the general prosperity and the measures of social reform which are characteristic of post-war Britain. Social factors influencing educational selection reveal themselves in more subtle forms today.

The present situation at its most favourable is illustrated by the position in South West Hertfordshire where a generally high minimum degree of material comfort is enjoyed at all social levels. In that area, in 1952, material conditions in their homes did not, at a given social level, distinguish the successful from the unsuccessful candidate in the selection examination. At a given social level, the children who secured grammar school places were not those whose parents earned the highest income, nor those who enjoyed superior standards of housing. On the other hand, differences in the size of the family, and in the education, attitudes and ambitions of parents were reflected in the examination performance of children in all classes. In Middlesbrough the situation was less favourable. In 1953 in that area, purely material conditions at home still differentiated the successful from the unsuccessful children even at the same social level. If poor parents were favourably disposed towards their children's education this attitude was less likely than in South West Hertfordshire to be reflected in the performance of their children in the selection examination. Moreover, the traditional association between poor homes and poor schools persists in Middlesbrough, and places an additional handicap on the child of poor but educationally well-disposed parents. There is still scope for attack on gross economic disabilities. In South West Hertfordshire, however, virtually everyone enjoys an adequate basic income and good housing which, together with the security of the social services, provide something like the basic ingredients of a middle-class or at least lower middle-class existence. The influence of the home on children's educational prospects is more subtle, and the problem of developing and utilizing their ability to the full is educational rather than social.

Once the grosser material handicaps are eliminated, the size of the family emerges as the most important single index of the favourable or unfavourable influence of home environment on educational prospects. Very little is known as to what determines the size of families at different social levels, but there is no doubt about the existence of a relationship between family size and educational opportunity. This relationship obviously has its economic aspect, even in the Welfare State. It is a well-established fact, however, that children from small families, at all social levels, tend on the average to do better in intelligence tests and therefore also in the selection examination for secondary education. Dr Nisbet has suggested that the child of a large family learns verbal skills less effectively from his peers than does the child of a small family from adults, and that he carries the handicap at least until the age of eleven. But the evidence from Middlesbrough suggests that the educational disadvantages of a large family are far less marked for the children of Catholic parents, and if generally true this would cast doubt on the notion that there is some distinctive quality of educational value in the environment of a small family. It may be suggested that family limitation amongst Catholic parents does not correspond so closely to intelligence as it tends to do amongst non-Catholic parents, so that the average level of ability of children from large Catholic families is likely to be higher than of those from large non-Catholic families. In fact, the mean IQ of the children of Catholic unskilled workers, who constituted the largest single social group amongst the Catholic children, was found in 1953 to be slightly higher than that of others at this social level. This finding cannot be interpreted without more information, particularly as to the geographical origins of Catholic parents, and their length of residence in Middlesbrough. Recent immigrants to the area might be temporarily employed in occupations below their capacities, so that their offspring might show greater ability than the average for the unskilled group. However that may be, this problem, and others in the same field of the relations between social class, family environment and educational opportunity, can only be effectively examined through intensive enquiry into children's home environment on case-study lines.

Social Class Differences in Attainment and Ability at Seven

(From Davie, R., Butler, N. and Goldstein, H., 1972, *From Birth to Seven*, London, Longman, pp. 98–105.)

The previous passage provided data and comment on social class differences in access to selective secondary education. This one gives information on pupils' attainments in infant schools and departments and relates these to social class (defined here in terms of the occupational group of the children's fathers). The figures come from the National Child Development Study which examined the overall development of about 16,000 children born between 3 March and 9 March 1958. This particular study of the children at the age of 7 was followed up when they were 11 (Wedge and Prosser, 1973) and again at 16 (Fogelman, 1976). Each of the studies revealed a similar picture, suggesting that 'whatever the factors are which social class indirectly measures, they are fairly sharply differentiated as between middle-class and working-class homes, at least as far as their effect on attainment or ability is concerned'. The particular figures reproduced here indicated the extent of class-related differences in attainment after only two years of compulsory education. A similar longitudinal study of a 1946 cohort of children (Douglas, 1964; Douglas, Ross and Simpson, 1968) indicated that the gap between social classes continued to widen during the period of formal schooling, at least as far as scores on reading and arithmetic tests were concerned.

This particular extract has been chosen as an example of the kinds of data which were provided by psychologists, medical personnel and others, and which required sociological study. In the event, the social determinants of educability proved elusive to pin down.

In interpreting the data in the extract, readers need to know the classifications of occupations adopted by the National Child Development Study as an indicator of social class:

Social Class I	Higher professional
II	Other professional and technical
III (non-manual)	Other non-manual occupations
III (manual)	Skilled manual
IV	Semi-skilled manual
V	Unskilled manual

References

DOUGLAS, J. (1964) *The Home and the School*, MacGibbon and Kee.
DOUGLAS, J. ROSS, J. and SIMPSON, H. (1968) *All Our Future*, Peter Davies.
FOGELMAN, K. (Ed.) (1976) *Britain's Sixteen-Year-Olds*, National Children's Bureau.
WEDGE, P. and PROSSER, K. (1973) *Born to Fail?*, Arrow Books (in association with National Children's Bureau).

Figure 26   *Percentage of children with below average oral ability (teachers' ratings)*

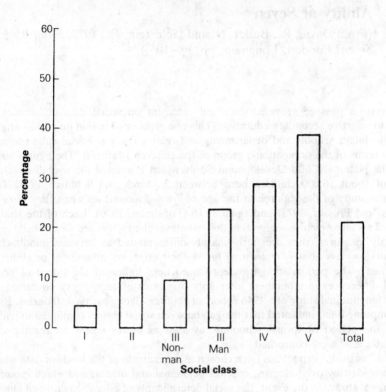

Social Class Differences in Attainment and Ability

There has been a great deal of discussion in recent years about the relationship between social class and school attainments. This has tended to centre upon the issue of social inequality which, it has been alleged, is reinforced by our educational system.

For example, Douglas's (1964) results indicate that during the years of primary schooling the gap in attainment between children from different occupational groups widens. Although this finding has been subjected to criticism on statistical grounds (e.g. Carter, 1964), there seems little doubt that the phenomenon is a real one. Douglas's later work (Douglas, Ross and Simpson, 1968) suggests that this process is continued in the secondary school.

However, in the discussions and controversies which have followed these and other findings, relatively little thought has been given to the role of the primary school. Attention has tended to centre upon the eleven-plus examination and the selective secondary education which follows. In particular, the laudable attempts to provide equal educational opportunity for

Figure 27   Percentage of children with below average 'awareness of the world around' (teachers' ratings)

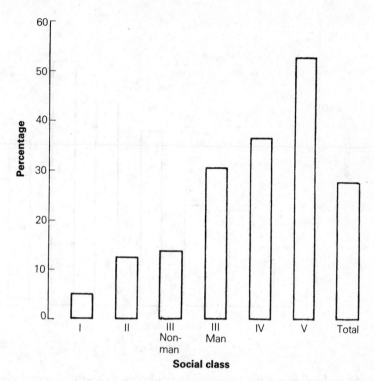

all children have perhaps overlooked the very marked inequalities which exist even before children transfer to junior school. This is partly because very few studies have been concerned with attainments in infant schools or departments, and even fewer have related these attainments to social class. . . .

. . . It is not difficult to see why there should be some relationship between a father's occupation and his children's progress at school. . . .

First, heredity is likely to play a part. The relative contributions of heredity and environment to children's abilities and attainments is a difficult question and psychologists, sociologists, geneticists and others will no doubt continue to debate it until we know a great deal more about brain function. However, that heredity plays some part in perhaps setting limits to the rate of intellectual development or to its ultimate peak can hardly be doubted. Since, in general, parents in a competitive society who have risen to occupations demanding a high level of skill will show a higher level of general intelligence than those in less skilled occupations, it would follow that there will be corresponding differences in their children.

Over and above this, environmental influences will shape a child's

Figure 28 Percentage of children with 'little' or 'no' 'creativity' (teachers' ratings)

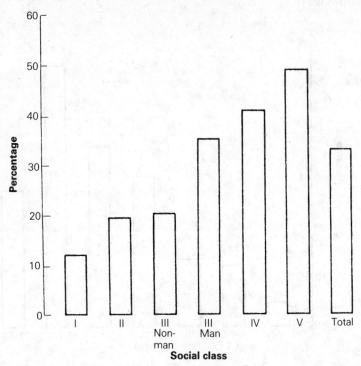

abilities and influence his capacity or readiness to learn. A great deal — if not the major part — of learning takes place outside of school and much of this is accomplished even before the child enters school. The vocabulary and concepts used by those around him are vital in providing a framework within which his own intellectual growth can take place. If this framework is bare or impoverished, his own development is likely to be slow; a rich framework of words and ideas will provide the food for more rapid growth. More advanced or abstract thought processes are usually clothed in more elaborate and highly structured language (Bernstein, 1961). A home conducive to learning is one where there is a feeling for the spoken and written word as a tool for conveying precise meaning; and where children are stimulated to question the world around them and receive explanations appropriate to their age.

There are two senses in which a child from such a home comes to school ready to learn. He is intellectually ready in that his language and concepts are already well structured, so that the school is building upon established foundations. But he is also psychologically ready to acquire new skills. For example, he has learned that reading provides pleasure and he wants to be a part of the literate community as soon as possible. His whole attitude to school is conditioned by his parents' high regard for education.

Figure 29   Percentage of children with 'poor' copying designs score (0–5)

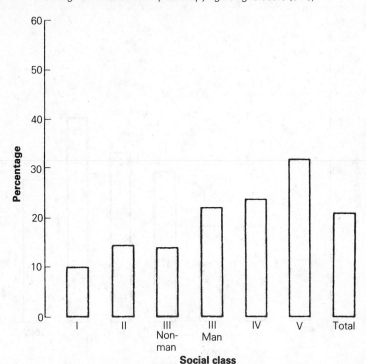

This kind of home is certainly not a monopoly of professional or other non-manual workers. However, it is more frequently found amongst occupational groups which possess a high level of education and skill. Thus, in examining social class differences, we are examining the effects both of environment and of heredity upon children's abilities and attainments.

The results in Figs 26 to 31 show the relationship between poor ability and attainment and social class. The groups of children included are by no means at the extremes. For reading and arithmetic, where test results were available, the children whose results appear in the histograms are those whose score placed them in the bottom 30 per cent of the sample.

Two important points emerge in these two analyses. First, there is clearly a strong association between social class and reading and arithmetic attainment at seven years of age. The chances of an unskilled manual worker's child (Social Class V) being a poor reader are six times greater than those of a professional worker's child (Social Class I). If the criterion of poor reading is made more stringent, the disparity is much larger. Thus, the chances of a Social Class V child being a *non*-reader are fifteen times greater than those of a Social Class I child.

A second point which emerges is that the gradient from Social Class I through to Social Class V is not regular. There are little or no differences

Figure 30 *Percentage of children with 'poor' problem arithmetic test score (0–3)*

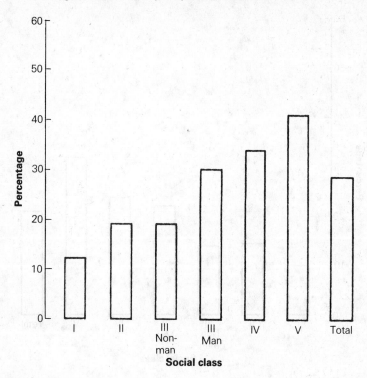

between the results for Social Class II and Social Class III (non-manual) children but very considerable differences between the results of these groups and those for Social Class III (manual) children.

The results for the abilities assessed by teachers' rating and for the copying designs test show the same general pattern with increasing proportions of children with poor ability accompanying lower social class. Again, the gradient of proportions through the social classes is not regular.

It is difficult to draw firm conclusions about the relative differences in the proportions in the social class groups since these are dependent upon the abilities being assessed, the measures used and the stringency of the criteria adopted. However, there appears to be a substantial division between the children from non-manual, or middle-class, homes on the one hand, and those from manual, or working-class, homes on the other. This suggests that whatever the factors are which social class indirectly measures, they are fairly sharply differentiated as between middle-class and working-class homes, at least as far as their effect on attainment or ability is concerned. The results also suggest that there is a meaningful division within the middle-class group between Social Class I children and the others. In the

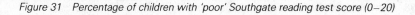

Figure 31   Percentage of children with 'poor' Southgate reading test score (0–20)

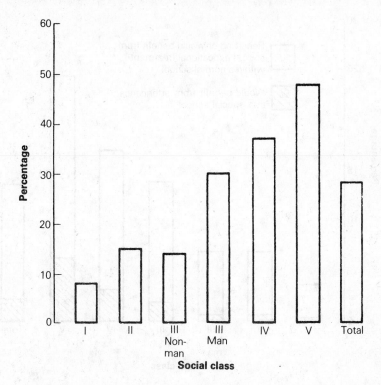

working-class group, the Social Class V children appear to be at a particular disadvantage in respect of poor ability or attainment in school.

Of course, these speculations do not throw light directly on the reasons for the differences. Some of the results in [a previous chapter] might suggest that environmental factors are relevant. For example, the proportions of parents who discussed their children with the schools followed the same social class pattern as for the children's abilities and attainments. However, hereditary factors cannot be entirely ignored.

Social Class and the Need for Special Educational Treatment

The teachers were asked whether the children were receiving any help within the school because of educational or mental backwardness, 'apart from anything which the teacher may be able to do in the normal way'; and, if No, they were asked whether the children would benefit from such help. Five per cent of the children were receiving help and a further 8 per cent were not but would have benefited. The size of this last figure, as was

Figure 32   *Percentage of children needing special educational treatment by social class*

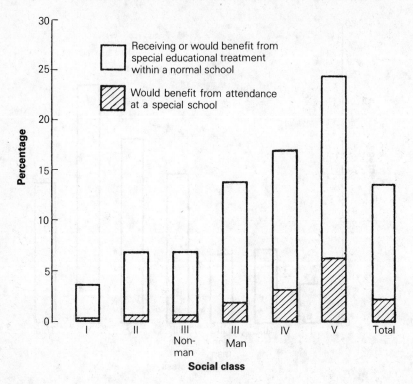

pointed out in the first report ... indicates an urgent need to re-examine the provision of special educational treatment in infant schools.

A further question asked of the teachers was whether the children 'would benefit *now* from attendance at a special school'. Some 2 per cent of children fell into this category. The teachers were not asked to choose between special schooling and special educational treatment within the normal school, so that virtually all of the children who would have benefited from special schooling were also said to be in need of help in the normal school.

The results presented in Fig. 32 show the proportions in the social classes. The proportion of children in Social Class V who, it was reported, would have benefited from attendance at a special school was forty-five times larger than the corresponding proportion in Social Class I.

References

BERNSTEIN, B. (1961) 'Social structure, language and learning', *Educational Research* 3, pp. 163–76.

CARTER, C. (1964) review of *The Home and the School, Eugenics Review*, 56, 2, pp. 93–6.
DOUGLAS, J. (1964) *The Home and the School*, MacGibbon and Kee.
DOUGLAS, J., ROSS, J. and SIMPSON, H. (1968) *All Our Future*, Peter Davies.

Factors Affecting Children's Performance in Primary Schools

(From Central Advisory Council for Education (England), 1967, *Children and Their Primary Schools*, Vol. 1, London, HMSO, pp. 31, 32, 33–4, 35, 36.)

Concern over the 'wastage' of ability, particularly working-class ability, created an alliance between sociologists and policy-makers, as illustrated by this passage from the Plowden Report. The Committee accepted the sociological findings concerning the relationship between social class and educational disadvantage and believed that the publication of their report presented 'an opportunity for reform'. The part of the report dealing with the relationship between home and school was imbued with a 'social democratic' stance towards the reduction and, preferably, elimination of inequality (see p. 77).

As part of the background to its deliberations, the Plowden Committee insti-gated a national survey to investigate the relationship between home and school and the attainment of children. Data were collected on about 3,000 children in 173 schools through interviews with the pupils' mothers, information on their schools from headteachers and HMIs, information on the children from their class teachers and assessments of children's attainments on reading comprehension tests and, for top juniors, on a picture intelligence test.

The passage reproduced below stresses as 'the most striking feature' of the comparisons made in the survey the large part played by parental attitudes in accounting for the variation in children's performance within and between schools. The Committee optimistically claims that since parental attitudes are not monopol-ized by any one class, the attitudes of large numbers of parents can be altered in the direction of supporting their children's efforts to learn. Some sociologists, however, later criticized the Committee's loose definition of 'parental attitude' and argued that parental attitudes might be more resistant to change than the report suggested, since attitudes could be regarded as dimensions of deep-rooted social class differences (Bernstein, B. and Davies, B., 1969, 'Some sociological comments on Plowden', in Peters, R. (Ed.) *Perspectives on Plowden*, London, Routledge and Kegan Paul, pp. 55–83).

... we are far from realizing the potential abilities of our children. To reveal the influence of parental occupation is a criticism of society; but it is also an opportunity for reform. There must always be a great diversity of parental occupations; but they need not continue to have their present severe discriminatory effect on children's educational prospects. The grosser deprivations arising from poverty can be removed. More parents can be brought to understand what education can do for their children, and how they can work with the schools. The educational disadvantage of being born the child of an unskilled worker is both financial and psychological. Neither handicap is as severe as it was. Both are more severe than they need be. Educational equality cannot be achieved by the schools alone: but the schools can make a major contribution towards ensuring (as Sir Edward Boyle wrote in his foreword to the Newsom Report) 'that all children should have an equal opportunity of acquiring intelligence'.

86. The last three reports of the Council drew attention to the numerous exceptions to the rule that they established. They pointed to the homes and the schools which produce good or even brilliant results in spite of adverse circumstances. Our own enquiries have been directed to throwing light on the reasons for these exceptions. If we can pinpoint the factors which make good work possible in apparently unlikely circumstances, we may see what most needs to be done to enlarge the numbers of those who succeed. What is it about the home that matters so much? That was the main question we wished to have explored. . . .

89. The main purpose of the survey was to relate what we could learn about home and school to the attainment of the children. For the summarized table in this chapter [Table 1] the variables used are grouped into three categories. . . . The first category is broadly called 'Parental Attitudes'. These attitudes were assessed by parents' answers to such questions as the age at which they wanted children to leave school and the secondary school they preferred. The initiative shown by parents in visiting the school, in talking to heads and class teachers and asking for work for children to do at home was also taken into account. Parents were asked about the time they spent with children in the evening and whether they helped children with school work. There was also an assessment of the literacy of the home as judged by what parents and children read, whether they belonged to a library and the number of books in the home. The second category is 'Home Circumstances', including the physical amenities of the home, or lack of them, the occupation and income of the father, the size of family, the length of parents' education and the qualifications they had obtained. The third category is the 'State of the School'. It covers facts about school organizations such as size of school, size of class and the ways children were put into classes. It also includes facts provided by the head about the experience of the staff and their attendance at short courses, and judgments by HMIs on the quality of the school and the competence of teachers. . . .

91. The figures given in Table 1 show, for different ages, the percentage of the variation in performance which can be accounted for by the three main categories of variable. For each age group the comparisons made in the table are of two kinds, between pupils *within* schools and *between* schools. The object of this division was to bring out the extent to which a school's situation depends on the neighbourhood it serves. For comparisons between

Table 1   Percentage contribution of parental attitudes, home circumstances and
state of school to variation in educational performance

	Infants	Between Schools Lower Juniors	Top Juniors	All Pupils
Parental Attitudes	24	20	39	28
Home Circumstances	16	25	17	20
State of School	20	22	12	17
*Unexplained	40	33	32	35
	100	100	100	100
	Infants	Within Schools Lower Juniors	Top Juniors	All Pupils
Parental Attitudes	16	15	29	20
Home Circumstances	9	9	7	9
State of School	14	15	22	17
*Unexplained	61	61	42	54
	100	100	100	100

* The unexplained variation is due to differences between children which have not been covered by our
variables, and also to errors in measurement. That so much variation has been explained — the amount in
the between-schools analysis is remarkable for an enquiry of this kind — is due in part to the
comparatively simple nature of the criterion variable, a reading comprehension test.

schools the unit of analysis was the school, and the variables were based on
the average for each school of the original variables. For comparisons within
schools the variables were the deviations of each pupil from the school
average. If neighbourhood were unimportant, and the parents, pupils and
teachers in each school were merely random samples of the general population, the two kinds of analysis would give the same result. In fact, they do
not; the comparisons between schools account for more variation than those
within schools. This is because pupils, parents and teachers in the same
school and neighbourhood resemble one another more than they resemble
pupils, parents and teachers in general, just as apples growing on the same
tree resemble one another more than they resemble apples in general. The
apples on a tree in a good situation will do better than those on a tree in a
poor situation, unless the latter receives special attention —....

92.   The most striking feature of both these sets of comparisons is the large
part played by parental attitudes, and the fact that it tends to be greater
among the older than the younger children. Not surprisingly, there are
changes of emphasis within the attitudes of parents as children grow older.
Parents' interest is likely to be greater in the children's early years at school

when, as the interviewers found, they were more confident about helping children in their work, because they understood it better. It yields some ground to parental aspiration as the children reach the top of the junior school. By that time the children's very success or failure in school work may increase or weaken parental aspiration.

93. The influence of the home has always been known to be important, and the importance of parental attitudes began to emerge in earlier studies such as those of Fraser (1954), Floud, Halsey and Martin (1956), but now its importance can be better understood. Broadly the same results stand out from other surveys made for us by Professor Wiseman in Manchester on a small group of children (1967), and by those responsible for the National Child Development Study (1967), which deals with a national sample, considerably larger than ours, of children born in one week in 1958....

98. Some explanation may be needed about the relatively low weight which attaches to two of the three variables in Table 1. Some readers may be surprised at what they suppose to be the comparatively small influence of the school. To feel thus is to misunderstand the table. What emerged as important about the schools was the experience and competence of teachers. Most teachers have had a similar education and training, and differ less from one another than parents. The parents have usually had their children in their care for their whole lives, whereas most of the class teachers about whom information was collected had been with the children only for the best part of one school year. It must, therefore, be expected that differences between parents will explain more of the variation in children than differences between schools. It is obvious, too, that parental attitudes may themselves be affected by children's performance at school and by the contacts parents have with schools....

100. [A] point that will occur to readers is whether the differences in circumstances account for the differences in attitudes. Our evidence ... suggests that parents' occupation, material circumstances and education explain only about a quarter of the variation in attitudes, leaving three-quarters or more not accounted for. This implies that attitudes could be affected in other ways, and altered by persuasion.

101. Our findings can give hope to the school, to interested parents, and to those responsible for educational policy. Parental attitudes appear as a separate influence because they are not monopolized by any one class. Many manual workers and their wives already encourage and support their children's efforts to learn. If there are many now, there can be even more later. Schools can exercise their influence not only directly upon children but also indirectly through their relationships with parents.

References

FLOUD, J., HALSEY, A. and MARTIN, F. (1956) *Social Class and Educational Opportunity*, London, Heinemann.

FRASER, E. (1954) *Home Environment and the School*, University of London Press.

NATIONAL CHILD DEVELOPMENT STUDY, (1967) 'First Report', in Central Advisory Council for Education (England), *Children and Their Primary Schools*, Vol. 2, Appendix 10, London, HMSO.

WISEMAN, S. (1967) 'The Manchester Survey', in Central Advisory Council for Education (England), *Children and Their Primary Schools*, Vol. 2, Appendix 9, London, HMSO.

Policy Informed by Research: Proposals for the Establishment of Educational Priority Areas

(From Central Advisory Council for Education (England), 1967, *Children and Their Primary Schools*, Vol. 1, London, HMSO, pp. 50, 51, 52–3, 57, 65.)

Within education, the relationship between sociological research and proposals for educational policy was never more clearly demonstrated than in the Plowden Committee's recommendations for the establishment of educational priority areas. Drawing on sociological research and the findings of their own national survey (pp. 206–10), the Committee acknowledged the 'central' role played by schools in disadvantaged areas, either in helping maintain a 'vicious circle' of 'cumulative deprivation', or in helping create a 'virtuous circle' of increased parental interest in education and higher standards of performance from children. In the passage below the Committee makes very strong claims for the importance of the primary school in combatting disadvantage: 'What these deprived areas need most are perfectly normal, good primary schools alive with experience from which children of all kinds can benefit.' Arguments are then advanced for 'positive discrimination' for schools in areas of educational priority and for both an increase in, and a redistribution of, resources devoted to education to help achieve this priority.

132. In a neighbourhood where the jobs people do and the status they hold owe little to their education it is natural for children as they grow older to regard school as a brief prelude to work rather than an avenue to future opportunities. Some of these neighbourhoods have for generations been starved of new schools, new houses and new investment of every kind. Everyone knows this; but for year after year priority has been given to the new towns and new suburbs, because if new schools do not keep pace with the new houses some children will be unable to go to school at all. The continually rising proportion of children staying on at school beyond the minimum age has led some authorities to build secondary schools and postpone the rebuilding of older primary schools. Not surprisingly, many teachers are unwilling to work in a neighbourhood where the schools are old, where housing of the sort they want is unobtainable, and where education does not attain the standards they expect for their own children. From some neighbourhoods, urban and rural, there has been a continuing outflow of the more successful young people. The loss of their enterprise and skill makes things worse for those left behind. Thus the vicious circle may turn from generation to generation and the schools play a central part in the process, both causing and suffering cumulative deprivation. . . .

What these deprived areas need most are perfectly normal, good primary schools alive with experience from which children of all kinds can benefit. What we say elsewhere about primary school work generally applies equally to these difficult areas. The best schools already there show that it is absurd to say, as one used to hear, 'it may be all very well in a nice suburb, but it won't work here'. But, of course, there are special and additional demands on teachers who work in deprived areas with deprived children. They meet special challenges. Teachers must be constantly aware that ideas, values and relationships within the school may conflict with those of the home, and that the world assumed by teachers and school books may be unreal to the children. There will have to be constant communication between parents and the schools if the aims of the schools are to be fully understood. The child from a really impoverished background may well have had a normal, satisfactory emotional life. What he often lacks is the opportunity to develop intellectual interests. This shows in his poor command of language. It is not, however, with vocabulary that teaching can begin. The primary school must first supply experiences and establish relationships which enable children to discriminate, to reason and to express themselves. Placing such children in the right stance for further learning is a very skilled operation....

138.   In our cities there are whole districts which have been scarely touched by the advances made in more fortunate places. Yet such conditions have been overcome and striking progress has been achieved where sufficiently determined and comprehensive attack has been made on the problem. In the most deprived areas, one of H.M. Inspectors reported, 'Some heads approach magnificence, but they cannot do everything ... The demands on them as welfare agents are never ending'. Many children with parents in the least skilled jobs do outstandingly well in school. The educational aspirations of parents and the support and encouragement given to children in some of the poorest neighbourhoods are impressive. Over half of the unskilled workers in our National Survey want their children to stay at school beyond the minimum leaving age. One third of them hoped their children would go to a grammar school or one with similar opportunities. The educational aspirations of unskilled workers for their children have risen year by year. It has been stressed to us that the range of ability in all social classes is so wide that there is a great reservoir of unrealized potential in families dependent on the least skilled and lowest paid work. A larger part of the housing programme than ever before is to be devoted to rebuilding and renewing obsolete and decaying neighbourhoods. The opportunity must be seized to rebuild the schools as well as the houses, and to see that both schools and houses serve families from every social class. It will be possible to make some progress in reducing the size of classes in primary schools in these areas as well as elsewhere. Colleges of education which have taken a special interest in deprived areas report that their students respond in an encouraging fashion to the challenge of working in these neighbourhoods. Most important of all, there is a growing awareness in the nation at large,

greatly stimulated, we believe, by our predecessors' Reports, of the complex social handicaps afflicting such areas and the need for a more radical assault on their problems. These are the strengths on which we can build. How can they be brought to bear?

139. We propose a nation-wide scheme for helping those schools and neighbourhoods in which children are most severely handicapped. . . .
 The principle, already accepted, that special need calls for special help, should be given a new cutting edge. We ask for 'positive discrimination' in favour of such schools and the children in them, going well beyond an attempt to equalize resources. Schools in deprived areas should be given priority in many respects. The first step must be to raise the schools with low standards to the national average; the second, quite deliberately to make them better. The justification is that the homes and neighbourhoods from which many of their children come provide little support and stimulus for learning. The schools must supply a compensating environment. The attempts so far made within the educational system to do this have not been sufficiently generous or sustained, because the handicaps imposed by the environment have not been explicitly and sufficiently allowed for. They should be. . . .

173. Positive discrimination accords with experience and thinking in many other countries, and in other spheres of social policy. It calls both for some redistribution of the resources devoted to education and, just as much, for an increase in their total volume. It must not be interpreted simply as a gloss upon the recommendations which follow. . . . This would not only be a misunderstanding of the scheme; it would destroy all hope of its success. For it would be unreasonable and self-defeating — economically, professionally and politically — to try to do justice by the most deprived children by using only resources that can be diverted from more fortunate areas. We have argued that the gap between the educational opportunities of the most and least fortunate children should be closed, for economic and social reasons alike. It cannot be done, unless extra effort, extra skill and extra resources are devoted to the task.

Policies and Practices in Pursuit of Equality

(From Halsey, A. (Ed.) 1972, *Educational Priority, Vol. 1: EPA Problems and Policies*, London, HMSO, pp. 3, 6, 7–8, 8, 9, 11–12, 12, 180, 198.)

Some sociologists have not only been concerned to investigate the relationship between social class and the educational system, but have gone further and partici- pated in the formulation of and, less often, the enactment of policies directed towards reducing inequalities. For example, in the late 1960s A.H. Halsey who had made a major contribution to demonstrating the relationship between social class and educational opportunity (see pp. 193–6) became national director of an action-research programme set up in response to the Plowden Committee's call for 'research to discover which of the developments in the educational priority areas have the most constructive effects, so as to assist in planning the longer term programme to follow'. Action-research projects were carried out in five urban areas between 1968 and 1971, and their findings published in a series of books. The material reproduced below is taken from the introductory volume to the series, which analyzes 'the EPA problem' and reflects on the work undertaken in relation to pre-schooling, the community school curriculum, and links between the community school, the family and the community. The first passage is a hard-hitting review of past policies and principles used 'to find a strategy for educational roads to equality'. It asserts firmly that 'egalitarian policies have failed' and it outlines how the debate about education and equality has shifted ground over the years. It clearly demons- trates the complex interconnections between political ends and educational means. The second passage outlines the major conclusions of the action-research programme and is curiously optimistic compared with the pessimistic policy analysis presented earlier. In the event, its optimism proved largely misplaced and its initial analysis largely justified. The 'framework of organization for pre-schooling and community schooling' which it advocated did not materialize on a national scale.

Political Ends and Educational Means

To find a strategy for educational roads to equality! That has been a central theme of educational discussion from the beginning of the twentieth century. It has produced a prolific sociology of education over the last generation in which the centrality of educational systems to the structure and the function- ing of industrial societies has become a commonplace. In the nineteen fifties education in these societies was seen as having a crucial role for economic growth and change. More recently the emphasis has shifted to the part played by formal educational organizations in defining what is and what is not knowledge, and as selective agencies allocating individuals to social positions, moulding their social personalities and their definitions of the world around them. But the underlying question is whether, and if so under what circumstances, education can change society ... the essential fact of twentieth century educational history is that egalitarian policies have failed. This must be the starting point for understanding the significance of our studies and to reach it we must review past principles and policies. There appears to us to have been a developing theoretical and practical debate in three stages about the way education can be used as a means towards the political and social end of equality.

In the first phase, from the beginning of the century to the end of the nineteen fifties, the definition of policy was liberal — equality of opportunity. It meant equality of access to the more advanced stages of education for all children irrespective of their sex or social origin in classes, religious and ethnic groups or regions. It therefore expressed itself in such measures as building the scholarship ladder, abolishing grammar school fees, doing away with a system of separate secondary education for the minority and elementary education for the majority and substituting a system of common schooling with secondary schools 'end-on' to primary schools. In the later years of this phase it also meant expansion of higher education....

The essential judgement must be that the 'liberal' policies failed even in their own terms. For example, when, in a large number of the richer countries during the nineteen fifties, a considerable expansion of educational facilities was envisaged, it was more or less assumed that, by making more facilities available, there would be a marked change in the social composition of student bodies and in the flow of people from the less favoured classes into the secondary schools and higher educational institutions. This has certainly not happened to the degree expected. While expansion of education was accompanied by some increase in both the absolute numbers and the proportions from poor families who reached the higher levels and the more prestigious types of education, nevertheless progress towards greater equality of educational opportunity as traditionally defined has been disappointing. It is now plain that the problem is more difficult than had been supposed and needs, in fact, to be posed in new terms (Frankel and Halsey, 1971).

Too much has been claimed for the power of educational systems as instruments for the wholesale reform of societies which are characteristically hierarchical in their distribution of chances in life as between races, classes, the sexes and as between metropolitan/suburban and provincial/rural populations. The typical history of educational expansion in the nineteen fifties and nineteen sixties can be represented by a graph of inequality of attainment between the above-mentioned social categories which has shifted markedly upwards without changing its slope. In other words relative chances did not alter materially despite expansion.... There has been a tendency to treat education as the waste paper basket of social policy — a repository for dealing with social problems where solutions are uncertain or where there is disinclination to wrestle with them seriously. Such problems are prone to be dubbed 'educational' and turned over to the schools to solve. But it was now increasingly plain that the schools cannot accomplish important social reforms such as the democratization of opportunity unless social reforms accompany the educational effort. And it also became more evident that the schools are hampered in achieving even their more traditional and strictly 'educational' purposes when, in societies changing rapidly in their technologies and in the aspirations of their populations, a comparable effort to make the required change in social structures and political organization is lacking.

In summary, it may be said that liberal policies failed basically on an inadequate theory of learning. They failed to notice that the major determinants of educational attainment were not schoolmasters but social situations, not curriculum but motivation, not formal access to the school but support in the family and the community.

So the second phase began with its new emphasis on a theory of non-educational determination of education. In consequence of the experience of the first phase in trying to bring about greater equality of educational opportunity, there had to be a change in the meaning assigned to the phase. Its earlier meaning was equality of access to education: in the second phase its meaning gradually became equality of achievement. In this new interpretation a society affords equality of educational opportunity if the proportion of people from different social, economic or ethnic categories at all levels and in all types of education are more or less the same as the proportion of these people in the population at large. In other words the goal should not be the liberal one of equality of access but equality of outcome for the median member of each identifiable non-educationally defined group, i.e. the *average* woman or negro or proletarian or rural dweller should have the same level of educational attainment as the average male, white, white-collar, suburbanite. If not there has been injustice....

The Plowden Report belongs to this phase in the development of our understanding of the egalitarian issues in education and relates them to the social setting of the school.... In reading the Plowden Report, one could hardly escape the view that equality of opportunity was without equality of conditions, a sham. Home circumstances were obviously critical and these in turn were adversely affected by class and neighbourhood patterns. The school, where, after all, the children spent only five hours of the day, seemed comparatively powerless to alter matters radically of its own volition. Assuredly, a decision to consider the EPA school in its communal setting was a wise one, and the Plowden Committee had been well advised to recommend that community schools should be developed in all areas but especially in EPAs.

Our own definition of the problem in 1968 was consonant with the debate up to this point and was in accord with the Plowden approach accepting that positive discrimination held out the hope of further steps towards the new definition of equality of opportunity.

But in the early months of our work we began to realize that there were unsolved issues behind the equality debate even in its advanced formulation and especially when applied to the children of the educational priority areas. The debate could be taken beyond equality of educational opportunity to a third phase which involves reappraisal of the functions of education in contemporary society. Education for what? The debate over equality as we have summarized it — a movement from preoccupation with equality of access towards concern with equality of outcomes as between social groups — is essentially a discussion about education for whom and to do what. In planning our intervention in schools we were forced sooner or later to consider both questions and in doing so to question whether an EPA programme is anything more than a new formula for fair competition in the educational selection race.

What assumptions could or should be made about the world into which our EPA children would enter after school? Were we concerned simply to introduce a greater measure of justice into an educational system which traditionally selected the minority for higher education and upward social mobility out of the EPA district, leaving the majority to be taught, mainly by a huge hidden curriculum, a sense of their own relative incompetence and impotence — a modern, humane and even relatively enjoyed form of gentling the masses? Or could we assume a wide programme of social reform which would democratize local power structures and diversify local occupational opportunities so that society would look to its schools for a supply of young people educated for political and social responsibility and linked to their communities not by failure in the competition but by rich opportunities for work and life? Even short of the assumption of extra-educational reform how far should we concentrate on making recognition easier for the able minority and how far on the majority who are destined to live their lives in the EPA? And if the latter did this not mean posing an alternative curriculum realistically related to the EPA environment and designed to equip the rising generation with the knowledge and skills to cope with, give power over and in the end to transform the conditions of their local community?

It was, and is, commonly felt that a discriminatory boost was needed in the backward areas to bring education up to scratch.... The Plowden Report argued this respectable and widely held thesis with admirable spirit. It detailed a programme of 'positive discrimination' and 'a new distribution of educational resources', through priority building and minor works, improved staffing and auxiliary help, supplemented salaries and so on. This was designed to cater for 'a great reservoir of unrealized potential', for 'what these deprived areas need most are perfectly normal good primary schools'. Twice over Plowden decreed that the EPA schools should be as good as the best in the land.

Because the national system of education was seen not to operate efficiently in its uniform application across the country, it was accepted that a differential application would help close, to quote Plowden again, 'the gap between the educational opportunities of the most and least fortunate children ... for economic and social reasons alike'. But, logically, an alternative existed. It was worth considering that what was wrong was a uniform system, and that differing areas required different educational formats.

This viewpoint, Eric Midwinter insisted in our early conferences, does no disservice to the pioneers who campaigned for parity of opportunity. They doubtless imagined that equality of opportunity would beget conditions in which forthcoming generations would automatically start at par. This has not, unhappily, transpired. Those working in a deprived area are typically sympathetic to the egalitarian tradition and find the alarums and the postures of the anti-egalitarian commentators laughable. They shout before they are hurt. One might recall the words of R.H. Tawney (1921): of the nation's children, he wrote '... if, instead of rejuvenating the world, they grind corn for the Philistines and doff bobbins for the mill-owners, the responsibility is ours into whose hands the prodigality of nature pours life itself'. Eventually an EPA community must stand on its own feet like any other and rejuvenate its world, and that is a dogma which might hold good on both political wings...

Conclusions

Our major conclusions from the four English EPA action-research projects are that:

1 The educational priority area, despite its difficulties of definition, is a socially and administratively viable unit through which to apply the principle of positive discrimination.

2 Pre-schooling is the outstandingly economical and effective device in the general approach to raising educational standards in EPAs.

3 The idea of the community school, as put forward in skeletal outline by Plowden, has now been shown to have greater substance and powerful implications for community regeneration.

4 There are practical ways of improving the partnership between families and schools in EPAs.

5 There are practical ways of improving the quality of teaching in EPA schools.

6 Action-research is an effective method of policy formation and practical innovation.

7 The EPA can be no more than a part, though an important one, of a comprehensive social movement towards community development and community redevelopment in a modern urban industrial society....

We must finally return to the fundamental question raised [at the beginning of this extract] — the limits of an educational approach to poverty. These limits cannot be removed by any kind of EPA policy. But within them we think we can see a viable road to a higher standard of educational living for hundreds of thousands of children in the more disadvantaged districts.

We have outlined a wide range of policies around the development of pre-schooling and the community school, and we have called for a co-ordinated advance of statutory and voluntary effort. The action-research project method, adroitly constituted to work with 'the system' but with a small but essential element of independence from the normal administrative procedures, has proved itself to be an effective agent of educational change and a magnet for voluntary effort from a wide range of public and private organizations. Such projects, perhaps linked in some cases to the current Community Development Projects, could carry forward the development of EPA policy as we have done in three years from its inception in the Plowden Report. At the same time we would hope that there is sufficient confidence in our results from the first projects for the Government and the local education authorities to create the framework of organization for pre-schooling and community schooling that we have advocated. If so there will be a new landmark in British educational progress.

References

FRANKEL, C. and HALSEY, A. (1971) 'Introduction', *Educational Policies for the 1970s*, Paris, OECD.
TAWNEY, R. (1921) *The Acquisitive Society*, Bell.

Language and Educability

(From Bernstein, B., 1971, *Class, Codes and Control, Vol. 1: Theoretical Studies Towards a Sociology of Language*, London, Routledge and Kegan Paul, pp. 194–5, 196–7, 199–200.)

The theoretical work of Bernstein 'is not only complicated and subtle but extremely general and comprehensive' (Banks, O., 1976, *The Sociology of Education*, 3rd ed., Batsford, p. 110). In his work on a sociology of language, he has been concerned with the interrelationships among culture, social organization, orientation towards certain uses of language, and social class differences in school achievement. He has argued that there is a relationship between social class, forms of family control and communication, and the linguistic codes used by parents and children. Elaborated codes, characteristic of many middle-class homes, involve speakers in elaborating their meanings and making them both explicit and specific; such codes give children access to universalistic orders of meaning conveyed by teachers in schools. Restricted codes, found particularly but not only in lower working-class homes, are characterized by implicit meaning, simplification and rigidity; such codes give children access to particularistic orders of meaning, which are discontinuous with the universalistic meanings transmitted and developed by teachers in schools. Such linguistic discontinuity forms a crucially important part of the total cultural discontinuity between the culture of the school and that of the working-class child. Though difficult to follow and requiring background reading to fill out and explain many of its points, the extract below summarizes Bernstein's sophisticated explanation of how social class differences in language-use are related to social class differences in school achievement. (For a critique see pp. 224–6.)

We can distinguish between uses of language which can be called 'context bound' and uses of language which are less context bound. Consider, for example, the two following stories which Peter Hawkins,... constructed as a result of his analysis of the speech of middle-class and working-class five-year-old children. The children were given a series of four pictures which told a story and they were invited to tell the story. The first picture showed some boys playing football; in the second the ball goes through the window of a house; the third shows a woman looking out of the window and a man making an ominous gesture; and in the fourth the children are moving away.

Here are the two stories:

1 Three boys are playing football and one boy kicks the ball and it goes through the window the ball breaks the window and the boys are looking at it and a man comes out and shouts at them because they've broken the window so they run away and then that lady looks out of her window and she tells the boys off.

2   They're playing football and he kicks it and it goes through there it breaks the window and they're looking at it and he comes out and shouts at them because they've broken it so they run away and then she looks out and she tells them off.

With the first story the reader does not have to have the four pictures which were used as the basis for the story, whereas in the case of the second story the reader would require the initial pictures in order to make sense of the story. The first story is free of the context which generated it, whereas the second story is much more closely tied to its context. As a result the meanings of the second story are implicit, whereas the meanings of the first story are explicit. It is not that the working-class children do not have in their passive vocabulary the vocabulary used by the middle-class children. Nor is it the case that the children differ in their tacit understanding of the linguistic rule system. Rather, what we have here are differences in the use of language arising out of a specific context. One child makes explicit the meanings which he is realizing through language for the person he is telling the story to, whereas the second child does not to the same extent. The first child takes very little for granted, whereas the second child takes a great deal for granted. Thus for the first child the task was seen as a context in which his meanings were required to be made explicit, whereas the task for the second child was not seen as a task which required such explication of meaning. It would not be difficult to imagine a context where the first child would produce speech rather like the second. What we are dealing with here are differences between the children in the way they realize in language-use apparently the same context. We could say that the speech of the first child generated universalistic meanings in the sense that the meanings are freed from the context and so understandable by all, whereas the speech of the second child generated particularistic meanings, in the sense that the meanings are closely tied to the context and would be fully understood by others only if they had access to the context which originally generated the speech. Thus universalistic meanings are less bound to a given context, whereas particularistic meanings are severely context bound....

We can ... say that certain groups of children, through the forms of their socialization, are oriented towards receiving and offering universalistic meanings in *certain contexts*, whereas other groups of children are oriented towards particularistic meanings. The linguistic realization of universalistic orders of meaning are very different from the linguistic realization of particularistic orders of meaning, and so are the forms of the social relation (e.g. between mother and child) which generate these. We can say then that what is made available for learning, how it is made available and the patterns of social relation are also very different.

Now when we consider the children in school we can see that there is likely to be difficulty. For the school is necessarily concerned with the transmission and development of universalistic orders of meaning. The school is concerned with the making explicit and elaborating through language, principles and operations, as these apply to objects (science subjects) and persons (arts subjects). One child, through his socialization, is already sensitive to the symbolic orders of the school, whereas the second child is much less sensitive to the universalistic orders of the school. The second child is oriented towards particularistic orders of meaning which are context bound, in which principles and operations are implicit, and towards a form of language-use through which such meanings are realized. The school is necessarily trying to develop in the child orders of relevance and relation as these apply to persons and objects, which are not initially the ones he spontaneously moves towards. The problem of educability at one level, whether it is in Europe, the USA or newly developing societies, can be understood in terms of a confrontation between the universalistic orders of meaning and the social relationships which generate them, of the school, and the particularistic orders of meanings and the social relationships which generate them, which the child brings with him to the school....

I have stressed that the school is attempting to transmit uncommon-sense knowledge, that is, public knowledge realized through various meta-languages. Such knowledge I have called universalistic. However, it is also the case that the school is both implicitly and explicitly transmitting values and their attendant morality which affect educational contents and contexts of education. They do this by establishing criteria for acceptable pupil and staff conduct. Further, these values and morals affect the *content* of educational knowledge through the selection of books, texts, films *and* through examples and analogies used to assist access to public knowledge (universalistic meanings). Thus the working-class child may be placed at a considerable disadvantage in relation to the *total* culture of the school. It is not made for him; he may not answer to it.

Now I have suggested that the forms of an elaborated code give access to universalistic orders of meaning in the sense that the principles and operations controlling object and person relationships are made explicit through the use of language, whereas restricted codes give access to particularistic orders of meaning in which the principles and operations controlling object and person relationships are rendered implicit through the use of language.... Because the sub-culture or culture through its forms of social integration generates a restricted code, it does not mean that the resultant speech and meaning system is linguistically or culturally deprived, that the children have nothing to offer the school, that their imaginings are not significant. Nor does it mean that we have to teach the children formal grammar. Nor does it mean that we have to interfere with their dialect. There is nothing, but nothing, in the dialect as such, which prevents a child from internalizing and learning to use universalistic meanings. But if the contexts of learning, the examples, the reading books, are not contexts which are triggers for the children's imaginings, are not triggers on the children's curiosity and explorations in his family and community, then the child is not at home in the educational world. If the teacher has to say continuously, 'Say it again darling, I didn't understand you', then in the end the child may say nothing. *If the culture of the teacher is to become part of the consciousness of the child, then the culture of the child must first be in the consciousness of the teacher.* This may mean that the teacher must be able to understand the child's dialect, rather than deliberately attempt to change it. Much of the contexts of our schools are unwittingly drawn from aspects of the symbolic world of the middle class, and so when the child steps into school he is stepping into a symbolic system which does not provide for him a linkage with his life outside.

It is an accepted educational principle that we should work with what the child can offer: why don't we practise it? The introduction of the child to the universalistic meanings of public forms of thought is not compensatory education — *it is education.* It is in itself not making children middle class. The implicit values underlying the form and contents of the educational environment might. We need to distinguish between the principles and operations, that is our task as teachers to transmit and develop in the children, *and* the contexts we create in order to do this. We should start knowing that the social experience the child already possesses is valid and significant, and that this social experience should be reflected back to him as being valid and significant. It can be reflected back to him only if it is a part of the texture of the learning experience we create. If we spent as much time thinking through the implications of this as we do thinking about the implications of the Piagetian developmental sequences, then possibly schools might become exciting and challenging environments for parents, children and teachers.

Continuity or Discontinuity between Home and School Experience of Language: A Critique of Bernstein's Views

(From Edwards, A., 1976, *Language in Culture and Class*, Oxford, Heinemann, pp. 145–7.)

The previous extract and its editorial introduction could not do justice to the subtlety and complexity of Bernstein's contribution to a sociology of language. Likewise, this passage is simply illustrative of the critiques of Bernstein's work undertaken by linguists, socio-linguists and sociologists of education. Much of the criticism has centred on the ambiguous concept of 'code' and on the interpretation of 'restricted code' as referring to an inferior form of speech. For examples of criticisms the reader is referred to Coulthard (1969), Jackson (1974), Grimshaw (1973) and Rosen (1972). The passage below, taken from an extended scrutiny of Bernstein's work, has been chosen to complement the previous extract where Bernstein suggested a cultural and linguistic discontinuity experienced by lower working-class children in schools. Edwards argues that 'the school end of this discontinuity of experience is described with infuriating vagueness'. He maintains that in the absence of extensive research into the forms and functions of classroom language, it could equally well be argued that in some schools (described as 'highly ritualized' and 'hierarchical'), there might be 'too much continuity between home and school experience of language'. At the very least, Edwards throws doubt on the adequacy of Bernstein's account of how social class differences in language-use are related to social class differences in school achievement.

References

COULTHARD, M. (1969) 'A discussion of restricted and elaborated codes', *Educational Review*, 22, 1, pp. 38–50.

GRIMSHAW, A. (1973) 'On langue in society, Part 1', *Contemporary Sociology*, 2.

JACKSON, L. (1974) 'The myth of elaborated and restricted codes', *Higher Educational Review*, 6, pp. 65–81.

ROSEN, H. (1972) *Language and Class: A Critical Look at the Theories of Basil Bernstein*, Falling Wall Press.

Bernstein's argument is *not* reducible to a matter of stylistic elaboration because of its emphasis on the functions of language, and the kinds of meaning being transmitted. The 'discontinuity' which he identifies is not 'linguistic', but what he calls 'cultural' and might have called 'sociolinguistic'. The lower working-class pupil is described as having had less experience of elaborated speech variants in two areas of experience obviously relevant to school, those of control and instruction. He has learned to look to adults as the source of directives, but not for the reasons for their orders, or the principles by which he should control his own behaviour. He faces problems in school because he is not used to feeling a personal responsibility for his actions, or to lengthy probing of his motives, or to subtly-phrased and indirect commands. He has special difficulties in learning because his curiosity has been less often rewarded, his questions have less often been answered in ways directly relevant to them, his awkward questions have been more often evaded, and his attention has been drawn less often to the general principles underlying concrete examples. Above all, he has had less experience of being offered alternatives to explore, and problems to solve for which the solutions are diverse or uncertain. He will be ill at ease with the universalistic orders of meaning which are emphasized in schools.

There are two main directions from which this summary can be questioned. Are the lower working-class children like this? And are schools like this? The school end of this discontinuity of experience is described with infuriating vagueness. Justifiably enough, the main efforts of the SRU [the Sociological Research Unit] went into the intensive investigation of family roles and relationships. The orientation of the lower working-class child was towards 'closed' roles and particularistic meanings. Schools, however, 'are predicated upon an elaborated code and its system of social relationships' (1973, p. 212; also 1970, p. 117). Does this mean *all* schools, at all age levels, in all degrees of selectivity, in all varieties of expressive or instrumental orientation? There is an interesting contrast between the 'global' assumptions about schools in Bernstein's writing on language, and the carefully differentiated analysis to be found in his writing on organization and curriculum (Bernstein 1967; 1971). If disbelief is suspended, the idealization takes the following shape. In formal education, principles and operations are made verbally explicit. They are freed from their immediate context, and from the implicit background knowledge made available by a shared cultural identity. Such universalistic meanings can be self-consciously examined, the grounds for them scrutinized. Though at some risk of insecurity and even alienation, alternative realities can be contemplated. Meanings are therefore provisional, open to change. They can arise only from relationships that are themselves open to change — which are personal and achieved, not positional and ascribed. Entering such an environment, the lower working-class child steps into a symbolic system which provides few links with his life outside (Bernstein 1970, p. 120). Yet all this would not be true of the highly ritualized hierarchical school; or the 'closed' school; or the school where what counted as knowledge was strongly 'classified' and 'framed'. Selecting some 'traditional' characteristics of schools (such as are described in Bernstein's own writing), it could be argued that meanings are too often 'given' as part of a natural order which cannot be questioned; that children are too rarely encouraged actively to enquire, experiment, and 'create their own world on their own terms in their own way'; that the boundary between teacher and learner is too clear, the latter having too little discretion; and that the individual child is so submerged in the pupil role that meanings relate not to him but to the category in which he is fitted. The counter-argument is as tendentious and over-generalized as the original target. But when Bernstein describes, in relation to the critical contexts of socialization, the underlying system of communication which is regulated through a restricted code, it is tempting to see some schools as fitting that picture without undue distortion. In so far as they do, their lower working-class pupils should, in Bernstein's own terms, feel perfectly at home. An underlying restricted code is found where communication is 'realized through forms of speech where meanings are implicit, principles infrequently elaborated, qualified or explored, infrequently related to the specific experience of the child or the specific requirements of the local context, where alternative possibilities are infrequently offered, where questioning is less encouraged' (in Gahagan and Gahagan 1970, p. 116). If *some* schools resemble this description, then extending their working-class pupils' range of control over language (crudely, 'teaching them' an elaborated code) will require new roles, functions and communicative tasks more demanding than the traditional classroom routines. Otherwise there will be too *much* continuity between home and school experience of language. That suggestion must be tentative because we know so little about the forms and functions of classroom language, and about how the sociolinguistic rules relevant to them are learned and applied.

References

BERNSTEIN, B. (1967) 'Open schools, open society', *New Society*, 14 pp. 351–3.
BERNSTEIN, B. (1970) 'A critique of compensatory education', in RUBINSTEIN, D. and STONEMAN, C. (Eds) *Education for Democracy*, Harmondsworth, Penguin.
BERNSTEIN, B. (1971) 'On the classification and framing of educational knowledge', in YOUNG, M. (Ed.) *Knowledge and Control: New Directions in the Sociology of Education*, Collier-Macmillan.
BERNSTEIN, B. (1973) *Class, Codes and Control; Vol. 1: Theoretical Studies towards A Sociology of Language*, Paladin Books.
GAHAGAN, D. and GAHAGAN, G. (1970) *Talk Reform: Explorations in Language for Infant School Children*, London, Routledge and Kegan Paul.

The Sociological Study of Educational Knowledge

(From Bernstein, B., 1975, *Class, Codes and Control. Vol. 3: Towards a Theory of Educational Transmissions*, 2nd ed., London, Routledge and Kegan Paul, pp. 85, 86–7, 87–9, 90–1, 91, 93–4.)

As indicated in the general introduction to this section of the source book, one of the 'new directions' taken by the sociology of education during the last decade or so has been the study of educational knowledge, including teachers' professional knowledge (see pp. 246–50) and knowledge enshrined in curricula. Bernstein has made a major contribution to this study, as he has done to the sociology of language. In his (1981) *Perspectives on the Sociology of Education* (Routledge and Kegan Paul), Robinson argues that Bernstein's 'work on the organization of knowledge is an extension of [his] earlier work and has been running parallel to the language theories since 1964. The essential problem that he addresses is common to both aspects of his work, namely the reproduction of the conditions through which social control is managed, how consciousness is structured by the pattern of class relationships in which the individual is located'. The passage below is taken from an influential paper in which Bernstein makes a number of important conceptual distinctions to aid in the study of curricula as socially organized knowledge. In the paper he distinguishes between curriculum, pedagogy and evaluation, and then (in this extract) goes on to use his concepts of 'classification' and 'framing' to generate a typology of educational knowledge codes which can be used to conceptualize the curricula of primary or secondary schools. In a later part of the paper (not reproduced here) he speculates on the consequences of the use of these knowledge codes for the exercise of social control and the shaping of children's consciousness in schools.

Introduction

How a society selects, classifies, distributes, transmits and evaluates the educational knowledge it considers to be public, reflects both the distribution of power and the principles of social control. From this point of view, differences within, and change in, the organization, transmission and evaluation of educational knowledge should be a major area of sociological interest (Bernstein, B., 1966, 1967; Davies, D.I., 1970a, 1970b; Musgrove, 1968; Hoyle, 1969; Young, M., 1971). Indeed, such a study is a part of the larger question of the structure and changes in the structure of cultural transmission. For various reasons British sociologists have fought shy of this question. As a result, the sociology of education has been reduced to a series of input-output problems; the school has been transformed into a complex organization or people-processing institution; the study of socialization has been trivialized....

Two Types of Curricula

Initially, I am going to talk about the curriculum in a very general way. In all educational institutions there is a formal punctuation of time into periods. These may vary from ten minutes to three hours or more. I am going to call each such formal period of time a 'unit'. I shall use the word 'content' to describe how the period of time is used. I shall define a curriculum initially in terms of the principle by which units of time and their contents are brought into a special relationship with each other. I now want to look more closely at the phrase 'special relationship'.

First, we can examine relationships between contents in terms of the amount of time accorded to a given content. Immediately, we can see that more time is devoted to some contents rather than others. Second, some of the contents may, from the point of view of the pupils, be compulsory or optional. We can now take a very crude measure of the relative status of a content in terms of the number of units given over to it, and whether it is compulsory or optional. This raises immediately the question of the relative status of a given content and its significance in a given educational career.

We can, however, consider the relationship between contents from another, perhaps more important, perspective. We can ask about any given content whether the boundary between it and another content is clear-cut or blurred. To what extent are the various contents well insulated from each other. If the various contents are well insulated from each other, I shall say that the contents stand in a *closed* relation to each other. If there is reduced insulation between contents, I shall say that the contents stand in an *open* relationship to each other. So far, then, I am suggesting that we can go into any educational institution and examine the organization of time in terms of the relative status of contents, and whether the contents stand in an open/closed relationship to each other.... I shall now distinguish between two broad types of curricula. If contents stand in a closed relation to each other, that is if the contents are clearly bounded and insulated from each other, I shall call such a curriculum a *collection* type. Here, the learner has to collect a group of favoured contents in order to satisfy some criteria of evaluation. There may of course be some underlying concept to a collection: the gentleman, the educated man, the skilled man, the non-vocational man.

Now I want to juxtapose against the collection type, a curriculum where the various contents do not go their own separate ways, but where the contents stand in an open relation to each other. I shall call such a curriculum an integrated type. Now we can have various types of collection, and various degrees and types of integration.

Classification and Frame

I shall now introduce the concepts, classification and frame, which will be used to analyze the underlying structure of the three message systems, curriculum, pedagogy and evaluation, which are realizations of the educational knowledge code. The basic idea is embodied in the principle used to distinguish the two types of curricula: collection and integrated. Strong insulation between contents pointed to a collection type, whereas reduced insulation pointed to an integrated type. The principle here is the strength of the *boundary* between contents. This notion of boundary strength underlies the concepts of classification and frame.

Classification, here, does not refer to *what* is classified, but to the *relationships* between contents. Classification refers to the nature of the differentiation between contents. Where classification is strong, contents are well insulated from each other by strong boundaries. Where classification is weak, there is reduced insulation between contents, for the boundaries between contents are weak or blurred. *Classification thus refers to the degree of boundary maintenance between contents.* Classification focuses our attention upon boundary strength as the critical distinguishing feature of the division of labour of educational knowledge. It gives us, as I hope to show, the basic structure of the message system, curriculum.

The concept, frame, is used to determine the structure of the message system, pedagogy. Frame refers to the form of the *context* in which knowledge is transmitted and received. Frame refers to the specific pedagogical relationship of teacher and taught. In the same way as classification does not refer to contents, so frame does not refer to the contents of the pedagogy. Frame refers to the strength of the boundary between what may be transmitted and what may not be transmitted, in the pedagogical relationship. Where framing is strong, there is a sharp boundary, where framing is weak, a blurred boundary, between what may and may not be transmitted. Frame refers us to the range of options available to teacher and taught in the *control* of what is transmitted and received in the context of the pedagogical relationship. Strong framing entails reduced options; weak framing entails a range of options. *Thus frame refers to the degree of control teacher and pupil possess over the selection, organization, pacing and timing of the knowledge transmitted and received in the pedagogical relationship.*

There is another aspect of the boundary relationship between what may be taught and what may not be taught and, consequently, another aspect to framing. We can consider the relationship between the non-school everyday community knowledge of the teacher or taught, *and* the educational knowledge transmitted in the pedagogical relationship. We can raise the question of the strength of the boundary, the degree of insulation, between the everyday community knowledge of teacher and taught and educational knowledge. Thus, we can consider variations in the strength of frames as these refer to the strength of the boundary between educational knowledge and everyday community knowledge of teacher and taught. . . .

A Typology of Educational Knowledge Codes

In the light of the conceptual framework we have developed, I shall use the distinction between collection and integrated curricula in order to realize a typology of types and sub-types of educational codes. The *formal* basis of the typology is the strength of classification and frames. However, the sub-types will be distinguished, initially, in terms of substantive differences.

Any organization of educational knowledge which involves strong classification gives rise to what is here called a collection code. Any organization of educational knowledge which involves a marked attempt to reduce the strength of classification is here called an integrated code. Collection codes may give rise to a series of sub-types, each varying in the relative strength of their classification and frames. Integrated codes can also vary in terms of the strength of frames, as these refer to the *teacher/pupil/student* control over the knowledge that is transmitted.

Figure 5.1 sets out general features of the typology.

Collection Codes

The first major distinction *within* collection codes is between specialized and non-specialized types. The extent of specialization can be measured in terms of the number of closed contents publicly examined at the end of the secondary educational stage. Thus in England, *although there is no formal limit*, the student usually sits for three 'A' level subjects, compared with the much greater range of subjects which make up the Ábitur in Germany, the Baccalauréat in France, or the Studente Exam in Sweden.

Within the English specialized type, we can distinguish two varieties: a pure and an impure variety. The pure variety exists where 'A' level subjects are drawn from a common universe of knowledge, e.g. Chemistry, Physics, Mathematics. The impure variety exists where 'A' level subjects are drawn from different universes of knowledge, e.g. Religion, Physics, Economics. . . .

Within the non-specialized collection code, we can distinguish two varieties, according to whether a subject or course is the basic knowledge unit. Thus the standard European form of the collection code is non-specialized, *subject*-based. The USA form of the collection is non-specialized, *course*-based. . . .

Figure 5.1

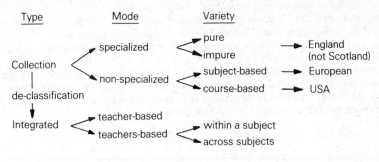

Integrated Codes

Integration, as it is used here, refers minimally to the *subordination* of previously insulated subjects *or* courses to some *relational* idea, which blurs the boundaries between the subjects. We can distinguish two types. The first type is *teacher*-based. Here the teacher, as in the infant school, has an extended block of time with often the same group of children. The teacher may operate with a collection code and keep the various subjects distinct and insulated, or he can blur the boundaries between the different subjects. This type of integrated code is easier to introduce than the second type, which is *teachers*-based. Here, integration involves relationships with other teachers. In this way, we can have degrees of integration in terms of the number of teachers involved.

We can further distinguish two varieties according to whether the integration refers to a group of teachers *within* a common subject, or the extent to which integration involves teachers of different subjects. Whilst integrated codes, by definition, have the weakest classification, they may vary as to framing. During the initiating period, the frames the teachers enter will be weak, but other factors will affect the final frame strength. It is also possible that the frames the *pupils* enter can vary in strength.

Thus integrated codes may be confined to one subject or they can cross subjects. We can talk of code strength in terms of the range of different subjects co-ordinated by the code, or if this criterion cannot be applied, code strength can be measured in terms of the *number* of teachers co-ordinated through the code. Integrated codes can also vary as to frame strength as this applies to teachers or pupils or both.

References

BERNSTEIN, B. (1967) 'Open schools, open society?', *New Society*, 14 September.
BERNSTEIN, B., ELVIN, L. and PETERS, R. (1966) 'Ritual in education', *Philosophical Transactions of the Royal Society of London*, Series B, 251, No. 772.

DAVIES, D.I. (1970a) 'The management of knowledge: A critique of the use of typologies in educational sociology', *Sociology*, 4, 1.
DAVIES, D.I. (1970b) 'Knowledge, education and power', paper presented to the British Sociological Association Annual Conference, Durham.
HOYLE, E. (1969) 'How does the curriculum change? (1) A proposal for enquiries (2) Systems and strategies', *Journal of Curriculum Studies*, 1, 2; 1, 3.
MUSGROVE, F. (1968) 'The contribution of sociology to the study of the curriculum', in KERR, J. (Ed.) *Changing the Curriculum*, University of London Press.
YOUNG, M. (1971) 'Curricula as socially organized knowledge', in YOUNG, M. (Ed.) *Knowledge and Control*, Collier-Macmillan.

Visible and Invisible Pedagogies:
An Introductory Overview

(From Robinson, P., 1981, *Perspectives on the Sociology of Education: An Introduction*, London, Routledge and Kegan Paul, pp. 120–1.)

Bernstein's interest in the sociology of educational knowledge has involved not just the curriculum (the focus of the previous extract) but also pedagogy — the way the curriculum is transmitted. In this summary by Robinson, Bernstein's distinctions between 'visible' and 'invisible' pedagogies are discussed and related to his previous work on classification, framing, and educational knowledge codes (pp. 227–32). An 'invisible' pedagogy, believed by Bernstein to be institutionalized at the level of the infant school, is seen to be a pervasive influence for the exercise of social control and thus important in the process of social reproduction in capitalist society. For further elaboration, readers are referred to Bernstein's original paper, 'Class and pedagogies: Visible and invisible', in Bernstein, B. (1975) *Class, Codes and Control, Vol. 3: Towards a Theory of Educational Transmissions*, 2nd ed., London, Routledge and Kegan Paul, pp. 116–56.

[In his discussion of pedagogy, Bernstein] suggests three factors which regulate the teacher-pupil relationship. These are the factors of hierarchy, sequencing rules, and criteria, each having an explicit and implicit dimension. Hierarchy refers to the power within the relationship, either unambiguously explicit as in 'I am in control because I am the teacher', or implicitly where there are no *overt* rules. The stress on 'overt' is crucial — the paradox of implicit hierarchies is that although on the surface there may appear to be no rules nevertheless rules exist. In the infant classroom the teacher may invite the children to 'do your own thing', to take responsibility for their own learning. The children quickly come to appreciate, however, that 'doing your own thing' does not include setting fire to the Wendy House or throwing sand across the classroom! Under the apparent freedom there is control and the child must learn the markers to that control.

The second aspect to the teacher-pupil relationship is the sequencing rules which regulate the order in which transmission takes place. If the rules are explicit, there is a clear recognition of what is appropriate to the child at any particular stage. Every teacher has experienced, for example, going into a noisy classroom and saying, 'What class is this?' and, on being told a fourth-year class, responding, 'I thought it was the first year, the amount of noise you were making.' There is appropriate behaviour at appropriate stages; if the rules are implicit, 'the sex and chronological age of the child do not become strong marking features of the sequencing rules'. In this case only the teacher will be aware of what is appropriate, picking up cues from the child's behaviour as to his reading readiness or developmental stage.

Finally the transmission realizes criteria of accomplishment which also may be explicit or implicit. If explicit the teacher on asking, for example, the child to draw a house will criticize the production if it does not have windows, or if the windows are in the 'wrong' place. If the criteria of accomplishment are implicit, the child is invited to 'Tell me all about your painting'. The criteria are apparently the child's. However the paradox reappears when at the end of the lesson not every picture is put on the wall for all to see; or if we had given the example of a piece of written work, not every piece is typed-up and placed in the class story book. Under the openness of the relationship there are criteria, there is control though its nature changes. Where the hierarchy, sequencing rules and criteria are *explicit* Bernstein labels the form of transmission one of *visible pedagogy*; where they are *implicit* he labels the form of transmission one of *invisible pedagogy*.

... Bernstein argues that under an integrated code, more of the pupil and teacher enter the pedagogical relationship. This can now be expanded by linking to his discussion of visible and invisible pedagogies. As the strength of classification weakens, so what counts as knowledge becomes more open to negotiation, the child may bring more of his world into the classroom. But in doing so he introduces more of himself as a unique person. Within a visible pedagogy (that is strong framing and strong classification) the teacher need not know her pupils as people; symbolically she enters the classroom through one door and the pupils through another and the two need never meet. This type of relationship is epitomized by the mass lecture in higher education — the personal biography of both lecturer and student is not relevant to the occasion. Within an invisible pedagogy, (weak framing and weak classification), the teacher knows more about the child as a person and must also reveal more of herself, if only to admit ignorance in answer to a pupil's question. But as more of the pupil is available so less of his unique self is protected from the school's influences, hence the paradox that although the invisible pedagogy appears to be the open, liberal pedagogy, it is also more pervasive in its control, the child begins to internalize the requirements of the classroom.

Bernstein is talking about the curriculum [and pedagogy] at a high level of theoretical abstraction, necessarily so if we are to begin to understand the place of education in the process of social reproduction. The curriculum is not a neutral package of knowledge which responds to the natural demands of the wider society. [Together with pedagogy] it is a vehicle both for increasing the child's knowledge of the world but also for moulding her stance towards that world, as Wylie puts it, 'From the attitude of teachers, from the way in which school work is presented, from the textbooks, the children learn to make basic assumptions concerning the nature of reality and their relationship to it' (1973, p. 73).

Bernstein has begun an exploration of how children might come to make basic assumptions about the nature of reality; the strength of his model lies in bringing together content and form, curriculum and transmission, and linking both to the process of social reproduction within society. Its weakness is that some of the links in the argument are ambiguous and await further development.

Reference

WYLIE, L. (1973) *Village in the Vaucluse*, Harvard University Press.

Control, Accountability and William Tyndale

(From Dale, R., 1981, 'Control, accountability and William Tyndale', in Dale R. *et al.* (Eds), *Education and the State, Vol. 2: Politics, Patriarchy and Practice*, Falmer Press/The Open University, pp. 308–14, 314–16.)

The increasing prominence of neo-Marxist scholarship in the sociology of education has helped redirect attention to the relationship between the educational, political and economic systems at national level. Because of Marxist preoccupation with problems of historical change and process, it has also led to a renewed emphasis on historical perspectives to this relationship. Dale's paper, from which this extract has been taken, analyzes aspects of the recent history of education and relates these to political forces. It is an example of what Ahier and Flude (1983) term 'a more policy-oriented and politically aware sociology of education'. In it, Dale examines changes in the control of schooling and the accountability of teachers, and the role played in these changes by the William Tyndale affair (pp. 45–50). He argues that the affair facilitated, but did not cause, changes in the structure of the educational system towards greater central control. In particular, it dealt a final blow to the basis of the management of the English educational system enshrined in the 1944 Education Act (pp. 35–7); it helped justify the replacement of teachers' professional judgement by bureaucratic accountability; and it contributed to the erosion of the teaching profession's influence on educational policy.

Reference

AHIER, J. and FLUDE, M. (Eds) (1983) *Contemporary Education Policy*, London, Croom Helm.

The Management of Education

The Tyndale affair has been widely regarded as a management problem. It is seen as posing questions both about how conflict between individuals and groups can be settled, and about what institutional machinery is most likely to bring about this desirable end. Yet, as in so many other areas, what happened at William Tyndale served to bring concentrated attention to bear on a problem which was far from novel, through a dramatic demonstration of some of the more extreme difficulties the problem might entail.

It was already clear before 1975 that the basis of the management of the English education system, enshrined in the 1944 Education Act, was in a rapidly advancing state of decay. The social, economic and educational context of 1944 had been transformed by the late 1960s, placing an increasingly unabsorbable strain on the assumptions on which the system was based. The two most crucial assumptions were those of a balance of power, and a supra-political consensus. The 1944 Act sought to create a balance between central and local government and the teaching profession such that:

> power over the distribution of resources, over the organization and context of education was to be diffused among the different elements and no one of them was to be given a controlling voice ... the DES was not given strong formal powers to secure the implementation of its policies because it was assumed that both central government and local education authorities were managed by men of good will whose main concern was to improve the service and whose reflective judgements remained untainted by the intrusion of party ideology (Bogdanor, 1979).

The second part of that quotation is shot through with an ideology of supra party consensus on education; this was to be achieved through consultation with all interested parties. Thus, as Bogdanor (1979) further states:

> Were any element in the system to seek to use its formal powers to the full, the system could not work. Mutual constraint, as in the Hobbesian universe, is the precondition of success, and the war of all against all would make progress in education impossible. There must, therefore, be limits on the degree of politicization of the education service if it is to operate successfully.

There are at least five shortcomings to be noted with respect to this system of education management. First of all, it quite clearly does not reflect the situation in the system it was set up to control at all accurately. The comprehensive schools issue alone, culminating in the Tameside judgement, knocks the props out completely from under a system premissed on the exclusion of party politics from educational matters and some sort of permanently available central-local consensus. Second, as Bogdanor too points out, the system is ineffective in directing the education system into new pathways. Since 1944, the potential contribution of education to both individual and national economic prosperity has been widely acknowledged, but a system which rests on no one party taking an undue initiative in its direction has responded only slowly to the challenges contained in the role of education in the development of human capital. (This is not to suggest that the system of education management alone is responsible for this failure, very far from it.) Third, again as noted by Bogdanor, such a system is able to operate much better in periods of expansion than in periods of retrenchment, when squabbles between the parties to the consensus over the distribution of even scarcer resources may become inevitable. Fourth, there has been in recent years evidence of a change in the style of education management, at both national and local level, towards a 'managerialism' emphasizing efficiency rather than broadening access (see David, 1978), with the DES coming under the influence of a manpower planning ideology (see Tapper and Salter, 1978). At a local level this has been accompanied by a growth in the size of local authorities following the 1974 reorganization of local government, and by the introduction in many of them of a system of 'corporate management' drawn from industrial and business use and intended primarily to increase efficiency (see Cockburn, 1977). Finally, the assumptions have been challenged by an increasing desire for participation in the control of the education system by many of the groups affected by it but excluded from influence over it. As Bogdanor (1979) puts it:

> in particular the move towards greater participation in education has done much to undermine traditional arrangements. For the system of consultation worked best, when only a small number of interests were involved whose rank and file were content to defer to elites, and could, therefore, be relied upon to act 'sensibly'.

(And what did William Tyndale do to that?!) As David has shown, pressure towards greater participation in the control of education was already building up in the late 1960s. At that time such pressure was associated with radical efforts at securing greater community control over schools; it is interesting that such moves were nowhere near as successful as the articulation of 'parent power' to a much more conservative political stance in the past three or four years, and it is difficult to avoid seeing an effect of William Tyndale here. What the Tyndale case was used to demonstrate was the importance of parents having some say in what was going on at their children's school, rather than an example, albeit rather flawed, of an attempt to set up a school more responsive to its local community than to perceived national priorities.

It is fairly clear that the Tyndale affair did have some effects in the area of the management of education. It served to deliver the final blow to the 1944 system by demonstrating that its several shortcomings could jointly lead to disaster. It had, perhaps, two particular effects in this area. First, it appeared to show that the pursuit of national economic goals could be not merely ignored but actually frustrated in a system where clear central leadership was absent; in this way it made the path to greater DES intervention in the education system much smoother. And second, it greatly enhanced the likelihood that the progress of parent participation in schooling would be articulated in a conservative rather than any kind of progressive or radical philosophy of schooling.

Teachers' Classroom Autonomy

The assumption that the education system was governed by a more or less implicit consensus about aims and objectives, strategies and tactics had considerable effects at the level of the management of individual schools, too. For, as Pateman (1978) argues, where the goals of schooling were expressed in terms of implicit understandings rather than explicit targets, this:

> increased the power of both teachers and inspectors. In the case of teachers it made it difficult for them to be held to account by either parents or managers with whom it was possible, if desired, to play a 'catch us if you can' game. In the case of inspectors, it required of them a hermeneutic understanding of the schools, the efficiency of which they were assessing . . . Education, like medicine and the law, had its mysteries to which teachers and inspectors were privy, and parents and politicians were not.

This approach is developed further in Dale and Trevitt-Smith (1976). In a consensual situation teachers' classroom autonomy has plenty of space to develop — in such a situation:

> the extent to which a school board can hold teachers or a school to account for its performance is strictly limited, since by definition its members are not expert and can at best only claim to be able to identify cases of gross incompetence, gross inefficiency and plain corruption — and even here they may well feel constrained to rely on the advice of the head teacher or an inspector.

Two common explanations of the Tyndale case, one from 'sympathetic liberals', and the other from more cynical radicals, become pertinent here. A common argument from people not unsympathetic to the Tyndale teachers is that what they were attempting was fine in theory (and some versions go on to indicate that similar things are being done with impunity in other schools) but they just were not very good at carrying through these admittedly very difficult practices and policies. Chaos inevitably ensued, to a degree that was interfering with any kind of effective education of the children. The more cynical view suggests that what happened to the Tyndale teachers merely confirms what we knew all along, namely that all the talk about professional autonomy was just a hoax — when it is put to the test, when someone actually treats it seriously, then its bogus nature is immediately revealed.

Both these arguments seem to be too simple and to ignore some of the complexities of the situation. The first argument assumes the persistence of a consensus about education; according to Pateman (1978), a logical precondition for teacher autonomy '. . . when the ends of education cease to be consensual . . . the claim to professional freedom logically collapses. For in such a situation there is no longer a neutral professional dealing in expertly-assessable means', albeit one that has changed over the years and is now represented, in primary schools at any rate, by what might be called 'Plowdenism'. John White (1977) puts this very clearly: 'It is one of the ironies of this case that they were, after all, only putting into practice in a radical form the theories that had been pumped into them in their own training and which have, between Hadow and Plowden, become the official gospel of the primary world'. Two points need to be made about this. First, the teachers at William Tyndale saw themselves as going well beyond Plowdenism — in April 1975 Brian Hadow had attacked 'the late 1960s style of informal progressive repression', advocated the abolition of 'point-less structure' and called for more egalitarian systems for staff and children. (The teachers' views on progressive education are set out in Ellis *et al.*, 1976). Thus, 'incompetent Plowdenism' seems an ineffective charge to lay at their door. Second, I have argued elsewhere (1979a, 1979b) that the period of dominance of the Plowden consensus was already very much on the wane, and was yet another educational phenomenon whose end was has-tened rather than directly brought about by its being dragged into the Tyndale affair. Effectively, then, teacher autonomy was being treated under a form assuming a consensus regime some time after a consensus could in fact be established. Hence the conditions for the kind of teacher autonomy premissed on consensus were absent; it was only a matter of time before their absence was discovered.

The other pat response to the Tyndale affair — its exposure of the hoax of teacher autonomy — also rests on a number of rather fragile and vague assumptions about the nature of teacher autonomy. Essentially, they make the exercise of teacher autonomy far too voluntaristic, indeed far too easy. What they miss is the situated nature of teachers' classroom autonomy, and even, indeed, its political nature. Only its suppression is seen as a political act; its practice by teachers in situations like that at William Tyndale is seen rather as the expression of inalienable professional rights. Yet Pateman's argument shows that it is only in the relatively narrow — and in a sense self-defeating — context of working within a consensus framework that the assertion of teacher classroom autonomy — if that means doing something different from what is officially expected of them, which it usually implicitly does — is anything other than a political challenge which must be inter-preted and acted on as such.

Oddly similar in some ways to this cynical interpretation of the Tyndale affair is the more popular and more right wing view which sees the teachers as abusing their power and deserving everything they got. This account, too, turns on a particular interpretation of teacher autonomy. There are very many, very widely recognized, constraints on teacher autonomy, some of which it is impossible for individual teachers to overcome — such as the teacher pupil ratio, the inability of schools to choose whom they will teach and so on — others of which it is possible, if very difficult, to overcome — such as the expectation that children will be taught the 3 R's or that they will not be tortured. Teachers have an implicit mandate to combat ignorance and indiscipline and they have to carry it out in particular circumstances (such as the teacher — pupil ratio, external examination demands) which themselves entail certain constraints (Dale, 1976, 1977). Within these constraints, teachers are relatively free to carry out their duties as they will. They are only relatively free since, first, they remain at the bottom of a hierarchy of authority and subject to the immediate control of their head teacher and, second, the ways in which they exercise the freedom available to them are subject both to the constraints of the classroom situation, its 'hidden curriculum', and to the assumptions about what it is to be a teacher which they distil from their own pupil experience, their teacher training and their teacher experience (Dale, 1977). One result of this, for instance is to make a cognitive style of individualism very prominent among teachers (Dale, 1978). It is for this reason, rather than any lack of imagination or initiative on the part of teachers, that what autonomy teachers have has both tended to be minimized in much writing about teaching, and to have had a confirmatory, rather than disruptive effect on the education system. Consequent to this modifying of possible autonomy, it was possible for teachers to be granted a 'licensed autonomy' within the education system without danger of this leading to a revolutionary, or even radical, transformation of the system.

What the Tyndale teachers appear to have done, however, and what led to the charges of abuse of autonomy, was to step outside the implicit and internalized guidelines as to how what autonomy they had should be used, as much as to extend the area of autonomy itself. In exercising their autonomy, the Tyndale teachers both ignored their mandate (by reversing the priorities it contained) and ignored the prescriptions for practice contained within the sedimented common sense of the teaching profession. This dual negation in the exercise of their professional autonomy is the basis of the accusations of its abuse.

The effects on educational policy of this perceived abuse of their autonomy by the Tyndale teachers have derived from the two sides of that negation. Steps have been taken to ensure both that the mandate (to teach certain subjects like maths and reading) is actually made mandatory (through the specification of the remit of the APU) and to reinforce the already potent effect of experience and professional common sense (through more frequent and more detailed monitoring of teachers and school activities). It has led to an increasing emphasis on how educational knowledge is *consumed* at the expense of how it is *produced* — symbolized in the waxing of the Assessment of Performance Unit while the Schools Council wanes. It has led to a recognition of the political nature of teachers' classroom autonomy in a period when there is no clear consensus on educational goals, and a consequent attempt both to specify the aims and objectives of the education system more clearly and more explicitly, and to routinize teachers' accountability for the performance of their (newly specified) roles. What is involved is the replacement of teachers' professional judgement by bureaucratic accountability. No longer will teachers be able to use their professional expertise to play 'catch me if you can'; they will now have to play 'jumping through the hoops'.

The Influence of the Teaching Profession

The effect which the Tyndale case had on teacher autonomy was not, however, limited to the moves to limit teachers' classroom autonomy just outlined. The affair also had a notable effect on the whole standing of the teaching profession and on its power and influence in the corridors and conference rooms where education policy is made. This is particularly important, for it is possible to distinguish two rather different conceptions of teacher autonomy which frequently are combined with consequent confusion and lack of clarity. The first conception of teacher autonomy, which we might call the weak conception, would limit it to the free exercise of acknowledged expertise in executing in the school and classroom educational programmes designed elsewhere, over which teachers should have no greater say than anyone else. It is this conception which underlay the discussion in the previous section. The second, 'strong', conception would include the creation as well as the execution of educational programmes within the scope of teacher autonomy, on the basis that the teachers are the experts about education and that they alone, or they best, can decide what should be taught as well as how to teach it. Now these issues are the subject of a continuing philosophical and political debate which is not strictly relevant here. What is relevant is that the Tyndale affair had an important effect not only on the weak conception of teacher autonomy, an effect which as we saw in the previous section led to it being curtailed, but also on the strong conception. This is not because the Tyndale teachers were in any way closely associated with those levels of the teaching profession which exercise its influence over educational policy, or because they were in any way attempting directly to bring pressure to bear on national educational policy themselves. Far from it. They were, in fact, repudiated by their union, the National Union of Teachers, which represented not them, but the Deputy Head, Mrs Chowles, at the Auld Inquiry and, though they received some initial support from their local association of the NUT in the form, for instance, of asking other local primary schools not to enrol children removed from William Tyndale, this appears not to have continued in the same way.

The two conceptions of teacher autonomy broadly divide the two major teachers unions, with the NUT holding very much more to the strong conception than the NAS/UWT.... It had been and continues to be, however, increasingly difficult to sustain [the strong conception], for a number of reasons, several of which appeared to be strengthened by what happened at William Tyndale. One basic cause was the generally declining economic state of the country. This inevitably led to ever more severe cuts in budgets for education, affecting both resources and manpower. The zenith of the NUT's influence had been reached, inevitably, in the decade of rapid educational expansion from the late 50s on, and such contraction not only closed off possible avenues of further expansion, but made it very difficult even to maintain the *status quo*. Again the Tyndale affair had no direct effect on this, but the atmosphere it created made it very much easier for such cuts to be implemented. That atmosphere had a similar effect on the teaching profession retaining its central role in educational decision making. As has been hinted above, the DES was very keen to give a more decisive lead to the education service, to bring it more into line with perceived national priorities, and 'clipping the teachers' wings' seems to have been regarded as an important part of this. Before Tyndale, though, this would have been politically very difficult to achieve, given the very entrenched and apparently well legitimated position the teaching profession held. Tyndale, together with other evidence (such as the alleged decline in literacy) of the failure of the schools to do what the nation required of them made this 'wing clipping' much more feasible. It did this through creating a situation where the scapegoating of the education system for the nation's parlous economic condition could be converted into the scapegoating of the teachers, and thus absolve all other levels of the system from responsibility. Thus, the educational policy makers and implementers emerged from the attacks on the system they directed scot free, while the reputation of the teaching profession received a very damaging blow.

As well as being squeezed from the one side by the more aggressive stance being taken by central government, the NUT's influence was also being pressured from the other side by the development of 'parent power', and once more this development was far from being hindered by the Tyndale affair.

So, notwithstanding the NUT's explicit repudiation of the Tyndale teachers, what they are popularly interpreted as having done has made a significant contribution to the erosion of the teaching profession's influence on education policy. Its wings *have* been clipped by the DES — note, for instance, the Schools Council's new (1978) constitution which effectively removed it from teacher control. It has been forced onto the defensive both by cuts in educational budgets and by falling rolls, with the pressure they put on the maintenance of teachers' jobs. And the public reputation of the teaching profession has not been lower for a long time, something which has further weakened its ability to defend its influence and its interests; this is symbolically reflected in a public mention, however tentative — in the Green Paper — of the possibility of setting up machinery to sack incompetent teachers, a further erosion of teacher power which the effect of Tyndale made it much more difficult to resist.

Conclusion

It should by now be clear that the role attributed to the William Tyndale affair in respect of changes in the control of schools and the accountability of teachers is essentially a facilitative one. What happened at the school did not initiate or cause these shifts, whose consequences are not yet clear, but whose broad aim quite clearly is to restructure and redirect the education system. Both the successful completion and an intended outcome of this process involve cutting back the influence of the teachers at both classroom and policy levels. However, stating that the Tyndale affair enabled rather than caused these changes is not an entirely satisfactory way to conclude this analysis and I would like in this final section to examine, extremely briefly, what might be some of those causes.

... many of the trends and tendencies which Tyndale brought to fruition were present long before the school achieved its notoriety, and I want now to look at some of these trends and tendencies. Why, for instance, did the DES want to increase central control over education? Why did the dominant consensus break down? Why did parents want more say in their children's education? In sum, how had all these problems arisen and why was it necessary to solve them in these particular ways?

Very briefly (the arguments in this paragraph are spelled out much more fully in Dale, forthcoming), over the period since 1944, the economic, political, and ideological climates in which education operates had changed, and so had the contributions which it was assumed education could make at each of these levels. However, the changes at these levels are far from being mutually complementary but are in fact contradictory; it is from these contradictions that the education system gains its dynamic. Similarly, changes at one level do not always, or often, keep pace with changes at other levels, which results in considerable strain during the catching-up period. Concretely, over this period both the pressure for national economic success, and the contribution which it seemed education could make to it, increased. The manpowering function of education became dominant. Yet, because it was governed by a system set up with a different set of priorities in mind, and dominated ideologically by approaches which were often hostile to the manpowering function, the implementation of what the priority of that function entailed was substantially obstructed. Furthermore, the removal of these obstructions was no easy matter; what were seen as obstructions from the viewpoint of an increasingly frustrated central government were widely legitimated features of a well established education system. As I have suggested some of these features were beginning to lose their legitimacy well before the Tyndale affair blew up. There is, though, no doubt that it hastened the pace of educational change, even if the broad direction of that change was already clear.

References

BOGDANOR, V. (1979) 'Power and participation', *Oxford Review of Education*, 5, 2, pp. 157–68.
COCKBURN, C. (1977) *The Local State*, Pluto Press.

DALE, R. (1976) *The Structural Context of Teaching*, E202, Unit 5, Open University Press.

DALE, R. (1977) 'Implications of the rediscovery of the hidden curriculum for the sociology of teaching', in GLEESON, D. (Ed.) *Identity and Structure: Issues in the Sociology of Education*, Driffield, Nafferton Books.

DALE, R. (1979a) 'From endorsement to disintegration: Progressive education from the Golden Age to the Green Paper', *British Journal of Educational Studies*, 28, 3, pp. 191–208.

DALE, R. (1979b) 'The politicization of school deviance: Reactions to William Tyndale', in BARTON, L. and MEIGHAN, R. (Eds) *Schools, Pupils and Deviance*, Driffield, Nafferton Books, pp. 95–112.

DALE, R. (forthcoming) *The State and Education Policy*, London, Routledge and Kegan Paul.

DALE, R. and TREVITT-SMITH, J. (1976) 'From mystique to technique: Completing the bourgeois revolution in education', unpublished paper.

DAVID, M. (1978) 'Parents and educational politics in 1977', in BROWN, M. and BALDWIN, S. (Eds) *The Year Book of Social Policy in Britain 1977*, London, Routledge and Kegan Paul, pp. 87–106.

ELLIS, T. *et al.* (1976) *William Tyndale: The Teachers' Story*, Writers and Readers Publishing Cooperative.

PATEMAN, T. (1978) 'Accountability, values and schooling', in BECHER, A. and MACLURE, S. (Eds) *Accountability in Education*, NFER.

TAPPER, E. and SALTER, B. (1978) *Education and the Political Order*, Macmillan.

WHITE, J. (1977) 'Tyndale and the Left', *Forum*, 19, 2, pp. 59–61.

Teachers and Their Pupils' Home Background

(From Goodacre, E., 1968, *Teachers and Their Pupils' Home Background*, Slough, NFER, pp. 15–18, 18–19.)

This material comes from an investigation of infant teachers' attitudes towards their pupils' home backgrounds and their expectations and assessments of individual pupils. In the passage, a summary analysis is provided of replies from infant teachers in middle-class, upper working-class and lower working-class areas. The extract has been chosen to illustrate two areas of interest in the sociology of education, one long-established, and the other more recent. The latter involves the examination of the origins, content and consequences of teachers' 'professional knowledge', including the labels and categories teachers employ which help define reality for them and, in part, for their pupils. The way the infant teachers categorized pupils into those from 'good' and 'poor' homes is discussed, and the argument is advanced that teachers' stereotypes of the type of pupil and home they could expect 'were related to their ideas concerning the relationship of occupational level, social conditions and intellectual ability'. The second area of interest illustrated by the extract is the concern of sociologists to provide explanations for working-class failure in schools. Goodacre's evidence suggests that, in the case of some of the teachers, their knowledge of children's social class background influenced their conceptions of pupils' ability and might have lowered their expectations of what pupils could achieve. Some sociologists certainly argue that a partial explanation of why working-class children underachieve in schools is the result of lowered expectations on the part of their teachers.

1.   *What importance do infant teachers attach to pupils' home background in the teaching of reading?*

Generally the teachers considered that the pupils' home background was an important factor in learning to read; they described those aspects of the home which they believed could actively assist that process, and the abilities pupils used in learning to read which they most readily associated with differences in home conditions. They most valued the provision of suitable reading material in pupils' homes on which pupils could practise their newly acquired skill, and the type of atmosphere in which it was taken for granted by parents and child that reading was a desirable skill to be acquired. Differences in home background were most readily connected with a child's desire to learn to read and his rate of learning.

2.   *How do teachers categorize their pupils in relation to home background?*

The teachers in this study appeared to be familiar with the terms 'good' and 'poor' homes as a means of categorizing pupils. When asked to describe them in their own words, they used more motivational and cultural characteristics in describing the 'good' home. The 'good' home tended to be described as one which facilitated the teacher's task of instruction by preparing the child for participation in the formal learning situation and also for acceptance of the teacher's role in it. If a child showed no eagerness to learn to read, teachers believed that the difficulty of imparting the techniques of the skill was increased, because not only did they have to provide the appropriate systematic instruction (difficult enough if teacher and pupil used different types of language systems, dialect etc.) but they had also to demonstrate to pupils that reading was a desirable and necessary skill.

When teachers rated the different characteristics of a 'good' home, the school's social area assumed importance. For instance, there was little difference between the ratings of teachers in middle and upper working-class areas, but particular motivational and cultural items assumed importance as distinguishing characteristics between the two working-class groups. These items were the ability of the parents to answer their children's questions, to provide stimulating experiences in the home and to help with school work; parents' own levels of education and intelligence, and the presence of 'good' conversation and manners in the home. Comparing the extreme social area groups, the items regarded as most important were a religious faith, parental help with school work, stable emotional home life, and a mother who did not go out to work.

Each teacher's ratings for the various items were added up to give a total score for this question, and if high scores can be interpreted as indicative of an interest in the contribution of the 'good' home, it seems likely that such an interest is related to the individual teacher's age and general personality type. The findings suggest that it is more likely to be the older or more authoritarian type of teacher, with unfavourable attitudes to pupils and their homes, who is most likely to categorize pupils in terms of 'good' or 'poor' homes.

3. *What is the extent of teachers' personal contacts with pupils and their homes, and what clues do they use as a basis for their impressions of pupils' home conditions?*

It was found that amongst these urban infant teachers, contacts with parents seldom extended beyond meetings on school premises. Few school heads had established parent-teacher organizations, and few teachers ever visited pupils' homes. Two out of three parents[1] were said to visit the school, usually for reasons connected with the child's physical well-being, and since these questions were asked of teachers of young children, parental interest at this stage was largely an expression of maternal concern.

Pupils' records of attendance and lateness were not indicative of social class differences in attitudes towards the value of education, but pupils' reasons for being away or their excuses for lateness provided teachers, to some extent, with information about the pupils' home circumstances. There was, however, some evidence to suggest that certain types of schools might find particular reasons more 'acceptable' than others.

Teachers seemed to have little difficulty in finding evidence of a child's economic circumstances. Conversations, class 'News', or actual observations of personal belongings, etc. brought to school were considered to be indications of a family's pattern of conspicuous consumption. The type and quality of a child's clothing, even in today's welfare state, still seems to be a major 'clue' for most teachers. Obvious signs such as the bare feet of the nineteen-thirties have disappeared, but indications such as the suitability of clothing from the point of view of climate and weather conditions, and the care and quality of underclothing provide a basis for comparison to the practised eye of the observer.

The teachers suggested a variety of ways in which the actions of parents could be construed as constituting parental interest in the child's reading progress. However, analysis of their answers indicated areas of difference which could well be the basis of misunderstandings between teachers and parents. There were, for instance, the different responses to the practical suggestion that parents should provide pupils with a copy of the reader in the school reading scheme, so that the child could practise at home. Firstly, provision of the reader and parents 'hearing' their children read at home was more often suggested as a sign of parental interest by the heads than by the class teachers. Secondly, the head's views as to whether the parent was expected to borrow or to buy the book appeared to be related to his own social class origin. A head of working-class origin would be likely to consider a request from a parent to borrow a school reader as a sign of interest, but the same request to a head of middle-class origin might be considered as a 'trivial' reason for a visit to the school.[2]

There was evidence to suggest that the type of school organization has a bearing on the role expected of parents. For instance, more heads of the smaller, combined department school expected parents to take an active interest in the work of the school to the extent of visiting the school to ask about the methods in use, whereas more class teachers in the infant only schools emphasized the parents' supportive role, expecting them to encourage and sustain their children in their efforts but not, at this early stage in their children's education, to want to help with school work.

5.   *What inferences do teachers make about pupils whose parents follow different types of occupation?*

The teachers' lack of knowledge regarding the gradients of status in the manual classes was reflected in the tendency for teachers in lower working-class areas to see their classes as homogeneous groups, and pupils as predominantly children of fathers with manual occupations. Their tendency to stress the power and responsibility of occupations which, in the past, were related to educational mobility and hence intellectual capacity, also led them to think of pupils from the lower working-class areas not only as *socially* homogeneous groups, but also as being *intellectually* homogeneous; more teachers in the lower working-class areas tended to accept that they had no pupils of above average intellectual ability. Further, it appeared from the teachers' comments that their own language system and academically biased education might make it extremely difficult for many of them to recognize unfamiliar forms of intellectual functioning.

6.   *To what extent do such inferences affect teachers' ratings of individual pupils?*

In reply to the request to complete estimates, records and predictions of individual pupils' abilities, attributes, reading attainment and progress, it was found that the teachers in the extreme social areas were less reluctant to supply information about pupils' home conditions than the teachers in the upper working-class areas. This suggested that the teachers in the extreme social areas tended to have well-structured stereotypes of the type of pupil and home they could expect. It seemed likely that these expectations were related to their ideas concerning the relationship of occupational level, social conditions and intellectual ability. . . .

Notes

1   Since one in three parents are not seen by the teachers at school (even from the beginning of the child's schooling), one wonders to what extent lack of face-to-face relationships influences the teachers' assessments of parental interest — it may well be that the unknown, unmet parent soon comes to be regarded as the parent who 'takes little interest'. Douglas (1964) assessed parental encouragement by using the class teachers' comments at the end of the first and fourth years in the primary school and their records of the number of times parents visited the school to discuss their children's progress. It was found that on the basis of this assessment of parental interest, when parents took little interest, their children lost ground in tests and gained rather fewer places in the selection examinations than would have been expected from their measured ability.

2   DEPARTMENT OF EDUCATION AND SCIENCE (1967). 'National Survey of Parental Attitudes and Circumstances Related to School and Pupil Characteristics', Appendix 3, *Children and Their Primary Schools* (Plowden Report) reported that just over a third of the parents had *bought* copies, to have at home, of some of the textbooks their children were using at school. Considerably higher proportions of parents from the non-manual than manual worker families had bought textbooks.

References

CENTRAL ADVISORY COUNCIL FOR EDUCATION (England) (1967) *Children and Their Primary Schools* Vol. 2, Appendix 3, London, HMSO.
DOUGLAS, J. (1964) *The Home and the School*, MacGiddon and Kee.

Primary Education and Social Control

(From Sharp, R. and Green, A., 1975, *Education and Social Control*, London, Routledge and Kegan Paul, pp. vii–viii, 216–7, 217, 217–18, 218, 221–2, 224, 224–5, 227.)

English infant education has been the subject of two important sociological case-studies, which are featured in this extract and that by King (pp. 258–62). Sharp and Green's study was conducted with the headteacher and infant teachers in one junior and infants school and, though small-scale and exploratory, raised a number of important issues, both for theoretical work in the sociology of education and for primary school policy and practice. The authors provided an abstruse but thought-provoking critique of 'progressive education'. Their main argument (summarized in the first paragraph of the extract) is that such an approach may not be as liberal or emancipatory as it appears; they suggest it 'is an aspect of romantic radical conservatism', since it involves a subtle process of sponsorship and stratification among pupils (equally as effective as the process of differentiation in traditional approaches to education) and it provides enhanced opportunities for the exercise of social control 'in both the narrow sense of achieving discipline in the classroom and the wider sense of contributing to the promotion of a static social order generally' (see also pp. 233–5). Their interpretations (both sociological and educational) have not gone unchallenged.

The child centred teacher sees him, or herself, as engaging in a radical critique of the authoritarian-élitist assumptions of the more formal, traditional approaches to education. He does not wish to subordinate the child's individuality to some predefined social requirements or impose 'high culture' upon the child in an arbitrary fashion because these would frustrate the realization of the child's inner potential. We attempt to show some of the ways in which the well-intentioned 'radical practices' of the progressive educator produce effects very similar to the hierarchical differentiation of pupils characteristic of formal methods. Whilst laying emphasis upon the freedom of the child, the teacher who has adopted the ideology of child centredness may well find himself unwittingly constrained to act in ways which pose serious problems concerning the efficacy of accommodating to and encouraging the 'spontaneous development of the child from within himself'. In our explanation of these and other phenomena which we have researched, what is being suggested is that the child centred educator, with his individualistic, voluntarist, and psychologistic solution to the problem of freedom fails to appreciate the ways in which, even in his own practice, the effects of a complex, stratified industrial society penetrate the school. It is suggested that the radicalism of the 'progressive educator' may well be a modern form of conservatism, and an effective form of social control in both the narrow sense of achieving discipline in the classroom and the wider sense of contributing to the promotion of a static social order generally....

In our analysis of the theory and practice of the teachers in their classroom activity, we observed them subject to conflicting expectations and ambivalencies stemming from several sources. The practical implications of the child centred methodology were not clearly articulated amongst the staff community. In operation they tended to mean the 'free day' or the 'integrated curriculum', both these and other notions being loosely formulated. These became, in practice, organizational precepts whereby children tended to be given wide discretion to choose between many activities, and in so far as they appeared to choose to do things, i.e. satisfied the conditions for 'busyness', the child centred approach was assumed to be in operation. The teachers seemed to be left unclear as to their precise role in interacting with their pupils to further their development in various approved areas of knowledge. The vocabulary appealed to such concepts as 'needs', 'interests' and children's 'readiness' without specifying their operational indicators. The teachers' rationales fall back upon the idea that 'what children do they need to do', 'it is important for children to be happy at school' or 'play is work'. These are operationalized or informed in practice by the teachers' common sense concerning how normal children behave, derived from their immediate colleagues, from the wider context of their professional relationships and from their continuing biography as lower middle class members of society.... [In the primary school studied] the teachers are able to organize the environment of their classrooms to allow a wide range of choice but have to generate their own theory of instruction for the children.

The headmaster publicly endorses the view that the school is committed to the teaching of both traditional and new types of knowledge. As a progressive school the children should be allowed to integrate their own knowledge, develop at their own pace, according to their own present needs and interests. But the school has also to account for itself in the established way by teaching literacy and numeracy. The teaching of reading, writing, mathematical concepts and computing skills are thus recognized as important in the teacher's work. The teachers are, however, in a difficult position because it is not immediately clear how these can be 'developed from within' the child rather than through the routine intervention and structuring by the teachers of their pupils' activities. They are confronted with the complex problem of cognizing, monitoring and further facilitating the children's development without adopting a too directive or formal approach. This is compounded by the age range of the children and their clearly differentiated levels of achievement.

The solution adopted by the different teachers we have observed consists of operationalizing in varying ways the 'integrated day' with a tendency to adopt the therapeutic ethos or image of the school as presented by the headmaster. Publicly, the school operates as a progressive educational establishment while in the practice of these teachers and in the private views of the headmaster, it is also a socializing institution, civilizing a deprived portion of the population....

Perhaps the central paradox of the substantive level of our study relates to the operationalization of the child centred methodology and the relationship between intentions and outcomes. In the abstract, child centred ideology, the teacher operates by 'knowing the child'. . . . The individual child in this situation, unlike in more formal and traditional approaches to education, really matters. At the level of the teachers' classroom practice and in the ethos of the school, the aim is towards a fluid harmony of co-operative actors allowing full and free expression on the part of the children. . . . We have tried to show how the constraints beyond and within the classroom situation prevent the teacher from achieving the high degree of consociality which the abstract ideology requires . . . whilst the teachers display a moral concern that every child matters, in practice there is a subtle process of sponsorship developing where opportunity is being offered to some and closed off to others. Social stratification is emerging.

We have tried to show how these practices are a function of the constraints both ideological and material which influence the practice of the individual teacher. . . .

. . . The processes we have observed in the classroom and referred to as the social structuring of pupils' identities can be seen as the initial stages of the institutionalization of social selection for the stratification system. As studies of differential achievement have shown, early success and failure in the classroom is of crucial importance for entry into the occupational structure, and hence the class structure at different levels. Moreover we have suggested not merely that there is a developing hierarchy of pupils but also the content of education is being selectively organized and socially transmitted. The social stratification of knowledge and ignorance which characterizes the wider society thus impinges on the child in his earliest encounters with formal institutional mechanisms. In addition within the school, social control is being maintained through the initiation of pupils, teachers and parents into appropriate attitudes and modes of action and, when these break down, through the operation of constraint against those who challenge established interests. . . . Whilst educators and parents may view the educational system as the locale where talent is developed and individual needs responded to, its 'real' function may be very different and related more to the social demands of established interests in the macro structure than to the requirements of individual pupils. As we have observed in the classroom, the social advancement of the few depends upon a denial of the same for the many, as pupils' careers are socially structured through the activities of educators who are themselves enclosed within a wider structure of constraints over which they have little control.

It is here that the real irony and paradox of child centred progressivism as an educational ideology is revealed. Developing as a reaction to what was held to be the rigidity of traditional educational structures which denied opportunity to the many, the progressive child centred movement was impelled by a moral rhetoric which sought to re-establish the rights of the individual for freedom, self-development and individual expression over and above the demands of the society....

We suggest that the rise of progressivism and the institutional supports it receives are a function of its greater effectiveness for social control and structuring aspirations compared with more traditional educational ideologies whose legitimacy was already being questioned. Within child centred progressivism, far wider ranges of the child's attributes become legitimate objects of evaluative scrutiny and explanatory variable in the construction of success and failure. Not merely intellectual but social, emotional, aesthetic and even physical criteria are often employed in the processing of pupils in educational institutions, the social control possibilities thus being enhanced.... We are suggesting that modern child centred education is an aspect of romantic radical conservatism.

Classroom Interactions and Pupils' Perceptions

(From Nash, R., 1973, *Classrooms Observed*, London, Routledge and Kegan Paul, pp. 16–17, 90–2, 101–2.)

This material has been taken from the report of a three-year observational study in primary and secondary schools, which explored how children through day-to-day interactions with teachers and fellow pupils formed concepts of themselves (their ability, status, identity) and developed consistent patterns of behaviour appropriate to their self-concepts. As Nash argues elsewhere in his book, 'the essential cultural messages of the school are conveyed through an incalculable number of interactions between teachers and pupils. These messages are only marginally concerned with school learning in the normal sense of the term but they have everything to do with the child's status, with his self-image, and with his aspirations for the future'. The two small-scale studies reported here (the first in a primary school and the other in a secondary school) support the author's interactionist stance and demonstrate how close were children's and teachers' perceptions of the class positions of individual pupils. Nash's work suggests a partial explanation of why working-class children are in general less successful in school than their middle-class counterparts. It may be that teachers' lower expectations for working-class children, documented in a number of studies, are conveyed directly or indirectly through day-to-day interactions to the pupils who use them to build up their identities which in turn influence their future behaviour and progress in school (see also pp. 246–50).

I set out to establish precisely how accurate children's perceptions of their class positions were. First of all I obtained from three teachers rank orders of ability on three measures; number, writing, and reading, for the children in their classes. Each child was then seen individually and asked to point to the names, written on cards arranged randomly on the desk before him, of the 'people a wee bit better than you at number'. The same procedure was followed for testing whom the child thought better than himself at reading and writing. From these data it was possible to estimate each child's self-perceived class position. For example, if a child pointed to ten children as a 'wee bit better' than himself, he was assumed to regard his position in the class as eleventh. It is necessary to be quite clear about what was happening here. The teachers' rankings were made at my request and were not communicated to their pupils. In theory the children should have had no idea of their class positions and had I directly asked children what their positions were I suspect I should have got some strange answers. But tested in this indirect way children aged as young as eight gave themselves positions which correlated highly with those assigned them by their teacher. The complete figures are given in Table 1....

[A similar investigation was carried out in a secondary class.] ... Each pupil was seen individually and presented with a set of thirty-five cards on

Table 1   Correlations between teachers' ranks on school subjects and pupils' own estimates of their positions

Age	Reading	Writing	Number	Totals	N
8	0.69	0.44	0.64	0.85	28
10	0.31	0.20	0.45	0.46	30
11	not applicable	0.47	0.80	0.82	33

each of which was written the name of one of the children in his class. The pupil was asked to sort the cards into three groups: (i) a group 'a bit more clever than you', (ii) a group 'about the same as you', and (iii) a group 'not so clever as you'. The names of the pupils placed in each group were noted. To establish the child's estimate of his position he was given those he had named 'about the same' as himself and asked to 'put them in the right order'. His own name is included in this group. If, for example, a child placed ten pupils in group (i), and twelve in group (iii), his estimate of his position must lie between eleventh and twenty-third. If the pupil then places himself fourth in group (ii) his position must be fourteenth. This procedure avoided giving children the rather tedious task of ranking thirty-five cards. The resulting positions were rank-ordered. Ties were permitted.

A second measure was obtained by counting the number of times each pupil was named by his classmates as 'more clever than me', subtracted from the number of times he was mentioned as 'slower than me'. For example, a child named as 'more clever than me' by twenty of his classmates and as 'slower than me' by twelve would receive a score of +8. These scores which ranged from −31 to +34 were ranked. Ties were permitted. This rank was assumed to correspond to the position each child was collectively seen to hold.

There are now two ranks: (i) derived from pupils' estimates of their own positions, and (ii) derived from pupils' estimates of each other's positions. These were found to be significantly correlated, r. 0.72. Analysis of the data shows that for thirteen of the thirty-three pupils tested (two were absent) the two ranks were within plus or minus 3 points. Another eleven pupils saw themselves as within plus or minus 6.5 points of their position as seen by others. Five children badly underestimated their position as seen by others and were not thought to be as poor as they thought themselves. Four overestimated their positions and thought themselves better than their classmates believed.

The interactionist theory discussed [previously] predicts that children perceived unfavourably by their teachers will develop unfavourable self-concepts and that these will be reflected in the low class positions these children will believe themselves to have. Conversely it predicts that children favourably perceived will believe themselves to be highly placed in the class. This hypothesis may be tested by correlating the teachers' perceptions of their pupils (construct rank) with the rank derived from the pupils' own estimates of their positions. The correlation was r. 054, which is significant at the 0.05 level. From this it follows that the correlation between the teachers' perceptions and the pupils' estimates of each other's class positions will be high. It is, in fact, r. 0.69, a result which may be taken to reflect the high degree of agreement between the pupils' and the teachers' perceptions of the relative abilities in the classroom. . . .

. . . I have argued that from an interactionist standpoint the child can be understood to be actively engaged in working out through his day-to-day interactions in the classroom a pattern and style of behaviour from which he and others build up expectations for his future behaviour. That others in the classroom are engaged in a continual process of evaluation has been demonstrated by the high correlation between the perception a child has of his class position and the perception his classmates have of it. It is becoming clear that within the classroom there is a commonly agreed body of knowledge about the relative abilities of all its members. These results may be taken to support the interactionist theory that children are continually engaged in forming a concept of themselves and developing a consistent pattern of behaviour appropriate to this self-concept. There is evidence that the firmer these patterns of behaviour become the more unshakeable the models of them constructed by others will be and the more power their expectations will have in confirming the others' behaviour. And the models and expectations children have of each other may be as important in determining academic behaviour as those of the teacher.

The Nature of Infant Education:
A Sociological Perspective

(From King, R., 1978, *All Things Bright and Beautiful?: A Sociological Study of Infants' Classroms*, Chichester, Wiley, pp. 143–6, 146, 147, 148–9.)

In his book from which this extract is taken, King provides a detailed sociological account of English infant education based on close observation and discussion of practices in three infant schools, including one (Burnley Road) designated as a social priority school because of its high proportion of disadvantaged children. In describing and explaining the activities occurring in the classrooms, he relates teachers' actions to the 'child-centred' educational ideology they hold with its elements of (i) developmentalism (belief in the existence and importance of physical, intellectual and emotional development); (ii) individualism; (iii) play as learning; and (iv) childhood innocence. (This constitutes a variant of 'liberal romantic' ideology discussed on pp. 79–94.) He shows how this ideology gives teachers a sense of what infant children and infant education are and how they should be. He argues that where (as at Burnley Road) there is a discrepancy between how children actually behave and how teachers assume they should behave, the latter resort to a 'family-home background theory' which, in crude summary, suggests that children's poor behaviour and progress are due to the conditions and the way they are brought up by their families (see Goodacre's 'good' and 'poor' homes, pp. 246–50). Through this means teachers preserve their belief in the innocence of childhood and their own identity as effective practitioners. The passage below indicates some of King's summary reflections on the nature of infant education in the light of his empirical work.

I pointed out that the child-centred ideologies which represent what is 'real' about children and their learning to infants' teachers, are social constructs; there was a time when they did not exist and they are not accepted by everyone. Children have learnt and still learn, in some parts of the world, basic skills by methods far removed from those I have described. Within this perspective, classroom practices and ideologies may be discussed and evaluated independently of any claims for their being the best or the truth.

Play

Among the many purposes they attributed to play, the teachers emphasized 'play as learning'. Children have learnt and do learn the three R's in other times and places without any play elements, so that this cannot be essential. Since all children did 'learning by playing' I have no adequate way of estimating its effectiveness in the three schools. The only easy judgement possible is whether it is desirable. Whether they learnt what their teachers thought they did or not, most children seemed happy when they played, and on this account alone it could be considered worthwhile, particularly at Burnley Road, especially if the teachers' ideas about the limited nature of their activities outside school were correct.

But does play get in the way of learning? Would the children at Burnley Road have mastered the basics better if they did them all day and never played? This idea was part of the pre-school intervention programme described by Bereiter and Engelmann (1966) in the USA. English infants' teachers would find the old-fashioned didactic methods they used an affront to their child-centred ideologies, but of all the programmes tried, it seems one of the most effective in terms of improved test scores.

Classroom Control

[Previously] I suggested that a major element in the oblique forms of social control used by teachers was the idea that young children were innocent in their intentions, even if their behaviour was defined as naughty. There are two important considerations that follow from this practice, one theoretical and the other practical.

This particular view of innocence touches upon the relationship between man and society and the issue of free will. It is recognized that men make society but are also constrained by it. The phenomenologists stress the first part of the relationship, the marxists and functionalists the latter. Weber tried to contain both in his sociology, in that, given the inseparable nature of man and society, it was still possible to pose that an individual may freely choose a course of action against societal constraints. At what point may children be regarded as being in this position? When may it be judged that a child has freely chosen to break the rules established by the powerful in the society of the classroom? I have suggested that the teachers' actions were such that the children tended to conform with the definitions that informed those actions, which were based upon child-centred ideologies. At Burnley Road the definition of innocence was difficult for the teachers to sustain. Would their dilemmas about the children's behaviour have been eased or solved if they had interpreted naughty behaviour as an outcome of the children's free choice, that they intended or chose to be naughty? Would the occasional pinching, punching, and pushing have stopped if they had not ignored it?

The forms of child behaviour approved by the teachers included being quiet, busy, tidy, helpful, kind, and conventionally polite, and much of their control was directed towards promoting them. Are these desirable qualities in a child, or should they be changed?

Children's Interests

Many classroom activities were based upon teachers' imputations of children's interests, but [elsewhere] I described how interests could be induced and others ignored by the teacher. Should the children's 'true' interests have been completely acknowledged and incorporated into the educational process as part of the idea of child-centredness? At Burnley Road this would have meant a curriculum for the boys which legitimated their manifest interest in fighting, wars, and violence in general, an interest which posed a problem for the teachers because it contradicted the definition of the children as innocent.

Given that many interests were induced by the teachers, the range and nature of these could be questioned. This might involve enquiry into the education of infants' teachers, and how, in my observations, its products claimed no special body of knowledge other than that of children and their learning, but were sometimes ignorant of that knowledge which they defined everyone should have. This implies that the child-centred education of teachers requires supplementing with more general education.

The Three R's

[In a previous chapter] I reported the primacy that teachers gave to the three R's. It may be thought an absurd question to pose whether children should learn to read, write, and do sums. Most people would regard these as being basic competences for adult life in contemporary British society, although Neil Postman (1973) has questioned the necessity of being able to read, a skill required in order to understand the argument he has written.

The child-centred ideology does not justify the learning of the three R's, but the methods of teaching and learning them were based upon the presumed nature of the child, and his presumed interests. Given the varying definitions of reading readiness by teachers and their invariably real consequences, the concept of readiness would appear to be very questionable, indeed at Burnley Road some teachers had laid it aside. This suggests that some children not manifesting 'readiness' could be started reading earlier in their school careers. This does not automatically mean that they would become better readers.

The content of the reading provided for children is based upon their imputed interests and upon assumptions about the need to protect their innocence. Does the nature of the story worlds so presented contribute to the sex and social class differences in reading attainment? (The latter was suggested by the Plowden Committee.) The worlds of Peter and Jane, and of Ken, Pat, and Pipkin are clearly more middle class than working class. Would their reading levels rise if the children of Burnley Road read stories reflecting their own family lives, including absent fathers and successions of 'uncles'?

The Family-Home Background Theory

Teachers created and managed classroom situations in which children exhibited behaviour and progress which the teachers sometimes found incompatible with their definition of what children should be, and they explained the discrepancies by means of the family — home background theory, which preserved the innocence of the children and their own identities as good teachers and left unquestioned their child-centred ideologies and practices. The posing of the family — home background theory was made easier, if not actually made possible, by their child-centred practices, which presented them with the 'evidence' of the children's homes and families through their writing, drawing, and talking. Taking an interest in the whole child legitimated knowing about his or her life outside the classroom. Thus the child-centredness permitted the family-home background theory and was protected by it.

It is not easy to imagine a case where a teacher would know nothing of a child's background without changing many established practices. If teachers were to abandon the family-home background theory they would have to conclude that any 'problems' were either due to the children's deficiencies or to their own. The acceptance of either would seriously question their ideologies.

Infant Education — A Middle-Class Institution?

The nature of infant education has been explored mainly in terms of the children's behaviour and progress that were defined as problems by the teachers. From this it might be concluded that it is basically a middle-class institution. There are a number of initial reservations that should be made about this view. Firstly, although there were social class differences in mean reading ages and in teachers' assessments of behaviour and attitude to work, it was not the case that all or even most middle-class children did better than all or most working-class children in the same school. Many working-class children were assessed as well behaved and hard working, and had high reading quotients. Statistical differences between social groups draw attention away from their similarities. Secondly, the sex differences in these assessments were arguably bigger than the class ones. Do these make infant education a female education or even a middle-class female one, since it is this group who are assessed most highly?

The analysis of the existing system of infant education cannot ignore its relation to the social and economic structure, but this relationship is not a sufficient criterion for its evaluation, which depends principally upon the acceptability of the value-judgements upon which it is based. In the teachers' terms these were that children should be able to read, write, and do sums; they should experience painting, drawing, craft work, singing, dancing, and physical exercise; they should be happy, helpful, quiet, tidy, clean, and kind. They should learn through play and through their presumed interests, and be treated in such a way as to protect and respect their imputed innocence. These are posed as intrinsically valuable for all young children irrespective of their sex, social origins, or social destinies. From this point of view infant education may be regarded as the most egalitarian sector of English education.

References

BEREITER, C. and ENGELMANN, S. (1966) *Teaching Disadvantaged Children in the Pre-School*, Prentice-Hall.

POSTMAN, N. (1973) 'The politics of reading', in KEDDIE, N. (Ed.) *Tinker, Taylor: The Myth of Cultural Deprivation*, Harmondsworth, Penguin.

Making Sense of School

(From Jackson, M., 1987, 'Making sense of school', in Pollard, A. (Ed.) *Children and Their Primary Schools*, Lewes, Falmer Press, pp. 74, 76, 80, 82–3, 84, 85–6.)

In this extract, Margaret Jackson argues for the significance of understanding the ways in which children attempt to make sense of their experience of school. It is a further example of a 'social constructionist' perspective, linking sociological study of social processes at the classroom level to psychological interest in learning. She sees children as active participants in their own learning, formulating hypotheses, testing them out, reformulating their ideas in the light of their experience and new knowledge. In the process of this they develop understanding of the social context and the parameters within which they have to live and work. In doing so they develop ideas about norms, rules, social conformity and the power of the teacher. Language is seen as a major factor in the child's attempts to come to terms with this new world. There are considerable similarities in the views expressed with a liberal romantic interpretation of how knowledge is acquired and modified by the learner (p. 85) and in Vygotsky's interpretation of the role of language in learning (see the article by Britton on pp. 317–22).

When starting school young children enter an environment very different from anything which they have previously known. King (1978) described infant classrooms as an 'educational casbah' full of a rich variety of furniture, displays, materials, games, etc. These rooms are constantly changing spheres of activity, reflecting not only the children's work but also the aspirations and ideals of the teachers' ideologies. In addition, classrooms can be seen as communities where roles and rules become defined and social groups are formed and maintained, challenged and reformed. In this chapter I will argue that children's academic performance in school is closely related to their competence within the social organization of the classroom.

Willes's work (1983) suggested that, for a young child entering school, the organization routines of classrooms have a crucial vitality and importance. These routines form a large part of the pattern for each child's time in school and place the control of activity firmly in the hand of the teacher. It seems then that for young children, an important aspect of starting school is concerned with becoming familiar with the rules and routines of daily classroom life. It is about the development of a level of social competence which allows access to the learning patterns of the classroom. It must also be remembered that learning experiences at school are very different from typical learning experiences at home — a difference which Cashdan (1980) describes as being similar to that between an *a la carte* menu and a *table d'hote* menu. I would argue that an important part of making sense of school is being able to use previous experiences and adapt them to the different ways of learning.

Making Sense

In considering how young children make sense of school, it is necessary to spend some time considering how they have previously made sense of the world around them and of the extent to which language plays a part in this process. A young child who is beginning formal education comes to school already possessing considerable knowledge about the world. Almost from birth children are making sense of their environment and the sense-making process is an active one, involving previous experiences and encounters in learning about the new.

A young child starting school can show well developed thinking skills and throughout life may have been engaged in creating hypotheses and then testing and reformulating them in the context of the social and physical environment. Effective early teaching is likely to take into account the characteristics of children's thinking and the social nature of the learning process. Language is a vital component of this process and has been used to learn about the world, to control behaviour and to establish roles. Halliday (1978) defined language as 'meaning potential' and so included the social environment of the child as an important factor in the learning process. It is difficult to separate general learning about the world from learning about language at these early stages. The language we use to talk about the environment gives meaning and definition to our experience and activity. As Wells and Nicholls (1985) says,

> . . . just as children learn the language system through experience of using it as a resource, so in increasing their control of the resources of language, they also increase their understanding of the experiences that are encoded by those resources. (p. 35)

Language can thus be seen as a functional resource and so the emphasis is placed on shared responsibility for learning within the social context. It then becomes apparent that within this model, the adult is seen as collaborator and facilitator rather than instructor.

One way in which an adult can facilitate learning is by providing an environment conducive to active learning, which allows children to test and reformulate the hypotheses formed from past experiences. In school, children progressively need to be able to turn language and thought in upon themselves; in Donaldson's terms (1978) to cope with disembedded language. Play is one way in which children are able to do this and to make new discoveries about the environment. In imaginative play children take themselves into new and exciting worlds and their knowledge of spoken language serves as a means for creating story, exploring new situations, developing relationships and acquiring new knowledge. It is this excitement of exploration which needs to be extended and providing opportunities for play can be one way of leading children into new worlds beyond the immediate and allowing them to be involved in their own learning.

As children actively interact with the environment their past experiences exert a strong influence on the learning process, as is illustrated by some current research in early literacy learning. The work of Fox (1983) showed that the beginnings of future literacy competencies can be found within the child's existing narrative competencies. Young children are able to use the literary conventions of story-telling and to demonstrate a range of understandings clearly related to the organization of text. In many different ways children are able to use their literary experience for their own narrative purposes. Dombey (1983) related the experience of being read to aloud to the experience of learning to read. She showed how the child learns relationship with the author, creation of meaning through written text alone, syntactic patterns to help prediction, pleasure from the experience and taking an active role in gaining meaning from the texts.

Sense-making can thus be seen as a continuum of learning and making sense of school becomes part of the continuum. New experiences build upon old as children test and reformulate hypotheses they have created. The question then arises of the extent to which children's past experiences are exploited in school and also of how appropriate the ways in which children use past experiences are to classroom activities.

Classroom activity is by its very nature problematic; the teacher controls the activity in that she decides on the resources and the aims but the children bring to bear their own understandings on the learning process. Teacher and children bring different meanings to the situation. To children the aims of the activity may not always be immediately apparent and they will use their own understandings to make sense of the situation. It may be that often the transition between home and school learning is so great that children perceive it as two distinct 'methods' rather than a gradual development and thus they do not see that their past experiences have an important bearing on their learning in school.

Children need to become aware of the expectations and demands of the school situation so that their own learning will become appropriate to the constraints of the situation in the classroom.

We can consider the children's developing social competence in three main areas:

   (i)   in procedural and organizational routines;
  (ii)   in interpersonal relations;
 (iii)   in learning 'how to be taught'.

Procedural and Organizational Routines

The organization of the classroom environment, both in management of time and materials, is an important part of life in a reception class. Hamilton's account (1977) of first days in school show how, during this time, much of the teacher's concern is with procedure. These procedural routines are an integral part of the transition from being an individual at home to being one of a large group at school. A young child's capacity to grasp the organizational procedures of the classroom has an influence on the learning process. As Cook-Gumperz (1986) says,

... familiarity with the subtleties of classroom social organization is a pre-condition for gaining access to learning opportunities. (p. 60)

However, in the classroom, the ultimate power rests with the teacher. Thus a child has to conform to the organizational norms of the classroom to exploit the full learning potential of the situation. It seems then, that for a child, active learning and relevant use of past experience and knowledge are not enough in the classroom. Conformation to expected behaviour patterns is what is also required by busy teachers.

Interpersonal Relations

A classroom can be seen as a social community and the relationships which are formed in that community have influence on the learning which takes place. A model of collaborative learning requires children to use language for negotiation, questioning, identifying issues, planning actions and establishing learning relationships and making sense of school demands a social competence within this interpersonal context. It involves forming understandings, not only of the physical but also of the social environment. Children are required to collaborate with each other and with adults and to recognize and respond to different roles in different situations. The range of social relationships with an adult is just one illustration of the complexity of social understanding required. Being in the school assembly, working in a small group with the teacher and sharing an activity on an individual basis are all very different social contexts and require different responses. The child whose past experience does not include using language in these ways or for whom the school experience is so strange could find this difficult.

Learning in the reception class is very much about collaboration with others and a lot of interaction with others is expected and encouraged. It seems that until young children are able to use language as a resource for negotiation with others and as a means for establishing collaborative learning relationships, the pattern of learning in the classroom remains inaccessible.

Learning 'How to be Taught'

Children come to school as active learners. They have probably had experience of investigating their own environment and learning through real and important problem-solving. Frequently they have had the sole attention of a concerned adult who has been learning alongside the child. Learning has been 'embedded' in concrete situations of everyday life.

In school children are required to conform to the pattern of learning of their classroom and this may not be the same as their previous active learning.

An important part of 'making sense of school' is learning to confine active learning to the constraints of the situation.

School learning rarely expects children to be completely passive and frequently there are clear patterns of participation.

I would thus argue that social competence in learning 'how to be taught' requires discernment of and compliance with the accepted learning patterns of the classroom.

Conclusions

I began by describing the 'recognizable social world' of the classroom and suggested that any description or analysis of classroom action must take into account the social elements of that classroom. 'Making sense of school' involves an increasing awareness of the social environment and an increasing ability to participate effectively in that social environment. Children, as active learners, bring to bear their past experiences and their own understandings and perceptions of the situation. These perceptions may not necessarily match the perceptions of the teacher, for learning in school can be a very different thing from learning at home. As children begin to make sense of school so they become aware of the perceptions and expectations of the teacher and frequently adapt their own behaviour to comply. As Stebbins (1981) says:

> Effective classroom participants have the requisite skill and knowledge to interpret the speech and behaviour of other participants there and to respond sensibly. (p. 258)

I have considered how children as active learners begin to make sense of school, how they begin to adapt and refine their learning strategies to comply with the expectations of the school and also how they adapt and refine the classroom activities to comply with their own understandings and past experiences. Thus they become effective classroom participants. I would argue that this sense-making is an essentially social process and is centred on the development of social competence within the classroom. The young child comes to an understanding of the different relationships and roles which exist within the classroom, of the expectations that the teacher holds, including those behaviours which are valued and those which are discouraged, and of the value and relevance of past experience. These understandings are reached within the social context as children interact with other participants and, at the same time, social competence is assessed by their behaviour within the classroom in response to the social and learning environment.

I would want to go on to argue that the same criteria for effective classroom participation should and do also apply to teachers. They also need the ability to interpret the behaviour of others and respond accordingly. Adopting this way of seeing and reflecting on classroom activity could be one way of enabling teachers to modify their behaviour in the classroom to take account of the child's perspective and thus ensure that classroom action is fully effective. It is because teachers have the power to control children and structure the classroom situation to which the children must respond that this sensitivity to the perceptions of the children is so vital. An awareness of the messages about learning and the curriculum which are conveyed through the social context of the classroom can only help teachers to help children to become more effective classroom participants.

References

CASHDAN, A. (1980) 'Teaching, language and reading in the early years', in BRAY, G. and HUGH, A.G. (Eds) *The Reading Connection*, Ward Lock.

COOK-GUMPERZ, J. (1986) *The Social Construction of Literacy. Studies in Interactional Sociolinguistics 3*, Cambridge University Press.

DONALDSON, M. (1978) *Children's Minds*, Fontana.

HALLIDAY, M.A.K. (1978) *Language as Social Semiotic*, E.J. Arnold.

HAMILTON, D. (1977) *In Search of Structure*, London, Hodder and Stoughton.

KING, R. (1978) *All Things Bright and Beautiful? A Sociological Study of Infant Classrooms*, Wiley.

STEBBINS, R. (1981) 'Classroom ethnography and the definition of the situation', in BARTON, L. and WALKER, S. (Eds) *Schools, Teachers and Teaching*, Falmer Press.

WILLES, M.J. (1983) *Children into Pupils: A Study of Language in Early Schooling*, Routledge and Kegan Paul.

Racism and Sexism

(From Davies, L., 1987, 'Racism and sexism', in Delamont, S. (Ed.) *The Primary School Teacher*, Lewes, Falmer Press, pp. 162–3, 164–5, 166–7, 173–4.)

The concern of sociologists with inequality has been complemented in recent years by the study of the ways in which gender and cultural background influence expectations and experience of schooling. The article by Lynne Davies emphasizes the need to acknowledge the complexity of children's individuality and the extent to which teacher bias and prejudice can influence their expectations and experience of school. Every teacher needs to be aware of their own racist and sexist tendencies and the racism and sexism which exists in the curriculum experiences of children.

In this chapter I want to look at manifestations of racism and sexism in the primary classroom.

It is conventional to begin by defining terms, although even that is not easy here. Racism and sexism are sometimes used as mere synonyms for discrimination and prejudice; there are at the other extreme sometimes intricate debates as to, for example, the difference between racism and racialism, and whether one refers to attitudes and the other to actual behaviour (Jeffcoate, 1985), or whether one relates to institutional and the other to personal treatment (Kumria, 1986). I suspect that we all carry around our own working definitions, and recognize different things as instances; so I shall simply provide one definition, to show where I begin from, but without any claims to universality. Racism or sexism (or indeed classism) I see as the individual, collective or institutional treatment of, or attitudes towards people based on shared stereotypes which are oppressive or limiting, and do not recognize people's complex identity.

This is, therefore, more than 'prejudice', for that may be individualistic and occur without damaging effects; it is more than simple 'discrimination', for it is essential for a teacher to be discriminatory if she or he is to diagnose and treat learning needs. Racism and sexism refer to behaviour which is based on sufficiently *shared* oppressive beliefs (for these are most influential); and which is discriminatory *in negative or irrelevant ways*.

What are the manifestations of this racism and sexism in the primary classroom? I shall classify(!) them into two types, first-hand and second-hand — although of course they converge.

First-hand Racism and Sexism

This refers to the daily and personal interaction between participants in the classroom, teachers and pupils. The possibly racist/sexist base to these interactions is now reasonably well documented and researched, and I merely present a shopping list with references to show I am not just making it all up.

Differentiation by Teachers

(i) Teachers unconsciously spend about twice as much time with boys than they do with girls. This may be 'positive' reinforcement of boys in terms of seeing them as more important; it may be 'negative' reinforcement in terms of having to respond to boys' deviance or disruption; it may be reactive behaviour in that boys *demand* more attention (Whyte, 1983; Clarricoates, 1980). However, this differential attention does vary according to subject, with some studies showing girls receiving more time on reading activities, boys on maths (Leinhardt *et al.*, 1979).

(ii) Teachers have different expectations of performance from boys and girls (Delamont, 1980) and from children of different ethnic groups (Brittan, 1976; HMSO, 1981). These expectations are communicated in subtle and not-so-subtle ways that lead to different tasks being set, or differential praise/support being given for similar work. We do not know how far these 'expectations' are internalized by pupils, but it is likely that at least in some cases there will be a self-fulfilling prophecy whereby pupils will prefer to act according to expectations rather than demonstrate lack of conformity to teachers' definitions. Teachers react negatively to dialect or West Indian speech, and judge such speakers as having the least academic potential (Edwards, 1979).

Stereotypical Views of Race and Culture

(i) Teachers will use different language in describing or talking to boys and girls and different labels for the same behaviour (i.e. what is bold or adventurous in a boy is aggressive or unlady-like in a girl). Boys are naughty, girls are devious (Davies, 1984).

(ii) In streamed primary schools, Asian and Caribbean origin children (but particularly the latter) tend to be clustered in the lower streams (Townsend and Brittan, 1982). There is a misplacement of Caribbean children into ESN schools which is at least partly the outcome of stereotypes by primary school heads (Tomlinson, 1982).

(iii) Teachers believe that the presence of a large number of black children will hold back white children's achievement, although there is no evidence for this (Little, 1975).

Abdication of Responsibility

(i) Even when pursuing multicultural programmes, teachers may not recognize the long-established diversity of UK citizens, and use a notion of 'our' culture which excludes black groups. In an 85 per cent black school, teachers would talk of giving respect to 'their' cultures, or of children being allowed to cook 'their own food' (Crozier, 1987). A deputy head in a predominantly Punjabi school introduced an assembly with a Punjabi theme by saying 'Now you're going to hear a funny language and some funny music'. Thus teachers may subvert the intentions of pluralist multicultural curricula by presenting particular cultures or religions as deviations from 'normality', and hence reinforce notions of 'us' and 'them'.

(ii) Children from a very early age have an awareness of race, which 'in some areas takes the form of open hostility based on a confused version of the facts' (Schools Council Draft Report, 1978). However, teachers are reluctant to accept that prejudice starts from pre-school age, and that teachers play a part in its subsequent development (Milner, 1983).

(iii) Teachers will prefer to ignore instances of racist or sexist behaviour between children, and thus do nothing to restore the self-esteem of the child subject to abuse, and implicitly condone the act (Mahoney, 1985; Suleiman and Suleiman, 1985). Boys monopolize physical space in the classroom and playground, and teachers condone this too (Holly, 1985).

Teachers as Role Models

(i) Teachers themselves may be subject to racism and sexism in their recruitment and promotion, in that while women are 77 per cent of all primary teachers, only 7 per cent of them hold headships, compared to 31 per cent of men (DES, 1983b). Little systematic empirical evidence exists on the employment situation of black teachers, since neither the DES nor LEAs maintain ethnic records (Dorn, 1985); yet single surveys begin to show indicative trends, such as in the London Borough of Brent, where the population is more than 50 per cent black, out of a total of 3000 teachers only 200 are black (*The Guardian*, 11 September 1986). Any underrepresentation of ethnic minorities in teaching, and of both women and Blacks in positions of authority, must have an effect on children's role modelling.

Naturally all these manifestations interact with and (together with social class) compound or confound each other, so that the process of the reproduction of inequality is not continuous. How a teacher interacts with a middle-class Asian girl may vary according to the classroom activity, the style of communication required, previous meetings with parents, or simply the time of day. All we can do at this stage is note the researched trends and try to identify and systematically assess our own behaviour as teachers, as for example Thomas (1986) and her colleagues did in nursery and infant classrooms. Observation schedules of children's behaviour and of teachers' sharing of time provide some uncomfortable data for teachers convinced of their own and their pupils' impartiality.

Second-hand Racism

Less threatening, and hence more popular with teachers, is the examination of others' racism and sexism as manifested in educational artefacts. This is a well-trodden field, and for this chapter again needs no more than the usual ticklist or criteria by which to examine books, toys, games, posters, films, ETV programmes, tests, assessment questions, jokes and even library cataloguing systems. I call it second-hand because it is not a direct personal experience for the child, nor always a direct product of the teacher; it is a vicarious discrimination, but none the less salient for that.

The usual areas to investigate are:

(i) *Numerical representation*: the actual number of women/Blacks in stories, illustrations, maths problems etc. and whether the proportions are representative of those in wider society, or whether women/Blacks are marginal or even invisible.

(ii) *Stereotyping*: when females/Blacks do appear, whether there are exaggerated or narrow depictions of their typical occupations, roles, activities, language or skills.

(iii) *Ethnocentrism/male domination*: whether history/geography books portray the world as centring only round white male achievement, and ignore Black history or female social history; whether tests and examinations are 'normed' on a white, middle-class, male culture and its expression.

(iv) *Negative images*: whether people in different countries are given a patronizing or derogatory image (simple peasant, coolie Chinese etc.); whether females are portrayed in negative ways (dumb blonde, fearful/tearful girl, wicked witch, awful stepmother etc.).

(v) *Language*: whether the constant use of the masculine speech form reinforces the notion of 'Man and his world'; whether there are still references to 'West Indians in *our* schools', or the word 'black' always used as a negative epithet.

Racism and sexism are limiting experiences for both the perpetrators and the receivers. My view is that the primary school should challenge any unfairness towards, or confinement of its participants, and publicize its stance. We also have to acknowledge, however, that we are working within a system which is competitive, hierarchical, selective and — in spite of GCSE and TVEI — operates a gradual gate-closing mechanism for future aspirations. One person's openness (i.e. academic success) has to be bought at the expense of another's limitation (i.e. failure). All we can do at the primary level is keep everyone's options open as long as possible, and give children the skills and confidence to prevent others — inside and outside their own 'culture' — closing them off for them later on.

This chapter has thus argued that we do need something called an anti-bias, equal rights or equal value policy in the primary school to counter both racism and sexism and all their combinations. This is not 'equal' in the sense of making children the same — for this leads to pointless arguments about Asian girls wearing trousers or forcing boys into the Wendy House. It is more a commitment to fair trading. An equal value policy does not mean making sure children have identical goods in their trolleys at the primary school checkout, any more than it means merely providing them all (as in 'equal opportunities') with the same empty ones at the entrance. A real caring sharing cooperative primary school aims at full, balanced but variable loads for each child, with no-one being able to sneak through an eight-items-only exit. Equally, an anti-bias school must acknowledge that its customers are subject to all manner of consumer apartheid on the High Street and within its own doors, and therefore that its political task includes a long-term external 'equal value' advertising campaign as well as every teacher being an inhouse store detective for the apprehension of racist and sexist practices.

References

BRITTAN, E. (1976) 'Multiracial education 2. Teacher opinion on aspects of school-life: Pupils and teachers', *Educational Research*, 18, 3, pp. 182–91.
CLARRICOATES, K. (1980) 'The importance of being Ernest, Emma ... Tom and Jane', in DEEM, R. (Ed.) *Schooling for Women's Work*, Routledge and Kegan Paul.
CROZIER, G. (1987) 'Multiracial education or anti-racist education: A case of mistaken identity'. Paper presented at the 10th International Sociology of Education Conference, Westhill, Birmingham.
DAVIES, L. (1984) *Pupil Power: Deviance and Gender in School*, Falmer Press.
DELAMONT, S. (1980) *Sex Roles and the School*, Methuen.
DES (1983) *Statistics of Teachers in Service in England and Wales*, HMSO.
DORN, A. (1985) 'Education and the Race Relations Act', in ARNOT, M. (Ed.) *Race and Gender: Equal Opportunities Policies in Education*, Open University Press/Pergamon.
EDWARDS, V. (1979) *The West Indian Language Issue in British Schools*, London, Routledge and Kegan Paul.
HMSO, (1981) *Committee of Inquiry into the Education of Children from Ethnic*

Minority Groups: Interim Report: West Indian Children in our Schools, Cmnd 8273, London, HMSO.

HOLLY, L. (1985) 'Mary, Jane and Virginia Woolf: Ten year-old girls talking', in WERNER, G. (Ed.) *Just a Bunch of Girls*, Milton Keynes, Open University Press.

JEFFCOATE, R. (1985) 'Anti-racism as an educational ideology', in ARNOT, M. (Ed.) *Race and Gender: Equal Opportunities Policies in Education*, Oxford and Milton Keynes, Pergamon/Open University Press.

KUMRIA, M. (1986) 'Establishing co-operation between parents and staff: A parent's view', in BROWNE, N. and FRANCE, P. (Eds) *Untying the Apron Strings: Anti-sexist Provision for the Under Fives*, Milton Keynes, Open University Press.

LEINHARDT, S. *et al.*, (1979) 'Learning what I taught: Sex differences in instruction', *Journal of Educational Psychology*, 11, 4.

LITTLE, A. (1975) 'The educational achievement of ethnic minority children in London Schools', in VERMA, G. and BAGLEY, C. (Eds) *Race and Education Across Cultures*, London, Heinemann Educational.

MAHONEY, P. (1985) *Schools for Boys?*, London, Hutchinson.

MILNER, D. (1983) *Children and Race Ten Years on*, London, Ward Lock Educational.

SCHOOLS COUNCIL DRAFT REPORT, (1978) 'Multi-racial education: Curriculum and content 5–13, Chapter 1, Assumptions and Contradictions', *New Society*, 16 February.

SULEIMAN, L. and SULEIMAN, S. (1985) 'Mixed blood — that explains a lot of things: An education in racism and sexism', in WEINER, G. (Ed.) *Just a Bunch of Girls*, Milton Keynes, Open University Press.

THOMAS, G. (1986) 'Hallo Miss Scatterbrain, Hallo Mr Strong: Assessing attitudes and behaviour in the nursery', in BROWN, N. and FRANCE, P. (Eds) *Untying the Apron Strings: Anti-sexist provision for the under fives*, Milton Keynes, Open University Press.

TOMLINSON, S. (1982) *A Sociology of Special Education*, London, Routledge and Kegan Paul.

TOWNSEND, H. and BRITTAN, E. (1982) *Organization in Multi-racial Schools*, Slough, NFER.

WHYTE, J. (1983) *Beyond the Wendy House: Sex Role Stereotyping in Primary Schools*, London, Longman for the Schools Council.

5　Primary Education:
Psychological Perspectives

Introduction

Psychology is regarded by many educationalists as:

... the oldest and largest of the foundation disciplines in the study of education, dealing with important issues of relevance to the teacher. (Salmon, 1985)

It is an area of understanding concerned with human behaviour, addressing questions of how and why we act as we do. It is not surprising therefore that psychology is regarded as having much to offer to the thinking and professional development of teachers. Salmon (1985) suggests, for example, that:

... all teachers, during their professional training and in their everyday professional practice, are characteristically concerned with issues such as how to engage childrens' interest and enthusiasm, how to help children who are struggling, or how, through social experience, to build a sense of confidence and resourceful in living.

Psychology contributes to our understanding in each of these areas. It has established strengths in the study of child development, with the acquisition and use of language, of how we think and come to solve problems and how social and emotional development occurs.

This section attempts to provide an overview of the contribution of psychology to thinking about primary education. We have already seen its influence earlier in this publication. For example, psychological evidence is used to justify practice within the liberal romantic tradition (pp. 79–94), through reference to the findings of Piaget in particular. There is also evidence of drawing upon the psychology of learning and group interaction in sociological studies of classroom processes (see the extract by Nash, pp. 255–7, and Jackson, pp. 263–8).

This chapter opens with an overview of psychological traditions by Claxton (pp. 279–82), and introduces us to the varying perspectives adopted by psychologists, notably cognitive, behaviourist and humanist. This is followed by a series of extracts reflecting each of these traditions. The work of Jean Piaget is used to represent a cognitive perspective, which sees the child as an active participant in his/her own learning. This work is explored in some detail via extracts by Isaacs (pp. 283–8) and Adibe (pp. 289–96) because of the significant influence of his work on primary education in the 1960s and early 1970s.

Although later on in his research Piaget considered the effect of the social situation and the significance of language in cognitive development his theory tended to under value the importance of language. Extracts on the ideas of Bruner (pp. 312–6) and Vygotsky (pp. 317–22) redress this balance and contributions from Tamburrini (pp. 297–300), Donaldson (pp. 306–11) and Boyle (pp. 301–5) consider the implications of his ideas for education from a critical perspective. The study by Mercer and Edwards (pp. 323–31) synthesizes the ideas of Bruner and Vygotsky as a way forward.

The Behaviourist tradition in psychology, sees the child as passively receiving and reacting to stimuli. All behaviour, including language is viewed as learned by the reinforcement which the environment provides. B.F. Skinner is notable amongst behaviourist psychologists and his article on the technology of teaching (pp. 332–6) demonstrates the application of behaviourist principles to the classroom context. This is followed by an extract on behaviour modification in the primary classroom (Presland, pp. 337–40), which is also based upon behaviourist principles.

An attempt to draw the cognitive and behaviourist perspective together is provided by extracts on Reception, Discovery and Meaningful Learning (pp. 341–5) proposed by David Ausubel.

The discussion of psychological traditions is concluded by reference to the work of Carl Rogers (pp. 346–51) who advocates that learners need to be 'free to learn' and is an indication of humanism in psychology. The only learning which significantly influences behaviour Rogers argues, is that which is self-discovered, self-appropriated personal learning. The function of the teacher in this context is as a facilitator and enabler, which reinforces the views expressed in the liberal romantic tradition discussed earlier (pp. 79–94).

Successful learning and development however, is as dependent on the learner as it is on the context and atmosphere in which learning takes place. The extracts from Yamamoto (pp. 359–62), Ainscow (pp. 363–7), Conner (pp. 368–72), Schaffer (pp. 379–84) and Rubin (pp. 385–8) explore different facets of individual difference to which psychological research has contributed.

Alister Fraser's extract (pp. 373–8) looks at some of the features discussed in earlier articles, in particular what happens when children take responsibility for structuring the context of their learning. This issue is also explored in problem solving situations in extracts by Fisher (pp. 389–92) and Easen (pp. 393–4).

The penultimate extract considers the complexity of matching learning tasks to children's competence, (Desforges, pp. 395–402) and the section concludes by discussing recent developments in psychological research. Just as we saw in the section on sociological and philosophical perspectives, important questions are asked about the relevance and pertinence of psychology to the solution of educational problems.

References

SALMON, P. (1985) 'Educational psychology and stances towards schooling', in CLAX-TON, G. *et al.*, *Psychology and Schooling: What's the matter?*, Bedford Way Papers 25, University of London Institute of Education.

Psychological Traditions

(From Claxton, G., 1984, *Live and Learn: An Introduction to the Psychology of Growth and Change in Everyday Life*, London, Harper and Row, pp. 8–9, 10–11.)

As was explained in the introduction to this section of the reader, there are varying ways in which psychologists attempt to explain human behaviour and this extract provides an introduction to them. Cognitive psychologists investigate how learning takes place and focus upon the ways in which the learner constructs meaning from experiences. Behaviourist psychology on the other hand is concerned with how particular organisms acquire specific behaviours.

> Techniques used emphasize the influence of the environment (situation) on these behaviours. Reflexes and conditioned reflexes are seen as the basic units on which more complex actions are based. Internal mechanisms of the mind are largely ignored by extreme behaviourists as hypothetical and/or irrelevant. (Campbell, 1988)

Claxton also identifies a 'social and personality' tradition within psychology concerned to investigate the formation and development of attitudes and an attempt to account for differences in the ways in which individuals make sense of the world. Finally, there is the 'humanistic' tradition which stresses the education of the whole person, and emphasizes the importance of learning being meaningful.

Reference

CAMPBELL, R.J. (1988) *The Routledge Compendium of Primary Education*, Routledge.

Science is the activity of creating communicable theories about physical reality. Psychology creates communicable theories about people's theories about reality — both physical and social. And the psychology of learning creates theories about how people's theories change and develop. It is theorizing about how people develop their personal maps, about how they come to know things, and to see and do things differently. All the comments we have made about theories apply to learning theories, but a couple of points are worth drawing special attention to. First, the domain of learning is so big that there are not just different theories around, but different *kinds* of theories. They differ not just in their basic model or language but in their scale, scope, purpose, and focus of convenience. We might identify four traditions that arose from very different beginnings.[1] There are *cognitive* learning theories, which grew out of experimental interest in the way adults remembered things — usually lists of unrelated words or 'nonsense syllables' or numbers. This tradition was born with Ebbinghaus in the last century and held sway until the late 1960s, when the range of convenience of its 'associative' and 'information processing' models was expanded to cover more complicated kinds of learning like solving problems and understanding language. The 1970s produced a lot of research that mapped the bounds beyond which such simple theories began to falter and fail to be useful or productive.

Then there are *behavioural* learning theories, that began with the attempt to predict and explain the behaviour of animals in simple situations, like learning to press a lever to get food, or to recognize and respond to a new signal for food. Gradually these 'conditioning' models were extended to more general concerns, like the development of physical skills and the role of reward and punishment in the education of children. A third tradition, that of *social and personality* development, started in the 1940s with an interest in how attitudes are formed and changed, and, even earlier, with the desire to account for the differences between individuals in the ways they learn, relate to and make sense of their world. Subsequent decades saw the growth of a wider study of the role of society in the formation of personality, the nature of our sense of 'self', and other more general and profound issues linking the individual to his social world. Finally, again in the 1940s and 1950s, *humanistic* learning theories were born from the attempt to explain how people's feelings and their capacity to feel were changed by various sorts of group or one-to-one counselling experiences. Here too the scope grew broader and broader as the concern with 'personal growth' threw up basic questions about the limits of human development and the importance of such slippery concepts as love, vulnerability, acceptance, and the like.

These four approaches to learning were bound, given their initial observations and aims, to go shooting off in different directions. Cognitive theories took over the domain of words, logic, language, reasoning, and knowledge. They become preeminent in the field of education, seeing the role of the teacher as that of instructor and communicator of facts and arguments. They became theories about the *head*, we might say. Behavioural theories, in contrast, paid little if any attention to the intellect, and preoccupied themselves with changes in physical competence that happened outside conscious thought. The important thing was practice and the teacher, if one existed, was seen as a trainer and orchestrator of rewards and punishments. These theories we might symbolize as being to do with the *hands*. Social and personality theories are concerned with matters of the *heart* in the sense that they focus on people's beliefs, opinions, attitudes, judgements about themselves and others. The teacher is often seen here as a model or example or 'exuder' of a certain personal style that is not directly taught but which may nonetheless be picked up by his students. Such theories fall between the two poles of pure reason and raw emotion, the latter being the central preserve of the humanistic theories. It is only within this last tradition that the role of awareness in learning has been studied, and the nature of conscious and unconscious experience, especially of feelings, has emerged as the main concern.

One problem in psychology has been the attitude of theorists to their theoretical progeny. Failing to keep sight of the fact that theories have foci and ranges of convenience, they have sometimes assumed that their particular brain-child must be applicable to the whole field of learning. Instead of investigating its limits they assert its limitlessness. And this breeds trouble. Thus conflicts between different approaches — that between Skinner and Rogers is a classic one[2] — have often been spurious. The electron, though one, sometimes looks like a particle and sometimes like a wave. The human being, though an integrated whole, sometimes appears as an actor, sometimes a thinker, sometimes a believer, sometimes a confused and agitated seeker of emotional aid. The kind of learning on which each tradition focuses is neither the only nor the 'best' kind of learning there is, and it is by no means certain that an elegant and successful model of a rat learning to run through a maze will be much good at explaining how children learn language. It may be worth trying it out (as Skinner has done)[3] but there is no reason why the exercise has to succeed, and we need not protest too much if it fails.

The story of the blind men and the elephant is well known. Each grabbed hold of a different bit and asserted that elephants were like hose-pipes, or walls, or tree-trunks, or bits of rope. Each produces a metaphor for the elephant's trunk, flank, leg, or tail that is hopelessly inadequate for the elephant as a whole. Not so well known is the occasion on which a primary-school teacher decided to discuss this cautionary tale with her class, but without telling them that the men were blind. Afterwards she asked the children, 'What kind of people do you think they were?' One child replied tentatively 'Please, Miss ... experts?' Learning is a large, strange, many-faceted elephant, and we will do well to remember these stories as we proceed.

This preamble is important for the way we as psychologists approach learning. But it also applies directly to the learner himself. We are all theory makers, theory dwellers and theory testers. We live on the basis of a personal theory — a personal map — of what things are like, and we could not live without it. All our knowledge, beliefs, attitudes, expectations, values, opinions, and prejudices are part of this giant theory. All our thoughts, actions, feelings, and sensations are produced by it. It is the vital and unavoidable go-between that mediates all our dealings with the outside world. Nothing has significance in that world; it only has significance *for* somebody. And unless I make a guess about what is significant, what matters, I have no basis on which to act. I cannot achieve anything that is desirable, not avoid anything that is harmful until I interpret whatever-it-is as desirable or harmful. Without my theory, my distillation of what matters out of the raw material of my past experience, I could not even get to the bathroom, let alone order a meal or make friends. Learning happens when I make mistakes, but without the map I would have no idea of what the right road looks like, nor how to find my way back to it.

So it is not hard to see that what we *do* to the world depends on what we consider that world to be: what it contains and which bits are significant. It is a little more tricky to appreciate that all our perceptions are products of the theory, too. Common sense says we see things the way they are, then we make decisions about what's important, and finally we select actions that will get us what we want and avoid what we don't. Common sense is wrong. What we see is an output of our personal theory, not an input to it. The Gestalt psychologist Koffka summed it up when he said 'We see things not as they are but as *we* are'.

Notes and References

1 EBBINGHAUS, H. (1985) *Memory: A Contribution to Experimental Psychology*, New York Teachers' College.
2 See for example, the debate in *Science*, Vol. 124, 1956, pp. 1057–1066.
3 SKINNER, B.F. (1957) *Verbal Behaviour*, New York, Appleton-Century-Crafts.

The Implications of Piaget's Work

(From Isaacs, N., 1961, *The Growth of Understanding in the Young Child*, London, Ward Lock, pp. 9–14.)

The work of Jean Piaget is an example of the cognitive perspective in psychology and the study of his findings has been a major element of primary students' and teachers' psychology courses for many years and as was demonstrated in the section on the liberal romantic tradition (pp. 79–94) his views have been used to justify educational practice in primary education. More recently, however, his ideas have been the subject of considerable criticism (see for example the extracts by Tamburrini (pp. 297–300), Donaldson (pp. 306–71) and Boyle (pp. 301–5)). Despite these criticisms, many of his proposals have stood the test of time and, as Piaget has suggested, theories should not be seen as static, they are ever-evolving and should be subject to modification in the light of new knowledge. His major contribution is likely to have been the questions he raised for others to study. Piaget did not really see himself as an educationalist, rather his interest was in 'genetic epistemology', the study of the nature and acquisition of knowledge. Applications of his ideas to education have depended to a great extent on others.

Isaacs was one of a number of psychologists who have interpreted the writings of Piaget and have discussed their implications for education. Here he draws the readers' attention to the importance of not misunderstanding Piaget's work so to constrain expectations of what a child can or cannot do by virtue of chronological age. Development proceeds in stages which are only very approximately age-related. Piaget merely cited the ages at which children in Geneva solved particular problems. These ages are not to be generalized to all children irrespective of culture and individual differences. Of special importance are the implications that the present level of thought structure sets limits to what can be meaningfully learned at a given time, and, from that, that the teacher needs to match work sufficiently closely to extend from existing understanding. This point recurs in other extracts. Isaacs rightly stresses that environment is not ignored by Piaget, but is very much a feature of his theory. According to the latter, development is essentially a question of the child's actions upon the environment, and higher levels of thought represent internalized action in which language comes to substitute for overt action. The weakness here, which is not drawn out by Isaacs, is that Piaget did not differentiate qualitative nor quantitative features of the milieu in which the child grows.

The Piagetian Picture of the Child's Development

1. Keys to the Child's Mental Growth

The main keys to the child's mental growth, as Piaget brings them out, are (i) the paramount part played from the start by his own *action* (ii) the way this turns into a process of *inward building-up*, that is, of forming within his mind a continually extending *structure* corresponding to the world outside.

(i) The Child As Agent

(a) Piaget shows how from the beginning, the infant himself takes a controlling hand in procuring and organizing all his experience of the outside world. He follows with his eyes, explores with them, turns his head; explores with his hands, grips, lets go, pulls, pushes; explores with his mouth; moves his body and limbs; explores jointly and alternately with eye and hand, etc. All this brings experiences which come to him as the products of his activities and are formed into psychic schemes or patterns *keyed* by them. That keying becomes even more clearly marked when, happening upon an interesting experience, he is stimulated to repeat the activity that led to it, and then *goes on* with it or, after an interval, returns to it. This process of absorbing and organizing experiences round the activities that produce them Piaget calls '*assimilation*'. He regards it as our most fundamental process of learning and growth, which indeed goes on for the rest of our lives. However, assimilation is always being modified by an accompanying process of *accommodation*. Many situations or objects resist the activity patterns the child tries on them, and in so doing impose some changes on these patterns themselves. Still others yield *new* results which go to enrich the range or scope of the patterns.

Thus the assimilative processes constantly extend their domain whilst at the same time accommodation steers them into ever more successful *adaptation* to the world. This dual process, and the endeavour to maintain an equal balance between the two sides, are for Piaget the chief controlling factors of intellectual growth.

(b) To begin with, the activities that organize patterns of resulting experiences round them can only be physical, directed to outward objects and situations. Their scope indeed widens all the time, as the child's powers grow and above all as he masters locomotion and his range of exploration and action is thus immensely multiplied. But in the course of the second year, these external activities also develop a great new inward dimension. Language comes in and with it a more and more settled power of evocation and representation of absent things. This power is the main foundation for the unfolding activity of thought. The latter begins essentially as a form of *action in terms of internal images*, and presently of their verbal symbols, extending the range of the child's *physical action on outward objects*.

Thought is in fact for Piaget just action carried on inwardly and thus started on a new career of internal organization and growth.

(c) That story goes on developing through all the child's activities, outward and inward, during the next few years; but his most decisive advance usually comes only towards 7–8, when, by various related moves forward, he establishes himself on the level of *structured thinking*. This Piaget calls the stage of *concrete* operations of thought, because it still remains tied to tangible starting-points and goals, taken over from the real world. In the years that follow, the child exploits and consolidates these new-found powers of controlled thinking; but at the same time he prepared the ground for his next and final advance. Between 11 and 14 he attains the power of *abstract* thought — that is, thought emancipated from the given facts of the real world and able to operate freely with its own imagined possibilities and hypotheses. It can work out the logical consequences of these, or vary them or even reverse them, and draw a fresh set of consequences. How much use the child makes of this ability will depend on his bent, interests and native capacity; but in suitable subjects it can lead all the way to the most abstruse forms of logical, mathematical or scientific thought. Yet the link with action remains unbroken. All thought, as Piaget sees it, is operation, and operation is internalized action; it is this that determines the whole of our human experience, all our thought-life and learning, and all human mental growth.

(ii)   The Child as Inward Builder
Piaget thus directs our attention to what in fact lies behind our characteristic behaviour as human beings. Right from the start we build up in our minds a kind of working model of the world around us; in other words, a model of a world of persisting and moving objects and recurring happenings set in a framework of space and time and showing a regular order. Piaget shows how far this model-building is carried, in a functional yet unmistakable way, even in our first eighteen months, that is, prior to the help of language or explicit thought. Once the basic model is in our minds, the rest is merely a matter of building on, filling in and organizing; the structure remains the same, even though it is immeasurably expanded and enriched. In fact we carry it with us for the rest of our lives and although we normally take it for granted, it continually *regulates* all our planning and action. We are drawing on it — and relying upon it — whenever we start to *think out* any course of action: its space aspect when we want to get somewhere; its scheme of material objects when we want to make or construct something; its order of events when we want to bring about or to prevent some happening.

From the appropriate part of the model in our minds we then work out the actual sequence of movements or actions which we shall have to follow. In a great number of cases this process is virtually automatic; our purposes bring into our thoughts the programmes needed to give effect to them, and we get on with these without worrying how we have come by them. If, however, we stumble on a difficulty and need to stop for some real thinking, this may well make us explicitly aware, first, of the scheme in our minds which has carried us so far, secondly, of the nature of the present gap in it, and thirdly of what help we might be able to get from bringing further parts of our thought-resources to bear.

If then we consider the whole range of planned courses of action on which we constantly launch ourselves, we can get some measure of the connected and organized scheme of things in our minds on which they must rest. Our plans of course always contemplate the real world itself, in which they are to be realized; but the point is that when we are making them, we are *fore*seeing, *fore*thinking and *fore*planning, and can therefore ony be doing so from the model of that real world in our *minds*. We are naturally thinking of the real world, but at that stage we are only *thinking* of it. However our model so truly corresponds to it, at any rate in its main structure, that we can pass straight over from the model to the real world without any further thought. It is only in matters of comparative detail that it is liable to prove wrong or insufficient.

2. The Main Building Stages

(i) First 18 Months; Sensori-Motor Phase
Through a series of revealing tests on his own three infants, Piaget brings out the stages by which the first building up proceeds. The earliest behaviour shows not the least sense of persisting objects or of the most rudimentary space or time relations. But presently it is seen to change, and month by month it takes more account of these features of the world, until the child clearly has in his mind a scheme that corresponds to them. We see him *recognizing* different objects as such and expecting them to persist, to move in space and to display spatial characters and relations. Similarly he *recognizes* different happenings and expects them to take a certain course, expects some of them to lead on to others, and so on. The infant's conduct is now visibly *pre*-adjusted to all this; i.e. it is controlled by something in his mind which regularly anticipates just those features. How he is led to form that controlling schema has already been referred to; he learns by doing and trying, by assimilating all the different experiences that thus come to him, and by constantly varying and extending his experimental activities. And by eighteen months the range and variety of his purposive behaviour already bears witness to the controlling presence in his mind of the sort of basic world-model I have described.

(ii) 18 Months to 4–5 Years: Stage of Intuitive Thought
So much having already been achieved, the child has only to go on to exploit all the further instruments and powers that come to him. He now incessantly

expands and enriches, works over, organizes and re-organizes, his inward model of the world. He does so mainly through imaginative play on the one hand and through more exploring and experimenting, combined with questioning, listening and talking, on the other hand. The different kinds of objects and happenings which he can recognize, pre-adjust to, remember and imagine continually increase, whilst at the same time his sense of space-relations and time-relations becomes more varied and better articulated. Yet most of the detailed images and ideas in his mind tend to remain vague and unstable, and his thinking cannot move away from present situations without losing itself.

(iii)   4–5 Years to 7–8 Years: Advance to Stage of Concrete Operations
Piaget now concentrates above all on the state of the child's main *framework* notions and what happens to them. Thus he examines how children progress in their notions of different aspects of space, of time, of movement and speed, of number and measure, and of elementary logical relations such as those of whole and part, classes and sub-classes, or serial order, etc. By numerous experiments he shows that most 4–5 year olds of average intelligence have as yet no settled notions in any of these fields. Everything is still in a state of flux, nothing is clear or stays put. Size, shape, arrangement, etc. are mixed up with number; distance and length with movement; rate of movement with overtaking or catching up; time with speed, and so on.

The same experiments, however, carried out with children only about a year older show the *beginnings* of a notable change. At least in the simpler cases they can, by trial and error, sort their ideas out, and thus get some first inklings of the true meaning of distance, length, number and the rest. Thereafter there is usually further piecemeal progress and then, perhaps another year on, the scene is transformed. By 7–8 years children deal with most of the concrete experimental situations much as an ordinary adult would. Each of the basic structural concepts is now clear and stable. In Piaget's language, the level of 'conservation' has been reached. That is, distance, length, number, speed, mass, class-inclusion, etc., now each stand for something *constant*, whichever way round it is taken, however it is sub-divided, and, in the case of number however it is arranged in space, concentrated or spread. Moreover we have here concepts that can be linked together in larger structures which in turn have the same character of conservation. In fact various sets of these concepts taken together come to form distinctive schemes of operational thought. That means, schemes of connected relational *reasoning*, either mathematical or logical, such as eventually make up geometry, arithmetic, mathematics at large, mechanics, and the formal logical aspects of all other sciences. That may seem to be looking a long way ahead, and is not properly realized till the stage of full abstract reasoning is reached at 11–14 years. What Piaget establishes, however, is that the first prototypes of these operational ideas, that is, concepts that possess the minimum characters needed, are present in most children's minds from the age of 7–8 years. Thus the basic structure of their world is now properly laid down in their thought, not of course in words, but in functioning ideas. Therefore they can think out, flexibly and successfully, the simple everyday space relations (distances, sizes, etc.), time-relations (intervals, successions, overlaps, etc.), or mechanical, numerical and logical relations which we all continually need.

Piaget and Education

(From Adibe, N., 1978, 'The many implications of Piaget's work for education', *New Era*, 59, 3, pp. 80–5.)

The article by Nastine Adibe attempts to draw together the many dimensions of Piaget's work that relate to the processes of teaching and learning. In particular, the article demonstrates the ways in which Piaget's ideas might serve as a basis for assessing children's cognitive development with his theory of stages, and how a teacher might explore changes in children's competence via the 'clinical method' developed by Piaget. We are also introduced to Piaget's view of the role of language in cognitive development, an area which has been the subject of much critical debate. (See the extracts by Tamburrini (pp. 297–300), Donaldson (pp. 306–11), Boyle (pp. 312–16), Conner and Britton (pp. 317–22).

Introduction

Piaget's publications are numerous and widely dispersed. Only a small percentage has been translated into English. His findings on the nature of knowledge, on the genesis of intelligence and its development from infancy to adulthood are the result of over half a century of continuous research. His methods are unique and manifest his great empathy and sensitivity to the mental activities of the subjects he has observed. His solid background in biology, logic, mathematics, philosophy, and psychology have enabled him to integrate ideas and research from various disciplines in formulating his theories. He continually revises and refines his conclusions in the light of the new evidence for or against his findings.

Because Piaget's findings provide insight into the complex and mysterious working of the human brain, his observations have particular significance for universal education: by studying his findings teachers are sensitized to student's mental processes. In Elkind's words, 'after becoming acquainted with Piaget's work, teachers can never again see children in quite the same way as before'.[1] Or, as another author puts it, the effect is like 'taking the top off the child's head and watching the wheels go round'.[2] We become sensitive to the importance of a real understanding of concepts as opposed to the memorization of facts by learners, and we reexamine our traditional views regarding intelligence, experience, and maturity. As a result we become more critical of the existing instructional strategies and the innovative practices introduced in education.

It is only since the 1960s that Piaget's work has become popular among educators. Since then, we have witnessed an acceleration in the translation of Piaget's work into English and the mushrooming of publications in English interpreting Piagetian theory.

As Piaget's work has been popularized and simplified, it has often been misinterpreted, taken out of context of his overall view and prematurely applied. Piaget's formulation is not easy to understand. In formulating his theories Piaget draws models and synthesized information from the fields of biology, mathematics, philosophy, physical sciences, and psychology. Therefore, a knowledge of the major concepts in these fields is essential and a knowledge of French is helpful to grasp fully Piaget's theories.

[Adide then goes on to indicate the main elements of Piaget's ideas in terms of their significance to education.]

Assessing Student's Cognitive Levels

In order to adjust his teaching strategies to the class as a whole, and to plan for appropriate activities to meet different individual needs, a teacher utilizes various diagnostic techniques to assess his students' conceptual level. As the experienced teacher knows, not all of these techniques are effective.

Piaget has made two important contributions, one theoretical the other practical, to help the teacher in this assessment (a) by delineating four critical stages of development which the teacher can look for in his studies, and (b) by providing a simple but effective clinical method of listening to student's errors so that their appropriate level of development can be assessed.

Piaget's Developmental Stages

Piaget describes intellectual development as evolving through various stages in the individual development of the child. In Piaget's words: 'development is achieved by successive levels and stages',[3] each of which lays the foundation for its successors. The four most important stages he recognizes are now well known: the sensory-motor stage, the pre-operational stage, the concrete operational stage, and the stage of formal operations. [Detail of these stages is provided in the previous extract by Isaacs (pp. 283–8).]

> Let us note he writes that these stages are precisely characterized by their set order of succession... That is, in order to reach a certain stage, previous steps must be taken, and the prestructures which make for further advance must be constructed.[4]

This is one of Piaget's most popular formulations. But what is often overlooked is that these stages do not correspond with absolute chronological age, but each stage succeeds its precursor in a set order.

They are not stages which can be given a constant chronological date. On the contrary, the ages can vary from one society to another.[5]

He explains elsewhere:

The maturation of the nervous system can do no more than determine the totality of possibilities at a given stage. A particular social environment remains indispensible for the realization of these possibilities. It follows that their realization can be accelerated or retarded as a function of cultural and educational conditions.[6]

Researchers using Piaget's operational tests with different groups of children have found that all children do not reach the same developmental stage at the same chronological age. For example, there is as much as four years time lag between children in Martinique and children in France in reaching the same stage.[7]

It is often erroneously assumed that students in secondary schools, because of their chronological age, have reached the formal operational stage. However, many secondary school teachers know that a large number of their students do not manifest the cognitive skills characteristic of this stage. Several studies have confirmed this: some college students as well as many secondary school students have not acquired the cognitive skills appropriate to the stage of formal operations which potentially they should be at.[8] Many students at the seventh and eigth grades assumed to be at the formal operational stage may still be in a period of transition from the concrete operational to the formal operational stage.

Another observation by Piaget which is often overlooked by teachers is that when a learner is confronted with an unfamiliar or difficult problem he reverts to a previous stage of thinking.

Teachers at all levels of instruction must realize that not all of their students develop all their cognitive potential. Understanding Piaget's developmental stages, the sequence of these stages and the various tasks devised by Piaget to evaluate the students' intellectual stage will help teachers become more effective in sequencing the content to be taught and in planning instructional strategies that will involve and interest a larger number of students.

Listening to Student Errors

Piaget's 'clinical method' of exploring intellectual development is ingenuously simple. He listens to his subjects respond as each is given a task, and observes and analyzes the correct answers as well as the errors made by them. As Freud has gained insight into the working of the unconscious mind in the affective field by observing the slips of the tongue of his patients, so

Piaget has collected valuable information on the working of the conscious mind in the intellectual field by analyzing his subjects' errors.

Most teachers are busy correcting their students' errors with little thought as to what an error indicates. Such errors when examined can reveal the students' thinking process, their logic, and their past experiences. They can also provide an excellent source of informatioin about the effectiveness of the strategies used by the teacher. Students' errors are often caused by faulty sequencing of the content, by overdramatization of an application of a concept, by use of words and expressions not in the repertory of the students' language, or by introducing new content with little empathy exercised towards the students' previous experiences and knowledge. Analysis of students' errors can be an effective diagnostic tool for teachers at all levels.

The Role of Language in Teaching and Learning

Most teachers rely on language as a medium for teaching and consider the students' verbal definition of terminology or verbal explanation of concepts as an indication of the students' understanding of the underlying concepts being taught. Piaget's observations have shown that language is deceptive with respect to thought and understanding. He argues that logical thinking is essential for understanding which is primarily non-linguistic. It involves representations such as images and mental symbols, and the internalized actions which he terms '**operations**'.

Language does not constitute the source of logic but is, on the contrary, structured by it. The roots of logic are to be sought in the general coordination of actions.[9]

However, he does not underestimate the role of language in the course of intellectual development. He considers language exercises only one of many semiotic functions affording us the ability to represent something by a sign or symbol. In addition to language, semiotic functions also include imitation, play, drawing, and mental images. 'The semiotic function makes thought possible by providing it with an unlimited field of application',[10] he emphasizes.

Elsewhere Piaget states:

Language can constitute a necessary condition for the completion of logico-mathematical operations without being a sufficient condition for their formation.[11]

It is important for teachers to realize that language is deceptive with respect to thought and understanding. Teachers are often misled by the verbal facility of some students into believing that these students comprehend the concept and are capable of handling more advanced concepts than they are actually able to. On the other hand, they are often fooled by the language handicaps of some students into thinking that such students have lower mental ability than they actually possess.

It is also important to remember that during the course of intellectual development, reasoning about things (concrete operation) develops prior to reasoning about verbal propositions (formal operation).

Such realization may enable the teacher to depend less on verbal explanations and more on providing concrete experiences.

Global Exploration: Analysis and Synthesis

Piaget's observations of the way a child **explores** objects have implications at all levels of instruction. 'Perceptual or sensory-motor activity develops noticeably with age.' During the early stages 'the child remains almost passive when confronted with objects he has to identify.... There is no decentration so that he does not really explore them at all'.[12]

Later the child learns to explore the object as a whole, what Piaget terms '**global exploration**'. At a later stage the child analyzes specific features. Finally, at the level of genuine operations the child is able to explore the object systematically and with some kind of synthesis.

In order to study an area of knowledge in greater depth, it becomes necessary to isolate it from the main concepts it is related to. For example, considerable time may be devoted to the study of the structure of the cell, to the study of life functions, to the study of leaves, to the study of the sun, in such a way that the pupils remain completely oblivious of the fact that each of these topics are only parts of a whole. We assume that somewhere during their previous experiences, students have learned that a cell is a unit of structure in all living organisms, that a life function is only one of all the other functions of an organism, that a leaf is a part of a whole plant, and that the sun is a part of a universe.

We also assume that the student is capable of integrating the newly acquired knowledge into what he may have been exposed to previously. However most students are not able to perform this task without assistance from the teacher. When the teacher presents the concept in its 'global' aspect first, then takes the part to be analyzed and elaborated further (but being sure to constantly refer to its relationship to the whole) the final task of synthesis can become a simple task for students and the whole process of learning becomes more meaningful.

Motivation

The importance of motivation for learning is recognized by every teacher. Piaget provides insights into this much discussed topic. He believes in intrinsic motivation, observing that the child actively seeks out new stimulation. Piaget explains motivation in terms of his equilibration theory. A state of disequilibration must exist for the child to be intellectually stimulated. Although the child is seeking out stimulation, he is selective. It is only the type of stimulation which can disequilibrate him which becomes motivational.

Piaget says that objects, ideas, situations or events to catch a child's attention must be 'moderately novel'. The child is not interested in what is 'too familiar', nor can he notice what is 'too new which does not correspond to any of his schemes'. Plays and puzzles, according to Piaget, are excellent sources for disequilibrating the child.

Students can be motivated in school work when teachers become better acquainted with a student's cognitive process and remember the role of surprise and play in stimulating curiosity.

Humanistic Education

Although Piaget is best known for his studies on intellectual development, he recognizes the inter-relationship of emotions with intellect. In his foreward to Décarie's book he asserts: 'the inseparability of the affective and cognitive aspects of the assimilatory scheme'.[13] The following statement also confirms his view that as emotions colour intellect, emotions are also influenced by the intellect:

> All interaction with the environment involves both a structuring and a valuation. We cannot reason, even in pure mathematics, without experiencing certain feelings; and conversley, no effect can exist without a minimum of understanding or discrimination.[14]

In the following statement Piaget explains the effect of emotions on the intellectual development:

> Affectivity or its privations can certainly be the cause of acceleration or delay in cognitive development ... but this does not mean that affectivity produces or even modifies the cognitive structures whose necessity remains intrinsic. Actually the affective and cognitive mechanisms always remain indissociable, although distinct; and it goes without saying that if the affective stems from an energetic then the cognitive stems from structures.[15]

Some teachers persist in believing that their role is to teach content regardless of all other considerations, completely oblivious of the fact that the teaching-learning process at any level is a human interaction activity in which the affective aspect cannot be neglected.

The Goals of Education

The following statement by Piaget states his educational goals:

The principal goal of education is to create men who are capable of doing new things, not simply of repeating what other generations have done — men who are creative, inventive, and discoverers. The second goal of education is to form minds which can be critical, can verify, and not accept everything they are offered. The great danger today is of slogans, collective opinions, ready-made trends of thought. We have to be able to resist individually, to criticize, to distinguish between what is proven and what is not. So we need pupils who are active, who learn early to find out by themselves, partly by their own spontaneous activity and partly through material we set up for them; who learn early to tell what is verifiable and what is simply the first idea to come to them.[16]

Admittedly, these goals are highly idealistic, yet they do support many of the goals of education embraced by educators for a long time.

To help today's youth grow into adults who can assume the challenge of individual responsibility and survive in an increasing technological world, we must consciously strive to attain these goals. It is through a society composed of such individuals that we can lift the human race above and beyond the fear, ignorance, brutality, and isolation which exist in today's world. The establishment of freedom, justice and peace for all mankind demands the intellectual as well as the moral and spiritual achievements of each individual.

Notes

1 DAVID ELKIND (1972) 'Piaget and science education', *Science and Children*, November, pp. 9–12.
2 HELMORE, G.A. (1969) *Piaget a Practical Consideration*, Pergamon Press, p. VII.
3 PIAGET, J. (1973) *The Child and Reality*, New York, Grossman Publishers, p. 10.
4 *Ibid*; p. 10.
5 *Ibid*; p. 10.
6 INHELDER, B. and PIAGET, J. (1958) *The Growth of Logical Thinking from Childhood to Adolescence*, New York, Basic Books, p. 37.
7 JEAN PIAGET (1970) *Science of Education of the Psychology of the Child*, The Viking Press, New York, 1970, p. 37.
8 a) BUEL, R. and BRADLEY, G. (1972) 'Piagetian studies in science: chemical equilibrium understanding from study of solubility', *Science Education*, 56, (1), pp. 23–29.
   b) DAVID ELKIND (1961) 'Quantity conceptions in junior and senior high school students', *Child Development*, 32, pp. 551–560.
9 PIAGET, J. and INHELDER, B. (1969) *The Psychology of the Child*, N.Y., Basic Books, p. 90.

10   *Ibid*; p. 91.
11   PIAGET (1973) p. 113.
12   PIAGET, J. and INHELDER, B. (1967) *The Child's Conception of Space*, N.Y., Norton and Co., 1967, p. 39.
13   DÉCARIE, T.G. (1965) *Intelligence and Affectivity in Early Childhood*, New York, International University Press, p. XIV.
14   PIAGET, J. (1950) *The Psychology of Intelligence*, London, Routledge and Kegan Paul, p. 6.
15   PIAGET, J. (1973) *The Child and Reality*, p. 47.
16   RIPPLE, R. and ROCKCASTE, V. (Eds) (1964) *Piaget Rediscovered*, Cornell University School of Education, p. 5.

Piaget Revisited

(From Tamburrini, J., 1982, 'New directions in nursery education', in Richards, C. (Ed.) *New Directions in Primary Education*, Lewes, Falmer Press, pp. 102–5.)

In recent years, there has been increasing evidence to suggest that Piaget's proposals are inaccurate and inappropriate for decision making in the classroom. As the next extract by Tamburrini indicates, Piaget's description, especially of the young child, tends to be one of incompetence, what the child is presently unable to do. This clearly creates considerable difficulties for those working with young children who prefer to emphasize success in learning, starting with what children can do and understand. Tamburrini demonstrates that given the right kind of conditions, young children can demonstrate competence considerably in excess of those that Piaget's proposals would lead us to expect. Central to this are factors such as the language in which activities are explained, the appropriateness of the task to the child and his or her present stage of understanding, familiarity with the materials used, the context in which situations are explored and children's expectations of the participants in the situation.

The work of Piaget has dominated the psychology of intellectual develop-
ment for several decades. There is not the space here to go into details concerning his work. The important thing to note is that his description of the thinking of (young) children is mainly in terms of their incompetence; of how, that is, they cannot yet reason. The major characteristic of young children's thinking, according to Piaget, is that they are unable to 'decentre', that is they focus on a limited aspect of an object or situation, resulting in false conclusions or 'illogical' thinking. Just a few examples must suffice to illustrate this. The young child cannot put himself at the point of view of another person when it is different from his own: he 'centres' on his own point of view. If the shape of some malleable substance is changed, (if a ball of clay, for example, is rolled into a sausage shape) a young child believes the quantity has either increased or decreased. He does so because he centres either on the increase in length and ignores the decrease in width or *vice versa*. Young children generally centre on similarities between objects and ignore dissimilarities. Piaget's example is of a child who, on a walk, saw first one slug and then another slug and concluded they were the same slug. Conversely and paradoxically, a child may sometimes centre on dissimilarities and ignore similarities. This leads him to conclude, for example, that there are several suns because he has seen the sun in different places. This account of young children's thinking is in terms of incompe-
tence; of what they cannot yet understand; of how they cannot yet think. It creates a problem for those concerned with the education of young children, when their traditional wisdom has been that it is important to start with

what a child can do and understand; with his competencies rather than his incompetencies.

There is now, however, a considerable amount of evidence that, given certain conditions, young children's intellectual capabilities are greater than Piaget's tests might lead us to believe. Tamburrini (1982) has agrued that it should not be inferred from this evidence that Piaget's tests are invalid, but rather that Piaget's tests assess some overall generalized competence that will be shown by a child in all relevant contexts, whereas there are some specific contexts where a child will think at a higher level than he does in a standard Piagetian test. What the characteristics of these contexts are must therefore now be examined.

First, it would appear that, if we want a young child to function intellectually at his most capable, we must ensure that the way we ask him to express his understanding is appropriate to his level of understanding and development. A comparison between children's responses on Piaget'a standard tests for egocentricity and those in a test devised by Borke (1978), which modifies the standard test only slightly, illustrates this principle. Egocentricity is the term Piaget uses for the inability of the young child to put himself at the point of view of another person when it is different from his own. In Piaget's test the child is shown a three dimensional model of three mountains each of which has a feature clearly distinguishing it from the other two. The child is required to select from photographs of the mountains from different points of view the one representing the perspective of a doll which is placed *vis-à-vis* the mountains in a position different from that of the child. On this standard test few children under the age of seven are able to select the correct photograph. Most young children select the photograph representing their own point of view. Borke modified the test in a simple way. Instead of selecting from photographs the child had to demonstrate the point of view of the doll by turning a turntable. Many children of four and some of three years of age were able to do this correctly.

A second condition favourable to children thinking at their most capable is the familiarity of the materials involved. In a further modification of Piaget's 'mountains' test for egocentricity Borke substituted for the three mountains a three dimensional model consisting of miniature people and animals in familiar domestic settings. As in the previous experiment the turntable was used instead of a selection of photographs. Under these conditions even more young children were able to give a correct response than in the other experiment by Borke discussed above.

A third important condition affecting the level of young children's thinking is one particularly stressed by Donaldson (1978) involving the extent to which they understand the intentions of the participants in a situation. She reports an experiment carried out by McGarrigle which again involved a minor modification to a standard Piagetian test. One of Piaget's tests for conservation of number involves showing the child two rows of five objects, say counters, aligned so that each counter in the second row is placed underneath the corresponding counter in the first row. The experimenter then spreads out the second row and the child, who has agreed that there was the same amount of counters in each row when they were aligned, is now asked whether there is still the same amount. In McGarrigle's version of the task the rearrangement was ostensibly the result of accident rather than of the intentional act of an adult. This was achieved by introducing a teddy bear, called 'naughty Teddy' who rearranged the elements. In this modified version more young children gave the correct response than normally happens in the standard test. Donaldson comments that in the standard test the young child tries to make sense of the experimenter's intention in terms of his experience of adults' intentions in his everyday transactions with them. If an adult arranges some objects, asks if they are the same amount, rearranges them, and then again asks if there is the same amount, a young child is likely to assume that the answer must be that the amount has changed, because in his experience adults do not carry out an action on things if their state is to remain the same as it was before. [A further extract from this influential book is to be found on pages 306–11]

A fourth condition affecting young children's understanding is, perhaps obviously, the complexity of relationships involved in a stituation. For example, Light (1979), investigating egocentricity or role-taking abilities in a group of four year old children, used a number of tasks varying in complexity but each one requiring the child to identify another's point of view that was different from his own. One of Light's tasks used a three-sided pyramid with a different toy illustrated on each of its faces. The child was required to say which toy the experimenter who sat opposite him could see. In a more elaborate version of the task a doll was used and placed in each of five positions from two of which it would 'see' only one toy and from the other three of which it would 'see' two toys. The child was required to identify the toy or toys the doll would 'see' from the various positions. Out of a group of sixty children only five gave the correct response on all trials in the second task, whereas twenty-three did so in the first task.

These findings lend support to the conventional wisdom that children need to explore and play with materials in their own way and in their own time. Further support for this practice comes from a comparative study carried out by Sylva, Roy and Painter as part of the Oxford Preschool Project. A comparison was undertaken between preschool centres in Oxfordshire and in Miami, Florida. In the Oxfordshire schools a large range of equipment was available from which, for the most part, a child selected what he wanted when he wanted it. By contrast, in most of the Miami centres a limited range of materials, such as three Rs materials, was laid out at any one time, and choice was firmly controlled by the teacher for large parts of the day, even in some cases in so-called free play periods. Sylva and her associates found that the Miami children were not stretching themselves intellectually as much as the Oxfordshire children, and this was in spite of the greater emphasis in the Miami centres on school-like activities and in spite of the much greater frequency in them of prescribed work as compared with the Oxfordshire centres.

While the evidence suggests the need for children to have ample opportunity to explore and play with materials in their own way and in their own time, it would be wrong to conclude that all the adult needs to do is to provide appropriate materials and then to adopt only a supervisory role. Evidence is beginning to accrue of differences in children's social experience that are associated with differences in their intellectual functioning. This evidence supports the view that teachers should adopt an active rather than passive role with respect to the cognitive domain.

References

BORKE, H. (1978) 'Piaget's view of social interaction and the theoretical construct of empathy', in SIEGEL, L.S. and BRAINERD, C.J. (Eds) *Alternatives to Piaget*, London, Academic Press.

DONALDSON, M. (1978) *Children's Minds*, London, Fontana.

LIGHT, P. (1979) *The Development of Social Sensitivity*, Cambridge, Cambridge University Press.

SYLVA, K., ROY, C. and PAINTER, M. (1980) *Childwatching in the Playgroup and Nursery School*, London, Grant McIntyre.

TAMBURRINI, J. (1982) 'Some educational implications of Piaget's theory', in MODGIL, S. and MODGIL, C. (Eds) *Jean Piaget: Consensus and Controversy*, Eastbourne, Holt, Rinehart and Winston/New York: Praeger.

The Myth of Piaget's Contribution to Education

(From Boyle, D., 1983, 'The myth of Piaget's contribution to educa-tion', in Modgil, S. and Modgil, C. (Eds) *Jean Piaget: An Interdisci-plinary Critique*, London, Routledge and Kegan Paul, pp. 71–5.)

The critique of the application of Piaget's ideas for education continues with Boyle's consideration of the importance of 'activity' in children's learning. Cognitive psy-chology stresses the importance of the meanings an individual makes of learning experiences (see the introduction to this section pp. 276–7 and the extract by Claxton pp. 279–82). This is a view strongly advocated by those supporting the liberal romantic tradition (see the extracts by Blyth, pp. 79–82; Marshall, pp. 83–6, and Nias, pp. 91–4). Such meanings should be personally and actively developed.

Boyle reminds us however, that activity need not always be physical activity. In cognitive development, mental activity is as important, if not more important. Boyle draws upon evidence to question the Piagetian assertion that children need to actively manipulate objects to ensure that successful cognitive development occurs. As he concludes, verbal explanation is fundamental and that, 'in the Piagetian scheme of things actions come first, words a very poor second'.

I shall illustrate some of the confusions that may arise when teachers attempt to base instruction on Piagetian theory by reference to three books written to illustrate such attempts. The first is by Furth and Wachs (1974) and concerns the 'Tyler Thinking School' in Charleston, West Virginia, where they have created an environment 'to implement Piaget's theory by providing the child with experiences best designed to develop his thinking'. They distinguish development (i.e., 'general mechanisms of action and thinking') from learning ('the acquisition of specific skills and the memoriz-ing of specific information'). They call 'learning' the result of teaching that does not basically alter the child's intelligence; and 'development' the result of teaching that brings about intellectual change. In practice, of course, one cannot teach without transmitting specific skills, but Furth and Wachs claim that the conceptual distinction between general and specific changes has value. However, it does appear from what they say that development can be brought about by teaching, and their conceptual distinction is valuable only in maintaining the Piagetian dogma that development is spontaneous.

Let us pause to consider what spontaneous development might mean. Piaget's model is that of maturation of the neuro-muscular system. A baby deprived of the opportunity to walk will nonetheless develop the neuro-muscular apparatus to make this possible at a certain age. Can we really believe this to be true of the intellect? Would a child growing up without direction, in however intellectually rich an environment, develop into a skilled thinker? Is it not more likely that he would formulate faulty hypo-theses and draw wrong conclusions? We cannot experiment to find out, but we conduct the business of living on the assumption that our errors are corrected by the interchange of ideas through language. This is the whole purpose, not only of schooling, but also of publishing books, scholarly papers and rebuttals, and of holding conferences at which contentious issues are debated.

An example makes clear the disastrous consequences of a determination to fit data into a Piagetian framework. An eight-year-old living in Washington, DC at a time when the mayor was named Washington believed that the mayor of Philadelphia would be a Mr Philadelphia. Furth and Wachs assumed that the child 'would have been capable of thinking at a more mature level if ... motivated to do so' (1974, p. 17). It is quite unwarranted to describe this thinking as 'low-level' and the result of inadequate motivation. The boy was drawing an inference from facts at his disposal, and he was wrong because the facts were insufficient. On the basis of those facts the inference was quite reasonable. Being right or wrong could have nothing to do with motivation in this instance; improvement in the child's performance (if, indeed, the idea of improvement has any meaning here) would be contingent upon an increase in the sort of factual knowledge that would allow the boy to realize that his first experience of towns, mayors and their names embodied a coincidence.

My second book for discussion is by Schwebel and Raph (1974) and is a collection of chapters by different authors. The one I have singled out is by Sinclair, and I have chosen it because it clearly illustrates the tendency of the Piaget shop-floor to use words in their own special way. Here is a quotation (1974, pp. 57–8):

> Piaget and his collaborators did not conclude that any kind of learning procedure would be useless.... [They] meant only that empirical methods, whereby the subject has to accept a link because this is imposed upon him, do not result in progress; progress results only when the subject himself discovers the link. This active discovery of links is what happens in development; it is therefore called spontaneous — maybe unfortunately — for development is always the result of interaction.... Learning is dependent on development, not only in the sense that certain things can be learned only at certain levels of development, but also in the sense that in learning — that is, in situations specifically constructed so that the subject has active encounters with the environment — the same mechanisms as in development are at work.

I maintain that this argument is little short of dishonest. In the first place, there is a false dichotomy between imposition of a link and discovery of that link. Most teachers, if not all, would regard effective teaching as the explanation of links, but Piaget's theory requires Sinclair to hold that whatever is not discovery is imposition. Presumably if a teacher successfully explained a link to a child this would count as the child's having discovered it! Sinclair's reference to 'activity' amounts to no more than saying that intellectual development occurs only when children understand what they are doing, a proposition with which few would disagree, whatever their persuasion. This trumpeting of banalities as if they were logical implications solely of Piaget's theory is typical of the narrowness and arrogance of the Piaget factory. As for the reference to 'spontaneous' development (another Piagetian sacred cow), this shows that 'spontaneous' development is not spontaneous at all, but is dependent upon the environment provided by the teacher. The advice to teachers to provide environments in which children can discover things for themselves is not exclusively Piagetian.

My third example (Wadsworth, 1978) confirms the suspicion that the major activity of the Piaget-for-education industry is sticking its own label on other people's tried and tested goods. Wadsworth, a Piagetian scholar, and a teacher, attempts to apply Piaget's theory to the practice of education, calling on the theory 'only to the extent necessary to provide a rationale for the teaching practices and principles presented'. He claims that 'Piagetian methods are a more efficient set of methods than traditional methods for acquiring skills and knowledge'. If we ask what these methods are, we have great difficulty in discovering precisely what is Piagetian about them. For example; 'Reading about and talking about things are not neglected, though they are not emphasized to the exclusion of everything else, as in traditional classrooms.' What tradition is this that excludes everything except reading and talking? Where are these classrooms? Certainly not in Britain, where Froebel and Montessori had exercised a liberating influence long before Piaget became a cult figure; nor, I suspect, in many parts of Europe where, of course, they were influential even earlier.

Piaget has recognized that the stress on activity is not new. Writing on the genesis of the 'new methods' (Piaget, 1971), he acknowledges that the importance of activity was recognized by Montessori, Froebel, Pestalozzi, Rousseau and even Socrates. He conceives his own unique contribution as being the objective establishment of the truth of the principle that activity is vital. Unfortunately the truth of this principle has recently been questioned.

Anthony (1977), writing in the same symposium as Smedslund, who has already been mentioned, argues that Piaget's claim that children need actively to manipulate objects is not supported by empirical research. Nor, as Anthony points out, does Piaget's commitment to this view appear to be shared by his close collaborators (Inhelder and Sinclair, 1969; Inhelder, Sinclair and Bovet, 1974). While some active handling can be beneficial, Anthony concludes that 'The extreme Piagetian insistence on physical activity has been excessive.'

Here is part of the quotation from Inhelder, Sinclair and Bovet (1974) which Anthony (1977, p. 25) uses to make his point:

being cognitively active does not mean that the child merely manipulates a given type of material; he can be mentally active without physical manipulation, just as he can be mentally passive while actually manipulating objects. Intellectual activity is stimulated if the opportunities for acting on objects or observing other people's actions or for discussions correspond to the subject's level of development.

The clear implication of this is that there can be physical activity or intellectual activity, and that intellectual activity is more important. To talk of 'intellectual activity' is to talk figuratively; it means that the child must think about what he is doing if he is to learn from any experience, a proposition that is hardly a revelation. Piaget does not seem to be referring to intellectual activity when he says (Schwebel and Raph, 1974, pp. ix–x):

> It is absolutely necessary that learners have at their disposal concrete material experiences (and not merely pictures), and that they form their own hypotheses and verify them (or not verify them) themselves through their own active manipulations. The observed activities of others, including those of the teachers, are not formative of new organizations in the child.

While what Piaget says does not rule out the requirement that the child be intellectually active, he is adamant that the child must actively manipulate material, 'with all the tentative gropings and apparent waste of time that such involvement implies' (Schwebel and Raph, 1974, pp. ix–x). This unambiguously means that insight cannot arise from observation, a proposition that is not confirmed by empirical studies, as Anthony demonstrates. As Anthony points out, the importance of physical manipulation is not a logical deduction from Piaget's theory, but it is a principle that has been made the basis of some teaching techniques. Herein, I think, lies a great danger. If it should become an accepted dogma that physical manipulation is essential for learning, then able children who could learn efficiently and quickly from demonstration and explanation would be held back by the insistence on frustrating and time-wasting activities. Of course there must be activity at some stage: children must be encouraged actively to apply their knowledge. However, there has long been a distinction made in psychology between learning and performance: improvement in performance certainly requires practice, but chimpanzees can learn by observation, and even rats can learn while apparently doing nothing. There is no reason to suppose that children are less gifted.

Human beings have a great advantage over animals in that language makes observation more efficient, because it can be accompanied by verbal explanation. Unfortunately in the Piagetian scheme of things actions come first, words a very poor second. Recommending that children be made to discover things through active manipulation rather than by talk and discussion is tantamount to refusing to accept the essentially verbal nature of human intellectual functioning. The recommendation would, if widely applied, be intellectually stultifying to our brightest children.

References

ANTHONY, W.S. (1977) 'Activity in the learning of Piagetian operational thinking', *British Journal of Educational Psychology*, 47, pp. 18–24.

FURTH, H.G. and WACHS, H. (1974) *Thinking Goes to School: Piaget's Theory in Practice*, New York, Oxford University Press.

INHELDER, B. and SINCLAIR, H. (1969) 'Learning cognitive structures', on MASSEN, P., LANGER, J. and COVINGTON, J. (Eds) *Trends and Issues in Developmental Psychology*, New York, Holt Rinehart and Winston.

INHELDER, B., SINCLAIR, H. and BOVET, M. (1974) *Learning and the Development of Cognition*, London, Routledge and Kegan Paul.

PIAGET, J. (1971) *Science of Education and the Psychology of the Child*, London, Longman.

SCHWEBEL, M. and RAPH, J. (Eds) (1974) *Piaget in the Classroom*, London, Routledge and Kegan Paul.

WADSWORTH, B. (1978) *Piaget for the Classroom Teacher*, London, Longman.

Comprehending the Task:
A Re-Examination of Piaget

(From Donaldson, M., 1978, *Children's Minds*, London, Fontana, pp. 18–24.)

This extract is taken from an influential book which seeks to modify and reinterpret the Piagetian view of children's development outlined earlier (pp. 288–9). This re-interpretation is based partly on a number of studies with children carried out by Donaldson and her associates. One such investigation is described here and relates to children's ability to take account of someone else's spatial perspective. Not only is Piaget's claim disputed, but an important point is made about factors affecting children's performance on tasks. When a child understands what is wanted, perform-ance is better than when the task is not clearly comprehended. This truism is tested in experimental form by Donaldson and her associates, and except for its significance for education, might have been thought to be too obvious to merit research. The extract outlines two important implications for teaching. First, if a task is outside our comprehension, if it does not make sense, then we have only our own point of view to fall back on — an egocentric view. Donaldson argues that this is the case with tests of egocentricity in understanding spatial relations in Piaget's Three Mountains Task. A second implication is that understanding is at first specific to the context in which it occurs and in order to abstract general principles or to form what Piaget called '*structures d'ensemble*' a child needs a variety of related experiences. Experi-ences of counting with acorns, buttons, peanuts and the like, as examples from the classroom, are necessary to the formation of concepts about ordinal and cardinal number. Each separate experience, rooted in everyday life, provides the '*aliment*' from which concepts develop in a fusion of nature and nurture.

It has been claimed that children under the age of six or seven are very bad at communicating, precisely for the reason that they are bad at decentring — or that they are highly 'egocentric'.

This claim has been made most forcibly by Jean Piaget, and it has been backed by much supporting evidence. He has made it central to his theoriz-ing about the capacities of children in the pre-school and early school years. He has constructed such a far-reaching and closely woven net of argument, binding together so many different features of the development of be-haviour, that it is hard to believe he could be wrong.

Yet there is now powerful evidence that in this respect he *is* wrong. In recent years Piaget has collected most of his data by devising tasks for children to do and then observing their behaviour when they deal with the task, questioning them about it, noting what they say. One of the best known of these tasks is concerned with the ability to take account of someone else's point of view in the literal sense — that is, to recognize what someone else will see who is looking at the same thing as oneself but from the other side.

For this task, a three-dimensional object or set of objects is needed. Piaget uses a model of three mountains. (See *The Child's Conception of Space* by Piaget and Inhelder.) The mountains are distinguished from one another by colour and by such features as snow on one, a house on top of another, a red cross at the summit of the third.

The child sits at one side on the table on which this model is placed. The experimenter then produces a little doll and puts the doll at some other position round the table. The problem for the child is: what does the doll see?

It would clearly be hard for the child to give a verbal description ('He sees a house on top of the mountain on his right ...' etc.) for that description would have to be of consideration complexity. So in one version of the task the child is given a set of ten pictures of the model taken from different angles, and he is asked to choose the one which shows what the doll sees. In another version he is given three cardboard 'mountains' and he is asked to arrange them so that they represent what would be seen in a snapshot taken from the doll's position. Children up to the age of around eight, or even nine, cannot as a rule do this successfully; and there is a powerful tendency among children below the age of six or seven to choose the picture — or build the model — which represents their own point of view — exactly what they themselves see.

Piaget takes this to indicate that they are unable to 'decentre' in imagination. He points out that in one sense they know perfectly well that the appearance of a thing changes when you walk round it. And yet he maintains that they are bound by what he calls 'the egocentric illusion' as soon as they are called upon to form a mental representation of some view which they have not actually seen. They 'really imagine that the doll's perspective is the same as their own'. They all think the doll sees the mountains only as they look from the child's position. What the child lacks is held to be the ability to see his own momentary viewpoint as one of a set of possible viewpoints, and to co-ordinate these possibilities into a single coherent system, so that he understands the ways in which the different perspectives relate to one another.

We are urged by Piaget to believe that the child's behaviour in this situation gives us a deep insight into the nature of his world. The world is held to be one that is composed largely of 'false absolutes'. That is to say, the child does not appreciate that what he sees is relative to his own position; he takes it to represent absolute truth or reality — *the world as it really is*. Notice that this implies a world marked by extreme discontinuity. Any change in position means abrupt change in the world and a sharp break with the past. And indeed Piaget believes that this is how it is for the young child: that he lives in the state of the moment, not bothering himself with how things were just previously, with the relation of one state to those which come before or after it. His world is like a film run slowly, as Piaget says elsewhere.

This is by no means to say that Piaget thinks the child has no memory of the earlier 'stills'. The issue for Piaget is how the momentary states are linked, or fail to be linked, in the child's mind. The issue is how well the child can deal conceptually with the transitions between them.

All this has far-reaching implications for the child's ability to think and reason ... let us consider how children perform on a task which is in some ways very like the 'mountains' task and in other extremely important ways very different.

This task was devised by Martin Hughes. In its simplest form, it makes use of two 'walls' intersecting to form a cross, and two small dolls, representing respectively a policeman and a little boy. Seen from above, the lay-out (before the boy doll is put in position) is like this:

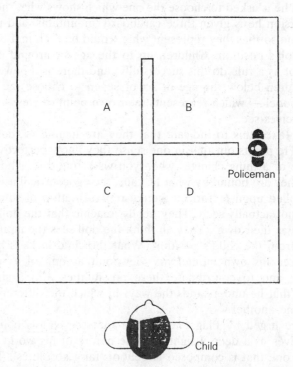

In the studies which Hughes conducted the policeman was placed initially as in the diagram so that he could see the areas marked B and D, while the areas A and C were hidden from him by the wall.

The child was then introduced to the task very carefully, in ways that were designed to give him every chance of understanding the situation fully and grasping what was being asked of him. First, Hughes put the boy doll in section A and asked if the policeman could see the boy there. The question was repeated for sections B, C and D in turn. Next the policeman was placed on the opposite side, facing the wall that divides A from C, and the child was asked to 'hide the doll so that the policeman can't see him'. If the child made any mistakes at these preliminary stages, his error was pointed out to him, and the question was repeated until the correct answer was given. But very few mistakes were made.

Then the test proper began. And now the task was made more complex. Another policeman was produced and the two were positioned thus:

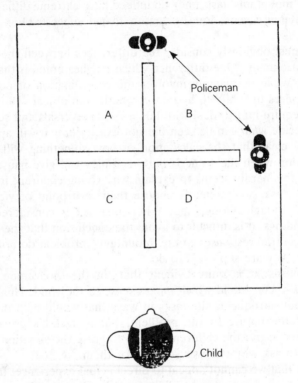

The child was told to hide the boy from both policemen, a result which could only be achieved by the consideration and co-ordination of two different points of view. This was repeated three times, so that each time a different section was left as the only hiding place.

The results were dramatic. When thirty children between the ages of three-and-a-half and five years were given this task, 90 per cent of their responses were correct. And even the ten youngest children, whose average age was only three years nine months, achieved a success rate of 88 per cent.

Hughes then went on the further trials, using more complex arrangements of walls, with as many as five or six sections, and introducing a third policeman. The three-year-olds had more trouble with this, but they still got over 60 per cent of the trials correct. The four-year-olds could still succeed at the 90-per-cent level.

It seems to be impossible to reconcile these findings with Piaget's claim that children under the age of seven are very bad at appreciating the point of view of some other person in the literal sense of being unable to figure out what that other person can see. However, though Hughes' findings cannot be reconciled with Piaget's *claim*, some way must be found of reconciling them with Piaget's *findings* — for these are not suspect. Research by other investigators has fully confirmed that, if children are given the Piaget 'mountains' task, they do indeed have extreme difficulty with it — but not, it now seems, for the reason Piaget suggests. For what reason, then?

One must obviously consider the differences between the two tasks — and these are many. One difference which Hughes noted is that the 'policemen' task, while it certainly involves the co-ordination of points of view, merely requires the child to figure out whether an object will be visible and does not require him to deal with left — right reversals and so on. That is, he must decide *what* can be seen but not exactly *how* it will appear. Now it is perfectly clear that the calculation of how something will look from a given position when the scene is fairly complex will give pause to many an adult. But this hardly seems to explain why young children, in tackling the 'mountains' task, so frequently choose their own point of view instead of a different, though wrong, one. When this fact is considered along with Hughes' findings, it is difficult to avoid the conclusion that the children who make 'egocentric' responses to the 'mountains' problem do not fully understand what they are supposed to do.[1]

By contrast it is quite evident that, in the 'policemen' problem, a situation has been found which *makes sense* to the child. Hughes was very careful about introducing the tasks in ways that would help the children to understand the nature of the problem, but in fact his precautions were largely unnecessary: the children seemed to grasp the situation at once. We have then to ask why this was so easy for them.

Notice that we cannot appeal to direct actual experience: few, if any, of these children had even tried to hide from a policeman. But we *can* appeal to the generalization of experience: they know what it is to try to hide. Also they know what it is to be naughty and to want to evade the consequences. So they can easily conceive that a boy might want to hide from a policeman if he had been a bad boy; for in this case it would be the job of the policeman to catch him and the consequences of being caught would be undesirable.

The point is that the *motives* and *intentions* of the characters are entirely comprehensible, even to a child of three. The task requires the child to act in ways which are in line with certain very basic human purposes and interactions (escape and pursuit) — it makes *human sense*. Thus it is not at all hard to convey to the child what he is supposed to do: he apprehends it instantly. It then turns out that neither is it hard for him to do it. In other words, in this context he shows none of the difficulty in 'decentring' which Piaget ascribes to him.

Reference

PIAGET, J. and INHELDER, B. (1963) *The Child's Conception of Space*, London, Routledge and Kegan Paul.

Note

1   In another study, Hughes used a simplified version of the mountains task and found that it was possible, by taking great care over the way in which the problem was introduced, to get a high proportion of correct responses from pre-school children. So this lends further support to the view that Piaget's subjects did not understand.

An Outline of the Contribution of Jerome Bruner

(An article produced for this volume by Colin Conner, Cambridge Institute of Education)

Jerome Bruner, like Piaget, describes development in terms of stages, but unlike Piaget sees them related to the technological advance of a culture. According to Bruner, cognitive development is the process by which human beings increase their mastery in achieving and using knowledge and cognition includes strategies for reducing the complexity of the world. He identifies three modes of representation which allows this to happen: the active, the iconic and the symbolic. Each of these has a powerful effect on mental life at different ages and each continues to function and interact with the others throughout later life.

In 1959, following the concern with the state of American education generated by the launch of the Sputnik by the Russians, Bruner chaired the 'Woods Hole Conference on Education'. This stimulated his interest in education and resulted in the *Process of Education* published in 1960, in which he outlined a theory of the organization and structure of education on a set of basic premises. It was partly as a result of this conference that Bruner became involved in the development of a social studies course, 'Man: A Course of Study' (MACOS) aimed primarily at children in the middle years. Whilst he was Guggenheim fellow at the University of Cambridge he studied cognition and cognitive development and visited Piaget in Geneva.

The article which follows was written specifically for this publication and attempts to draw together the major features of Bruner's contribution to our understanding of important educational issues. As will be seen, a major difference between the views of Piaget and those of Bruner is the importance Bruner attaches to language in cognitive development. The influence of language on learning has been the focus of much of Bruner's most recent work, in particular his studies of young children's talk and their learning to use language. His ideas have significantly influenced the work of Mercer and Edwards in this area (pp. 323–31).

References

BRUNER, J.S. (1960) *The Process of Education*, Harvard University Press.
BRUNER, J.S. (1983) *Child's Talk: Learning to Use Language*, Oxford, Oxford University Press.

Bruner's researches have contributed to the study of education in four main directions:

(i)   His studies of the process of Conceptual Development.
(ii) His comments on the process of Intellectual Development.
(iii) His comments on the structure and organisation of the Curriculum.
(iv) His comments on the most appropriate learning and teaching methods.

Concept Development

Bruner's researches into the formation and development of concepts are reported in *A Study of Thinking*, published in 1956 with Goodnow and Austin. As a result of their experiments they identified two categories of concept formation:

   (i) *Focussing* An individual investigates situations and experiences by considering one attribute at a time. They tend to be cautious and not necessarily particularly methodical.

  (ii) *Scanning* An individual investigates situations and experiences *either* (a) Simultaneously by looking at the whole picture; (b) Successively by looking at the situation one aspect at a time. After such initial deliberations *Scanners* then begin to set up hypothetical solutions to the problem which they then test to arrive at a final solution.

Bruner and his colleagues concluded that *Focussing* tends to be the most frequently employed strategy.

In the discussions based upon this research, Bruner concluded that all cognitive activity is dependent on the process of *categorisation*, and we each build up a *Generic Coding System* to deal with the multitude of stimuli that impinges upon us. Success in cognitive activity depends upon the breadth of our Generic Coding System.

Intellectual Development

For Bruner the development of the mind is dependent upon the mastery of intellectual techniques which are embedded in the culture in which a person is reared. No matter what the culture, the techniques which Bruner isolates are those of Action, Imagery, and Symbols. Thus he hypothesises three levels of representation:

Enactive — the representation of experience through motor responses of various kinds

Iconic   — dealing with events by using imagery and perceptual models

Symbolic— the use of the symbol systems of words and numbers

Bruner's stages or levels of development seem to have obvious similarities to Piaget's stages. For Bruner, as for Piaget, the child passes through the modes gradually, integrating and combining past experience in the transition to the next one. When organising and manipulating past experience each individual is dependent upon his own unique cognitive structure, but Bruner feels that the extension of this cognitive structure can be assisted by the teacher. Hence his interest in the curriculum, whose proper design and sequencing he sees as fundamental to aiding children's intellectual growth. Bruner sums up his views, as compared with those of Piaget, in this way:

> At the Institute in Geneva, cognitive development is seen almost purely as a matter of maturation, maturation that takes place by a process of internalisation of logical forms; first expressed motorically, is gradually internalised until it can be used symbolically — at which time physical action becomes no longer necessary for thought ... At the Cognitive Centre at Harvard, cognitive development is conceived more in terms of the internalisation of technologies from the culture, language being the most effective technique available. (Bruner *et al.*, 1966, p. 214.)

The Significance of Language

Bruner's general description of stages of representation parallels Piaget's sensorimotor, concrete operational, and formal operational stages, but differs in his interpretation of the role of language in the development of thought. Piaget believes that thought and language are closely related, but different, systems. He regards the thinking of the child as based on a system of inner logic that evolves as a child organises and adapts to experiences. He also believes that the symbols of the younger child are based on visual images and imitation. This is an hypothesis based on observations that two-year-old children are able to engage in accurate imitations of complex behaviour at a time when their language skills are quite primitive. Bruner, however, maintains that thought is internalised language and that syntactical rules of language rather than logic can be used to explain mastery of conservation and other principles. He bases this on experiments reported in *Studies in Cognitive Growth* (1966) by Bruner, Olver and Greenfield. The most well known experiment in this field was undertaken in collaboration with Francoise Frank, in which they modified Piaget's conservation experiment involving transfer of liquid from one container to another. Instead of allowing the visual impression to confuse the children, they poured the water behind a cardboard screen which allowed the child to see only the tops of the jars and not the amount of water. When children were asked if there would be the same amount of water in tall and short jars, most were able to give the correct answer, although many were unable to conserve their thinking when the screen was removed and they could actually see the jars being filled. Bruner explains that children who see the water being poured are impelled by the visual prescence of the pouring to concentrate on visual cues, whereas children who are asked to describe what will happen without seeing the whole array use symbolic representation, which frees them from the concrete.

The Structure of Knowledge and the Spiral Curriculum

According to Bruner, in teaching, one of the principal tasks is to communicate *structual* elements. These elements comprise the main ideas, the key concepts, characteristic modes and methods of enquiry, of any subject, which should be taught with learner in mind. 'The task of instruction is to translate the subject matter's basic ideas into a language appropriate to the learner.' Bruner believes that any subject can be taught effectively in some intellectually honest form to any child at any stage of development.

It is a necessary feature of these suggestions that the child has the opportunity to revisit these basic ideas in progressively more complex form, thus Bruner envisages a 'Spiral Curriculum', in which learning is presented on several different levels, each of which builds upon and extends the last.

One important way in which structure often needs to be translated for young learners is into the mode of representation appropriate to their stage of development. Children not yet operating within the symbolic mode may be able to grasp quite abstract relationships in iconic form. Bruner has attempted to do this in the curriculum package in which he became involved. (MACOS — Man: A Course of Study. For a useful review of the MACOS package see the article by Jean Ruddock in the *Cambridge Journal of Education*, 2, 2, 1972, pp. 118–126.)

Learning and Teaching Methods

Bruner strongly advocates the importance of activity and the involvement of the child in his own learning. This he suggests has a number of distinct advantages:

(i)   It will increase intellectual potency.
(ii) There will be a move from extrinsic to intrinsic rewards.
(iii) The child discovers how to discover.
(iv) There will be an improvement in memory.

Bruner accepts that this type of 'Discovery Learning', which has been criticized especially by Ausubel, implies that the teacher could be seen NOT to be involved in the child's learning. But he sees the teacher as a guide, a source of encouragement, and planner of the child's self activated discovery.

The teacher will become well practised in the art of 'intellectual temptation'. More recently Bruner has attempted to draw together ideas which have developed over an extensive career. In his study, *Actual Minds, Possible Worlds* (1986) he comments on the changes in his own thinking about education. 'I have come increasingly to recognise that learning in most settings is a communal activity, a sharing of the culture' (p. 127).

He sees the idea of education as a transmission of a body of unchanging facts from the teacher to a passive class of children as entirely inappropriate.

Bruner prefers the idea of education as an opportunity for teacher and learners to engage in a negotiated set of shared meanings.

> It follows from this view of culture as a forum that induction into the culture through education, if it is to prepare the young for life, as lived, should only partake of the spirit of a forum, of negotiation, of the recreating of meaning. But this conclusion runs counter to traditions of pedagogy that derive from another time, another interpretation of culture, another conception of authority — one that looked at the process of education as the transmission of knowledge and values. (1986, p. 123)

References

BRUNER, J.S., GOODNOW, J.J. and AUSTIN, G.A. (1956) *A Study of Thinking*, New York, Wiley.

BRUNER, J.S., OLVER, R.R. and GREENfiELD, P.M. *et al.* (1966) *Studies in Cognitive Growth*, New York, Wiley.

BRUNER, J.S. (1986) *Actual Minds, Possible Worlds*, London, Harvard University Press.

Vygotsky and Education

(From Britton, J., 1987, 'Vygotsky's contribution to pedagogical theory', *English in Education*, 21, 3, pp. 22–6.)

A major feature in the cognitive view of development concerns the importance attached to language. As we have seen, there are differences in the perspectives of Piaget and Bruner (see the extract by Conner, pp. 312–16). Another significant contribution to this debate comes from the work of Vygotsky, a Russian psychologist. Although his main writing dates back to 1929, his study of thought and language was not published in English until 1962. In this study he offered four discoveries, which subsequent research has confirmed. Firstly, that word meanings evolve throughout childhood, which implies that children's use and interpretation of language may not always be the same as adults. Secondly, that early concepts can sometimes be taken from others, without the Piagetian insistence on experience. Thirdly, that learning to read and write has a significant effect on the achievement of abstract thinking and finally that speech in infancy is a pre-cursor to thinking at a later stage. Vygotsky contradicts Piaget's bias that thinking and knowing are largely the result of children reflecting on their own activity. Instead he emphasizes how much is learned from interacting with others. We learn, he suggests, from being taught and by what we see others doing, and that language provides an important structure for organizing children's cognitions. The article by James Britton attempts to assess Vygotsky's contribution to educational thinking.

The story of Vygotsky's influence on educational thinking in the West is a fantastic one — it reads, as they say, like a fairy story. A young Russian intellectual — in the first instance a student of literature — at the age of thirty-eight writes a book on the relation of language to thought. Having previously worked on the ideas with colleagues for some ten years, he finishes the manuscript off in haste, a race against tuberculosis, and dies before it is published. Two years after its publication the book, *Thought and Language*, is suppressed by the Soviet authorities and remains so for twenty years — though not before the substance of a magnificent last chapter, presented as a paper at an American conference, finds its way — in English — on to the pages of a psychological journal. A long silence is finally broken when, in 1962, twenty-eight years after its original appearance, scholars in Cambridge, Massachusetts produce an English translation of the whole work and Bruner is on hand to write the introduction.

But that is hardly more than the beginning of the story. Perhaps as an effect of the 'cold war', recognition of the significance of Vygotsky's work is slow to develop: seminal works in language acquisition and development continue to be published with slight reference, or none, to his ideas — and surprisingly enough, particularly so in America. Cambridge (Mass.), however, continued to take the lead: in 1971 MIT Press brought out an English translation of a collection of Vygotsky's early writings on literary texts under the title *The Psychology of Art* — now, unfortunately, no longer in print. And in 1978 four American editors, working with A.R. Luria, Vygotsky's close colleague, disciple and friend (and in turn his successor in Moscow), produced an edited translation of seminal work by Vygotsky and gave it the title *Mind in Society*. Finally, there has this year appeared a revised and re-edited translation of *Thought and Language* from MIT Press.

In his introduction to the original Russian edition of *Thought and Language*, Vygotsky had written, 'we fully realize the inevitable imperfections of this study, which is no more than a first step in a new direction'. In which direction? Vygotsky has this answer: 'Our findings point the way to a new theory of consciousness' — and he goes on to indicate four aspects of the work that are *novel*, and — consequently — 'in need of further careful checking'. I have the sense here of someone embarking on an idea he knows he cannot himself carry through to a conclusion. His four discoveries, to state them as briefly as I can, are these:

(1) Word meanings *evolve* during childhood: it cannot be assumed that when a child uses a word he means by it what we as adult speakers would mean.

(2) While accepting Piaget's theory of the growth of *spontaneous concepts* — ideas arrived at by inference from (or evidenced by) our own experiences, Vygotsky adds the notion of *non-spontaneous concepts* — ideas taken over from other people (notably teachers) — taken over as problems needing solution, or as 'empty categories', so to speak, which need time to find embodiment in our own experience and ground themselves in our own knowledge base. Vygotsky sees this as a two-way movement, 'upward' of spontaneous concepts, 'downward' of non-spontaneous concepts, each mode facilitating the other — and the joint operation being characteristic of human learning.

(3) Vygotsky believed that mastery of the written language — learning to read-and-write — had a profound effect upon the achievement of abstract thinking. The *constancy* of the written language, grafted, so to speak, upon the *immediacy* of the spoken language, enables a speaker to *reflect* upon meanings and by doing so acquire a new level of control, a critical awareness of his/her own thought processes.

(4) Speech in infancy, Vygotsky claimed, is the direct antecedent of thinking at a later stage. When children discover that it is helpful to speak aloud about what they are doing, they begin to employ what Vygotsky termed 'speech for oneself'; and thereafter speech takes on a dual function and, in due course, develops differential-

ly; conversation becomes more effective *as communication*, while monologue or 'running commentary' (speech for oneself) changes in what is virtually the opposite direction. That is to say, in conversation children extend their control of the grammatical structures of the spoken language and increase their resources of conventional word meanings. In their monologues, on the contrary, they exploit the fact that they are talking to themselves by using as it were 'note form' — skeletal or abbreviated structures that would mean little to one who did not already share the speaker's thoughts — and *personal, idiosyncratic* word meanings — pet words, inventions, portmanteau terms, rich in meaning for the originator but minimally endorsed by convention.

Vygotsky observed these changes in the speech of children from about three years old to about seven — changes that set up a marked difference between their conversational mode and their use of 'speech for oneself'. On the strength of these observations he speculated that, rather than 'withering away' as Piaget had suggested, speech for oneself became internalized and continued to operate as the genesis of thought, perhaps moving through the stages of *inner speech to verbal thinking* and thence to the most elusive stage of all — thought itself.

By this account, then, we *think* by handling 'post-language symbols' — forms that began as speech but which have been successively freed from the constraints of the grammar of the spoken language and from the constraints of conventional, public word meanings. It is this freedom that characterizes the fluidity of thought — and accounts for the necessity of *imposing organization* upon our thoughts when we want to communicate them.

It was a brilliant insight on Vygotsky's part to realize that when speech for oneself becomes internalized it is in large part because the child, in handling the freer forms of speech that constitute that mode, begins to be capable of carrying out mental operations more subtle than anything he or she can put into words. I think we can become aware of the reciprocal process when as we listen to discussion we engender some response — a question to be asked or a comment we want to make — and have a clear sense that the process of moving from the fluid operation of thought units to the utterance of rule-governed 'public' speech using conventional word meanings is one that may demand strenuous mental effort on our part.

When *Mind in Society* appeared in 1978, a review by Stephen Toulmin in the *New York Review of Books* underlined Vygotsky's concern with consciousness. He saw Vygotsky as denying on the one hand that human consciousness can be regarded as simply an effect of the genes, of *nature*, or on the other hand as an effect of environment — of *nurture* — claiming that both influences must interact in the creation of mind in the individual. He gave his review the title, *The Mozart of Psychology* (nominating Luria in consequence as *The Beethoven*) and suggested that Western psychology urgently needed to take on the broader perspective that Vygotsky had initiated.

It is in this work that Vygotsky's central contention becomes clear — the claim that *human consciousness is achieved by the internalization of shared social behaviour*. A series of 'temporary connections' is made by the individual within the individual life-span; each link makes possible further links, each operation begins with external *observable social behaviour* — an exposed segment, as it were, of what is to become inner behaviour. Thus is indicated, surely, a new emphasis upon the observation and study of child-hood activities for the light they throw upon later behaviours not open to observation.

But social behaviour implies interaction within a group whose activities have been shaped to cultural patterns. The relationship between individual development and the evolution of society is a complex one, not a matter of mere recapitulation or parallelism. The familiar story of the psychologist Kellogg and his chimpanzee comes to mind: the chimpanzee had acted as companion to Kellogg's infant son and for a period of years both creatures developed, so to speak, in tandem — able to share each other's activities — but only up to the point where the boy learned to speak: the young Kellogg is today, I believe, himself a scientist — the chimpanzee remains — a chimpanzee! In the historical development from animal to man, the acquisition of language is a watershed: in the development of the individual child from birth to three or four years, the acquisition of language is a watershed.

Speech, that begins as a shared social activity on the part of the child and becomes a principal means of the mental regulation and refinement of his individual behaviour — this is the prime example of Vygotsky's theory of internalization to achieve consciousness. He gives us a further striking example when he claims that make-believe play in early childhood constitutes the earliest, and at that time only available form of *imagination*. It is nearer the truth, he says, to claim that imagination in adolescence and later is 'make-believe play without action' than it is to claim that make-believe play in young children is 'imagination in action'.

The implications of these ideas for pedagogy are, of course, enormous. If speech in childhood lays the foundations for a life-time of thinking, how can we continue to prize a silent classroom? And if shared social behaviour (of many kinds, verbal and non-verbal) is seen as the source of learning, we must revise the traditional view of the teacher's role. The teacher can no longer act as the 'middle-man' in all learning — as it becomes clear that education is *an effect of community*. Bruner, in a recent book, devoted a chapter to Vygotsky's ideas, and in a later chapter makes this comment: 'Some years ago I wrote some very insistent articles about the importance of discovery learning ... What I am proposing here is an extension of that idea, or better, a completion. My model of the child in those days was very much in the tradition of the solo child mastering the world by representing it to himself in his own terms. In the intervening years I have come increasingly to recognize that most learning in most settings is a communal activity, a sharing of the culture. It is not just that the child must make his knowledge his own, but that he must make it his own in a community of those who share his sense of belonging to a culture. It is this that leads me to emphasize not only discovery and invention but the importance of negotiating and sharing — in a word, of joint culture creating as an object of schooling and as an appropriate step en route to becoming a member of the adult society in which one lives out one's life' (Bruner, 1986, p. 127).

The notion that shared social behaviour is the beginning stage of learning throws responsibility upon those who interact socially with the growing child. By interacting in such a way that their awareness of approaches to skilled behaviour, their awareness of snags and obstacles to such behaviour are made available to learners, they are in fact (in Vygotsky's terms) *lending consciousness* to those learners and enabling them to perform in this relationship tasks they could not achieve if left to themselves. Again in Vygotsky's terms, this is to open up for the learner 'the zone of proximal development' — an area of ability for which one's previous achievements have prepared one, but which awaits assisted performance for its realization. That assistance may take the form of teacher/student interaction, or peer tutoring, or group activity — as well, of course, as in the give and take of social cooperation in and out of school.

Viewed thus broadly, we might add that a learner by taking part in rule-governed social behaviour may pick up the rules by means hardly distinguishable from the processes by which they were first socially derived — and by which they continue to be amended. On the other hand — along may come the traditional teacher and — with the best intentions, trying to be helpful — set out to observe the behaviour, analyze to codify the rules and teach the outcome as a recipe. Yes, this may sometimes be helpful, but as consistent pedagogy it is manifestly counter-productive.

Taking 'community' in a micro sense, it is likely that we all live in a number of communities. As teachers we are responsible for one of those — the classroom. It is clear we have a choice: we can operate so as to make that as rich an interactive learning community as we can, or we may continue to treat it as a captive audience for whatever instruction we choose to offer.

Wherever Vygotsky's voice can be heard, perhaps that choice constitutes a Zone of Proximal Development for many of us.

References

BRUNER, J. (1986) *Actual Minds, Possible Worlds*, Harvard University Press.
KELLOGG, W.N. and LOUISE, E. (1933) *The Ape and the Child*, McGraw Hill.
PIAGET, J. (1926) *Language and Thought of the Child*, Routledge and Kegan Paul.

TOULMIN, S. (1978) 'The Mozart of psychology', *New York Review of Books* Vol. XXV(14), 28 Sept.

VYGOTSKY, L. (1939) 'Thought and speech', *Psychiatry* Vol. 2, pp. 29–57.

VYGOTSKY, L. (1962) *Thought and Language*, MIT Press.

VYGOTSKY, L. (1971) *The Psychology of Art*, MIT Press.

VYGOTSKY, L. (1978) *Mind in Society*, Harvard University Press.

VYGOTSKY, L. (1987) *Thought and Language*, newly revised and edited, MIT Press.

Common Knowledge

(From Edwards, D. and Mercer, N., 1987, *Common Knowledge*, London, Methuen, pp. 160–70.)

In this extract Mercer and Edwards draw upon the ideas of Bruner and Vygotsky to suggest a way forward in the primary classroom which draws upon cognitive psychology for a set of basic principles. They argue that teachers need to become much clearer about children's interpretation and understanding of the expectations of the learning situation through the development of a set of shared meanings. Children need activities which are structured more carefully than 'the discovery sandpit of the Piagetian classroom'. In the successful classroom, they suggest,

> Talk between teachers and children helps build the scaffolding; children's activity, even 'discovery', in the absence of such a communicative framework may, in cognitive terms, lead nowhere. (p. 167)

There are obvious similarities in this interpretation with the ideas expressed by Tamburrini (pp. 297–300) and Donaldson (pp. 306–11).

They go on to suggest that the study of cognitive development, especially as a result of the influence of Piaget, has emphasized how knowledge and thought are represented in the mind of the individual, a kind of decontextualized 'lone organism' they suggest that the future emphasis should seek the essence of human thought in its cultural context, its communicability and our transactions with other people.

> The process of education, as Vygotsky and Bruner have always recognized is at the heart of all that. (p. 165)

1 We have adopted a perspective on human thought and understanding which emphasizes their basis in social relations and communication. Knowledge and thought are not just to do with how individuals think, but are intrinsically social and cultural. We have therefore focused on what we call 'common knowledge', looking at how this is constructed through joint activity and discourse.

2 Through discourse and joint action, two or more people build a body of common knowledge which becomes the contextual basis for further communication. Overt messages, things actually said, are only a small part of the total communication. They are only the tips of icebergs, in which the great hidden mass breath is essential to the nature of what is openly visible above the waterline. This is why *context* and *continuity* are essential considerations in the analysis of discourse.

3 'Context' is essentially a mental phenomenon. Things 'out there' become contextual only when they are invoked — that is, referred to, assumed or implied in what is communicated. The very act of naming things, or of assuming shared understandings of them, makes their reality for communicators a social and conceptual one, rather than one of simple

physical existence in the surrounding world. Context *is* the common knowledge of the speakers invoked by the discourse. It is problematical both for the participants and for any observing investigator. Participants' conceptions of each other's mental contexts may be wrong or, more likely, only partially right. The investigators similarly have the problem of determining what is contextual. Any physical set of circumstances could lend itself to an infinity of possible shared conceptions and relevances, and, in any case, the mental contexts of conversational communication are by no means restricted to the physical circumstances of acts of speech. 'Continuity' is likewise problematical because it too is mental (or, more accurately, inter-mental). Continuity is a characteristic of context, being context as it develops through time in the process of joint talk and action. It exists as shared memory and intention, the conceptions and assumptions that participants hold, of what they have done and said, of its significance, of what the interaction is all about and of where it is going.

4 One important function of education may be described as *cognitive socialization*. The particular research that we have discussed in this book has examined some features of this process within one particular cultural setting, that of some English primary classrooms. Within a society the education system has its own epistemological culture. This culture, and the institutional framework within which children are educated, are what distinguish education from other kinds of cultural learning. Teachers have the task of 'scaffolding' children's first steps towards and into this culture, of supervising their entry into the universe of educational discourse. This is done by creating, through joint action and talk with the child, a contextual framework for educational activities. One of the main purposes of education is thus to develop a common knowledge. This is a problematical process, not only because the creation of successful discourse is in itself problematical (involving as it does the development of adequate context and continuity), but also because education is necessarily ideological and predicated upon social relations in which power and control figure largely. The extent to which educational knowledge is made 'common' through classroom discourse is one measure of the effectiveness of the educational process. The importance of a teacher-child asymmetry of power also makes problematical one of the major goals of education — the eventual 'handover' of control over knowledge and learning from the teacher to the child, whereby the pupil achieves autonomy.

5 Educated discourse is not talk which is 'disembedded' from context and which differs from less elevated forms of discourse by being more explicit. On the contrary, it is talk which relies for its intelligibility on speakers' access to particular, implicit contextual frameworks. The discourse of educated people conversing about their specialism — mathematics, philosophy, literary criticism or whatever — is explicit only to the initiated.

6 An important part of the contextual basis of classroom discourse is a body of rules which define educational activities and which are required for

successful participation in educational discourse. These *educational ground-rules* have both social and cognitive functions. They represent both a set of social conventions for presenting knowledge in school, and also a set (or sets) of cognitive procedures for defining and solving problems. These rules are problematical for both teachers and pupils, for reasons which stem from the fact that they normally remain implicit. They form part of the 'hidden agenda' of school work which is rarely, if ever, available for scrutiny and discussion by teachers and children together. This means that they are tacitly contextual, and participants in education rarely check the adequacy of their assumed shared understanding of the requirements or purpose of their mutual pursuit. It is also difficult for teachers, or pupils, to judge the educational value of these rules in any general sense, or to assess the appropriateness of applying any particular rule or subset of rules to a particular activity or problem. Furthermore, we have argued that the maintenance of the tacit/implicit status of these rules is itself a tenet of the dominant pedagogy or educational ideology.

7 We have drawn a rather simple, but useful distinction between different kinds of educational knowledge. There is knowledge which is essentially procedural, routinized, expedient; we have called this *ritual knowledge*. There is also knowledge which is explanatory and reflective, which is not tied to specific courses of action; we have called this *principled knowledge*. A problematical aspect of education is that even well-intentioned joint action and discourse will not necessarily ensure that teachers and pupils establish a common understanding of both procedures and principles. The ritual-principle distinction is also one that we have tried to relate the matters of educational ideology and the practices that derive from it.

Two of the theoretical perspectives that have most influenced our analysis have been those of Lev Vygotsky and of Jerome Bruner. Bruner's recent writings serve as an excellent starting point for a discussion of some points that we have raised in our own study.

A Dialogue with Jerome Bruner

Jerome Bruner (1983, 1986) has recently been taking stock of a remarkably fruitful life's work on the nature of the human mind and its development in children, and on the process of education. In *Actual Minds, Possible Worlds* (1986) he remarks on a development in his own thinking: 'I have come increasingly to recognize that most learning in most settings is a communal activity, a sharing of the culture' (p. 127). Bruner's words, as usual, carry a great deal of wisdom, His depiction of the nature of education is intended to be both descriptive and prescriptive. He is interested not only in what education is, but also in what it could be. He is particularly clear on what it should not be — the notion of education as the transmission of a body of unchanging facts, from teacher to passive pupils, is clearly inappropriate. Bruner prefers the notion of culture (and therefore of education) as a 'forum', in which teacher and learners engage in a negotiation of shared meaning, the teacher interacting with her pupils in an essentially Vygotskyan manner, guiding them through successive zones of proximal development:

> It follows from this view of culture as a forum that induction into the culture through education, if it is to prepare the young for life as lived, should also partake of the spirit of a forum, of negotiation, of the recreating of meaning. But this conclusion runs counter to traditions of pedagogy that derive from another time, another inter-pretation of culture, another conception of authority — one that looked at the process of education as a *transmission* of knowledge and values. (1986, p. 123)

Much of our discussion of classroom talk has been an investigation of the problematics of this process. But the lessons we have examined were by no means the old-style didactic sort; they were the modern sort, characterized by exploration and discovery, joint activity and talk, scaffolded learning, and an educational ideology — notwithstanding Piaget's influence — not far removed from Bruner's own. A similar notion of education as a negotiation of meanings between teacher and pupils is characteristic of Hugh Mehan's work (Mehan, 1979; Griffin and Mehan, 1981), on which Bruner draws. It is an excellent depiction but, as we have stressed, an idealized one. Our own depiction has been of a more compromised process, where the negotiation is a rather one-sided affair in which the teacher's role as authoritative bearer of the ready-made knowledge simply finds alternative, more subtle means of realizing itself than the crudities of brute 'transmission'. Perhaps it is itself a cultural difference between Britain and the United States, whether of the classrooms studied or of the investigators themselves; in either case, our analysis of the compromises of the newer pedagogy clearly echoes that of another British study (Edwards and Furlong, 1978). The process that Bruner describes is indeed the one that we have investigated. We have simply been at least as interested in its problems and difficulties as in its actual or possible achievements.

It appears to be a major issue for research and theorizing about Vygots-ky's 'zone of proximal development' that there occurs within pedagogic activities a tension between the demands of, on the one hand, inducting children into an established, ready-made culture and, on the other hand, developing creative and autonomous participants in a culture which is not ready-made but continually in the making. An emphasis on one aspect or the other is what characterizes the familiar dichotomies of educational ideology, between transmissional teaching and the child-centred approach, 'traditional' and 'progressive' education, and so on. The value of Vygotsky's and Bruner's approach is to see the dichotomy as false, to stress the participa-tory, future-orientated process of culture and education. This is what Bruner's notion of a 'forum' implies. Peg Griffin and Michael Cole similarly merge description with idealization:

> Social organization and leading activities provide a gap within which the child can develop novel creative analysis ... a zoped [zone of proximal development] is a dialogue between the child and his future; it is not a dialogue between the child and an adult's past. (Griffin and Cole, 1984, p. 62)

We agree with Bruner's emphasis on the communal basis of knowledge and thought, a view that he uses to judge different pedagogies in terms of the sorts of thought and understanding they may be expected to foster. Bruner depicts knowledge and the educational process as essentially rhetorical:

> the language of education, if it is to be an invitation to reflection and culture creating, cannot be the so-called uncontaminated language of fact and 'objectivity'. It must express stance and counter-stance and in the process leave place for reflection, for metacognition. It is this that permits one to reach higher ground, this process of objectifying in language or image what one has thought and then turning around on it and reconsidering it. (1986, p. 129)

The expression of stance and counter-stance is again a negotiative depiction of education, a rhetorical, argumentative meeting of minds in which what is 'known' is merely what is claimed by somebody: it is open to scrutiny. And the scrutiny is a social process, not merely one of individual discovery but one of sharing, comparing, contrasting and arguing one's perspectives against those of others. We have commented on the difficulties that teachers may face in achieving such aims, against the easier demands of power and expedience, and supported by an ideology which encourages leaving children to discover things for themselves. But Bruner's statement offers other insights.

The notion of a metacognitive 'turning around on' one's own conceptions is surely a reference to that famous passage in Bartlett's classic *Remembering*, in which he ponders on the relation between memory and consciousness:

> to go to that portion of the organized setting of past responses which is most relevant to the needs of the moment ... an organism has somehow to acquire the capacity to turn around upon its own 'schemata' and to construct them afresh ... It is where consciousness comes in; it is what gives consciousness its most prominent function. I wish I knew exactly how this is done. (Bartlett, 1932, p. 206)

As we have argued elsewhere (Edwards and Middletor, 1986), the key to the process of remembering may well be the sort of discursive meeting of minds that Bruner writes of. The psychological study of cognition and of cognitive development has concentrated for several decades on how knowledge and thought are represented in the mind of a decontextualized 'lone organism', the individual experimental subject. We must surely now seek the essence of human thought in its cultural nature, its communicability, in our transactions with other people. The process of education, as Vygotsky and Bruner have always recognized, is at the heart of all that.

Some Educational and Psychological Implications

So far as the educational implications of the research can be summarized, they fall into two categories. First, there are the benefits to be gained from observing and analyzing the educational process as situated discourse — that is, applying the approach and methods we have used to examine classroom communication critically. Second, there are the consequences of questioning the adequacy of an accepted psychological model of cognitive development and learning, which legitimizes dominant educational ideologies and is used to justify particular educational practices. We shall consider each in turn.

By looking at education as situated discourse, as a process whereby teachers and children act and talk together to some supposed common purpose, the researcher (who may also be the teacher) can more easily identify ways in which, and occasions on which, this purpose is achieved or lost. Particular strategies for introducing topics, leading discussions, relating talk to action, consolidating shared experiences, resolving misunderstandings, and so on, may be developed with greater confidence. We have suggested elsewhere some ways in which practising teachers can begin to do this (Mercer, 1985). But the acquisition of this kind of analytic technique by teachers would best be done through the specialized use of video and audio recordings of teaching practice as part of initial and in-service training. Simply 'sitting in' on other teachers' lessons, or having access only to transcripts, would not be enough. Suitable audio-visual equipment is now common in schools and colleges of education, and is even used in some institutions for analogous purposes (e.g. 'micro-teaching' analysis and social skills training), so technical matters should pose no intractable problems. There is, however, still much for us to do before feeling confident in detailing the form any such scheme should take.

It is difficult to summarize the educational implications of abandoning an individualistic perspective on the development of knowledge and understanding, and taking up instead a psychological viewpoint which gives primacy to culture and communication (a goal pursued notably by Michael Cole and his colleagues at the Laboratory of Comparative Human Cognition at San Diego). One implication would seem to be that 'learning failures' are not necessarily attributable to individual children or teachers, but to the inadequacies of the referential framework within which education takes place. In other words, they are failures of context. These might be locatable in particular events within the dynamics of discourse in a particular class-room over a given period of time, or attributable to inherent, permanent features of the process of teaching and learning, as tacitly defined by partici-pants who must invoke their own conceptions of education to make sense of what they do. Good teaching will be reflexive, sensitive to the possibility of different kinds of understanding. It may be pursued through the careful creation of context, a framework for shared understanding with children based on joint knowledge and action which provides its own rationale for present activity and a strong foundation for future developments. This contextual edifice is the 'scaffolding' for children's mental explorations, a cognitive climbing-frame — built by children with their Vygotskyan teacher — which structures activity more systematically than the discovery sandpit of the Piagetian classroom. Talk between teachers and children helps build the scaffolding; children's activity, even 'discovery', in the absence of such a communicative framework may, in cognitive terms, lead nowhere. And if teachers insist on retaining tight control, dominating the agenda and discus-sion, determining in advance what should happen and what should be discovered, then even their more successful pupils will remain 'scaffolded' like some supported structure, unable to function independently or outside the precise context and content of what was 'done' in the classroom.

However, rather than simply recasting the process of classroom learning into Vygotskyan or Brunerian terms, we have sought to do so in a manner which raises the problematical nature of the process. If teachers and pupils are to engage fruitfully in scaffolded learning, then there are key features of the learning processes that we have observed which need to be emphasized and examined. These include the following:

1 There appears to be a fundamental dilemma for our teachers — that of balancing the conflicting demands of, on the one hand, a child-centred ideology of learning and, on the other hand, an essentially socializing role as the society's agents of cultural transmission in the context of a system of compulsory education. The pupils have to be seen to be learning the right sorts of things, but at the same time to be discovering them for themselves. The dilemma is resolved in ways that may make the educational process a more difficult one than the ideal of scaffolded learning would define as necessary. Pupils have to divine as best they can the unspoken and implicit ground-rules of the system, and must learn how to extract meaning from the teacher's hints and clues, how to play the classroom game. The child-centred ideology needs to be replaced with one that emphasizes the socio-cultural and discursive bases of knowledge and learning.

2 All of classroom education is conducted against a background of implicit rules, assumptions and knowledge. To some extent this is natural and inevitable; the construction of context and continuity is, as we have

emphasized, an intrinsic characteristic of education. But some things that could usefully be explicated remain unspoken. It appears to be a valued and common practice that teachers will conduct an entire lesson, or series of lessons, and never feel it appropriate to tell the pupils why they are doing particular activities, or where it all fits into what they have done and will do next. This appears to be no accidental state of affairs. The avoidance of explicit communication of the goals and contexts of classroom activity is a consequence of teachers' educational ideology — that pupils are essentially individuals in pursuit of a realization of their own individual potentials, that they are not to be 'told' things, that they should learn things for themselves.

3   The notion of experiential learning is clearly inadequate as a description of what actually happens in classrooms, and inadequate also as a pedagogic principle upon which to found pedagogic practice. The experiences and activities of the classroom are made meaningful by the sense made of those things by classroom talk. When teachers go out of their way to avoid offering to pupils overt help in making sense of their experiences, the consequences may be that the usefulness of those experiences is lost, or that teacher and pupils resort to more surreptitious means of communicating what is conventional sense. So we find teachers asking questions and miming the answers. For many pupils, learning from teachers must appear to be a mysterious and arbitrarily difficult process, the solution to which may be to concentrate on trying to do and say what appears to be expected — a basically 'ritual' solution. A greater emphasis on the importance of language and communication in creating a shared conceptual sense of the meaning and significance of experience and activity may help to make classroom education a more open and explicit business, and therefore a less mysterious and difficult process for pupils.

It seems to us that, despite practical constraints and resource limitations which must continually frustrate their intentions, the British primary school teachers we have observed try in good faith to carry out their interpretation of the progressive style of education advocated by the Plowden Report. This is their educational ideology, a set of beliefs about how children's cognitive development and learning are best assisted. They have good reasons for relying upon it, because it is an educational approach based on sensible criticisms of traditional didactic teaching methods, advocated by a high-status committee of educationists and legitimized by the most widely accepted theory of cognitive development. We believe along with other critics (e.g. Donaldson, 1978; Walkerdine, 1984), however, that the time is ripe for a reappraisal of this ideology, which remains dominant in British primary education. This is largely because the Piagetian theory upon which it stands has not withstood recent critical attacks; it no longer justifies educationists' trust. It encourages a pedagogy which overemphasizes the individual at the expense of the social, which undervalues talk as a tool for discovery, and which discourages teachers from making explicit to children the purposes of educational activities and the criteria for success. There is an alternative psychological approach which we believe offers more now to teachers and researchers, as we hope we have shown.

References

BARTLETT, F.C. (1932) *Remembering: A Study in Experimental and Social Psychology*, Cambridge, Cambridge University Press.

BRUNER, J.S. (1983) *In Search of Mind: Essays in Autobiography*, New York, Harper and Row.

BRUNER, J.S. (1986) *Actual Minds, Possible Worlds*, Cambridge, MA, Harvard University Press.

Donaldson, M. (1978) *Children's Minds*, London, Fontana.

EDWARDS, A.D. and FURLONG, V.J. (1978) *The Language of Teaching*, London, Heinemann.

EDWARDS, D. and MIDDLETON, D. (1986) 'Joint remembering: Constructing an account of shared experience', *Discourse Processes*, 9, pp. 423–59.

GRIFFIN, P. and COLE, M. (1984) 'Current activity for the future: The zoped', in ROGOFF, B. and WERTSCH, J.V. (Eds) *Children's Learning in the Zone of Proximal Development*, New York, Jossey-Bass.

GRIFFIN, P. and MEHAN, H. (1981) 'Sense and ritual in classroom discourse', in COULMAS, F. (Ed.) *Conversational Routine: Explorations in Standardised Communication Situations and Prepatterned Speech*, The Hague, Mouton.

MEHAN, H. (1979) *Learning Lessons. Social Organisation in the Classroom*, Cambridge, MA, Harvard University Press.

MERCER, N. (1985) 'Communication in the classroom', in *Every Child's Language: An Inservice Pack for Primary Teachers*, (Book 1), Clevedon, Multilingual Matters/Open University, p. 534.

WALKERDINE, V. (1984) 'Developmental Psychology and the child-centered pedagogy: The insertion of Piaget into early education', in HENRIQUES, W. *et al.*, *Changing the Subject*, London, Methuen.

The Technology of Teaching

(From Skinner, B.F., 1968, *The Technology of Teaching*, Appleton-Century-Crofts, pp. 14–21).

The contributions considered so far are regarded as supporting a 'cognitive perspective' in psychology. As was discussed in the first article by Claxton (pp. 279–82) in this section, an alternative perspective comes from the behaviourists. Notable amongst behaviourist psychologists who have considered the implications of their studies for education is B.F. Skinner. Skinner is regarded by many as the greatest living psychologist (Patterson, 1977):

> His thesis, presented in *Beyond Freedom and Dignity* (1971), that behaviour is under the control of environmental stimuli, and the proposal that therefore we should create an environment which will shape the kind of person, eliminating 'freedom', (which in any case according to Skinner does not exist), has resulted in attacks on him by psychologists and philosophers as well as layman.

The extract by Skinner which follows takes the basic behaviourist principle of 'reinforcement' and applies it to the teaching context.

Schoolroom Teaching

Let us consider, for example, the teaching of arithmetic in the lower grades. The school is concerned with imparting to the child a large number of responses of a special sort. The responses are all verbal. They consist of speaking and writing certain words, figures, and signs which, to put it roughly, refer to numbers and to arithmetic operations. [Obviously this is not the 'new math', but a similar analysis might be made of any material suitable for the same grades.] The first task is to shape these responses — to get the child to pronounce and to write responses correctly — but the principal task is to bring this behavior under many sorts of stimulus control. This is what happens when the child learns to count, to recite tables, to count while ticking off the items in an assemblage of objects, to respond to spoken or written numbers by saying 'odd', 'even', or 'prime'. Over and above this elaborate repertoire of numerical behavior, most of which is often dismissed as the product of rote learning, the teaching of arithmetic looks forward to those complex serial arrangements of responses involved in original mathematical thinking. The child must acquire responses of transposing, clearing fractions, and so on, which modify the order or pattern of the original material so that the response called a solution is eventually made possible.

Now, how is this extremely complicated verbal repertoire set up? In the first place, what reinforcements are used? Fifty years ago the answer would have been clear. At that time educational control was still frankly aversive. The child read numbers, copied numbers, memorized tables, and performed operations upon numbers to escape the threat of the birch rod or cane. Some positive reinforcements were perhaps eventually derived from the increased efficiency of the child in the field of arithmetic and in rare cases some automatic reinforcement may have resulted from the sheer manipulation of the medium — from the solution of problems or the discovery of the intricacies of the number system. But for the immediate purposes of education the child acted to avoid or escape punishment. It was part of the reform movement known as progressive education to make the positive consequences more immediately effective, but any one who visits the lower grades of the average school today will observe that a change has been made, not from aversive to positive control, but from one form of aversive stimulation to another. The child at his desk, filling in his workbook, is behaving primarily to escape from the threat of a series of minor aversive events — the teacher's displeasure, the criticism or ridicule of his classmates, an ignominious showing in a competition, low marks, a trip to the office 'to be talked to' by the principal, or a word to the parent who may still resort to the birch rod. In this welter of aversive consequences, getting the right answer is in itself an insignificant event, any effect of which is lost amid the anxieties, the boredom, and the aggressions which are the inevitable by-products of aversive control.

Secondly, we have to ask how the contingencies of reinforcement are arranged. When is a numerical operation reinforced as 'right'? Eventually, of course, the pupil may be able to check his own answers and achieve some sort of automatic reinforcement, but in the early stages the reinforcement of being right is usually accorded by the teacher. The contingencies she provides are far from optimal. It can easily be demonstrated that, unless explicit mediating behavior has been set up, the lapse of only a few seconds between response and reinforcement destroys most of the effect. In a typical classroom, nevertheless, long periods of time customarily elapse. The teacher may walk up and down the aisle, for example, while the class is working on a sheet of problems, pausing here and there to call an answer right or wrong. Many minutes intervene between the child's response and the teacher's reinforcement. In many cases — for example, when papers are taken home to be corrected — as much as twenty-four hours may intervene. It is surprising that this system has any effect whatsoever.

A third notable shortcoming is the lack of a skilful program which moves forward through a series of progressive approximations to the final complex behavior desired. A long series of contingencies is necessary to bring the pupil into the possession of mathematical behavior most efficiently. But the teacher is seldom able to reinforce at each step in such a series because she cannot deal with the pupil's responses one at a time. It is usually necessary to reinforce the behavior in blocks of responses — as in correcting a worksheet or page from a workbook. The responses within such a block must not be interrelated. The answer to one problem must not depend upon the answer to another. The number of stages through which one may progressively approach a complex pattern of behavior is therefore small, and the task so much the more difficult. Even the most modern workbook in beginning arithmetic is far from exemplifying an efficient *program* for shaping mathematical behavior.

Perhaps the most serious criticism of the current classroom is the relative infrequency or reinforcement. Since the pupil is usually dependent upon the teacher for being told that he is right, and since many pupils are usually dependent upon the same teacher, the total number of contingencies which may be arranged during, say, the first four years, is of the order of only a few thousand. But a very rough estimate suggests that efficient mathematical behavior at this level requires something of the order of 25,000 contingencies. We may suppose that even in the brighter student a given contingency must be arranged several times to place the behavior well in hand. The responses to be set up are not simply the various items in tables of addition, subtraction, multiplication, and division; we have also to consider the *alternative* forms in which each item may be stated. To the learning of such material we should add hundreds of responses such as those concerned with factoring, identifying primes, memorizing series, using short-cut techniques of calculation, and constructing and using geometric representations or number forms. Over and above all this, the whole mathematical repertoire must be brought under the control of concrete problems of considerable variety. Perhaps 50,000 contingencies is a more conservative estimate. In this frame of reference the daily assignment in arithmetic seems pitifully meagre.

The result of all this is, of course, well known. Even our best schools are under criticism for their inefficiency in the teaching of drill subjects such as arithmetic. The condition in the average school is a matter of widespread national concern. Modern children simply do not learn arithmetic quickly or well. Nor is the result simply imcompetence. The very subjects in which modern techniques are weakest are those in which failure is most conspicuous, and in the wake of an ever-growing incompetence come the anxieties, uncertainties, and aggressions which in their turn present other problems to the school. Most pupils soon claim the asylum of not being 'ready' for arithmetic at a given level or, eventually, of not having a mathematical mind. Such explanations are readily seized upon by defensive teachers and parents. Few pupils ever reach the stage at which automatic reinforcements follow as the natural consequences of mathematical behavior. On the contrary, the figures and symbols of mathematics have become standard emotional stimuli. The glimpse of a column of figures, not to say an algebraic symbol or an integral sign, is likely to set off, not mathematical behavior, but a reaction of anxiety, guilt, or fear.

The teacher is usually no happier about this than the pupil. Denied the opportunity to control via the birch rod, quite at sea as to the mode of operation of the few techniques at her disposal, she spends as little time as possible on drill subjects and eagerly subscribes to philosophies of education which emphasize material of greater inherent interest. A confession of weakness is her extraordinary concern lest the child be taught something unnecessary. The repertoire to be imparted is carefully reduced to an essential minimum. In the field of spelling, for example, a great deal of time and energy has gone into discovering just those words which the young child is going to use, as if it were a crime to waste one's educational power in teaching an unnecessary word. Eventually, weakness of technique emerges in the disguise of a reformulation of the aims of education. Skills are minimized in favor of vague achievements — educating for democracy, educating the whole child, educating for life, and so on. And there the matter ends; for, unfortunately, these philosophies do not in turn suggest improvements in techniques. They offer little or no help in the design of better classroom practices.

The Improvement of Teaching

There would be no point in urging these objections if improvement were impossible. But the advances which have recently been made in our control of the learning process suggest a thorough revision of classroom practices and, fortunately, they tell us how the revision can be brought about. This is not, of course, the first time that the results of an experimental science have been brought to bear upon the practical problems of education. The modern classroom does not, however, offer much evidence that research in the field of learning has been respected or used. This condition is no doubt partly due to the limitations of earlier research. But it has been encouraged by a too hasty conclusion that the laboratory study of learning is inherently limited because it cannot take into account the realities of the classroom. In the light of our increasing knowledge of the learning process we should, instead, insist upon dealing with those realities and forcing a substantial change in them. Education is perhaps the most important branch of scientific technology. It deeply affects the lives of all of us. We can no longer allow the exigencies of a practical situation to suppress the tremendous improvements which are within reach. The practical situation must be changed.

There are certain questions which have to be answered in turning to the study of any new organism. What behavior is to be set up? What reinforcers are at hand? What responses are available in embarking upon a program of progressive approximation which will lead to the final form of the behavior? How can reinforcements be most efficiently scheduled to maintain the behavior in strength? These questions are all relevant in considering the problem of the child in the lower grades.

In the first place, what reinforcements are available? What does the school have in its possession which will reinforce a child? We may look first to the material to be learned, for it is possible that this will provide considerable automatic reinforcement. Children play for hours with mechanical toys, paints, scissors and paper, noise-makers, puzzles — in short, with almost anything which feeds back significant changes in the environment and is reasonably free of aversive properties. The sheer control of nature is itself reinforcing. This effect is not evident in the modern school because it is masked by the emotional responses generated by aversive control. It is true that automatic reinforcement from the manipulation of the environment is probably only a mild reinforcer and may need to be carefully husbanded, but one of the most striking principles to emerge from recent research is that the *net* amount of reinforcement is of little significance. A very slight reinforcement may be tremendously effective in controlling behavior if it is wisely used.

If the natural reinforcement inherent in the subject matter is not enough, other reinforcers must be employed. Even in school the child is occasionally permitted to do 'what he wants to do', and access to reinforcements of many sorts may be made contingent upon the more immediate consequences of the behavior to be established. Those who advocate competition as useful social motive may wish to use the reinforcements which follow from excelling others, although there is the difficulty that in this case the reinforcement of one child is necessarily aversive to another. Next in order we might place the good will and affection of the teacher, and only when that has failed need we turn to the use of aversive stimulation.

In the second place, how are these reinforcements to be made contingent upon the desired behavior? There are two considerations here — the gradual elaboration of extremely complex patterns of behavior and the maintenance of the behavior in strength at each stage. The whole process of becoming competent in any field must be divided into a very large number of very small steps, and reinforcement must be contingent upon the accomplishment of each step. This solution to the problem of creating a complex repertoire of behavior also solves the problem of maintaining the behavior in strength. We could, of course, resort to the techniques of scheduling already developed in the study of other organisms, but in the present state of our knowledge of educational practices scheduling appears to be most effectively arranged through the design of the material to be learned. By making each seccessive step as small as possible, the frequency of reinforcement can be raised to a maximum, while the possibly aversive consequences of being wrong are reduced to a minimum. Other ways of designing material would yield other programs of reinforcement. Any supplementary reinforcement would probably have to be scheduled in the more traditional way.

Behaviour Modification: Theory and Practice

(From Presland, J., 1978, 'Behaviour modification: Theory and practice', *Education 3–13*, 6, 1, pp. 43–4.)

An example of the principles of behaviourist psychology applied to the classroom is seen in attempts at behaviour modification. This refers to a set of procedures in which knowledge derived from learning theory and in particular Skinner's notions of 'instrumental' or 'operant' conditioning are used in a planned and systematic way to change an individual's classroom behaviour. In this article, by Presland, we see theory and practice meeting. The article outlines a series of workshops with primary teachers who draw upon the knowledge gained to improve the learning opportunities for children in their class by introducing a programme to change behaviour in a specified direction. The procedure described has been especially successful with children who have emotional, motivational or behavioural difficulties. (For a further example of classroom application of the principles readers are referred to, 'A plain guide to behaviour modification', by Mary Robertson, *Primary File*, 1, 1987.)

Research and Theory

In classrooms, pupils and teachers have modified one another's behaviour for generations. The term 'behaviour modification' is, however, a relatively new one which refers to a range of techniques in which applications of the psychology of learning are used in a planned and careful way to change the behaviour of oneself or others. The classroom has been one of the more fruitful environments for this kind of activity.

There are many different theories of learning, each with its own associated body of knowledge and research. However, practically all classroom applications have been based on B.F. Skinner's notion of *instrumental* or *operant* conditioning. This involves the concepts of a *stimulus*, which is anything which impinges on a living organism; a *response*, which is anything the organism does, thinks or feels; and a *reinforcer*, which is anything which increases the probability of a particular response being made to a given stimulus. One of the earliest demonstrations that the notion of reinforcement applied to children as well as to animals[1] showed that children trained to press a lever for machine delivery of pieces of candy continued to do so when the machine stopped providing it. The candy reinforcer had made the pressing response to the lever stimulus more likely to occur. The greater the number of such reinforcements a child experienced, the more often he pressed the lever after reinforcement had ceased.

Early critics could be forgiven for doubting whether such an absurdly simple principle applied to behaviours more complicated than the mere pressing of levers; and whether it could be utilised in a planned way to make significant differences to the ways in which children behaved in classrooms. Now, however, there is a considerable body of research[2] demonstrating, not only its efficacy in influencing children to attend to the teacher, get on with work, remain in their seats, attend school more regularly, and interact socially (where they were initially withdrawn); but also that it is helpful to reinforce children for *not* doing something. Such unwelcome behaviours as getting out of their seats when they're supposed to be staying in them, tapping, knocking things off desks, hitting and kicking, talking when not permitted, whistling, running around, grimacing and gesturing, throwing things and inappropriate crying have all been reduced in frequency by reinforcement procedures. More recently, children have even been taught to modify the behaviour of their classmates[3] and even of their teachers![4]

The variety of ways in which reinforcement and other learning principles have been shown to be applicable in the classroom cannot be described here. A brief account[5] and more detailed treatments[6] may be found elsewhere. My purpose here is to give some idea of how the most straightforward approaches work in practice with children in ordinary schools by reference to the happenings in three workshops for teachers run by educational psychologists in Birmingham in 1975.

The workshops followed the same broad lines as have already been described by Harrop[7] and Cook.[8] Each consisted of six weekly meetings and a follow-up meeting after an interval of several weeks. Methods of implementing the techniques were described in lectures, and discussion groups were used to guide each participant to select a child in his or her class who showed some problem of behaviour, devise and implement a programme to change the behaviour in a specified direction, and measure its occurrence before and during the programme and at follow-up.

Illustration

To show how the techniques were applied, I will describe Miss W's work with Gordon, aged 8, in a junior school. (The names, like all others mentioned, are fictitious.) Miss W. was first asked to identify behaviours displayed by Gordon which she wished to change and behaviours she wished to engage in more. She noted that he hid classroom equipment, would leave his seat to ask unnecessary questions or say he could not do work when he could, threw sticks and stones at other children in the playground, and argued when corrected about his behaviour or work. He needed to learn to put equipment away in the normal place, stay in his seat, play with other children without hurting them, and accept correction without arguing or becoming tense.

To simplify the task, Miss W. was asked to select one or two very specifically defined behaviours to work on as a first step. She chose *one* — leaving his seat to ask unnecessary questions. The frequency with which this behaviour occurred was then measured. Miss W. recorded each incident and calculated the number of times he left his seat unnecessarily each morning. These measurements formed a 'baseline' with which later measures could be compared.

The next steps were to decide upon certain reinforcers which would be sufficiently appealing to Gordon to motivate him to change his behaviour; and to incorporate them in a programme in which they were awarded systematically for instances of desired behaviour. Where behaviour is to be eliminated, the rewards can be given either for defined periods of abstinence, or for engagement in other behaviours incompatible with the one to be eliminated. Miss W. chose the former initially. During each timed twenty-minute period, he was praised intermittently for staying at his desk. At the end of each of these periods, he was given a choice of classroom jobs (e.g. holding and locking the door, giving out and collecting books, tidying up the book corner) if he had not left his seat at all. If he won the job for two twenty-minute periods, he was given a school team point. (All children in the class could, in fact, win such points for good behaviour and endeavour, as well as good work.) This system was put into operation every morning for a week, and then extended to the whole day for another week.

While this programme was in operation, Miss W. continued to record the frequency of the behaviour to be eliminated. The results for the two weeks baseline and two weeks programme were presented in a graph. From this can be calculated that the average number of interruptions per morning was 2.6 during the baseline and 0.4 during the first week of the programme. During the second week of the programme, it was 0.2 for the whole day. At follow-up, it was 0.3 for the whole day. From being a daily occurrence, the behaviour became confined to a minority of days. Miss W. herself felt that the behaviour had improved, and was maintained at follow-up.

Once the desired change was obtained, Miss W. turned her attention to the other aspects of Gordon's behaviour. Before follow-up, she had changed the behaviour reinforced to doing an acceptable or reasonable amount of work. His work then improved. He also continued to remain in his seat, since the incompatible behaviour of getting on with his work was being reinforced — he could not leave his seat and get on with his work at the same time. The next step was to phase out the programme while retaining the improved behaviour. Miss W. explained that he no longer needed to be timed, but still praised him at intervals and rewarded him at the end of each school period. The job rewards were then gradually phased out, and at follow-up, his improved behaviour was maintained by team points and praise alone — the classroom norm. Miss W. then tackled another aspect of his behaviour.

Overall Results

Twenty-three out of twenty-nine teachers in ordinary schools implemented a programme of some kind with children varying in age from three to thirteen and reported back on their results. Twenty-two of them thought there had been some degree of improvement in the behaviour studied. Fifteen were able to make sufficiently useful measurements to check this opinion, and all confirmed it. Fourteen of the twenty-two 'successes' were judged by their teachers to have maintained their improved status at follow-up. (In nearly all of them, the teachers were still using some of the workshop techniques.) Nine of these were checked by useful measurements, all confirmatory. In two cases the improvement was subsequently regained to some extent. Only three teachers reported loss of improvements despite continuation of the programme.

It should be realised that objectives were often limited and there were reservations about the value of some of the behavioural changes. They were, however, all changes that the teachers wanted.

Notes

1 SIEGEL, P.S. and FOSHEE, J.G. (1953) 'The law of primary reinforcement in children', *Journal of Experimental Psychology*, Vol. 45, No. 1, pp. 12–14.
2 HANLEY, E.M. (1970) 'Review of research involving applied behaviour analysis in the classroom', *Review of Educational Research*, Vol. 40, No. 5, pp. 597–625; ALTMAN, K.I. and LINTON, T.E. (1971) 'Operant conditioning in the classroom setting: A review of research', *Journal of Educational Research*, Vol. 64, No. 6, pp. 277–86; O'LEARY, K.D. and DRABMAN, R. (1971) 'Token reinforcement programs in the classroom: A review', *Psychological Bulletin*, Vol. 75, No. 6, pp. 379–98; O'LEARY, K.D. and O'LEARY, S.G. (1972) *Classroom Management: The Successful Use of Behaviour Modification*, New York: Pergamon; McLAUGH-LIN, T.F. (1974) 'A review of applications of group contingency procedures used in behaviour modification in the regular classroom: Some recommendations for school personnel', *Psychological Reports*, Vol. 35, No. 3, pp. 1299–1303; LITOW, L. and PUMORY, D.K. (1975) 'A brief review of classroom group oriented contingencies', *Journal of Applied Behaviour Analysis*, Vol. 8, No. 3, 1975, pp. 341–7.
3 ROSENBERG, H. (1975) 'Children as psychologists', *Special Education Forward Trends*, Vol. 2, No. 4, pp. 8–9.
4 ROSENBERG, H. (1976) 'Modifying teachers' behaviour', *Special Education Forward Trends*, Vol. 3, No. 2, pp. 8–9.
5 PRESLAND, J.L. (1974) 'Modifying behaviour now', *Special Education Forward Trends*, Vol. 1, No. 3, pp. 20–22.
6 BLACKHAM, G.J. and SILBERMAN, A. (1971) *Modification of Child Behaviour*. Belmont, California: Wadsworth; MEACHAM, M.C. and WIESEN, A.E. (1969) *Changing Classroom Behaviour*, Scranton, Pennsylvania: International Textbook Co.
7 HARROP, A. (1974) 'A behavioural workshop for the management of classroom problems', *British Journal of In-Service Education*, Vol. 1, No. 1 pp. 47–50.
8 COOK J. (1975) 'Easing behaviour problems', *Special Education Forward Trends*, Vol. 2, No. 1, pp. 15–17.

Reception and Discovery Learning

(From Ausubel, D. *et al.*, 1978, *Educational Psychology: A Cognitive View*, 2nd ed., London, Holt, Rinehart and Winston, pp. 24–79.)

Ausubel is one of a number of psychologists who have attempted to draw together cognitive and behaviourist perspectives. In his discussion of reception and discovery learning, reception learning is more likely to benefit from interpretation in behaviourist terms, whereas discovery learning is related to principles advocated by cognitive psychology. The view of cognitive psychologists that children are able to discover knowledge has its justification in observations of spontaneous learning through play and activity. Piaget's conclusions for example, that thinking and intelligence develop from actions upon objects and events in everyday life, have lead to the suggestion that children should experience discovery methods in the classroom. In contrast to this arguments for learning based on 'rote learning' sees learning as received and allows no interpretation on the part of the learner. This implies that learning is merely a process of accretion, a continual adding on of new knowledge. Such learning is often seen as didactic, delivered in verbal terms.

In this extract from Ausubel, it becomes clear that the distinction between rote and active learning is not simple and that it is inaccurate to assume that material presented verbally is necessarily rote in nature. Concepts may be meaningfully incorporated into a learners' understanding or they can be rote and meaningless. It depends upon what is already understood by the learner and how the new learning is presented. The teacher's task is to present new learning in a meaningful way, linking it to existing understanding. In this way positive transfer from old to new learning is more likely to take place and by implication making the new understanding more readily available for application.

Reception versus Discovery Learning

In reception learning (rote or meaningful) the entire content of what is to be learned is presented to the learner in final form. The learning task does not involve any independent discovery on the student's part. The learner is required only to internalize or incorporate the material (a list of nonsense syllables or paired adjectives; a poem or geometrical theorem) that is presented so that it is available or reproducible at some future date. In the case of meaningful reception learning, the potentially meaningful task or material is comprehended or made meaningful in the process of internalization. In the case of rote reception learning, the learning task either is not potentially meaningful or is not made meaningful in the process of internalization.

Much of the confusion in discussions of school learning arises from the failure to recognize that rote and meaningful learning are not completely dichotomous. Although they are *qualitatively* discontinuous in terms of the psychological processes underlying *each* and therefore cannot be placed at opposite poles of the same continuum, there are transitional types of learning that share some of the properties of both rote and meaningful learning (for example, representational learning or learning the names of objects, events, and concepts). Further, both types of learning can take place concomitantly in the same learning task. This same qualification also holds true for the distinction between reception and discovery learning. In somewhat simplified terms, these relationships are shown in diagrammatic form in Figure 1, in which these two dimensions of learning are viewed as orthogonal to each other.

The essential feature of discovery learning, whether concept formation or rote problem solving, is that the principal content of what is to be learned is not given but must be discovered by the learner before it can be meaningfully incorporated into the student's cognitive structure. The distinctive and prior learning task, in other words, is to discover something — which of two maze alleys leads to the goal, the precise nature of the relationship between two variables, the common attributes of a number of diverse instances, and so forth. The first phase of discovery learning involves a process quite different from that of reception learning. The learner must rearrange information, integrate it with existing cognitive structure, and reorganize or transform the integrated combination in such a way as to generate a desired end-product or discover a missing means-end relationship. After discovery learning itself is completed, the discovered content is made meaningful in much the same way that presented content is made meaningful in reception learning.

Reception and discovery learning are thus two quite different kinds of processes. It will be shown later that most classroom instruction is organized along the lines of reception learning. . . . Verbal reception learning is not necessarily rote in character. Much ideational material (concepts, generalizations) can be internalized and retained meaningfully without prior problem-solving experience. And at no stage of development does the learner have to discover principles independently in order to be able to understand and use them meaningfully.

It is important to note at this point that reception and discovery learning also differ with respect to their respective principal roles in intellectual development and functioning (Ausubel, 1961). For the most part, large bodies of subject matter are acquired through reception learning, whereas the everyday problems of living are solved through discovery learning. Nevertheless, some overlap of function obviously exists. Knowledge acquired through reception learning is also used in everyday problem solving, and discovery learning is commonly used in the classroom both to apply, extend, clarify, integrate, and evaluate subject-matter knowledge and to test comprehension. In laboratory situations, discovery learning provides insight into scientific method and also leads to the contrived rediscovery of known propositions. When employed by gifted persons it may generate significant

Figure 1 *Reception learning and discovery learning are on a separate continuum from rote learning and meaningful learning*

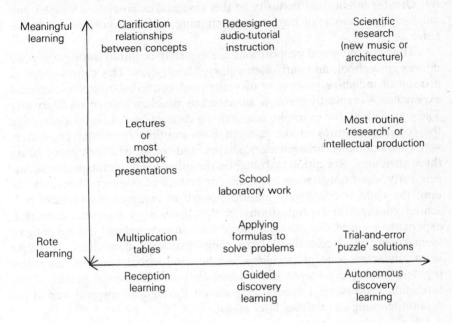

new knowledge. In the more typical classroom situation, however, the discovery of original propositions through problem-solving activity is not a conspicuous feature in the acquisition of new concepts or information. As far as the formal education of the individual is concerned, the educational agency largely transmits ready-made concepts, classifications, and propositions. In any case, discovery methods of teaching hardly constitute an efficient *primary* means of transmitting the *content* of an academic discipline.

One can justifiably argue that the school is also concerned with developing the student's ability to use acquired knowledge in solving particular problems systematically, independently, and critically in various fields of inquiry. But this function of the school, although constituting a legitimate objective of education in its own right, is less central than its related transmission-of-knowledge function. This is true in terms of the amount of time that can be reasonably allotted to this function, in terms of the objectives of education in a democratic society and in terms of what can be reasonably expected from most students.

From the standpoint of psychological process, meaningful discovery learning is obviously more complex than meaningful reception learning. It involves an antecedent problem-solving stage before meaning emerges and can be internalized (Ausubel, 1961). Generally speaking, however, reception learning, although phenomenologically simpler than discovery learning, paradoxically emerges later developmentally and, particularly in its more advanced and pure verbal forms, implies a higher level of cognitive maturity. Greater intellectual maturity in this case makes possible a simpler and more efficient mode of cognitive functioning in the acquisition of knowledge.

Thus concepts and propositions are typically acquired during the post-infancy, preschool, and early elementary-school years. This comes about as a result of inductive processing of verbal and nonverbal concrete-empirical experience — typically through autonomous problem solving or discovery. The young child, for example, acquires the concept of a chair by abstracting the common features of the concept from multiple incidental encounters with chairs of many different sizes, shapes, and colors, and then generalizing these attributes. Reception learning, on the other hand, although also occurring early, does not become a prominent feature of intellectual functioning until the child is cognitively mature enough to comprehend verbally presented concepts and propositions in the absence of concrete, empirical experience — until, for example, he or she can comprehend the meaning of 'democracy' or 'acceleration' from their dictionary definitions. In other words, inductive concept *formation* based on non-verbal, concrete, empirical problem-solving experience exemplifies early developmental phases of information processing. Concept *assimilation* through meaningful verbal reception learning exemplifies later stages.

Meaningful versus Rote Learning

Although the distinction between reception and discovery learning discussed above has absolutely nothing to do with the rote-meaningful dimension of the learning process, the two dimensions of learning were commonly confused. This confusion is partly responsible for the widespread but unwarranted twin beliefs that reception learning is invariably rote and that discovery learning is inherently and necessarily meaningful. Both assumptions, of course, reflect the long-standing belief in many educational circles that the only knowledge one *really* possesses and understands is knowledge that one discovers by oneself. Actually, each distinction (rote versus meaningful and reception versus discovery learning) constitutes an entirely independent dimension of learning. Hence a much more defensible proposition is that *both* reception *and* discovery learning can be *either* rote *or* meaningful depending on the conditions under which learning occurs (Ausubel, 1961). The relationships between rote and meaningful learning, as well as their orthogonal relationship to the reception-discovery dimension are shown diagrammatically in Figure 1.

In both instances meaningful learning takes place if the learning task can be related in nonarbitrary, substantive (nonverbatim) fashion to what the learner already knows, and if the learner adopts a corresponding learning set to do so. Rote learning, on the other hand, occurs if the learning task consists of purely arbitrary associations, as in paired-associate, puzzle-box, maze, or serial learning, if the learner lacks the relevant prior knowledge necessary for making the learning task potentially meaningful, and also (regardless of how much potential meaning the task has) if the learner adopts a set merely to internalize it in an arbitrary, verbatim fashion (that is, as an arbitrary series of words). . . . It is true that much potentially meaningful knowledge taught by verbal exposition results in rotely learned verbalisms. This rote outcome, however, is not inherent in the expository method, but rather in such abuses of this method as fail to satisfy the criteria of meaningful verbal learning (Ausubel, 1961).

There is much greater reluctance, on the other hand, to acknowledge that the conditions of meaningful learning just mentioned also apply to problem-solving methods. Performing laboratory experiments in cookbook fashion without understanding the underlying substantive and methodological principles involved confers little appreciation of scientific method. Neither does 'discovering' correct answers to problems in mathematics and science, without really understanding what one is doing, add to knowledge or problem-solving ability. Students accomplish this latter feat merely by rote memorizing 'type problems' and mechanical procedures for manipulating algebraic symbols. Nevertheless, it must be recognized that laboratory work and problem-solving are not genuinely meaningful experiences unless they meet two conditions. First, they must be built on a foundation of clearly understood concepts and principles; second, the constituent operations must themselves be meaningful.

Reference

AUSUBEL, D. (1961) 'In defense of verbal learning', *Education Theory*, 11, pp. 15–25.

Meaningful Learning

(From McClelland, G., 1983, 'Ausubel's theory of meaningful learning and its implications for primary science', in Richards, C. and Holford, D. (Eds) *The Teaching of Primary Science: Policy and Practice*, Lewes, Falmer Press, pp. 113–17.)

The ideas of Ausubel are explored and explained further in the next extract by McClelland. He argues that it is essential that teachers understand the processes of learning in order to improve judgments made in the classroom. Ausubel's theory, he suggests provides a useful framework for understanding learning, but has proved inaccessible to many teachers because of the technical nature of the language used. McClelland admits that in attempting to represent some of the main features of the theory there is a likelihood that it becomes distorted and less rigorous.

A central reason for teaching anything to a child is that the child, by learning it will gain understanding and control of some aspect of the world of experience. Through ideas of number and the four processes of arithmetic a truly enormous range of problems can be solved. Through ideas of right and wrong people learn to live together. Through science pattern and order may be inposed on apparently diverse and chaotic experiences. Through all of these and many more, but particularly through science, the idea that the world of experience is governed by rules, and that it is worth while to seek for such rules, can be developed. The more we have a theoretical grasp of how such learning takes place and how it fulfils these functions, the better the position we will be in to make decisions about what to teach, when, in what sequence, and how. Ausubel's theory of learning provides such a framework which, to date, has been neither widely understood nor disseminated, largely, I think, because it has been framed (Ausubel *et al.*, 1978) in very careful, but far from easily accessible language. By re-expressing some of the main aspects of the theory in less technical language I am bound to distort it and to lessen its subtlety and rigour.

Ausubel's Theory of Meaningful Learning

From the many changes of behaviour or capability which can be termed learning, Ausubel concentrates on a restricted range, that of learning meanings expressed in symbols, mainly words. This makes it particularly relevant to school learning. He distinguishes two independent aspects of the learning process as shown in Figure 1, the degree of meaningfulness and the way in which the material to be learnt is encountered.

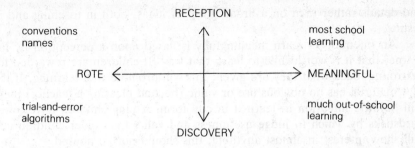

Probably no learning experience is ever entirely rote nor entirely meaningful, but pure rote learning would form no link with anything already known, would not help further learning, and would neccessarily be learnt 'by heart'. Learning is meaningful according to how well it fits into the network of what is already known, extends it, and improves the ability to learn still more. A child who can work out the exercise 12 × 23 to get 276, but cannot find the cost of 12 chocolate bars each costing 23 units or the area of a rectangle with sides of 12 and 23 units, and so on, has not learnt multiplication meaningfully. Meaningful learning is demonstrated by the appropriate use of the ideas in hitherto unseen situations.

Three Conditions for Meaningful Learning

Learning will not be meaningful unless three conditions are met.

1 What is to be learnt must make sense, or be consistent with experience. This is logical meaningfulness. (The material does not have to be true.)
2 The learner must have enough relevant knowledge for the material to be within grasp. This is psychological meaningfulness.
3 The learner must intend, or be disposed, to learn meaningfully, that is, to fit the new material into what is already known rather than to memorize it word-for-word.

While these conditions are seen as necessary, they are not sufficient. For example, inherently meaningful material will not automatically be learnt, given the other two conditions. There are problems of medium, sequence, timing, exemplification and expression to be solved.

Relevant knowledge and the way it is interconnected will vary from individual to individual. Learning is an individual, constructive activity leading to an end-product which is different for each person. It is easy, as a teacher, to think of the content of a lesson as being 'transmitted' but this is a misleading analogy. One product of this idea is to view errors or gaps in pupils' knowledge as being 'their fault' rather than as the results of failure to meet the second condition. Another is to focus attention on specific facts and details rather than on a broad grasp of ideas, both in teaching and in testing.

An intention to learn meaningfully is based upon a perception by the learner that it is worthwhile to learn that way. If children are rewarded for 'parroting' back what they are given, this will promote rote learning. If the new material has no obvious use or value (beyond pleasing a teacher) there will be little intention to learn it in any form. Young children have fewer yardsticks by which to judge usefulness and value than older children and will show interest in almost anything; this should not be abused.

It bears mention that the three conditions do not specify whether material is presented or discovered. This is seen as separate dimension, that is, didactic presentation and discovery methods can equally range across the spectrum of meaningfulness. Something essentially arbitrary, with little connection to any existing network of knowledge may be discovered by a child, while highly meaningful material can be learnt through being heard or read. Discovery is a double-edged weapon: it is perfectly possible to discover something which is false.

Concepts

Most areas of human understanding may be analyzed into hierarchies of concepts of ever greater degree of abstraction. An example from biology is Rover, dog, mammal, vertebrate, chordate. What is known by an individual is not open to such simple analysis. It is also organized hierarchically but in a much more confused and overlapping way so that different individuals have different structures covering the same general areas.

According to Ausubel, it is the concepts at the highest level of abstraction in an individual's organized knowledge which are the most stable and useful. That is, they are the most valuable for dealing with new situations and the most resistant to forgetting. Formation of high-level concepts, to draw together the many experiences we have, is the central feature of human ability. It is this rather than the ability to accumulate pieces of information which gives human thought its power, and it happens spontaneously. Children are natural theory-builders. High-level concepts are stable because they are used, and each successful use deepens and strengthens their base. Situations where they lead to inappropriate action give rise either to their modification or to avoidance behaviour. The higher the level of a concept, the greater the range of phenomena and situations to which it applies and the more likely it is to be used and stabilized. Part of the trade-off in this process is loss of exact recall of specific instances and information. Requiring precise memorization may well inhibit formation of higher-level and more beneficial ideas.

The task of the teacher is to help children to develop useful high-level concepts, that is, to organize learning experiences so as to promote rapid and efficient meaningful learning of the abstractions which link and underlie specific phenomena and experiences. If children study the life-cycle of a small animal or send table-tennis balls along the floor by blowing through straws, it should not be because we think they should be knowledgeable about these phenomena, but because they can exemplify more general ideas. Particular experiences are relatively unimportant and are freely interchangeable with others. They are not the content but the vehicle for learning it. If what we teach does not exemplify higher-level abstractions, children will invent their own, almost certainly incompatible with a modern view and often reminiscent of aspects of Aristotelian science. If what we teach is not perceived as useful by an individual, it will not be stabilized but forgotten.

Higher-level concepts cannot be pinned down by simple definitions or lists of attributes. Research on such trivial concepts as identifying 'blue triangles' from sets of coloured shapes can have little bearing on how children develop a concept of 'force' or 'adaptation'. High-level concepts are developed, not selected from alternatives. They can be more or less clear, cohesive, all-embracing and applicable to new situations. My concept of energy is probably more elaborated in these respects than yours, as I have spent a great deal of time thinking about it, but your concept of justice may be much more usable than mine. It is a matter of degree, not of absolutes. High-level concepts are more than a means for coping with existence; they also determine what we perceive out of the mass of information which constantly bombards our senses. Shelley's skylark blithely poured forth profuse streams of unpremeditated art: mine is on red alert defending its territory.

Learnability of New Material

The degree to which something new is potentially easy or difficult to learn depends on two factors: its internal complexity and its relationship to what is already known. These can be viewed as independent dimensions. Internal complexity is the quality which distinguishes the exercise 23×47 from 2368×4759. The direct effect of an internal complexity is to increase the time required to process the information. For an individual there may be a ceiling to the degree of complexity which can be tolerated. In what follows it will be assumed that internal complexity is kept constant, and below such a ceiling. Six levels of relatedness to pre-existing knowledge can be distinguished, each of which leads to different learning characteristics. The list is more or less in order of difficulty, given that reasonably large amounts of material are to be learnt:

1　deducible or derivable from what is already known;
2　extends, elaborates or recodes what is already known;
3　draws together low-level concepts into one higher-level abstraction;

4 although meaningful, cannot be directly related to what is already known;
5 arbitrary (or approached in this way);
6 meaningful but conflicting with or negating what is already known.

Although children bring to school a great deal of knowledge and experience, it is not usually highly elaborated nor organized, so much school learning is likely to fall into the fourth category. Some may fall into the sixth.

Strategy for Presenting New Material

Where new material does not link directly with what is already known it cannot be actively 'fitted in' and may be quickly forgotten unless some means is arranged to give it temporary stability. Ausubel describes a strategy designed for this purpose. The new material is presented as a short set of statements at a high level, followed by specific lower-level instances, used to develop their meaning. Initially the general statements have little meaning and the concepts they express are vague, limited and possibly confused. Experience with the widest possible range of situations to which they apply clarifies and refines them to the point where they can take over the task of explaining and incorporating further examples. At first the statements act as a clue that something worthwhile is to be learnt, and as a guide to what that learning will like. There is a considerable analogy with how a new word is learnt. Met in isolation it can only be learnt by rote and is soon forgotten. Met in context its meaning develops, and the wider and more complete the range of contexts, the more rapid and complete the process.

Unlearning

New information which conflicts with or negates existing concepts is the most difficult to learn and the process may even be painful. If the concept under threat has been hitherto useful, and so is highly stable, the most likely course of action is to try to deny or discount the new information, or to avoid circumstances in which it must be acknowledged. The reception given to evolutionary theories by Christian fundamentalists exemplifies these processes. It is for this reason that I would strongly argue against either allowing children to form their own scientific concepts through experience or taking their concepts as a starting point for lessons (Albert, 1977; Driver, 1980; Erickson, 1979; Harlen, 1980; see also Chapter 5 in this book). Most physical science is based on theories which fly in the face of naive observation, and later attempts to displace perfectly successful but incorrect theories may well contribute to the well-known flight from physical sciences at school. Even practising scientists are not immune to this problem. It has been said that ideas in science change not because individuals change but because old people die. The ideas which a person discovers or invents are more strongly held than those which are learned from others so if they are wrong they will be at least a stumbling block to further learning. Better a tentative and vague grasp of a useful idea than a firm and clear grasp of an erroneous one. As Mark Twain put it, 'It ain't what you don't know that causes the trouble. It's what you know that ain't so.'

As a general rule I should argue that any concept or theory which has not been discovered nor invented by adults in other societies than our own is unlikely to be discovered or invented by young children in ours, however well-planned the experiences given them. If misconception and error is to be avoided, such concepts and theories must be presented in contexts where they can be used to make sense of experience. If misconceptions already exist, it is vital to know about them, and this may mean quite careful probing of children's talk. The use of standard phrases and terminology may well disguise differences in meaning. Misconceptions cannot be expected to be uprooted quickly. Children do not usually have so elaborate, stable and interconnected ideas as adults. Also they are reasonably accustomed to having got things wrong, so the task is not impossible, but it can be expected to require more repetitions of the new ideas with accompanying experiences than would learning the same material from zero. It is not enough to present the new ideas and hope that the old ones will wither away.

Reference

AUSUBEL D., *et al.* (1978) *Educational Psychology: A Cognitive View*, 2nd Edition, Holt, Rinehant and Winston.

Freedom to Learn

(From Patterson, C.H., 1977, *Foundations for a Theory of Instruction and Educational Psychology*, London, Harper and Row, pp. 299–304.)

The final psychological perspective to be considered derives form the work of Carl Rogers. Although he began his work with children, much of his experience was with adults. He adopted a 'client-centred' approach to his work which was concerned with psychotherapy. He developed theories relating to the nature of the individual and human personality. In 1969 he wrote *Freedom to Learn* which brought together his thinking about education and teaching. As his work in psychotherapy has been concerned with the 'person', so his writing on education focuses upon the individual and the attitudes of the teacher rather than methods of instruction. This viewpoint is reinforced in his statement that the aim of education is the facilitation of learning.

Rogers comments,

> We know that the facilitation of such learning rests not upon the teaching skills of the leader, not upon his curricular planning, not upon his use of audiovisual aids, not upon the programmed learning he utilizes, not upon his lectures and presentations, not upon an abundance of books, though each of these might at one time or another be utilized as an important resource. No, the facilitation of significant learning rests upon certain attitudinal qualities which exist in the personal relationship between the facilitator and the learner.

The Crisis in Education

Education, says Rogers, is facing challenges the response to which will be one of the major factors in determining whether mankind moves forward, or whether man destroys himself on this planet, leaving this earth to those few living things which can withstand atomic destruction and radioactivity. The crisis is represented by a number of questions which he poses:

1 Can education free itself from the past and past goals and prepare individuals and groups to live in a world of accelerating change, if it is possible for human beings to do so?
2 Can education deal effectively with increasing racial tensions and prevent civil war among the world's races?
3 Can education prepare us to deal responsibly and communicatively with increasing irrational nationalism and international tension, and help us prevent nuclear destruction?

4   Can educators and educational institutions satisfy the revolt and objections of youth against the imposed curriculums and impersonality of secondary and higher education, or will learning move out of our institutions of learning, leaving them to indoctrinate conformity?

5   Can the conservative, traditional, bureaucratic, rigid educational system break out of the shackles of pressures for social conformity and deal with the real problems of modern life?

6   Will education be taken over by business, with more innovation and responsiveness, but with the motive of profit-making and emphasis upon producing profitable hardware?

These are not issues of technology; they are philosophical, social, and psychological issues. And they clearly relate not to the traditional subject matter of education, that is, information and knowledge, or even cognitive or intellectual development, but to the area of personal development and interpersonal relationships.

The Goal of Education

To resolve these crisis questions and to assure human survival, the goal of education must be the facilitation of change and learning. 'The only man who is educated is the man who has learned how to learn; the man who has learned how to adapt and change; the man who has realized that no knowledge is secure, that only the process of *seeking* knowledge gives a basis for security. Changingness, a reliance on *process* rather than upon static knowledge, is the only thing that makes any sense as a goal for education in the modern world.'

This goal includes, but goes beyond, cognitive or intellectual education, to include the education of the whole person. It involves personal growth and the development of creativity and self-directed learning. The goal of education is the same as the goal of psychotherapy: the fully functioning person. Openness to experience; an existential way of living in which life is not static but an ongoing, flexible, adaptive process; and trust in the organism as the basis for behavior are characteristics of the person who is capable of continuing to learn and to adapt to change, to meet the issues involved in the crisis in education. The traditional concept of the 'educated person' is no longer relevant to our modern society.

The educator of the future 'must know, at the deepest personal level, the stance he takes in regard to life. Unless he has true convictions as to how his values are arrived at, what sort of individual he hopes will emerge from his educational organization, whether he is manipulating human robots, or dealing with free individual persons, and what kind of a relationship he is striving to build with these persons, he will have failed not only his profession, but his culture.' This is a far cry from, but more fundamental and important than, concern with curriculums, methods, administration, and teaching techniques.

Two Kinds of Learning

Learning may be conceived of as falling along a continuum of meaning. At one end is meaningless learning — rote learning, exemplified by the learning, or memorization, of nonsense syllables. Such learning is difficult and does not last. Much of what is taught in schools involves such learning. The material has no personal meaning for the student, does not involve feelings or the whole person; it is learning occurring 'from the neck up'.

The learning which takes place in everyday life, experiential learning, has meaning and personal relevance. Such learning is quick and is retained. Learning a language in a native environment, as compared to learning it in a classroom, illustrates the difference. Even though the stimulus for learning in the first case may come from outside, from the necessity to adapt to the society, it is in a real sense self-initiated. It also represents a personal involvement. It is pervasive, influencing the total person, including attitudes and behavior. It is evaluated by the learner in terms of his or her needs — the locus of evaluation is internal. And its essence is meaning.

Education traditionally has involved the first, meaningless kind of learning, though many teachers and educators recognize the value of the second. To implement the second approach would amount to a revolution in education. The difficulties of implementing it in a practical way have stood in the way of those who accept it theoretically. Rogers proposes ways in which it can be implemented.

This second kind of learning is not noncognitive in nature. It involves cognitive elements or aspects; but it combines these with the affective elements involved in personal meaning. It recognizes that meaningful learning, even of a cognitive nature, involves the total person.

The Nature of Significant Learning

Significant — personal, experiential — learning is learning which makes a difference to the person, in behavior, attitudes, and personality. It is learning which leads to the individual becoming a more fully functioning person. Such learning involves certain principles (or hypotheses) which relate to the theory of human nature and of human behavior presented earlier.

1   Human beings have a natural propensity for learning. They are by nature curious; exploratory; desirous of discovering, knowing, and experiencing. Yet there is an ambivalence toward learning; significant learning involves some pain, either connected with the learn-

ing itself or with having to relinquish earlier learnings. Learning to walk involves bumps and bruises. Learning that some others are better than oneself in some respects is painful. But the gains and satisfactions of learning, of developing one's potentials, are usually greater than the pain, and learning continues.

2 Significant learning takes place when the subject matter is perceived by the student as having relevance for her or his own purposes. A person learns significantly only those things which are perceived as involving the maintenance and enhancement of the self. Two students of equal ability learn quite different things, or amounts, depending on how they perceive the material as relating to their needs and purposes. The speed of learning also varies. The time for learning may be reduced by as much as two-thirds to four-fifths when material is perceived as relevant to the learner's purposes.

3 Learning which involves a change in self-organization, or the perception of the self, is threatening, and tends to be resisted. The self includes one's values, beliefs, and basic attitudes, and when these are questioned they are defended. To recognize that something new and different may be better, that one is behind in things or inferior in some way, or inadequate, is defended against.

4 Those learnings which are threatening to the self are more easily perceived and assimilated when external threats are at a minimum. Pressure, ridicule, shaming, and so on, increase resistance. But an accepting, understanding, supportive environment removes or decreases threat and fear and allows the learner to take a few steps or to try something and experience some success. Teaching machines incorporate this idea.

5 When threat to the self or self-concept is low, experience can be perceived in a differentiated fashion, and learning can proceed. This is why learning is inhibited by threat and assisted by its lack. Threat disorganizes thinking: It leads to distortion of perception, restriction of the perceptual field (a kind of tunnel vision), even, in strong threat, to paralysis of thinking and action. Freedom from threat to one's security, or ego, frees one to see the total situation and to examine it — to 'take it apart', manipulate it, put it together — and to learn. Threats to the *organism* — even life-or-death threats — can be handled or responded to with all one's powers; but threats to the *self* or the self-concept interfere with learning. Another way to view it is that threat to the self leads to all-out efforts to *maintain* the self as it exists, but not to change or growth in the self.

6 Much significant learning is acquired through doing. Experiential involvement with practical or real problems promotes learning. Meaningfulness and relevance are inherent in such situations.

7   Learning is facilitated when the student participates responsibly in the learning process. When students choose their own objectives and directions, formulate their own problems, discover their own resources, decide on and follow their own courses of action, and experience and live with the consequences, significant learning is maximized. Self-directed learning is meaningful and relevant.

8   Self-initiated learning which involves the whole person of the learner — feelings as well as intellect — is the most lasting and pervasive. The learning is the learner's own, and becomes incorporated in her or him; it is not something external or accepted on authority, and thus vulnerable to questioning or another authority.

9   Independence, creativity, and self-reliance are all facilitated when self-criticism and self-evaluation are basic and evaluation by others is of secondary importance. Creativity needs freedom, freedom to try something unusual, to take a chance, to make mistakes without being evaluated or judged a failure.

10 The most socially useful learning in the modern world is the learning of the process of learning, a continuing openness to experience and incorporation into oneself of the process of change. Change is a central fact of current life, and learning must be continuous.

Significant learning requires that we focus upon something other than the usual concerns of teaching or education. It makes the question of what should be taught, the curriculum, minor. Teaching as the imparting of knowledge is useful in an unchanging environment. But in this modern world, are we justified 'in the presumption that we are wise about the future and the young are foolish? Are we *really* sure as to what they should know? Then there is the ridiculous question of coverage ... based on the assumption that what is taught is learned. ... I know of no assumption so obviously untrue.' In a continually changing world, information and knowledge quickly become out of date or obsolete.

Significant learning involves the whole person; it combines cognitive and affective-experiential elements. It is a unified learning, yet with awareness of the different aspects. It does not separate the mind from the heart, from feelings, as most education attempts to do. Rogers quotes Archibald McLeish in this regard: We do not feel our knowledge. Nothing could better illustrate the flaw at the heart of our civilization ... Knowledge without feeling is not knowledge and can lead only to public irresponsibility and indifference, and conceivably to ruin. Personal meaning, relevance, significance involve feelings, attitudes, and beliefs.

Teaching and Learning

If the only learning which can significantly influence behavior is self-discovered, self-appropriated personal learning, can learning be taught?

Rogers, on the basis of his experience both in psychotherapy and in teaching, has raised some serious questions. He states them personally as follows (not all are listed here):

It seems to me that anything that can be taught to another is relatively inconsequential and has little or no significant influence on behavior....

Self-discovered learning, truth that has been personally appropriated and assimilated in experience, cannot be directly communicated to another....

When I try to teach, as I do sometimes, I am appalled by the results, which seem a little more than inconsequential, because sometimes the teaching appears to succeed. When this happens I find that the results are damaging. It seems to cause the individual to distrust his own experience, and to stifle significant learning. *Hence I have come to feel that the outcomes of teaching are either unimportant or hurtful....*

As a consequence, *I realize that I am only interested in being a learner, preferably learning things that matter, that have some significant influence on my own behavior....*

I find that one of the best, but most difficult, ways for me to learn is to drop my own defensiveness, at least temporarily, and to try to understand the way in which his experience seems and feels to the other person.

I find that another way for me to learn is to state my own uncertainties, to try to clarify my own puzzlements, and thus get closer to the meaning that my experience actually seems to have.

Such experience, he concludes, would imply that we do away with teaching. Learning would take place in groups of people who wanted to learn. But can this be done with children? What is the place of the teacher in the learning of children?

The Teacher as the Facilitator of Learning

Teaching, as usually defined and practiced, involves instruction, imparting information, knowledge, or skill; it is 'to make to know', 'to show, guide, direct'. These are activities of the teacher. But are they necessary for learning, or even related to learning as defined earlier? 'Teaching', says Rogers, 'is a vastly over-rated function'.

The function of the teacher is to facilitate learning in the student by providing the conditions which lead to meaningful or significant self-directed learning. The objective is to develop a group, including the teacher, into a community of learners. In such a community, curiosity is freed, the sense of inquiry is opened up, everything is open to questioning and exploration. 'Out of such a context arise true students, real learners, creative scientists and scholars and practitioners, the kind of individuals who can live in a delicate but everchanging balance between what is presently known and the flowing, moving, altering, problems and facts of the future'. Such a community facilitates learning, or learning how to learn.

Reference

Rogers, C.R. (1969) *Freedom to Learn*, Columbus, Ohio, Merrill.

Primary Education: Psychological Perspectives

Self Concept and Motivation

(From Yamamoto, K., 1972, *The Child and his Image*, Boston, Houghton-Mifflin, pp. 80–4.)

A central feature of the humanist perspective in psychology is a concern for the individual, especially the relevance of learning to the individual. Fundamental to successful learning is the extent to which the child is interested in and motivated by his learning experiences. In fact, evidence exists that without adequate motivation even the brightest children fail to achieve. A significant factor in motivation is the extent to which the child expects to succeed, the feeling that a task or problem can be solved satisfactorily. The way a child views him or herself as a learner is an essential feature of the successful completion of school tasks. This suggests that an understanding of 'self concept', is of considerable importance for the intending teacher. As Conner suggests in a later extract (pp. 368–72), if a child is failing to learn, might it not be something to do with the perception the learner has of him or herself as well as the way in which the teacher has organized the learning activity. The next extract by Yamamoto attempts to explain what is meant by 'self concept' and discusses the importance of a knowledge of the self concept for the teacher. He argues that the way in which a child perceives him or herself is fundamental in their motivation to learn.

In recognizing the inevitability of rapid change in today's society, educators are challenged as never before to find the means of developing in youth a stable personality. The only predictions about the future that can be made with certainty are that it will be different and change will be a constant way of life. Supposedly the well-adjusting personality, the stable and flexible person, can adapt to change whereas the maladjusting personality feels threatened and becomes defensive, resistive, and often violent. The cure for these self-defeating coping strategies, so far as educators are concerned, lies not in emergency measures but rather in 'the steady, consistent effort to make education more responsive to the real needs and essential quality of all human beings'.[1]

Relevance in education is contingent first upon understanding the student, and secondly, upon individualizing the educational process. As a philosophical concept, individualized instruction meets little argument today. At the operational level, however, it provokes controversy — frequently quite heated — at the drop of a mortarboard.

Among several aspects of personality calling for better understanding, motivation possibly ranks first. Relative to achievement, motivation is perhaps even more complex and more significant than intelligence itself. Without adequate motivation the intelligent child is hardly a match for his less intelligent but highly motivated peer. A significant factor in motivation is anticipated success — the feeling that the task at hand can be completed.

In fact, the realization has recently emerged that the child's *concept* of ability may be as crucial to his success as his ability per se. If a person feels he cannot produce, then the actual ability to produce is reduced or negated. By the same token, a success-oriented individual will often plunge into a project with little past experience and more often than not be successful. This feeling about ability is based on past experiences, physical, emotional, and psychological.

Although the importance of the self concept is an established fact and the literature is becoming increasingly productive, the concept continues to be elusive. The research is relatively limited, standardized measures are largely nonexistent, and terminology is obscure. Albeit limited, the research is consistent in reporting the relation between self concept and achievement, whether it be academic or social. Brownfain[2] found that college students with a stable self concept were better adjusted and freer of inferiority feelings and nervousness, were more popular, knew more people and were better known, and showed less evidence of compensatory behavior of a defensive kind than those students who had an unstable self concept. Wattenberg and Clifford[3] report that at the kindergarten level a self concept evaluation is a more accurate predictor of second-grade reading achievement than is a mental age evaluation.

Glasser[4] makes perhaps the strongest argument of all for the importance of the relation between self concept and achievement. He says that the whole of our society today is dichotomized between those who identify with success and those who identify with failure; not between blacks and whites or rich and poor. Glasser believes a child creates some feeling of who he is, that is, an identity, which will be either positive or negative. Ages five to ten are the critical years for this development, with the home and school as the major agents. In his book, *Schools Without Failure*, Glasser is highly critical of schools and the role they play in blocking the achievement of a success identity. School policies tend to reward those children who perform well and expose those who are unable to compete, and then emphasize academic material giving little encouragement to learning about oneself.

The role of the responsible elementary teacher today is expanding far beyond the teaching of academics. It is essential that the teacher know more about the children in his classroom; specifically, it is important to know how they feel about themselves.

Self Concept in the Child's Life

The child's view of his environment and of his place in this environment determines his reactions and his behavior. One child may be challenged by the stimulation of environmental factors. Another child may see these same factors as overwhelming and thus will openly rebel, withdraw, or perhaps develop other defense systems in order to maintain himself psychologically.

To understand the child's judgment of self, we must look at the whole child and study every facet of his behavior. Appraising the self concept involves observing this behavior. The human organism is fundamentally consistent in its expression. Environmental conditions as well as a temporary internal state may influence responses. However, a general consistency of behavior is maintained throughout and is discernible in every mode of expression if the observer is insightful enough to interpret the meaning of the behavior accurately. Because the self image is a concept and not a concrete entity, an appraisal of this self image can be accomplished only by observing the behavior that allows insight into the system determining that behavior. In other words, the self concept per se cannot be directly measured.

Beatty[5] says that the nervous system is the basis for what we call intellect and that it is well developed at birth. As the child experiences his own body interacting directly with the environment, he begins to develop an image of what he is like. This is the self concept. Beatty further indicates that the young child reacts directly to his feelings rather than to a sophisticated interpretation of his feelings. As he grows he begins to see his feelings and reactions in terms of their impact on those around him. Thus the self concept develops. Further development stems from the feeling component generated in past encounters. The child indeed becomes that which he thinks he is. If environmental factors distort reality (e.g., parents overlooking successes and emphasizing failures), then a poor self concept results, which can inhibit his development. The child who experiences difficulty in reading may acquire an erroneous self image. Perhaps he is exposed to the task before he is developmentally or otherwise ready. Frustrated by his inability to learn, his teacher tells him he is a poor reader. To emphasize the point, the teacher reports the child's failure to his parents. Becoming anxious, they in turn tell him again that he is a poor reader. Because it has become a sensitive subject, he shuns every reading exposure. Lacking positive motivation, he dislikes the subject and practice is avoided. When he does try to read further difficulty is encountered, which serves to reinforce the feeling he had originally, 'I am a poor reader'. If reading had been presented so as to promote success rather than failure, the negative experience could have been prevented or reduced. The child's self concept would not have suffered a devastating blow. This example is not an isolated incident; it is a common experience in a majority of schools today for a significant number of children.

Role of the Teacher in Self Concept Development

While the self concept is established in the early years of childhood, it remains pliable during the elementary years. At this time the teacher plays an extremely important role in the development of the self image — both in handling the child and in reporting to his parents. Davidson and Lang[6] found that during the elementary years a significant correlation existed between the child's perception of his teacher's feelings toward him and his own self image. A positive perception resulted in a positive self image and vice versa. The academic achievement was higher and the classroom behavior more desirable for those children who saw themselves as adequate in the eyes of their teachers.

The teacher's role in the development of a child's self image is as important as are his methods of direct, cognitive teaching. In addition to noting potential and achievement, he needs to be mindful of other significant indicators, such as posture, voice quality and speech content, role in free play, conversation, drawings, and stories.

Notes

1 KUNZ, F.L. and SELLON, EMILY B. (1969) 'News and views', *Main Currents in Modern Thought*, 25, p. 145; May–June.

2 BROWNFAIN, JOHN J. (1952) 'Stability of the self-concept as a dimension of personality', *Journal of Abnormal and Social Psychology*, 47, pp. 597–606; July.

3 WATTENBERG, WILLIAM W. and CLIFFORD, CLARE. (1964) 'Relations of self concept to beginning achievement in reading', *Child Development*, 35, pp. 461–7; June.

4 GLASSER, WILLIAM. (1969) *Schools Without Failure*, New York: Harper and Row.

5 BEATTY, WOLCOTT H. (1969) '*The feelings of learning*', *Childhood Education*, 45, pp. 363–9; March.

6 DAVIDSON, HELEN H. and LANG, GERHARD. (1960) 'Children's perceptions of their teachers' feelings toward them related to self perception, school achievement, and behavior', *Journal of Experimental Education*, 29, pp. 107–8; December.

Meeting Special Educational Needs

(From Ainscow, M., 1987, 'The primary curriculum and special needs'. A paper presented to the Conference of the National Council for Special Education, April, pp. 2–6.)

Another area to which psychologists have made an important contribution to our thinking in primary education concerns children with special educational needs. The 1981 Education Act and the Warnock Report actively advocated the integration of children with special needs into 'normal' learning contexts. The next article by Mel Ainscow draws upon recent research into 'Co-operative Learning' as a means by which all children might become more successful learners. Although initially concerned with meeting special educational needs, the ideas proposed have practical applications for all primary classrooms and as can be seen extends the ideas of Rogers and Yamamoto, discussed earlier (pp. 352–8; 359–62). In particular Ainscow stresses the importance of considering the child as a learner and of their need to develop a positive self image. This is of special importance for children regarded as having special educational needs.

Meeting special educational needs is to a large extent a matter of seeking a match between the attainments and interests of individual pupils and the tasks and experiences with which they are provided. In other words it is about the curriculum.

In this short paper it is impossible to do justice to this broad topic. Consequently I have chosen to focus on certain issues which seem to me to be the concern of many teachers in primary schools.

Integration

It is generally agreed that the overall aims of education for children with special educational needs are the same as those for all children. The task is to find effective ways of achieving these aims.

Increasingly the emphasis is on doing this within the ordinary classroom and, indeed, it seems likely that in future children with more severe learning difficulties will be educated within integrated settings. The main arguments for this are:

(i)   Children must learn to live and work with all members of the community, whatever their disadvantages or disabilities;

(ii)   Children with learning difficulties are entitled to participate in a broad and balanced range of educational experiences; and

(iii)   They should have the benefit of working and interacting with children who are more successful in learning.

It has to be said, however, that where children with special needs become socially and intellectually isolated within mainstream classroom, there are strong possibilities of negative outcomes resulting from their own so-called integration. For example, they may:

— develop low self esteem as a result of being stigmatised and stereotyped
— avoid challenging situations, work at a slow rate, or indeed, spend periods doing very little work at all
— suffer social isolation or rejection by other pupils
— be treated with paternalistic care of the sort usually reserved for pets

The major question, therefore, is what teaching approaches are most successful in providing children with special needs with appropriate educational opportunities within the ordinary primary classroom? What we are seeking are approaches which facilitate constructive interactions between pupils and, at the same time, ensure success in learning.

Key issues that need to be considered are:

— How can we take account of individual differences when setting tasks?
— How can we help children to be actively engaged in educational tasks?
— How can we ensure that children are learning successfully?

Individual Differences

As I said, in meeting special needs we are attempting to achieve a match between the attainments and interests of individual children and the activities they are asked to do. Our concern is to take account of their individual differences?

What do we mean when we refer to individual differences. Four areas are particularly significant when considering children's educational needs. They are:

PREVIOUS EXPERIENCE
Every child brings to school a unique range of personal experience. Looked at from our perspective as teachers the experience of some children may seem limited or distorted, perhaps, for example, as a result of the circumstances of their families. Nevertheless each child has personal interests and preferences which can and should be used as a basis for enhancing learning, even if they seem to result mainly from the 'second-hand' experience of watching television.

EXISTING SKILLS AND KNOWLEDGE
Setting tasks at an appropriate level for each child is a fundamental skill of a teacher. Essentially this is a matter of knowing what the child can

already do in order to decide what he or she should do next. This might be a very obvious level, for example where a child must be able to count before carrying out tasks involving addition of numbers. On the other hand the skills and knowledge necessary for progression to some educational tasks are more complex, and difficult to determine.

ATTITUDES

On first admission to school most children are eager to learn and explore new experiences. It is sad that this initial enthusiasm and confidence seems to die in some cases. In considering children as individuals we need to be sensitive to their attitudes towards various types of learning tasks. Some may have a negative view of themselves as learners based upon previous experiences of failure; some may also have little confidence in teachers as people who can help them to succeed in learning.

DISABILITIES

Finally we must not ignore the fact that some children have disabilities or medical conditions which may hinder their educational progress. Sometimes these are obvious and well known to everybody involved, more often they are hidden and may be overlooked. Part of the responsibility of teachers must be to be on the look out for symptoms that might suggest such difficulties. It is also one of the important reasons for close teacher-parent collaboration.

Approaches

Most teachers in my experience when asked about how they try to help children with special needs seem to emphasise two main aspects. First of all they argue that central to their approach is rapport. In other words they believe that such pupils need to feel confidence in their teachers and that such confidence grows as a result of a warm and trusting relationship. The other main approach that is emphasised is the careful planning and preparation of tasks and materials. Here the aim is to provide children with activities within which they can be challenged and yet at the same time experience success.

I certainly would not wish to argue with either of these approaches. However there is, I believe, a third possibility that is worthy of consideration, the capacity of children to help one another.

Recently work in this country and North America (e.g. Johnson and Johnson, 1986; Lunzer and Gardner, 1984; Slavin, 1984) supports the view that where teachers structure their classrooms in order to encourage children to work together this can facilitate academic and social progress. Such a view is also consistent with recent thinking in the field of primary education. However such evidence as there is (e.g. Galton *et al.*, 1980), suggests that whilst children are often seated in groups in their classrooms they are rarely asked to work at their tasks in a collaborative manner.

Why is this so? It seems likely that the major explanation is that most teachers have not received training in ways of organising group work in the classroom.

Setting Tasks

The key to cooperative work in the classroom is the way in which tasks are set for the children. In general, task setting can take one of three forms:

1 *Competitive tasks*

This means that tasks are set in such a way that members of a class are placed in a win–lose struggle to see who is best. Consequently pupils:

— Work against each other to achieve a goal that only one or a few can attain.

— Are graded by their ability to work faster and more accurately than their peers.

— Seek outcomes that are personally beneficial but also are detrimental to others in the group.

— Either study hard to do better than their classmates or they take it easy because they do not believe they have a chance to win.

2 *Individualised tasks*

Here pupils are asked to work alone on tasks which have been carefully selected in order that they are suitable for the individual. As a result pupils:

— Know that their achievement is unrelated to the achievement of others.

— Are evaluated on a fixed set of standards.

— Seek outcomes that are personally beneficial and ignore as irrelevant the achievements of classmates.

3 *Cooperative tasks*

With this approach pupils are encouraged to collaborate in completing tasks so that they:

— Perceive that they can achieve their personal goals only if the other group members achieve theirs.

— Seek outcomes that are beneficial to all in a group.

Cooperative Learning

It is important to recognise that cooperative learning assumes a planned approach which goes well beyond a simple commitment to encouraging children to work together. Where such a policy is implemented the results are encouraging. Indeed Johnson and Johnson (1986) argue that cooperative approaches to learning should be used 'whenever teachers want students to learn more, like school better, like each other better, have higher self-esteem, and learn more effective social skills'.

When teachers have been successful in introducing this type of approach it often seems to be in the context of a planned school policy within which there is a staff development and support programme. In my experience cooperative learning in the classroom is facilitated by cooperative planning in the staffroom.

Issues that need to be considered when planning the introduction of cooperative learning methods include:

How do we prevent one or two pupils doing all the work?

Why should pupils help each other learn?

Why should they care what their classmates are doing?

What would keep the more successful pupils from belittling the contributions of others?

How can low attaining pupils make a significant contribution?

How can group work be structured to facilitate the greatest possible learning for all members?

What kinds of materials and activities should be used?

How can we encourage colleagues to try cooperative methods?

Conclusion

I have argued in this paper that in attempting to provide an appropriate curriculum for pupils with special educational needs in primary schools the emphasis must be on taking account of individual differences. My feeling is that this can be achieved by using cooperative learning methods to compliment traditional approaches. Such developments require careful planning and implementation.

References

GALTON, M.J., SIMON, B. and CROLL, P. (1980) *Inside the Primary Classroom*, London, Routledge and Kegan Paul.

JOHNSON, D.W. and JOHNSON, R.T. (1986) 'Mainstreaming and cooperative learning strategies', *Exceptional Children* 52 (6), pp. 553–61.

LUNZER, E. and GARDNER, K. (1984) *Learning from the Written Word*, Edinburgh, Oliver and Boyd.

SLAVIN, R.E. (1984) 'Team assisted individualization: Cooperative learning and individualized instruction in the mainstream classroom', *Remedial and Special Education* 5, pp. 33–42.

Learning Styles

(From Conner, C., 1988, 'Learning styles and classroom practice', in Conner, C. (Ed.) *Topic and Thematic Work in the Primary and Middle Years*, Cambridge Institute of Education, pp. 66–70.)

As our understanding of the nature of learning has improved, so we have come to realize that not everyone learns in exactly the same way. The study of preferred modes of learning is referred to as cognitive style, or individual variations in perceiving, remembering, thinking, and of organizing and processing information. The extract by Conner considers the implications of a knowledge of cognitive style in the context of topic work. As was suggested in the section on liberal romanticism (pp. 79–82) two major principles of this tradition and often embodied within topic work are concerned with creating opportunities for children to negotiate their own learning and to have control over their learning. This implies that all children are able to cope with the demands implied by this. The study of cognitive style indicates that this can create difficulties for some children. For the teacher, a knowledge of differences in learning preference might lead teachers to offer more varied opportunities in their learning. As Bruner (1966) has suggested, ... 'there should be many tracks leading to the same general goal'.

Reference

BRUNER, J.S. (1966) *Toward a Theory of Instruction*, Cambridge, Ma., Harvard University Press.

That's the trouble with David, he never does anything properly.

Oh, Julie is a delightful child. She writes beautifully and is very careful. I wish I had more like her in my class.

These two comments are offered as examples of an individual teacher's assessment of two children's topic work. We could begin to imagine the children the comments describe. It might even bring to mind similar children in our own classes. More careful analysis however could suggest other important avenues for our consideration about individual children and individual teachers in the topic work context. Is the response to David, for example, an indication of a conflict between his preferred way of working and that of his teacher? It could be argued that a comment such as that provided tells us as much about the teacher as it does about David. Similarly, the enthusiasm for Julie's working style might be an indication of obvious similarities between Julie's preferred approach and that of her teacher when engaged in classrooms activities. Topic work which provides opportunities for children to take responsibility for their own learning raises important questions about the competence of all children to cope with the demands involved in negotiationg, coordinating and influencing their own learning. Recent research into children's learning (Conner, 1982, 1986; Egan, 1986; Rowland, 1984; Claxton, 1984; Armstrong, 1980) reminds us of the ad hoc and often unsystematic nature of progress with phases of relative calm interspersed with amazing indications of development and progression. Alan Blyth (1987) succinctly describes this process of learning:

> To me, as a non-technical observer, the model of children's learning that makes sense is one in which children learn by fits and starts and some serendipity, now advancing rapidly, now resting on their oars or even drifting slightly backwards, and always liable to change direction and emphasis. Over the years, I believe, individual children learning in this way interact with the curriculum, sensitively conceived, in such a way as to make impressive general progress; but nobody can postulate a uniform process of learning, uniformly assessable, in the face of what is necessarily wayward and unplannable at the individual level. To do so would be to assume godlike powers and authority.

> Experienced teachers are of course aware of these incongruities.

What this suggests in the context of curriculum structure, therefore, is that for some children direction and suggestion are appropriate, whereas for others they need to be given opportunities without external influence, where they have considerable control over their own learning and this need not be just a result of their basic competencies. Witkin (1977), for example, described differences in terms of an *analytic* as opposed to a *global* approach to learning. Those adopting a global approach rely heavily on advice and direction, they need cues for successful learning, whereas the more analytic individuals are independent and prefer to approach learning in their own way (Goodenough, 1976). Differences of this kind, Witkin suggests, develop very early on in a child's life and such knowledge could be used by the teacher to improve the success of learning.

Cognitive styles are varied in their focus of attention, but tend to be described in bi-polar terms, with one extreme balanced against another extreme with a continuum between the two. Each end of a cognitive style continuum has positive as well as negative characteristics and, therefore, different implications for cognitive functioning. Many advocates of considering individual differences in terms of cognitive style continua suggest it is less threatening than scores of ability or measures on objective tests. However, it is the case that one end of a cognitive style continua can quickly assume superiority over its opposite, and it is important to avoid this and attempt to view them as a balance between the advantages and disadvantages, as well as recognise that many of us sit between the two extremes, tending towards one dimension or another. Examples of cognitive styles vary, but some of the best known are convergence/divergence (Guilford, 1959), focusers/scanners (Bruner, 1966), holists/serialists (Pask and Scott, 1976), analytic/global (Witkin *et al.*, 1977), reflective/impulsive (Kagan, 1975). For a more detailed digest see Messick (1976) or Kogan (1972). At present the levels of comparability between these styles are relatively low, yet intuitively an acceptance that children may vary in the way they approach learning has important implications for teaching. Watson (1980) demonstrated this beautifully in his investigation of children's errors in mathematics. It is common practice, he suggests, for teachers of beginning readers to hear individual children read, to ask questions of what they read, to analyse any errors and then organise teaching to overcome weaknesses, and take advantage of strengths indicated. He applied a similar technique to mathematics and discovered children arriving at correct answers with totally inappropriate processes:

> The most interesting feature of the results from the classroom teacher's point of view is that it was possible to see precisely how he or she approached the problem, to see where strengths and weaknesses lay and organise learning in a way which suited their preferred approach. (Watson, 1980)

One important benefit of a knowledge of research into cognitive styles is the challenge it offers to us as teachers, causing us to examine the learning environments we provide in school. If a child is failing to learn might it not be that the organisation of the learning experience has failed to take notice of the child's preferred way of learning? It suggests that we need to offer flexible learning environments with a range of alternative modes which allow children to choose; it also requires us to improve our observation skills of children at work. Just what are we seeing when children are engaged in learning activities? Similarly, it raises questions about the appropriateness and extent of our own intervention as teachers. Jerome Bruner (1966) suggested long ago that we need to become skilled in 'the art of observation and intellectual temptation'.

The comment quoted above reinforces the important message, that there are considerable differences likely to be apparent within any class of children and at any time in terms of the way they respond to different learning situations, and this need not be in terms of their ability.

I would argue that we do children a disservice if we do not respect their preferred ways of learning. Project work which is open ended and allows opportunities for children to initiate and contribute to the structure and organisation of their learning should at the same time take cognisance of their individuality. It seems important therefore to consider two fundamental issues as part of our reflection on the nature and organisation of topic and thematic work, which are concerned first with how we gain access to and develop our understanding of children's preferred learning styles, and secondly, to what extent can we cater for such individual differences that exist amongst children in our own classrooms in terms of such knowledge? It is to these questions that I would now like to turn.

The obvious and most important question we need to answer here is, *what do we mean by 'learning style'*?

Nathan Kogan (1972) has defined learning styles as,

Individual variations in modes of perceiving; remembering and thinking or as distinctive ways of apprehending, storing and utilising information

and Stephen Messick (1976) refers to cognitive styles as,

. . . consistent individual differences in the ways of organising and processing information and experience.

Here we can see that the terms 'learning style' and 'cognitive styles' are interchangeable.

Definitions of cognitive or learning style have several common elements. They refer to individual differences which are consistent, cutting across levels of general intelligence, and they refer to the organisation and processing of information, concerned with the structure rather than the content of thought. They can therefore be seen as an additional variable of individual difference which is likely to influence what one gains from a learning experience. As I have suggested elsewhere (Conner, 1986), all children bring something different to the learning situation which undoubtedly affects their response to what is presented as well as what they gain from the experience.

However, cognitive styles also represent the realisation that individuals may be consistent within themselves across subjects and situations in important ways.

These consistencies open up the possibility that we can tailor, or 'fine tune', teaching to match individual needs and approaches. (Squires, 1982)

For the teacher, an indicator of individual difference which pervades the personality, which is stable and consistent, and which is related to thinking processes rather than content, would appear immediately attractive in the context of modern educational thinking and could provide an important organisational principle for project work activities. Information derived from studies of the ways in which children learn would seem to have obvious practical educational applications which stem from a concern for the child, and which could demand radical rethinking about the structuring of educational experiences. For example, does the organisation of learning allow for varied approaches? If it doesn't, is this an important factor in children's failure to grasp or understand certain situations or experiences? Does the learning allow for the child to engage in the debate about his or her own learning? Is there an opportunity for children to elect for guidance or to lead, to take over responsibility for the organisation and structure of the learning in hand, or to draw upon the advice of teacher or peer group?

References

ARMSTRONG, M. (1980) *Closely Observed Children*, London, Chameleon Books.

BLYTH, A. (1987) 'Towards assessment in primary humanities', *Journal of Educational Policy*, 2, 4, pp. 353–60.

BRUNER, J.S. (1966) *Toward a Theory of Instruction*, Cambridge, Mass., Harvard University Press.

CLAXTON, G. (1984) *Live and Learn*, London, Harper and Row.

CONNER, C. (1982) An investigation into the relationship between children's cognitive style and their perception of the environment. Unpublished PhD thesis, University of London.

CONNER, C. (1986) 'Children's learning and project work', *Cambridge Journal of Education*, 16, 1, pp. 11–16.

EGAN, K. (1986) *Individual Development and the Curriculum*, London, Hutchinson.

GOODENOUGH, D.R. (1976) 'The role of individual differences in field dependence as a factor in learning and memory', *Psychological Bulletin*, 83.

GUILFORD, J.P. (1959) 'Three faces of intellect', *American Psychology*, 14.

KAGAN, J. (1975) 'Developmental studies in reflection and analysis', in WHITEHEAD, J.M. (Ed.) *Personality and Learning*, Sevenoaks, Hodder and Stoughton.

KOGAN, N. (1972) 'Educational implications of cognitive styles', in LESSER G.S. *Pychology and Educational Practice*, Glenville (Ill), Scott Foresman.

KOGAN, N. (1976) *Cognitive Styles in Infancy and Early Childhood*, London, Academic Press.

MESSICK, S. *et al.* (1976) *Individuality in Learning*, San Francisco, Jossey Bass.

PASK, G. and SCOTT, B.C.E. (1976) 'Learning strategies and individual competence', *International Journal Man Machine Studies*, 4, pp. 217–53, in WHITEHEAD, J.M. (Ed.) *Personality and Learning*, Sevenoaks, Hodder and Stoughton.

ROWLAND, S. (1984) *The Enquiring Classroom*, Lewes, Falmer Press.

ROWLAND, S. (1986) 'Classroom enquiry: An approach to understanding children', in HUSTLER, D. *et al.*, *Action Research in Classrooms and Schools*, London, Allen and Unwin.

SQUIRES, D. (1982) *Cognitive Styles and Adult Learning*, Nottingham, University of Nottingham.

WATSON, I. (1980) 'Investigating errors of beginning mathematicians', *Educational Studies in Mathematics*, 11.

WITKIN, H.A. *et al.* (1977) 'Field dependent and field independent cognitive styles and their educational implications, *Review Educational Research*, 47, 1.

Children and Their Learning

(From Fraser, A., 1987, 'A child structured learning context', in Dadds, M. (Ed.) 'Of Primary Concern', *Cambridge Journal of Education*, 17, 3, pp. 146–7, 150–1.)

The extent to which children are able to take responsibility for aspects of their own learning is also addressed in the next extract, by Alister Fraser. (This issue is also raised in discussions of liberal romanticism (pp. 83–6), liberal pragmatism in the extract by Conner (pp. 111–17) and in the previous extract on cognitive styles (pp. 368–72). It is also considered, in extracts from Bonnett's discussion of child-centredness and structure in learning in Volume 2 of this series.)

Fraser expresses concern that most opportunities provided for children to take control over their learning tend to be rhetoric rather than reality. Stimulated by a visit to Summerhill, he involved his class of third and fourth year junior children in a series of regular meetings for which they were responsible and in which they could make decisions about the organization and structure of aspects of their school life. It is an attempt to liberalize some of the features that typify educational provision in the primary school and attempts to place the teacher in the position of adviser and facilitator of children's learning rather than director of it. The evidence presented suggests that given the opportunity, children react extremely positively.

For some time I have reached the conclusion that teachers are far too autocratic in their approach to children's learning. There are a lot of myths around about tailoring the curriculum to the children's needs, about respecting children as individuals and about helping children to realize their potential. There is not much evidence to suggest that is what is actually happening. Grandiose claims are made but the reality pans out as something quite different. Tailoring the curriculum to the children's needs produces neat sets of difficulty graded worksheets; respecting children as individuals just means being even more aware that there are thirty plus of them in your class, and helping the children realize their potential means 'stretching' them with more of the same but with added tension. A lot of that is said tongue in cheek but it serves to make the point that rarely are the children themselves involved in the planning of their learning. Letting children take charge of their own learning is yet another myth that is bandied about. Children are rarely given that opportunity because the consequences mean letting go of the comfortable props that surround the orthodox teaching-learning situation.

Coincidentally I visited Summerhill. It left a great impression on me. I found myself attracted to a lot of what I saw. I also recoiled from a lot of what I saw. But it provided the motivation to start considering more seriously what I have felt for some time now, that children are not being allowed to be involved in the structuring of their own education and that I as a teacher am in a position to do something about that.

I determined, then, to change part of my practice. I would institute a 'Meeting' for the third and fourth year children. It wasn't going to be based on the Summerhill model — the schools are poles apart and what is good for one is most definitely in this case not good for the other. I want the children to become more involved in their own learning and to come to greater understanding of themselves and others, but how that happens is not at all clear.

I started off by talking with the children very generally about school and what they thought of it. It provoked a lot of interest. I told them about Summerhill and they became increasingly incredulous. Do schools with that degree of freedom really exist! From there I went on to describe the Summerhill Meeting. 'Why can't we do something like that here?' they asked. From that small seed something grew and is still growing and getting stronger.

It might be helpful to give a very brief description of the Barrington Meeting as it has evolved to date. The children of the third and fourth year are together in one class. Once a week they hold their Meeting. I say 'they' intentionally because in every sense it is the children's Meeting. There is a Chair who is nominated by the outgoing Chair of the previous week. The children have made it a rule that no person can serve again as Chair until everyone has had a turn (and everyone will have a turn whether they like it or not). From the early days they realised their Meeting needed some sort of control and the Chair was the answer. The Chair is at present all-powerful with the right to close any items of business at any time and to close the Meeting at any time. Members of the group are not allowed to speak unless invited to do so by the Chair. Children raise their hand if they have something to say. The Chair also takes proposals from the children and invites comments before the proposal is put to the Meeting for a vote. Meetings begin with notes being read from the previous meeting. The Chair then invites items of business. There are no explicit rules about what constitutes an item of business; the Chair decides what is appropriate or not. Many items are brought up which require planning and more thought. Very often they are suggestions with which all the children would like to become involved. The children realized that it was unworkable to do so with a large group and so they evolved the idea of setting up committees to deal with such situations.

The Meeting came into existence in a spontaneous way and it would be misleading to say that I had deliberately planned its beginning; at least, not in the accepted sense of the word. It is true that I had vaguely thought along those lines for some time before it actually happened, but there had been no careful consideration. The fact was that it just happened one day because the conditions were right for it to happen. And because it came about the way it did, the children and I had a great sense of joint ownership of something. We all positively wanted it to work. The children developed a sort of affection for it and indeed were very possessive about it. They talked about it in terms of 'our' Meeting and saw Class 4 as having sole rights to it. It conferred a certain status on those involved in it — the preserve of the elders of the tribe. After all, they had originated it so why should they not be jealous of it?

In many ways I colluded with the children. I remember very well the feelings of seclusion when the early Meetings were taking place; a kind of privacy and understanding behind closed doors. As one child commented:

This is a school but it doesn't feel like one. It's like a film this.

There was a sense of nurturing something that was too frail to expose to the outside world. I make no excuse for that. I don't think that I was in a position to defend something which I intuitively felt was right for the children's development but of which I had no clear understanding. It was necessary at the time.

The Meeting has survived its early infancy and has now been in existence for something like two years. During that time the children have covered much ground. It is not possible to go into detail but a short summary of the issues the children have addressed might serve to illustrate the nature of the learning experience, at the same time conveying something of the flavour of the Meeting.

Much of their deliberation has centred around organising systems to improve the quality of the school environment. For example, they established teams to look after cloakroom areas and to ensure that the school grounds were kept free of litter. It is interesting to note in passing, that to be a member of the cloakroom and playground committee was considered to be a mark of prestige. How the membership of these committees was achieved led to much consideration of the notions of fairness and co-operation.

It was suggested by one member of the class that the school would benefit from a conservation area. This idea began a lengthy period of discussion that lasted many weeks. During that time they wrote letters to the school governors, the school's grounds staff, the local gardening club, the Primary Inspector and various other bodies who could offer help in any way. It led to a project on conservation, structured by themselves, being included in their topic work. They invited various people into their Meeting to talk with them about their plans including the Primary Inspector who was obliged to observe the rules of the Meeting dutifully raising his hand when he wished to speak! They organised parents to do the harder labour and as a final result the school now has a conservation area complete with small pond.

The children have shown a remarkable degree of awareness of the needs of the younger children in the school. They have established 'on duty' members of the group who look after the infants during break and lunch times. In addition, they have organised welcoming parties for the in-coming children to the reception class. These events have been extremely successful and have involved the children in a great deal of organisational activity.

Many of their meetings are concerned with less tangible subject matter. They have spent many hours discussing such issues as discipline, crime, punishment and responsibility. What is significant to me is that they have confronted such issues within contexts that are authentic and that matter to them.

I suppose that what I am championing is the possibility of liberalising some of the characteristics that typify much of the educational provision in our primary schools. I am questioning the place of the teacher at the hub of all classroom activity, to whom everything refers. I am looking at a picture of a school where the relationship of teacher to pupil is not polarised by authority and where the learners' self-regulation is recognised as a powerful aid to learning. Lawrence Stenhouse (Stenhouse, 1983, p. 187) has this to say:

> Whenever we assert and bully with our authority instead of reasoning on an equal base with those we teach and helping them to liberate themselves from our authority as the source of truth, we invite them to faith rather than knowledge.

What I am reaching towards is a view of education where the child is released from the shackles of the teacher as final arbiter to a position of negotiated control over what is to be learnt and how it is to be learned.

It is my contention that the Meeting is educationally sound on many fronts. At a basic level it offers opportunity for linguistic, social, moral and personal development. On a higher plane, it offers the opportunity for the children to explore and to experience, in an authentic way, what it is to be an autonomous learner. It is only a beginning but a step towards what Stenhouse (Stenhouse, 1983, p. 186) describes as:

> ... the importance of the right of the learner to speculate, to learn autonomously to criticise and correct intelligent errors which they reach after understanding.

It seems to me that the Meeting affords the opportunity for a high degree of involvement by the children in a setting where problems of an authenic nature are addressed. The children set their own agenda grounding their thinking in their own experience. The context is childish — but not trivial. Its very strength lies in its relevance to the children taking part in it. On many occasions I have found it difficult to accept their subject matter. My inclination as a teacher or an adult, is to move them on to subject matter that I consider more suitable. It has been a difficult task to stand back and let the children define what is suitable and what is not. Nothing, either in my training or subsequent experience, has prepared me for this. All my life as a teacher, I have had 'teacher as prime mover in the classroom' reinforced to the point that it is virtually impossible to climb over that barrier and to look at new possibilities.

I do not claim the Meeting to be a panacea; it just happens to satisfy needs in this particular situation. What is important though, are the principles that underlie it and the implications they have for the confident belief in the ability of children to identify what is relevant to their learning needs. Furthermore, they point towards the need for a greater degree of trust in their potential to shape and control contexts in which such learning can take place.

There has been a steady movement since the Great Debate in 1976 away from the developing progressive education of the late fifties and sixties towards an education more suited to the needs of industry. The movement has continued unabated and in recent years we have seen an increase in central government intervention. The departure of Sir Keith Joseph from the DES has not seen any lessening of these trends. Quite the opposite, there has been an ever greater thrust towards centralisation, standardisation and a closer embrace of a utilitarian educational system.

The time has never been more crucial that antidotes to this particular direction be pursued. We are in danger of ignoring many of the hard-won lessons that have been learnt from the work of numbers of educationalists who strove to put the child at the centre of the education experience. What is now happening is that education is being seen more and more as something that is done to children and that their involvement is expected to be no more than a passive acceptance of what others have decided is relevant for them.

Nowhere in the recent documents from the DES is there any mention that the children themselves should play a part in the shaping of the curriculum. There is, to be sure, much play made of the necessity for the curriculum to be relevant to the needs of the children, but somehow the children themselves are left out of the process of identifying what those are — the 'needs' of children have already been defined and whether they are considered appropriate or not depends as much (if not more) upon political allegiance as upon what might constitute true educational experience.

It is my belief that when the emphasis is put upon learning as process within an authentic context, then what is learned is likely to be more potently formed. The Meeting provides such a context and invites the children to become actively engaged in their own learning. This is not at variance with some of the aims set out in the HMI document *The Curriculum from 5–16*, for example:

> Pupils need to understand that human beings, in shaping their
> world, making their living, planning their futures, developing forms
> of government and law, are influenced to a greater or lesser degree
> by ideas and beliefs, by their past, by the places and conditions in

which they live and by the ways in which they need to relate to each other. (Paragraph 41)

Part of the educational value of this initiative in my practice lies in its being a shared learning experience by the children and myself. A claim on my part to understand all that the Meeting is about, is to lose a vital component in the experiencing of it. The children (and I) have gained from a sense of trail-blazing together. There is a sense in which as long as the Meeting and the sort of implications I have referred to maintain a feature of the unknown, there will be a place for the children to shape and participate in the formation of their own learning experience. If there were no unknown, there is a very real danger that it could become yet another rigid teacher-directed enterprise, the substitution of one unyielding stimulus-response cycle for another. A shared experience of searching for understanding by teachers alongside children, forms a powerful learning environment.

What is suggested to me is that teachers need to let go of the comfortable props that surround the orthodox teacher-pupil patterns, and to invest more trust in the ability of children to identify their own needs and to participate in the structuring of learning contexts. I am not suggesting that the teacher has no part to play in this. What I am saying is that teachers could well consider a more oblique approach where negotiation and a shared quest for understanding are the hallmarks of their involvement with children's education.

> Yeh, it's ... see if ... if you didn't want something and somebody made you have it, it just means that you'd hate them even more. But if we get choices and things, we kind of ... we grow to like that person. It's like they're letting us have a say in something that we'll never probably have a choice in at all. So it is ... it's like getting a say in the whole world ... It's not just given to you on a plate.

References

HMI (1985) *The Curriculum from 5 to 16*. Curriculum Matters Series 2, London, HMSO.

NEILL, A.S. (1962) *Summerhill* (1973 ed.), London, Victor Gollancz Ltd.

STENHOUSE, L. (1983) *Authority, Education and Emancipation*, London, Heinemann.

Identification and Imitation

(From Schaffer, H., 1968, 'Identification', in Lunzer, E. and Morris, J. (Eds) *Development in Human Learning*, Granada Publishing Ltd., pp. 51–61.)

Psychologists are also interested in how society impinges on the growing child and how it shapes and canalizes his or her behaviour in some directions rather than others. Psychologists of education have a particular interest in the role of schools, especially teachers and a child's fellow-pupils, in this process. The extract below illustrates the 'social learning' perspective briefly referred to in the introduction to this section of the source book. Central to this perspective are the process of identification and the part played by imitation and modelling. It is argued that although parents have the most decisive influence on a child's identification, other individuals (such as teachers) and groups (such as the peer group, pp. 385–8) can, and do, serve as models. Two particular areas are examined in some detail: sex-typing, and the development of conscience. The reader may wish to compare the views offered on gender with those expressed in the extract by Davies (pp. 269–74).

Having formed a strong bond to certain selected individuals, the child will inevitably wish to conform to their standards of behaviour and avoid their disapproval of inappropriate conduct. He does so by becoming like them — by incorporating their standards and thus identifying with them.

The task of socialization is at first almost entirely in the hands of the child's family. This is the primary social group in which he is introduced to the mores of society and which helps him to acquire the basic skills necessary to cope with the environment. In so far as social learning is a function of social contagion, i.e. the extent to which the individual comes into contact with others, the family is likely to provide the most powerful formative influence on personality development, for in the early years, at the time of maximum susceptibility, the child will be in almost continuous contact with family members. On an overt level, their influence manifests itself in the child's tendency to imitate their ways of behaviour and consequently to become more and more like them in speech, dress, eating habits and other personal characteristics. Habits of imitation can, in fact, be learned if the child is suitably rewarded for doing so (Miller and Dollard, 1941). However, imitation is not merely conditioned by overtly given rewards and instructions but depends on the total parent–child relationship and the powerful, though often subtle, feelings which a child develops towards those on whom he is emotionally dependent. The whole process that leads the child to think, feel and act as though the characteristics of another person were his own is called identification. The person with whom the child identifies is known as the model, and identification may thus also be regarded as the wish to be the model. Two qualifications must, however, be added: in the first place, a child need not necessarily identify with the whole model but may do so with only certain of its parts or attributes, and in the second place this tendency can be a wholly unconscious process.

Most of the difficulties of studying identification arise from this latter point. Freud, to whom much of the credit must be given for drawing attention to this process, was mainly concerned with it as a defence mechanism, i.e. as a way of dealing with the anxiety which the child experiences as a result of the feelings of hostility that parental frustrations engender. Afraid of losing the parents' affection as a result of these hostile feelings, the child solves the conflict by repressing his aggression and instead adopts the safer course of himself, as it were, becoming the aggressor through incorporating the parents' characteristics. The Freudian theory thus views identification as being mainly based on the child's negative feelings towards his parents and in this way differs from the learning theory account, which proposes instead that the child's wish to be the parent arises from his past experiences of feelings of gratification and pleasure associated with the presence of the parent, as a result of which he adopts his characteristics in order, so to speak, to supply his own rewards.

Whichever view is the correct one, the process is clearly a very important one in making the child into an acceptable member of society. Most of the research dealing with it has investigated it in relation to two areas: sex-typing and the development of conscience.

From a very early age on boys and girls are expected to behave differently. Already at three and four years of age children have formed definite and sex-appropriate preferences when asked to choose from such toys as guns, dolls, kitchen utensils and soldiers (Hartup and Zook, 1960), and the strength of these sex-linked preferences tends to increase with age. To some extent learning the appropriate role is due to direct training procedures employed by the parents, but there is evidence suggesting that it is also a result of identification with the same-sex parent. The little boy is expected to be 'like daddy' and to engage in masculine activity like hammering in nails and kicking footballs, while the little girl is similarly encouraged to imitate her mother's interests in cooking, knitting, etc. Society thus guides the child towards the appropriate model and gives him or her the opportunity to form the relevant identification with it. This process involves, of course, not merely the imitation of certain interests and hobbies but also the incorporation of more basic personality characteristics. Aggression, for instance, is regarded as being a mainly masculine trait and therefore fostered in boys by contact with their father. In one investigation (Sears, 1985) pre-school boys whose fathers were away on military service were found to have developed less aggression than boys whose fathers were at home. No such difference was found between father-present and father-absent girls of the same age.

Many attempts have been made to ascertain those characteristics in a child's family environment which foster strong sex-identifications. There is general agreement that the quality of the relationship with the parent is the most decisive factor in this respect. In a study of five-year-old boys (Mussen and Distler, 1959) a test was administered to measure strength of masculine identification. The scores were then compared with the boys' perception of their fathers (as obtained from the endings which the children supplied to incomplete stories), and it was found that boys with high male identifications tended to see their fathers as warmer and more affectionate than boys with low male identifications. Similar evidence has come from another study (Payne and Mussen, 1956), this time on adolescent boys and using 'test similarity' as a criterion of father-identification: again the strength of identification and the perception of the father as warm, helpful and kind were related. The same finding also applies to girls, for those with high femininity scores on sex-role tests have been found to have warmer relationships with their mothers than girls with low scores. It is thus the rewarding, positive qualities of the parents that promote identification rather than their negative, fear-arousing characteristics.

Another parental quality which encourages the child to model himself on the parent can be described as the latter's 'power'. In the study of five-year-olds quoted above the boys with high male identifications described the father not only as warm but also as strong, powerful and competent: clearly all qualities which aroused the child's incentive to be like the father. Similarly, the parent's interest in the child and the amount of time spent with him promoted identification, suggesting that it is primarily those variables which describe the parents' salience in the child's experience that affect this process.

A child's parents will usually, of course, exercise the most decisive influence on the nature of his identifications. They are, however, by no means the only individuals who will serve as models, and indeed identifications may subsequently be formed with groups and institutions as well. In the case of sex-identification, a study by Koch (1956) shows the importance of family members other than parents. Girls who have older brothers, it was found, tend to be more 'tomboyish' than girls with older sisters, and likewise boys with older sisters have a somewhat higher proportion of feminine traits than boys with older brothers.

Whether sex-linked behaviour is, in fact, solely a function of social learning, as so many writers seem to assume, or whether constitutional factors do not also play a part, remains as yet an unsolved problem. Certainly anthropological material concerning the very different conceptions of sex-roles found in other societies indicates that behaviour regarded by us as 'natural' may turn out to be a product of socialization rather than inheritance. Yet in the area of sex-linked behaviour above all the assumption of the '*tabula rasa*' child ought to be avoided until more data have been gathered to enable us to make more precise statements regarding aetiology than we can make at present.

The other main area in which the process of identification has been studied is the development of conscience. The learning of moral standards and prohibitions starts early in life in relation to such mundane things as feeding, elimination and aggression, and it is here rather than on the lofty plane of morality and ethics that the foundations of conscience are laid. At first 'right' and 'wrong' are, from the child's point of view, purely arbitrary notions that are imposed on him by external agents. Sooner or later, however, he learns that these agents will follow 'right' actions with praise and 'wrong' actions with punishment and withdrawal of love. In order to avoid the latter consequences he begins to incorporate the rules of behaviour expected of him, so that his conduct is no longer exclusively governed by sanctions employed by other people but becomes increasingly regulated by the feeling of guilt which he experiences after all transgressions. Thus, in the adequately socialized child, the tendency to model his behaviour after that of his parents results in the incorporation of adult moral standards and the capacity for self-punishment.

The progression from external to internal regulation of behaviour takes a long time and may, in some individuals, never be completed. Again, a satisfactory relationship with the parents appears to be an essential prerequisite for such a development, for children with a highly developed conscience have mostly been found to have warmer, more accepting parents than children of the same age with less well developed consciences. A further influence, however, has also been isolated, namely the actual technique which parents employ in order to impose conformity. In general, withdrawal of love has been found far more effective in producing a strong conscience than physical punishment, deprivation of privileges, or the giving of tangible rewards (Sears, Maccoby and Levin, 1957). However, this relationship only holds in those cases where the parents are also generally warm and affectionate towards the child, for otherwise, presumably, there would be less love to take away and the child would not be as affected by the threatened loss as a child who has a rather more affectionate relationship with his parents. Thus the children most advanced in conscience development appear to be those whose parents are relatively warm towards them but who make their love contingent on the child's willingness to conform to their demands.

Once again one must remember, however, that parents are not the only models a child encounters. Influences outside the home also play their part in shaping conscience: a conclusion borne out by an interesting finding on boys with criminal fathers (McCord and McCord, 1958). This investigation showed that such boys are less likely to become criminals themselves if accepted by their fathers than if rejected by them. Where the parent model is found by the child to be opposed to society's norms, parents' acceptance may actually operate against identification.

Just in what way identification is to be differentiated from imitation is still an open issue. Some writers distinguish between these terms on the basis of the degree of specificity of the behaviour pattern which is learned; others consider that identification presupposes the existence of an attachment to the model, whereas this is not a necessary precondition in the case of imitation; and still others believe that imitation is a process that requires the model's presence at the time, whereas identification refers to the performance of the model's behaviour in the latter's absence. However, one recent body of research stemming from the work of Bandura and Walters (1963) has proceeded from the assumption that the two terms refer in fact to the same set of behavioural phenomena and to the same learning process, and that no useful purpose is served by making any distinction between them. Both terms, according to these writers, apply to the manner in which patterns of social behaviour are acquired through a process that may most suitably be labelled as *observational learning*. Whereas previous theories had stressed the need for rewards to be made available if imitation is to occur, these investigators have shown that, through simple exposure to a model and the opportunity to observe him perform certain activities, children will acquire new responses that match those of the model and which can, moreover, be reproduced not only at the time but also be replicated at a later date. Thus, in a typical experiment (Bandura, Ross and Ross, 1963), nursery school children watched a model behaving aggressively in a play situation by showing, for instance a number of unusual hostile responses towards a large inflated rubber doll. When the children were subsequently allowed to play in the same situation it was found that they showed precisely matching responses and tended to behave far more aggressively than children who had not previously been exposed to a model. Moreover, there was no difference in the extent of imitation between children who had observed a real-life model and children who had observed a filmed model, suggesting not only that exposure to aggression can heighten and also shape the nature of children's aggressive reactions, but also that this influence can be exerted by means of pictorial as well as real-life stimulation.

From experiments such as these Bandura (1962) concludes that social behaviour is typically acquired by means of imitation, that this may take place merely on the basis of 'sensory contiguity' (i.e. the opportunity to observe and attend to the activities of others), and that such learning usually involves the imitation of large segments of behaviour or whole sequences of activities rather than proceeding through the slow, gradual acquisition of isolated responses, each of which must be differentially reinforced by a suitable programme of rewards and punishment. However, imitation is by no means conceived of as a purely passive process, as exposure of an individual to a set of stimuli is no guarantee that he will attend to and learn the relevant cues. It is, however, a virtue of this conceptual approach that it is possible, through a variety of laboratory experiments (cf. Bandura, 1965) to isolate the conditions under which imitating does occur and thus to specify both the environmental and the subject factors which make for optimal susceptibility to the influence of social models. In this way those adult–child similarities of behaviour, which have given rise to the concept of identification in psychodynamic theories, can be studied empirically and traced back to their developmental origins.

There can be little doubt that identification is an extremely complex process and that it is as yet little understood depsite the growing amount of research into it. This is partly because of the rather crude techniques that have been used to investigate it: for instance, parental identifications have been measured by the relative amounts of handling of father-dolls and mother-dolls in structured doll-play situation yet the validity of this technique remains unknown. Similarly in research on moral development the choice of criteria for conscience, such as the type of endings which a child supplies to uncompleted stories, is not based on any established association with actual behaviour. Nevertheless, this area does represent an earnest attempt to find out how society impinges on the growing child and the manner in which it shapes and canalizes his behaviour. At present our theories about identification may be rather more impressive than their empirical underpinnings, but at least they serve to draw attention to some of the more subtle forms of interaction between the child and his social environment and to the wide range of variables which may influence any one behavioural activity.

References

BANDURA, A. (1962) 'Social learning through imitation', in Jones, M.R. (Ed.) *Nebraska Symposium of Motivation*, Lincoln, University of Nebraska Press.
BANDURA, A. (1965) 'Behavioural modification through modelling procedures', in KRADNER, L. and ULLMANN, L.P. (Eds) *Research in Behaviour Modification*, New York, Holt, Rinehart and Winston.
BANDURA, A. and WALTERS, R.H. (1963) *Social Learning and Personality Development*, New York, Holt, Rinehart and Winston.
BANDURA, A., ROSS, D. and ROSS, S.A. (1963) 'Imitation of film-mediated aggressive models', *J. Abnorm. Soc. Psychol.*, 66, pp. 3–11.
HARTUP, W.W. and ZOOK, E.A. (1960) 'Sex-role preferences in three and four-year-old children', *J. Consult. Psychol.*, 24, pp. 420–6.
KOCH, H. (1956) 'Attitudes of young children towards their peers as related to certain characteristics of their siblings', *Psychol. Monogr.*, 70, 19.
MCCORD, J. and MCCORD, W. (1958) 'The effect of parental role model in criminality', *J. Soc. Issues*, 14, pp. 66–75.
MILLER, N.E. and DOLLARD, J. (1941) *Social Learning and Imitation*, New Haven, Yale University Press.
MUSSEN, P. and DISTLER, L. (1959) 'Masculinity, identification and father–son relationships', *J. Abnorm. Soc. Psychol.*, 59, pp. 350–6.
PAYNE, D.E. and MUSSEN, P. (1956) 'Parent–child relations and father identification among adolescent boys', *J. Abnorm. Soc. Psychol.*, 52, pp. 358–62.
SEARS, P.S. (1951) 'Doll play aggression in normal young children: Influence of sex, age, sibling status, and father's absence', *Psychol. Monogr.*, 65, 323.
SEARS, R.R., MACCOBY, E.E. and LEVIN, H. (1957) *Patterns of Child Rearing*, New York, Harper and Row.

Learning and the Peer Group

(From Rubin, Z., 1980, *Children's Friendships*, London, Fontana, pp. 93–7, 106–7.)

The importance of the peer group in the growing up process is explored in this extract from *Children's Friendships*. Children are beings in a social world, and friendship groups often characterized by rules, rituals and initiation ceremonies, provide a context for learning about self and developmental concerns. Developmental tasks, culturally mediated, are likely to form the substance of many same-sex groups in the later primary school years. Becoming a sexual being is of increasing importance as puberty approaches, and with it attitudes towards the other sex, adult relationships and self are formed. At younger ages the developmental concern is more with learning culturally accepted standards of behaviour in such areas as toileting, and the beginnings of cooperative behaviour in games. Flexible teaching approaches, where friendships rather than ability groups are used, have potential for harnessing the importance of the peer group for school learning.

In the early school years children often become especially interested in forming 'official' groups. A commonly observed pattern is for a group of eight- or nine-year-olds to form a club — typically admitting only boys or only girls — invest a tremendous amount of energy into deciding on officers and their official titles, find nothing to do after that, and then disband. For my own part, I was a charter member of a club for seven-year-olds called the Penguins whose two major activities were acquiring extensive information about penguins and standing outside in the freezing weather without a coat for as long as we could. Like most other groups of this sort, the Penguins did not last very long. But in the making and unmaking of such groups, children are conducting what may be informative experiments in social organization. Through such experiences, children develop increasingly sophisticated understandings of groups, from an early conception of a group as merely a collection of people in one place to a later conception of a group as a collective organization in which individuals are united by common interests and goals.

Children's groups characteristically take on their greatest importance in late childhood — the years between about nine and twelve. At a time when children must leave the safety of the family, to become more autonomous persons, a group of friends can lay a valuable supportive role, especially in the domains of sexual and emotional development. Despite the psychoanalytic notion that childhood is a period of sexual latency — the calm before the storm of puberty — sexual concerns are likely to the prominently revealed in groups of nine- to twelve-year-olds. American boys, for example, are likely to participate in 'bull sessions' devoted to the exchange of sexual information. According to Gary Fine, 'These sessions are filled with loud (almost hysterical) giggly laughter, insults, and bravado,' all of which may testify to the underlying significance of the topics being discussed. Although group discussions may arouse anxiety, they may also provide needed reassurance and support as children deal with the concerns of growing up.

At the same time, children's groups pose the central issue of inclusion and exclusion. Even among toddlers in the kibbutz, group membership is closely linked to the exclusion of nonmembers. On the kibbutz carousel, for example, the children always make room for members of their own group but do not let members of other groups join them. In nursery school,... inclusion and exclusion are constant themes of social life. It is through the continuing negotiation of who is 'in' and who is 'out' that children establish and maintain group boundaries. When Josh, Tony and Caleb want to play spaceship, they usually shout to one another and discourage any other children from joining in. A revealing exception comes on a day that Tony is absent from school and another boy, Eddie, is allowed on board:

When I inquire into the matter, Josh (Captain Kirk) tells me that Eddie is Spock, adding that 'He's on my crew.'

'But I thought Tony was Spock,' I protest.

Josh looks at me disdainfully and then explains the obvious: 'Tony's not here today.'

'Well, how about when Tony gets back?'

Josh glances at Eddie and replies, 'Then *he's* not playing.'

Eddie was not admitted to regular membership in the space group because he had relatively little in common with Josh, Tony, and Caleb. Eddie was slower-moving and slowing-talking than the other three boys and had trouble keeping up with their often frenetic pace. In addition, because of his shoulder-length hair, Eddie appeared 'girlish' to the other boys. These differences contributed to his exclusion from the space group. For if pairs of friends tend to be similar to one another, similarity of attributes and skills typically plays an even larger role in determining the membership of cliques and groups.

The membership of a group may take shape in several different ways. Sometimes an individual child with valued skills plays a central role, with others entering the group by gaining the leader's approval. In other cases the group begins with an existing pair of friends, who then proceed to include others in their activities. Josh and Tony became friends early in the year and only later took Caleb, a slightly younger and smaller boy, into their group as a sort of junior member. In still other instances the group is based primarily on joint participation in a particular activity.

Whether the activity is playing in a band or building sand-castles, children will be included only if they have the skills and interests that enable them to take part. All of these processes of group formation are likely to produce a relatively homogeneous membership. Just as in groups of adolescents and adults, moreover, there are strong pressures to exclude the 'deviant' child, whether the difference is with respect to appearance, skills, or temperament. In many school settings, race is another basis of group membership. 'They [other black girls] get mad because you've made a white friend,' a black twelve-year-old reports. 'They say that blacks are supposed to have black friends and whites are supposed to have white friends.' Indeed, the link between group solidarity and similarity is so prevalent as to approach the status of a universal law of social behaviour.

Groups also have the effect of *making* their members — or prospective members — similar to one another. There is usually strong pressure on children to conform to the expectations and standards of their groups, both because of concern about being accepted and because of the assumption that 'if everyone in my group is doing it, it must be right'. The influence of group membership on children's behaviour is especially striking in the kibbutz. Even in the youngest kibbutz groups, the children themselves play an important role in enforcing standards of behaviour. When one of the children has a toileting accident, for example, the others all look at him and shout, 'Haggai did a BM, Haggai did a BM! Not on the floor, Haggai, not on the floor!' Similarly, when one child has hit another and made him cry, all the other group members come up and hit the first child. 'How many times do I have to tell you not to hit other children?' one of them adds. Such peer influence proves to be extremely effective in regulating the children's behaviour.

The degree to which children conform to group norms and beliefs appears to increase during the years of childhood, often reaching its peak at about the age of twelve....

Why do boys' and girls' friendships differ in these ways? Douvan and Adelson try to explain the difference in terms of a psychoanalytically derived view that boys have a greater need to band together and rebel against paternal authority. Other behavioural scientists have speculated — albeit without solid evidence — that there are biologically based predispositions for males to bond in groups and for females to be concerned with intimate, nurturant relationships. But the different patterns of friendship seem to be best understood as outcomes of early learning experiences. Part of this learning may come from the different games and sports that boys and girls play. Janet Lever observes that girls' games (such as playing house or jumping ropes) are likely to involve close contact with a single, well-liked person, whereas boys' games (such as baseball or football) are more likely to be played in larger groups and to call for cooperation even with teammates who may not be well-liked personally.

Whether sex-typed games and sports are viewed as causing the differences or as reflections of already existing differences, it is clear that boys and girls grow up with somewhat different models of social relations. In their intimate friendships, girls develop their aptitude for nurturance and emotional expressiveness, social skills that are most relevant to close personal and family relationships. In their larger groups, boys learn to operate within systems of rules and to get along even with people they don't especially like; social skills that are most relevant to modern organizational life. Each sex learns something of importance, but at the same time each sex is deprived of opportunities to learn other important skills. I suspect, for example, that the social learning of childhood is responsible in large measure for the special difficulty that men often have in forming intimate friendships. My own view is that it would be valuable for both boys and girls to have more positively sanctioned exposure to the games, sports, and social patterns that are typically associated with the other sex, as a means of encouraging the fuller development of individual children's potential for rewarding social relationships.

Problem Solving

(From Fisher, R. (Ed.) 1987, *Problem Solving in Primary Schools*, Oxford, Blackwell, pp. 16–18, 242–3, and Easen, P. (1987) 'Developing real problem solving in the primary classroom', in Fisher, R. (Ed.) *Problem Solving in Primary Schools*, Blackwell, pp. 242–3.)

The Plowden report (1967) advocated the benefits of children working together collaboratively on tasks, arguing that such experience promoted enquiry and helped to stimulate thinking and communication skills. Evidence from a variety of research projects undertaken in the 1970s suggested however, that:

> While children were usually set in groups there were very few cases where children were given the kind of work which required them to collaborate together and to work as a team. (Galton, 1987)

A variety of evidence from psychological research has emphasized the fact that learning is as much a social act as it is a cognitive or individual activity. The studies of Tamburrini (pp. 297–300) and Donaldson (pp. 306–11) remind us of the importance of context in children's learning. The investigations of Paul Light (1979, 1986) emphasize the importance of the social world of children and the most recent studies emanating from the University of Geneva have demonstrated that children engaging in Piagetian tasks collaboratively make considerable gains in their understanding (Open University Course E3652, Cognitive Development).

The developments which have occurred in problem solving in the primary classroom attempt to take advantage of the social nature of learning and indicates a move from the emphasis on the individual which typified practice in many primary classrooms in the 1960s and 1970s. Keith Jackson (1983), the director of the Bulmershe-Comino Problem-Solving Project, argued that problem solving in the classroom created opportunities for — pupil centred learning; active participation; shared responsibility; the development of confidence, independence, and self-sufficiency; good reciprocal relations between teachers and pupils; and an opportunity for children to reveal their creativity and at the same time develop previously unrevealed talent and potential. The two articles which follow are offered as evidence to support these claims. The first by Fisher provides some of the evidence to justify the inclusion of problem solving activities in the classroom. As Alister Fraser (pp. 373–8) had attempted to do in his Summerhill type meeting, Fisher believes that problem solving attempts to make children partners in the learning process and to give them control over what they are doing. The second extract by Patrick Easen (pp. 393–4) reminds us, however, that many of the problems used as the basis of activity are not the children's problems. They are often artificial, contrived by the teacher. Real problem solving, he suggests, should be based upon the problems children themselves face.

> Real problems for children are those that have an immediate, practical effect on their lives, and in which the children themselves can effect some improvement of the situation. (Easen, 1987)

References

CENTRAL ADVISORY COUNCIL ON EDUCATION (England) (1967) *Children and their Primary Schools* (The Plowden Report), London, HMSO.
GALTON, M. (1987) 'Change and continuity in the primary school: The research evidence', *Oxford Review of Education*, 13, 1, pp. 81–93.
LIGHT, P. and RICHARDS, M. (Eds) (1986) *Children of Social Worlds*, Cambridge, Polity Press.
OPEN UNIVERSITY (1988) *Cognitive Development Course E362*, Milton Keynes, Open University Press.
JACKSON, K.F. (1983) *The Art of Problem Solving*, Bulmershe-Comino Problem Solving Project, Bulmershe College of Higher Education.

The accuracy of the work in standards 1 and 2 is all that can be desired, and in many cases marvellous; at the same time the oral test shows that the children are working in the dark. In these years, at least, far too much time is given to the mechanical part of the subject. The result of this unintelligent teaching shows itself in the inability of the upper years to solve very simple problems. (HMI Report, 1895)

We live in a changing society that is making increasing demands on the problem-solving skills of its citizens. The school curriculum is also changing in response to these new demands. Emphasis is moving away from the transmission of facts, the *products* of knowledge neatly packaged into separate subject areas, towards an approach which focuses on the *processes* of study, investigation and problem-solving. This approach moves from simply teaching children the facts of language, mathematics, history, geography, science and the other 'disciplines', towards encouraging children to be scientists, historians, geographers, linguists and mathematicians, through the use of appropriate problem-solving skills and processes. Such change is slow to take place, and it needs to be planned with care if it is to be effective. However it is a change which many of those involved in maintaining and evaluating the education system see to be one of profound importance.

The system of primary education in this country is widely regarded as being among the best in the world, with its emphasis on curriculum development and a 'child-centred' learning approach. But no system, or school, is perfect; many official reports on primary education produced in the last 50 years have repeated similar criticisms of primary school practice. These include that:

- Children are offered few opportunities to engage in problem-solving activities, and to apply basic skills in new contexts;
- Children are rarely required to use 'higher-order' thinking skills such as inference, deduction, analysis and evaluation;
- Children are given insufficient opportunity to develop the social

skills of co-operation and communication through discussion and group work;
- Brighter children are frequently given work which is not sufficiently demanding.

One way teachers may respond to the need to provide stimulus and challenge across the whole ability range is by introducing a problem-solving approach to class activities.

What does *problem solving* in primary schools mean? Problem solving is an activity that can be defined in a number of ways, for example 'dealing with a difficult situation', 'overcoming an obstacle', 'bringing about a desired effect', 'resolving a puzzling question', or 'getting a required result'. What problem solving involves is *thinking and doing*, or acting for some purpose. It is a way through which we can learn, practise and demonstrate essential skills and knowledge — and it can give purpose to a whole range of curriculum activities.

What are the skills and strategies of problem-solving, and how can they be taught? One scheme, devised by teachers in Oldham, is to introduce — to children as young as five — a systematic approach to the solving of everyday problems. This programme has been inspired by the Bulmershe-Comino Problem-Solving Project, as described in Professor Keith Jackson's book, *The Art of Solving Problems*.

The strategy teaches children to tackle problems in a logical sequence of steps, which Oldham teachers have translated into five questions:

1 What is my problem?
2 How can I explain it?
3 What can I do about it?
4 Which way is best?
5 Have I finished successfully?

This process can be drawn up as a table by the child or teacher with gaps to fill in for each stage of the problem as it is tackled, including the outcome. To help younger children, one school uses a five-colour rainbow as an aid. Another teacher has written a book about Splodge, a starfish who wanted to look like other starfish. In the story a wizard taught Splodge the five questions he must ask to overcome the problem.

Any problem from a child's home or school situation can be tackled in this way, whether it be having to sit next to an incompatible classmate, planning a nature trail or resolving a family argument. It is important for children to consider a variety of possible courses of action. Indeed, it comes as a surprise to some that there *are* several choices. Children are not restricted to the conventional, expected answers but are free to explore apparently bizarre and impractical solutions. Faced with the problem of how to get water out of a ditch one child suggested 'bringing in an elephant to suck it out'. Instead of thinking only in terms of draining the ditch, children suggested a variety of solutions which led on to the concept of pumping water — an example of the creativity that problem solving can inspire.

The Oldham teachers help children to apply the strategy not only in academic situations, but to other aspects of their everyday lives. Children are encouraged to be open to sharing their real-life problems. One approach is to provide a *Problem box* in the classroom into which they can pop an anonymous description of their personal problems and questions. For example:

- My sister is always fighting me at home
- I can't reach my train set which is kept on top of the wardrobe and my Mum and Dad won't get it for me
- My brother always rips up letters from school before I get home
- I would like a copy of Roald Dahl's *Revolting Rhymes* but I can't afford it

The problems can be tackled cooperatively or individually, and much lively discussion often ensues about possible plans of action. Some children keep a record of the problems they have tackled which can be used to monitor the quality and depth of their insights. In this way children develop resourcefulness and confidence in decision making.

Teachers in Oldham have introduced strategic thinking to children as young as five by using practical illustrations — for example, explaining how a problem has a purpose and an obstacle by 'planting' a sweet on an out-of-reach sill and asking 'How do we reach it?' Classes of seven-year-olds have been introduced to the terms 'strategy', 'strategic thinking', 'obstacle' and 'outcome'. Children are expected to use the problem-solving strategy not only in special lessons but whenever the need arises — during class work and in everyday situations. Just as children learn to look for their own ways of tackling a problem so teachers find their own way of teaching problem-solving and incorporate it into their everyday teaching.

As in all aspects of teaching children vary in their response and in their ability to understand a problem-solving strategy. We know from experience that abstract rules are far harder to understand than practical ones. These skills and strategies aim to make the abstract practical. The approach aims to make children partners in the learning process, and to give them more control over what they are doing. Whatever the situation, once a problem arises our control and mastery of the situation will first depend on identifying and defining the problem.

Reference

JACKSON, K.F. (1983) *The Art of Solving Problems*, Bulmershe-Comino Problem-Solving Project, Bulmershe College of Higher Education.

Real Problem Solving

(From Easen, P.R., 1987, 'Developing real problem solving in the primary classroom', in Fisher, R. (Ed.) *Problem Solving in Primary Schools*, Oxford, Blackwell.)

You are a busy teacher and among the many problems confronting you are trouble in the playground and disappointing mathematical performance in the classroom. What do you do? Probably few people would answer 'Get the children to tackle the first problem and it will help you solve the second' but that's exactly what Ann Jones did with her class of 10-year-olds (see Figure 12.1).

These school rules were devised by Ann's children ... and drawing them up gave the class plenty of opportunity to use their 'four rules'! That is not all they did. They built a marble area and a toy car track; they painted hopscotches, organized lunch-time clubs and instituted a football rota. In the process they used a considerable amount of mathematics in a way that helped them to see its relevance. The children were engaged in 'real problem solving'.

Real problem solving formed part of an Open University course, PME233: *Mathematics across the curriculum*. As members of the course team, we felt that the idea was sufficiently powerful to merit further attention in its own right. The article from which this extract comes describes an attempt to explore the impact of real problem solving when it becomes a regular feature of classroom life. The classroom in question belonged to a mixed ability class of 28 10- and 11-year-olds at a school in Buckinghamshire. We began during the second half of the autumn term, and, for the rest of the academic year, the children spent a minimum of one session (morning or afternoon) a week on real problem solving.

What is real problem solving?

Real problem solving aims to build up the confidence and ability of children to solve just the kind of problems that are characteristic of a rapidly-changing society. Confidence in one's ability to cope, as any adult knows, plays large part in tackling important problems. Again, as any adult also knows, the important problems are the real ones — the ones that will not go away on their own. While no-one would deny that adults should be capable of resolving their own problems, how well are children being prepared in the classroom for this need?

It is not as if children do not have real problems. These may well be different from those that concern adults, but many of the same characteristics remain. Real problems for adults are practical, immediate impediments

Figure 12.1

<u>Rules</u>

Bad Behaviour

1. No swearing on school premises.
2. No spitting on school premises.
3. No fighting in playground.
4. No going through unit 2 unless going to the toilet

Trouble Makers

1. No going on school roofs
2. No stealing peoples talls.
3. Never cut corners because grass is trying to grow.
4. You must never come into anyother cloakroom but your own.
5. No pushing off logs.

Prevent Accident

1. No going in sand or throwing sand on playground.
2. No running on paths round school
3. NO playing on logs in winter.

to safe or satisfying living — and the successful resolution of such problems actually makes a difference to the life of the adult involved. Similarly, real problems for children are those that have an immediate, practical effect on their lives, and in which the children themselves can effect some improvement of the situation.

Matching Tasks to Children's Attainment

(From Desforges, C. (1985) 'Matching tasks to children's attainment', in Desforges, C. and Bennett, N., 'Recent advances in classroom research', *British Journal of Educational Psychology*, Monograph Series, 2, pp. 92–6, 99–102.)

In an earlier extract in this section of the reader, Ainscow (pp. 363–7) introduced the concept of 'matching' which he defined as, 'a matter of seeking a match between the attainments and interests of individual pupils and the tasks and experiences with which they are provided' (Ainscow, 1987). In the 1978 Primary survey, HMI discussed the problems of matching curriculum experiences to the capacity of learners and concluded that 'mismatching' was a common feature of many primary classrooms, with serious underestimation for many able children and over-estimation for children with learning difficulties. These assertions stimulated the interests of a number of researchers, notably the psychologist Charles Desforges and his colleague, Neville Bennett. The extract which follows, summarizes the research undertaken into this topic by them and indicates that the whole topic of matching curriculum experiences to children's competence is considerably more difficult than HMI suggested. In fact what the research seems to reinforce is that classrooms are extremely complex places and that teachers should be applauded for the success that they presently achieve. In this extract they employ a variant of Piaget's clinical method (see the extracts by Isaacs pp. 283–7 and Adibe pp. 289–95) to explore children's understanding and suggest that teachers could benefit from developing their skills in this area as a means of monitoring children's progress and by implication improve the level of matching in their classrooms.

References

AINSCOW, M. (1987) The Primary Curriculum and Special Needs. Paper presented at the Conference of the National Council for Special Education, April.
DES (1978) *Primary Education in England: A Survey by HM Inspectors of Schools*, London, HMSO.

The term 'matching' appears to have been coined by Hunt (1961) in his work on the application of Piaget's psychology to education. In particular the term encapsulated the view that teachers should assign to children those tasks which capitalise on cognitive processes defined by their Piagetian stage of intellectual development. The notion that the cognitive demand of school materials should be mapped onto, or matched with, the cognitive stage of the learner continues to have considerable influence (ASEP, 1974; Karplus, 1975; Lovell and Shayer, 1978; Shayer and Adey, 1981).

However, in the general literature on teaching the term has a broader meaning. Here, matching work to children entails giving them those tasks which optimally sustain motivation, confidence and progress in learning. Teachers must '. . . avoid the twin pitfalls of demanding too much and expecting too little' (Plowden, 1967, para. 874). In this very general sense of the term matching, Ausubel has summed up the whole of educational psychology in the following statement, '. . . the most important single factor influencing learning is what the learner already knows. Ascertain this and teach him accordingly' (1968). As a version of the dictum that teachers should do the right thing at the right time the advice has a long history in the textbooks of educational prescription (Ausubel, 1968; Bain, 1879; Jensen, 1974 for example) and contemporary builders of models of classroom learning continue to make use of the term 'appropriate' in specifying the conditions of ideal learning environments (see Haertel et al., 1983 for a review). Perhaps because it is a truism that to foster learning it is necessary for learners to work on tasks appropriate to their attainments and abilities, the problems of actually following this prescription under the practical conditions of the classroom have rarely been researched.

Recently, however, HMI (1978) issued a report which brought matching to prominence as a serious educational problem. Mismatching was perceived to be a very common occurrence in primary classrooms. The report concluded that for high attaining children mismatching in mathematics was evident in almost half the classes observed and in geography, history and science, this figure rose to more than two thirds. HMI suggested that whilst teachers seriously underestimated higher attaining children, their capacity to assign appropriate work to lower attainers was much better, and particularly so in reading, writing and mathematics. However, even here, as many as 25 per cent of classes observed evinced less than satisfactory matching.

Although HMI did not make it clear how they had made their decisions on the match between a child's attainment and his assigned work and although they did not study how the perceived mismatching came about, they and others were not slow to suggest solutions to the problem. With specific reference to science, for example, Harlen (1982) has argued that the very poor level of matching is likely to be a consequence of several factors including the low priority given to science by primary teachers, the lack of time spent on science education in teacher training, the very low quality of teachers' own background knowledge in science and the dearth of appropriate teaching materials. It is assumed that attending to each of these factors would improve matching significantly.

These solutions have certain obvious attractions. Teachers, of course, will not teach what they do not value and cannot teach what they do not know. Yet the suggestion remains unconvincing for at least two reasons. First, the data in the HMI's report provide considerable grounds for scepticism about this approach to the improvement of matching, for whilst considerable time is allocated to mathematics education in teacher training and whilst schools are apparently very well equipped with mathematics schemes and materials, it was nonetheless found that matching was less than satisfactory for able children in more than half the classes observed. More materials and teacher training seem to have had little influence here. Secondly, the vast industry applied to curriculum development and in-service training of teachers seems to have had little identifiable impact on classroom learning (Sirotnik, 1983).

Thus, whilst HMI might have identified a significant problem in classroom learning their research made no contribution to understanding or ameliorating it. In the light of contemporary educational research, two fundamental errors were made. First, no clearly articulated view of learning was adopted. Without such a view it is an open question as to what constitutes a mismatch. Secondly, a naive view of classroom teaching in which, implicitly at least, the most significant feature is teacher knowledge, was adopted. Matching was consequently seen as an isolated, cognitive issue to be optimised by improving the characteristics of the teacher as a transmitter. Contemporary research on classroom teaching and learning would suggest this to be a gross over-simplification of the problem and cast doubt on the adequacy of solutions based on this narrow approach to the issue.

A more sophisticated approach to understanding matching as it proceeds in classrooms has recently been adopted by Bennett and Desforges (1984). Their study has been strongly influenced by recent developments in models of learning and teaching. Before commenting on the detailed findings it is necessary to describe the theoretical background to the research.

Conceptions of Learning in Research on Matching

Assessments of the match between the demands of a task and a child's attainment must be inextricably linked to models of learning and attainment. These links are rarely articulated in research on matching. In the work of HMI (1978), for example, over-expectation was '. . . evidenced by too many mistakes . . .' whilst '. . . under expectation often took the form of children being required or allowed to repeat work already understood . . .' (p. 208). Whilst it cannot be denied that 'too many' mistakes are to be avoided the notion of learning from mistakes is buried in the same rubric. Additionally the criterion for under-expectation seems to deny a role for practice in learning.

American researchers (see, for example, Fisher *et al.*, 1980) have used the notion of error rate more explicitly. If a student succeeds on every task then the tasks are too easy: if he fails on every task then they are too difficult. Good psychometric practice then leads to the conclusion that a 50 per cent error rate might be taken to be evidence of a student working at his optimal level. Psychometrically sound, this approach is nonetheless theoretically and educationally limited. It is based on no identifiable theory of learning or attainment. Additionally this operational definition of appropriateness does not transfer well to educational tasks. The reader who misread every other word would be in serious trouble. Considerable differences might be envisaged between one student who got every other sum in an exercise wrong and the student who got the first half of the exercise right and the second half wrong, although both students would have the same error rate of 50 per cent.

In so far as a view of learning can be discerned in this approach to mismatching, the notion of performing at the limits of competence seems to be implied. This notion has been most clearly articulated by Harlen (1982) who observed that 'The keynote of matching is thus finding the right challenge for a child ...' (p. 184).

Explicit or implicit, this is a unidimensional view of learning and probably represents the vestiges of an earlier era of learning research in which learning was considered to be by *gestalt* or association or to be reception or discovery or to be by rote or understanding. Contemporary models of learning, especially in respect of complex curriculum materials, indicate an important role for all these processes (see, for example, Norman, 1978; Resnick and Ford, 1981). In these models, a child stands to make important progress from practice just as much as he might from 'being challenged' or having his curiosity aroused (Resnick, 1976).

The most clearly articulated account of a multi-faceted view of learning has been developed by Norman (1978) and it is this view that influenced the research of Bennett and Desforges.

Three learning processes are identified by Norman: accretion, restructuring and tuning. Accretion is the direct acquisition of elements of knowledge or skill to existing knowledge modules; restructuring involves new insights or the otherwise reorganisation of knowledge already stored; whilst tuning is a process of automating intellectual routines. Tuning entails the elimination of unnecessary steps in procedures and an increase in the facility of the deployment of cognitive processes. The three processes of knowledge acquisition or reorganisation may occur singly or in concert. In this view of learning, the acquisition of facts, the growth of understanding and the deployment of procedural knowledge proceed together. Challenge and practice, rote acquisition and pattern recognition are all significant facets of learning.

From Norman's model, Bennett and Desforges designated four main types of task demand: incremental tasks, restructuring tasks, enrichment tasks and practice tasks. The chief characteristics of these tasks are shown in Table 1.

Incremental tasks correspond to the accretion process, restructuring and enrichment tasks encourage the process of reorganisation, whilst practice tasks enhance tuning processes.

In respect of this more sophisticated model of the cognitive demands teachers might make on children in the tasks they assign, the definition of matching becomes more complex. Whilst the general question 'What does

Table 1   Types of task demand

Task demand	Chief characteristics
Incremental	Introduces new ideas, procedures or skills, demands recognition, discrimination.
Restructuring	Demands the invention or discovery of an idea, process or pattern.
Enrichment	Demands application of familiar skills to new problems.
Practice	Demands the tuning of new skills on familiar problems.

this task contribute to the child's learning?' remains, it requires supplementary questions to decide whether the child might profit in terms of new insights, greater facility in the use of familiar routines or in the acquisition of strategic skills.

Bennett and Desforges drew up criteria as a function of task demand for designating tasks as matched or mismatched. For example, a practice task would be a match if it increased the facility with which a child used a familiar skill. It would be a mismatch if the child were already at maximum facility or if he did not possess the skill he was to practice. Enrichment tasks demand that recently acquired skills be deployed in novel, problem-solving contexts with a view to developing strategic skills, namely those skills which are required to recognise when and how to use a concept or procedure. Such tasks frequently take the form of problems in mathematics or comprehension tasks in language. These tasks may be ill-matched in two ways. It might be the case that the child already has the strategic skills. The intended task then underestimates him. On the other hand the child might not have the requisite core skill. Without this he cannot develop the strategic skill.

It should be clear from these examples of criteria that observed on-task error rates do not provide sufficient evidence on which to judge the match of a task to a child. In the case of enrichment tasks, for example, it is less the quantity than the quality of the child's errors which is informative. Two children could be making 100 per cent errors — one from random behaviour and the other from systematic and thoughtful effort. To establish the degree of preparedness of each child for the assigned task, Bennett and Desforges not only observed the on-task performance but also conducted a post-task interview with the pupil to assess his degree of understanding of the assigned task.

The Lancaster Study

In a project based at the University of Lancaster, Bennett and Desforges (1984) observed the process of task allocation and matching in 16 top infant classes. A follow-up study attempting to explore the problems of improving teachers' matching was conducted with a further 17 top infant teachers. All teachers in the study were volunteers and were judged by local education advisers as experienced and able.

In the initial matching study, the tasks allocated to six target children (two high attainers, two middle and two low attainers) in each class were observed. The teachers were asked to explain why these particular tasks were chosen, and what problems they expected the children to meet. The children were closely observed at work on the tasks by fieldworkers trained in observation techniques and clinical interviewing. All the fieldworkers were themselves experienced infant teachers. Data collected consisted of logs of the target children's conversations and activities, whether on or off task. On completion of the task the child's work or a facsimile was collected. A post-task interview was conducted with the child to ascertain his inter-pretation of what the teacher wanted, his evaluation of his work and the degree of understanding of the task presented. A post-task interview was conducted with the teacher who was invited to evaluate the child's perform-ance, judge the degree of appropriateness of the task and suggest what next would be allocated to the child. Data were collected on 212 number tasks and 205 language tasks.

Using the criteria generated from Norman's theory (briefly described earlier) each task was allocated to a demand category and then, by applying relevant criteria, judged to be a match, overestimate or underestimate. Inter–judge agreements on these decisions was in excess of 90 per cent.

There was found to be little difference between the levels of matching in number and language tasks. Approximately 40 per cent of all tasks were matched, 28 per cent too difficult and 26 per cent too easy.

Children at different levels of attainment, however, had radically diffe-rent experiences. High attainers were underestimated on 41 per cent of all tasks assigned to them. Low attainers were overestimated on 44 per cent of tasks assigned. This is consistent with a recent American study (Anderson, 1981) but not consistent with HMI (1978). The latter found higher levels of matching in maths and language than Bennett and Desforges and few problems with low attainers. Bennett and Desforges thus appear to have found mismatching to be a more serious problem than HMI (1978) in core areas of the curriculum although it must be recognised that the HMI study was concerned with older primary children.

Another important finding was revealed by Bennett and Desforges when judgements made on research criteria were contrasted with judge-ments made by teachers. Teachers saw more overestimation than did the researchers. That many children were in difficulty with tasks was very evident to their teachers. Conversely, no teacher saw any task as too easy. The problem of underestimation simply did not arise in their view.

Visible or not, mismatching caused problems, at least in the short term, for low attainers and wasted opportunities for high attainers. Low attainers produced very little work, concentrated on the production aspects of tasks, were slow to start, made extensive demands on the teacher and consequently spent a lot of time standing in queues. They had limited memory for the stimulus material in writing tasks and limited comprehension of the procedures in mathematics tasks. In contrast, high attainers were often held up by the production features of tasks. For example drawing coins as answers to money sums was frequently seen conducted by children who could do complex calculations in their heads.

The forces which initiate and sustain mismatching seemed to have little relationship to the schemes in operation in the classroom. The teaching of mathematics was dominated by attention to schemes and was highly individualised in the classrooms observed. Conversely, language lessons were highly idiosyncratic and largely delivered as class lessons in which children at all levels of attainment were assigned the same task. Despite these differences in approach in the two curriculum areas, levels of mismatching were almost identical.

Mismatching appeared rather to be sustained by a complex set of social processes. It was observed that regardless of the perceived level of mismatch, the children always appeared to be happy and industrious. They neither gave indication of nor claimed any emotional distress with their work. The level of pupil satisfaction was sustained by copious praise from the teacher for effort to fulfil procedural instructions rather than actual fulfilment or comprehension. Teachers laid emphasis on procedural aspects of tasks, e.g. layout, neatness, writing the date and following routines. So long as children strove to follow these requirements they met with approval.

Teachers saw some children having difficulty following routines. This constituted their recognition of overestimation. However, they rarely planned to go back to diagnose children's problems. Indeed they were not aware of the scale of these difficulties. This was because they saw only the product of the child's work rather than the processes which the child had used. This in turn was a consequence of the teachers' techniques for managing learning. They rarely asked children *how* they had worked tasks or asked them to give some account of their difficulties or interpretations of tasks. They simply had them bring their completed work to the teacher's desk. Unaware of the scale of the children's lack of comprehension and convinced that the children were responding emotionally well to the tasks, the teachers continued to overestimate low attainers.

Since high attainers followed procedures well and accumulated work in quantity they were perceived to be properly occupied. In the absence of discussions with the children about their work, the degree of underestimation remained hidden. Underestimation was thus not a problem.

In the second phase of the Lancaster study, attempts were made to enable teachers to conduct diagnostic work with children. The teachers evinced considerable difficulties with this. They found it difficult to create the necessary few minutes with an individual which such work entails. This again seemed mainly due to the teachers' determination to be instantly available to any child at any time. Secondly, they were of the view that diagnosis was hardly necessary: problems underlying children's errors were seen to be self-evident and remedies entailed re-instruction in terms which had already failed. The teachers could hardly resist the temptation to teach, i.e. to directly instruct. Additionally, when exchanges did occur between teacher and child in respect of children's work they proved frustrating for the teacher and confusing for the child. They demonstrated an almost total lack of skill on the part of teachers in the conduct of diagnostic interviewing.

In sum, mismatching appears to be initiated and sustained by (a) demanding concrete records of procedures rather than evidence of thought, (b) rewarding effort to produce rather than effort to conceptualise, (c) adopting management techniques which permit rapid responses to each child's immediate problems but leave the teacher ignorant of the child's confusions or potential, (d) teachers' inexperience with and lack of skill in diagnostic work and a taste for direct instruction, however informally put, rather than analysis.

The problem of mismatching thus appears to be serious and complex. It is not likely to be carelessness which moves teachers to set concrete goals. These are easy for the child to interpret and the tangible products permit tangible rewards. Specifying cognitive objectives is much more difficult and especially so with younger children. For example, it is easier to ask for and deliver a neat piece of writing than an exciting story.

It seems that solutions to the problem of matching will not come easily. Indeed it might be that the classroom as presently conceived has reached levels of productivity, in terms of learning outcomes and happy relationships, consistent with its design limitations. Improvements might require radical reconceptions of teaching and learning situations.

Whether these are forthcoming or not, extensive further research of both pure and technological kinds seems necessary. Work needs to be done on the specification of cognitive procedures essential to progress in curriculum areas. Applied research seems fundamental to enable teachers to understand and constructively manipulate the subtle accountability procedures which operate in classrooms.

References

ANDERSON, L.M. (1981) 'Student responses to seatwork: Implications for the study of students' cognitive processing.' Paper presented to AERA, Los Angeles.

ASEP (1974) *A Guide to ASEP*, Melbourne, Australian Science Education Project.

AUSUBEL, D.P. (1968) *Educational Psychology: A Cognitive View*, New York, Holt, Rinehart and Winston.

AUSUBEL, D.P. and ROBINSON, F.G. (1969) *School Learning: An Introduction to Educational Psychology*, New York, Holt, Rinehart and Winston.

BAIN, A. (1879) *Education as a Science*, London, Kegan Paul.

BENNETT, S.N., DESFORGES, C.W., COCKBURN, A.D. and WILKINSON, B. (1984) *The Quality of Pupil Learning Experience*, London, Lawrence Erlbaum Associates.

BLOOM, B.S. (1976) *Human Characteristics and School Learning*, New York, McGraw Hill.

BRUNER, J. (1966) *Toward a Theory of Instruction*, Cambridge, Harvard University Press.

CARROLL, J.B. (1963) 'A model for school learning', *Teachers College Record, 64*, pp. 723–33.

DESFORGES, C. (1981) 'Linking theories of cognition and cognitive development to educational practice', Lancaster University, unpublished Ph.D. thesis.

DOYLE, W. (1983) 'Academic Work', *Review of Educational Research, 53*, 2, pp. 159–99.

DOYLE, W. (1979a) 'Making managerial decisions in classrooms', in DUKE, D.L. (Ed.) *Classroom Management*, Chicago, University of Chicago Press.

DOYLE, W. (1979b) *The Tasks of Teaching and Learning in Classrooms*, R + D rep. no. 4103. Austin, University of Texas.

EISNER, E. (1983) 'Can educational research inform educational practice?', Paper presented to A.E.R.A., Montreal.

FISHER, C.W. *et al.* (1980) 'Teaching behaviours, academic learning time and student achievement: An overview', in DENHAM, C. and LIEBERMANN, A. (Eds) *Time to Learn*, Washington, National Institute of Education.

GAGNE, R.M. (1974) *Essentials of Learning and Instruction*, Hillsdale, Ill., Dryden Press.

GLASER, R. (1976) 'Cognitive psychology and instructional design', in KLAHR, D. (Ed.) *Cognition and Instruction*, Hillsdale, N.J., Lawrence Elrbaum Associates.

GLASER, R., PELLEGRINO, J.W. and LESGOLD, A.M. (1977) 'Some directions for a cognitive psychology of instruction', in LESGOLD, A.M. *et al.* (Eds) *Cognitive Psychology and Instruction*, New York, Plenum.

HAERTEL, G.D., WALBERG, H.J. and WEINSTEIN, T. (1983) 'Psychological models of educational performance: A theoretical synthesis of constructs', *Review of Educational Research, 53*, 1, pp. 75–91.

HARLEN, W. (1982) 'Matching', in RICHARDS, C. (Ed.) *New Directions in Primary Education*, Lewes, Falmer Press.

HMI (1982, 1983) 'Reports on particular schools', London, Department of Education and Science.

HMI (1978) *Primary Education in England*, London, HMSO.

HUNT, J. McV. (1961) *Intelligence and Experience*, New York, The Ronald Press.

JENSEN, A.R. (1974) *Educational Differences*, London, Methuen.

KARPLUS, R. (1975) *Proportional Reasoning and Control of Variables in Seven Countries*, Berkeley, C.A., Lawrence Hall of Science.

LOVELL, K. and SHAYER, M. (1978) 'The impact of the work of Piaget on science curriculum development', in GALLAGHER, J.M. and EASLEY, J.A. (Eds) *Knowledge and Development, Vol. 2: Piaget and Education*, New York, Plenum.

NORMAN, D.A. (1978) 'Notes towards a complex theory of learning', in LESGOLD, A.M. *et al.* (Eds) *Cognitive Psychology and Instruction*, New York, Plenum.

PLOWDEN (1967) *Children and Their Primary Schools*, London, HMSO.

RESNICK, L.B. (1976) 'Task analysis in instructional design: Some cases from mathematics', in KLAHR, D. (Ed.) *Cognition and Instruction*, Hillsdale, N.J., Lawrence Erlbaum Associates.

RESNICK, L. and FORD, W. (1981) *The Psychology of Mathematics for Instruction*, Hillsdale, N.J., Lawrence Erlbaum Associates.

SHAYER, M. and ADEY, P. (1981) *Towards a Science of Science Teaching*, London, Heinemann.

SIROTNIK, K.A. (1983) 'What you see is what you get — consistency, persistency and mediocrity in classrooms', *Harvard Educational Review, 53*, 1, pp. 16–31.

Does Educational Psychology Contribute to the Solution of Educational Problems?

(From Jacobsen, B., 1985, 'Does educational psychology contribute to the solution of educational problems?, in Claxton *et al.*, *Psychology and Schooling: What's the Matter?*, Bedford Way Papers, 25, pp. 62, 64, 65–7.)

This final extract raises an important question for these involved in the psychology of education. In the opening introduction to this chapter, claims were made that psychology contributed to teachers' understanding of children, their development and their learning. The article which follows questions some of the previously held assertions about the psychology of education and provides an indication of the current direction of much psychological study.

As with sociological study (p. 183) the classroom is becoming an important arena for psychological investigation, where the emphasis is upon attempting to interpret research findings in their social context. As Walkerdine (1985) suggests:

> Schooling and psychology have developed hand in hand: they have a joint and twin history. This means that when we look at schools we are not seeing a place where psychology is applied so much as a place where certain truths about children are continually produced.

In the past, Jacobsen argues, psychology's main contribution was the invention of labels. The pupil is 'gifted', 'retarded' or 'a high-or-low achiever'. These became categories for the teacher to use to explain problems in learning or development. They did not offer solutions however. Psychology, he believes dealt with individuals out of their social or historical contexts. Instead, he argues for psychology to emphasize human beings as changing subjects with capacities for doing something about their own situation. The influence of humanistic psychology and the work of Carl Rogers is of particular significance here (see the extract by Patterson on pp. 352–8).

Reference

WALKERDINE, V. (1985) 'Psychological knowledge and educational practice', in CLAXTON, G. *et al.*, *Psychology and Schooling: What's the Matter?*, Bedford Way Papers, 25, pp. 48–61.

The merits of educational psychology may be discussed from many angles. Imagine, however, that you were allowed to formulate only one question about it, which would be the most fruitful one? I would ask: '*Why should we have educational psychology at all?*' Or in other words: '*What is the good of educational psychology?*' Or: '*What good does educational psychology do?*'

The more one thinks about this question, the more difficult it is to find an answer. But an answer must be found. Otherwise any responsible person must favour the immediate abolition of all professorships, lectureships and other positions within educational psychology as well as corresponding curricula within teacher training and related areas.

Consider some of the words with which EP and other parts of psychology have 'enriched' our educational language: 'intelligence', 'high-ability', 'under-achiever', 'deprived childhood', 'emotional instability', 'low ego-control', 'level of aspiration', 'mentally deficient', 'backward reader', 'emotional blocking', 'learning disorder', 'deviant', 'late-developer', 'behaviour disruption', 'hyper-active'. What use can one make of such designations? What purposes could they serve?

It may be the case that terms like 'backward learner' and 'learning disorder', when first invented, served a human purpose. They may in the beginning have saved many pupils from the cane and led to a more humane treatment, for instance in a special class. Today, however, the terms do not function in that way. They have become easy categories for the teacher or the headteacher to apply in order to avoid disturbing and embarrassing problems. Put a label on a pupil and you have solved a problem. This pupil is 'retarded' or 'hyper-active' or 'an under-achiever', you may tell yourself, so he ought to get special treatment. The terms of EP are suitable instruments for categorizing and segregating pupils. They are less good instruments for arriving at a genuine understanding of pupils as human beings. And they are impossible instruments if the endeavour is to make pupils' life conditions better than they are at present.

The Fruitlessness of Traditional Psychology and Various Reactions to it

The very technical character of a discipline supposed to be about human beings may be responsible for educators' disappointment with psychology in general and EP in particular. That there is disappointment, or disillusion, I infer from the fact that within teacher training as well as within educational research in many of the Western countries, there has been a strong recent tendency to want to reduce the role of psychology. In connection with the attempts at reduction you hear arguments about psychology's lack of relevance or lack of fruitfulness for the problems of the classroom.

The decreased expectations as to what one may get from psychology at all, in particular from EP, appear to be an international phenomenon. Interestingly enough, though, there seem to be different national reactions to this emerging crisis of significance.

The main trend in the United Kingdom so far seems to be that psychology is maintained as it is, but that priority is given to other areas. In other words, when educationalists discover that psychology (especially EP) cannot solve their problems or tell them what happens in the classroom, they tend to leave it alone, and give priority either to sociology and philosophy or to a more practical focusing on methods, critical incidents and perhaps curriculum discussions. In this country, therefore, the emerging crisis or opposition is not primarily within psychology itself, it is between psychology and educational practice. Psychology has, one could say, a problem of justifying or legitimating its own existence.

In other countries you find a different pattern. In some parts of continental Europe, and rather strongly in the Scandinavian countries and West Germany, the crisis (or opposition) seems to have developed *within* psychology rather than *between* psychology and the rest. At some of the universities there, traditional psychology seems already to have come into discredit around 1970. At that time members of the general public and many young psychologists began to feel that what psychology had to say on the whole did not reflect the real world people were living in. Psychology, it was shown, dealt to a large degree with individuals abstracted from their social and historical contexts. When people's interplay with society was abstracted, it was thought, psychology came to give a false, ideological picture of real human lives. Furthermore, articles and textbooks in psychology were criticized for depicting human beings predominantly as passive objects to be manipulated, not as active, willing subjects able to co-determine their own fates.

In addition there were critical debates on the role of psychologists in society. Critics said that psychologists (together with psychiatrists) mainly performed destructive tasks of selection, i.e. naming different categories of 'deviants' and justifying their being put in various boxes.

In the mid-Seventies in Denmark much of the traditional psychological content (learning, perception, intelligence, motivation, etc.) was gradually discarded from university studies and teacher training. But there were still a lot of psychology lessons on the weekly timetables which were filled with various attempts to create alternatives to the traditional psychology. Two main trends among these alternatives can be distinguished.

The first is what could be called humanistic–therapeutic psychology, encompassing what is known as humanistic psychology in the United States together with some of its European predecessors and contemporaries within existentialist thought. In these classes students often talk about and analyze their own feelings, experiences, and problems. The focus is practical and personal rather than theoretical.

The other trend comprises various attempts to understand the individual as a social and historical phenomenon. These attempts are all related to Marxism. One school consists of authors from Soviet Marxism, i.e. authors codified and read in the Soviet Union and Eastern Europe (e.g. Rubinstein, Leontiew); another is based broadly on Western Marxism (for instance, Brückner, Krovoza, Ziehe). Authors in the latter school are trying to develop a Western Marxism and they are not read in Eastern Europe. The whole Marxist trend tends to be somewhat abstract and theoretical.

Feelings and experiences are rarely dealt with, although certain political activities may be connected to the theoretical studies.

There have been some difficulties connected with the attempts to develop these alternative psychologies. One is that to develop a new and substantial field of knowledge is a far bigger enterprise than is often first realized. Consequently, there has been a tendency to overestimate the contributions of some of the new schools. A certain tendency to look towards fashions and gurus has been noticeable and, together with that, a certain risk of superficiality in the quality of learning. An additional difficulty is the communication problem arising from the fact that people no longer read the same authors. On the other hand, when a science or a subject field dissolves or breaks down, as has been the case here, teachers and students alike are forced to focus upon basic problems and philosophical aspects of the field in question. This in itself tends to create a generation with sound theoretical and intellectual foundations.

The situation just described carries all the signs of a paradigm breakdown as described by Thomas Kuhn. There is first a normal science losing its credibility and then a vacuum with various schools competing for the terrain, each believing it has the strongest explanatory apparatus. A crisis comes about, according to Kuhn, when normal science is no longer able to explain the phenomena under investigation in a satisfactory way.

Towards a New Psychology?

It is time to approach an answer to the questions raised at the beginning of the article: 'Why should we have EP?' and: 'What would we miss if it were not there?'

For a start the administrative authorities would certainly miss a useful instrument for dividing the population up into a large number of categories corresponding in structure to the highly specialized division of labour in our society. And with the new development of psychological understanding as part of the pattern of soft control, the same authorities would probably miss a useful instrument for keeping the bottom layer of society in its place. But the ordinary teacher would miss very little. And the ordinary pupil might not miss anything at all.

In other words: society would miss an instrument for its frictionless technical functioning. But, as far as making society more truly human is concerned, it is hard to see any loss.

This leads to the question of whether EP could be fundamentally changed, which would mean also a fundamental change in psychology as a whole. I should emphasize that this is a project of a size which is easily underestimated. This is not however an excuse not to begin it. Two possible directions might be mentioned.

In order to be satisfactory from a human point of view, a new EP should be able to understand human lives in their real social, cultural and historical interrelationships, not as the postulated universal abstractions that now appear in the textbooks. Furthermore a new EP should develop a conceptual apparatus suitable for understanding human beings as changing subjects, with will, intentions, goals, aspirations, for a good life and a better world, together with capacities for doing something about their own situation. What traditional EP has never understood is that the EP you create helps to co-create in its turn the social world we all come to live in.

Reference

KUHN, T. (1970) *The Structure of Scientific Revolutions*, Second Ed. University of Chicago Press.

Index

The Study of Primary Education — A Source Book: Contents of Volumes 2, 3 and 4

Volume 2 The Curriculum

Volume 3 School Organization and Management

Volume 4 Classroom and Teaching Studies

Volume 2: The Curriculum

Is Primary Education Possible?
(From Oliver, D., 1984, 'Is primary education possible?', *Education 3–13*, 12, 2)

Ground Rules for a Community Curriculum
(From Midwinter, E., 1972, *Priority Education*, Penguin Books)

Education, Politics and the Neglect of Communality
(From Lawson, K., 1979, 'The politics of primary curricula', *Education 3–13*, 7, 1)

Bases for the Primary Curriculum
(From Blyth, A., 1984, *Development, Experience and Curriculum in Primary Education*, Croom Helm)

An Enabling Curriculum
(From Blyth, A., 1984, *Development, Experience and Curriculum in Primary Education*, Croom Helm)

A View of the Primary Curriculum
(From DES, 1980, *A View of the Curriculum*, HMSO)

2 'Official' Statements

Responsibilities for the Curriculum
(From DES, 1979, *Local Authority Arrangements for the School Curriculum*, HMSO)

Towards a Framework for the Curriculum
(From DES/Welsh Office, 1980, *A Framework for the School Curriculum*, HMSO)

Policy for the School Curriculum
(From DES/Welsh Office, 1981, *The School Curriculum*, HMSO)

The Organization and Content of the Primary Curriculum: A Note
(From DES, 1984, *The Organization and Content of the 5–16 Curriculum: A Note*, HMSO)

The Primary Curriculum: A National View
(From DES, 1985, *Better Schools*, HMSO)

The National Curriculum
(From DES, 1989, *From Policy To Practice*, HMSO)

HMI's Observations on the Primary Curriculum in England
(From DES, 1978, *Primary Education in England: A Survey by HM Inspectors of Schools*, HMSO)

The Primary Curriculum in Northern Ireland: General Considerations
(From DENI, 1980, *Primary Education*, HMSO)

The Primary Curriculum in Scotland: General Considerations
(From SED, 1980, *Learning and Teaching in P4 and P7*, HMSO)

HMI Observations on the First School Curriculum
(From DES, 1982, *Education 5 to 9*, HMSO)

3 Aims

Who Should Decide?
(From White, J., 1979, 'Aims and curricula: Do heads and teachers have the right to decide?', *Primary Education Review*, 7)

Primary Teachers' Aims
(From Ashton, P., 1978, 'What are primary teachers' aims?', in Richards, C. (Ed.) *Education 3–13, 1973–77*, Nafferton Books; and Ashton, P., 1981, 'Primary teachers' aims 1969–77', in Simon, B. and Willcocks, J. (Eds) *Research and Practice in the Primary Classroom*, Routledge and Kegan Paul)

4 Curriculum Issues

The Primary Curriculum: Perennial Questions and General Issues
(From Richards, C., 1981, 'The primary curriculum: Perennial questions and current issues', *Primary Education Review*, 12)

The Curriculum from 5–16: An HMI View
(From Richards, C., 1986, 'The curriculum from 5 to 16: Background content and some implications for primary education', *Education 3–13*, 13, 1; and Southworth, G. (Ed.) *Readings in Primary School Management*, Falmer Press)

Subjects, Specialist Teaching and Curriculum Overlay
(From Richardson, J., 1987, 'Subject to subjects', *Forum*, 29, 2)

Analyzing the Primary Curriculum
(From Alexander, R., 1984, *Primary Teaching*, Holt, Rinehart and Winston)

Continuity: Goals and Policies
(From Dean, J., 1980, 'Continuity', in Richards, C. (Ed.) *Primary Education: Issues for the Eighties*, A and C Black)

Continuity and Liaison: Primary-Secondary Practices
(From Findlay, F., unpublished manuscript)

Continuity Between Primary and Secondary Schools: A Proposal
(From Thomas, N. *et al.*, 1985, *Improving Primary Schools*, ILEA)

Primary-Secondary Transfer: The Experience of ILEA
(From ILEA, 1988, *Improving Secondary Transfer*, Bulletin 17, ILEA)

Continuities and Discontinuities in the Primary Curriculum
(From Blyth, W. and Derricott, R., 1985, 'Continuities and discontinuities in the primary curriculum', *Curriculum*, 6, 2)

The Range of the Primary Curriculum
(From DES, 1978, *Primary Education in England*, HMSO)

Curriculum Consistency
(From Richards, C., 1982, 'Curriculum consistency', in Richards, C. (Ed.) *New Directions in Primary Education*, Falmer Press)

Curriculum Diversity
(From Farquhar, C. *et al.*, 1987, 'Curriculum diversity in London infant schools', *British Journal of Educational Psychology*, 57)

Curricular Integration or Differentiation?
(From Dearden, R., 1976, *Problems in Primary Education*, Routledge and Kegan Paul)

Integration in the Curriculum: A Developmental View
(From Blyth, W., 1985, 'Integration in the curriculum: Some observations', in Day, C. *et al.* (Eds) *Prospects for Curriculum*, Association for the Study of the Curriculum)

The Problem of Match
(From DES, 1978, *Primary Education in England*, HMSO)

The Role of Assessment in 'Matching'
(From Harlen, W., 1982, 'The role of assessment in "matching"', *Primary Education Review*, 13)

Proposals for a National Assessment System
(From DES, 1988, *Task Group on Assessment and Testing: A Report*, HMSO)

Who's Afraid of Evaluation?
(From MacDonald, B., 1976, 'Who's afraid of evaluation?', *Education 3–13*, 4, 2)

An Accountability Model for Progressive Education
(From Elliott, J., 1979, 'Accountability, progressive education and school-based evaluation', *Education 3–13*, 7)

Approaches to Accountability at School Level
(From Becher, T. *et al.*, 1981, *Policies for Educational Accountability*, Heinemann)

An American Perspective on the Evaluation of the Primary Curriculum
(From Eisner, E., 1974, *English Primary Schools: Some Observations and Assessments*, National Association for the Education of Young Children)

School Self-Evaluation: Rationale, Scope and Participation
(From, Rodger, I. and Richardson, J., 1985, *Self-Evaluation for Primary Schools*, Hodder and Stoughton)

Factors Influencing Primary Schools' Effectiveness
(From ILEA, 1986, *The Junior School Project: A Summary of the Main Report*, ILEA)

How Do Teachers Plan?
(From McCutcheon, G., 1980, 'How do elementary teachers plan? The nature of planning and the influences on it', *The Elementary School Journal*, 81)

Curriculum Policy-Making
(From Garland, R., 1982, 'Curriculum policy-making in primary schools', in Richards, C. (Ed.) *New Directions in Primary Education*, Falmer Press)

Achievements in Primary Schools: Key Issues
(From Thomas, N., 1987, 'Achievement in primary schools: The Select Committee's Report', *Education 3–13*, 15, 2)

5 Other Aspects

Principles for Record-Keeping
(From Clift, P. *et al.*, 1981, *Record-Keeping in Primary Schools*, Macmillan)

Some Realities of Classroom Life
(From Jackson, P., 1968, *Life in Classrooms*, Holt-Rinehart)

Curriculum Schemes and Guidelines
(From Alexander, R., 1984, *Primary Teaching*, Holt, Rinehart and Winston)

The Place of 'Discovery Methods'
(From Bantock, G., 1969, 'Discovery methods', *Black Paper Two*, Critical Quarterly Society)

Learning How to Learn
(From Dearden, R., 1976, *Problems in Primary Education*, Routledge and Kegan Paul)

The Autonomy of the Primary School Teacher
(From Taylor, P. and Reid, W., 1973, 'Influence and change in the primary school', *Education 3–13*, 1, 1)

Curriculum Structure and Topic Work
(From Bonnett, M., 1986, 'Child-centredness and the problem of structuring project work', *Cambridge Journal of Education*, 16, 1)

The Curriculum — As Observed in Some Inner City Classrooms
(From Tizard, B. *et al.*, 1988, *Young Children at School in the Inner City*, Lawrence Erlbaum)

The Informal Curriculum
(From Blyth, W., 1984, *Development, Experience and Curriculum in Primary Education*, Croom Helm)

Messages Conveyed by Physical Forms
(From Evans, K., 1979, 'The physical form of the school', *British Journal of Educational Studies*, 27, 1)

Order and the Use of Space in Primary School Buildings
(From Cooper, I., 1982, 'The maintenance of order and use of space in primary school buildings', *British Journal of Sociology of Education*, 3, 3)

Gender Stereotyping: Another Aspect of the 'Hidden Curriculum'
(From Clarricoates, K., 1983, 'Some aspects of the "hidden curriculum" and interaction in the classroom', *Primary Education Review*, 17)

Learning at Home and at School
(From Atkin, J. and Goode, J., 1982, 'Learning at home and at school', *Education 3–13*, 10, 1)

Parents and the Curriculum
(From Tizard, J. *et al.*, 1982, 'Collaboration between teachers and parents in assisting children's reading', *British Journal of Educational Psychology*, 52)

The Primary Curriculum: Towards a World View
(From Blyth, W., 1984, *Development, Experience and Curriculum in Primary Education*, Croom Helm)

Index

The Study of Primary Education — A Source Book: Contents of Volumes 1, 3 and 4

Volume 3:
School Organization and Management

General Introduction

Compilers' Notes

Acknowledgments

Introduction

1 Roles and Responsibilities

Introduction

The Primary Head
(From Alexander, R., 1984, *Primary Teaching*, Holt Education)

Leadership in Primary Schools: The Role of the Head
(From DES (Welsh Office), 1985, *Leadership in Primary Schools*, HMI
Occasional Paper)

The Managerial Work of Primary Headteachers
(From Coulson, A.A., 1986, *The Managerial Work of Primary School
Headteachers*, Sheffield Papers in Education Management, No. 48,
Sheffield City Polytechnic)

Perceptions of Heads in Primary Schools
(From Southworth, G.W., 1987, 'Primary school headteachers and collegiality', in Southworth, G.W. (Ed.) *Readings in Primary School Management*, Falmer Press)

Primary Heads and School Culture
(From Nias, D.J., Southworth, G.W. and Yeomans, R., 1989, *Staff
Relationships in the Primary School: A Study of School Cultures*, Cassell)

The Deputy Head
(From Whitaker, P., 1983, *The Primary Head*, Heinemann)

The Role of the Deputy Head
(From DES (Welsh Office), 1985, *Leadership in Primary Schools*, HMI Occasional Paper)

A Deputy Head Observed: Findings from an Ethnographic Study
(From Nias, D.J., 1987, 'One finger, one thumb: A case study of the deputy head's part in the leadership of a nursery/infant school', in Southworth, G.W. (Ed.) *Readings in Primary School Management*, Falmer Press)

Class Teaching, Specialist Teaching and the Role of the Post-Holder
(From DES, 1978, *Primary Education in England*, HMSO)

The Duties of Teachers with Curricular Responsibilities
(From DES, 1982, *Mathematics Counts*, HMSO)

The Role of the Curriculum Post-Holder
(From Campbell, R., previously unpublished paper)

Curriculum Co-ordinators
(From The Third Report of the Education, Science and Arts Committee of the House of Commons, 1986, *Achievement in Primary Schools*, HMSO)

Teachers and Teaching
(From DES, 1985, *Education Observed: Good Teachers*, HMSO)

Moving Towards Partnership
(From Sallis, J., 1988, *Schools, Parents and Governors: A New Approach to Accountability*, Routledge)

2   School Organization and Management

Introduction

Managing the School as an Organization
(From ILEA, 1985, *Improving Primary Schools*, ILEA)

Characteristics of Good School Organization
(From DES, 1987, *Primary Schools: Some Aspects of Good Practice*, HMSO)

Curriculum Management and Organization: The Collegiate Approach
(From Wallace, M., 1988, 'Towards a collegiate approach to curriculum management in primary and middle schools', *School Organization*, 8, 1)

The Culture of Collaboration
(From Nias, D.J., Southworth, G.W. and Yeomans, R., 1989, *Staff Relationships in the Primary School: A Study of School Cultures*, Cassell)

Teacher Isolation and School Organization and Culture in the Small Rural School
(From Bell, A. and Sigsworth, A., 1987, *The Small Rural Primary School*, Falmer Press)

Inside Primary School Organization
(From Pollard, A., 1985, *The Social World of the Primary School*, Holt, Rinehart and Winston)

Supply, Temporary and Part-Time Teachers: Partial Members of the School?
(From Nias, D.J., 1989, *Primary Teachers Talking*, Routledge)

Classes: The Fundamental Unit of Organization
(From The Third Report of the Education, Science and Arts Committee of the House of Commons, 1986, *Achievement in Primary Schools*, HMSO)

Vertical Grouping
(From Lee, J., 1984, 'Vertical grouping in the primary school', *School Organization*, 4, 2)

Small Rural Schools and Peer Groups
(From Bell, A. and Sigsworth, A., 1987, *The Small Rural Primary School*, Falmer Press)

The Ages at which Children Enter School
(From The Third Report of the Education, Science and Arts Committee of the House of Commons, 1986, *Achievement in Primary Schools*, HMSO)

Local Education Authority Admission Policies and Practices
(From Sharp, C., 1987, 'Local education authority admission policies and practices', in *Four Year Olds in School: Policy and Practice*, NFER/SCDC)

Special Educational Needs in Infant Classes
(From Lewis, A., 1986, 'Meeting special educational needs in infant classes: A discussion of evidence from HMI reports on individual schools', *School Organization*, 6, 2)

Meeting Individual Needs: Towards a Whole School Response
(From Ainscow, M. and Muncy, J., 1989, *Meeting Individual Needs*, David Fulton)

Parents and Other Voluntary Helpers
(From The Third Report of the Education, Science and Arts Committee of the House of Commons, 1986, *Achievement in Primary Schools*, HMSO)

Parents and Partnership
(From Arkinstall, M., 1987, 'Towards a partnership: The Taylor Report, school government and parental involvement', in Lowe, R. (Ed.) *The Changing Primary School*, Falmer Press)

Parent-School Relationships
(From Tizard, B., Blatchford, P., Burke, J., Farquhar, C. and Plewis, I., 1988, *Young Children at School in the Inner City*, Lawrence Erlbaum)

Schools, Governors and Parents
(From Sallis, J., 1988, *Schools, Parents and Governors: A New Approach to Accountability*, Routledge)

3 Professional and School Development

Introduction

Staff Development
(From Schools Council, 1983, *Primary Practice*, Methuen Educational)

Headship Development
(From Coulson, A.A., 1988, 'Headship development through personal and professional growth', in Clarkson, M.W. (Ed.) *Emerging Issues in Primary Education*, Falmer Press)

Developing Collegiality Through Management Development
(From Wallace, M., 1988, 'Towards a collegiate approach to curriculum management in primary and middle schools', *School Organization*, 8,1)

Staff Relationships and Teacher Education
(From Nias, D.J., Southworth, G.W. and Yeomans, R., 1989, *Staff Relationships in the Primary School: A Study of School Cultures*, Cassell)

Learning in Staffrooms
(From Nias, D.J., 1989, *Primary Teachers Talking*, Routledge)

In-service Education for Teachers of Young Children
(From Abbott, L., 1987, 'In-service education for teachers of young children', in *Four Year Olds in School: Policy and Practice*, NFER/SCDC)

School Development Plans
(From ILEA, 1985, *Improving Primary Schools*, ILEA)

Characteristics of School Development Plans
(From Holly, P.J. and Southworth, G.W., 1989, *The Developing School*, Falmer Press)

Issues Arising from School Development Plans
(From Campbell, P., 1987, report prepared for Suffolk Education Authority)

Self-Evaluation for School Development
(From Rodger, I.A.S. and Richardson, J.A.S., 1985, *Self-Evaluation for Primary Schools*, Hodder and Stoughton)

Evaluation for the Developing Primary School: Learning from GRIDS
(From Holly, P.J., 1987, 'Evaluation for the developing primary school', in Southworth, G.W. (Ed.) *Readings in Primary School Management*, Falmer Press)

Teacher Appraisal: Contexts and Elements
(From Day, C., Whitaker, P. and Wren, D., 1987, *Appraisal and Professional Development in Primary Schools*, Open University Press)

Appraisal as Teacher Learning and Change
(From Day, C., Whitaker, P. and Wren, D., 1987, *Appraisal and Professional Development in Primary Schools*, Open University Press)

Learning and Teacher Appraisal
(From Dadds, M., 1987, 'Learning and teacher appraisal: The heart of the matter', in Southworth, G.W. (Ed.) *Readings in Primary School Management*, Falmer Press)

Effective Schools
(From Mortimore, P., 1988, *School Matters*, Open Books)

Index

The Study of Primary Education — A Source Book: Contents of volumes 1, 2 and 4

Volume 4: Classroom and Teaching Studies

General Introduction

Compilers' Notes

Acknowledgments

Introduction: Classroom and Teaching Studies

1 Teachers and Teaching

Towards a Revitalized Pedagogy
(From Simon, B., 1981, 'Why no pedagogy in England?', in Simon, B. and Taylor, W. (Eds) *Education in the Eighties: The Central Issues*, Batsford)

Teaching Styles
(From Bennett, N. *et al.*, 1976, *Teaching Styles and Pupil Progress*, Open Books)

Exploratory and Didactic Teaching
(From DES, 1978, *Primary Education in England: A Survey by HM Inspectors of Schools*, HMSO)

Teaching Styles: An Alternative Typology
(From Galton, M., 1982, 'Strategies and tactics in junior school classrooms', in Richards, C. (Ed.) *New Directions in Primary Education*, Falmer Press)

Dilemmas of Schooling and Formal/Informal Teaching
(From Berlak, A. and H., 1981, *Dilemmas of Schooling: Teaching and Social Change*, Methuen)

Teaching Styles and Children's Progress
(From Bennett, N. *et al.*, 1976, *Teaching Styles and Pupil Progress*, Open Books)

Teaching Styles and Pupil Progress: A Re-analysis
(From Aitkin, M. *et al.*, 1981, 'Teaching styles and pupil progress: A re-analysis', *British Journal of Educational Psychology*, 51, 2)

Teaching Styles and Children's Progress: Results from ORACLE
(From Galton, M. and Simons, B. (Eds) 1980, *Progress and Performance in the Primary Classroom*, Routledge and Kegan Paul)

Formal and Informal Teaching: What is More Effective?
(From Gray, J. and Satterley, D., 1981, 'Formal or Informal: A reassessment of the British evidence', *British Journal of Educational Psychology*, 51, 2)

Inside Primary Classrooms: A View from ORACLE
(From Simon, B., 1980, 'Inside the primary classroom', *Forum*, 22, 3)

Informal Primary Education: Teachers' Accounts
(From Nias, D.J., 1988, in Blyth, W. *Informal Primary Education Today: Essays and Studies*, Falmer Press)

Teaching Modes
(From Rowland, S., 1984, *The Enquiring Classroom*, Falmer Press)

Handling Classroom Complexity
(From Desforges, C. and Cockburn, A., 1987, *Understanding the Mathematics Teacher*, Falmer Press)

Vision and Reality of the Primary Classroom
(From Galton, M., 1989, *Teaching in the Primary School*, Fulton)

2 Children and Learning

Children's Behaviour in Junior School Classrooms
(From Boydell, D., 1975, 'Pupil behaviour in junior classrooms', *British Journal of Educational Psychology*, 45, 2)

Classroom Tasks
(From Bennett, N. *et al.*, 1984, *The Quality of Pupil Learning Experiences*, Lawrence Erlbaum)

Classroom Tasks: A Response
(From Pollard, A., 1985, *The Social World of the Primary School*, Holt)

Curriculum Provision: Priorities and Consistencies
(From Alexander, R.J., 1984, *Primary Teaching*, Holt)

Opportunity to Learn
(From Bennett, N., 1987, 'The search for the effective teacher', in Delamont, S. (Ed.) *The Primary School Teacher*, Falmer Press)

Time and Structure for Children to Write
(From Calkins, L.M., 1983, *Lessons from a Child*, Heinemann)

Children with Special Educational Needs
(From Croll, P. and Moses, D., 1985, *One in Five: The Assessment and Incidence of Special Educational Needs*, Routledge and Kegan Paul)

Society in the Classroom
(From Pollard, A., 1985, *The Social World of the Primary School*, Holt)

Making Sense of School
(From Jackson, M., 1987, 'Making sense of school', in Pollard, A. (Ed.) *Children and Their Primary Schools*, Falmer Press)

Starting School
(From Barrett, G., 1986, *Starting School: An Evaluation of the Experience*, Centre for Applied Research, University of East Anglia)

Gender and the Classroom
(From French, J.C., 1986, 'Gender in the classroom', *New Society*, 7 March)

Gender and the Classroom
(From Clarricoates, K., 1987, 'Child culture at school; A clash between gendered worlds', in Pollard, A. (Ed.) *Children and Their Primary Schools*, Falmer Press)

The Intellectual Search of Young Children
(From Tizard, B. and Hughes, M., 1987, 'The intellectual search of young children', in Pollard, A. (Ed.) *Children and Their Primary Schools*, Falmer Press)

Children's Control of Learning
(From Rowland, S., 1984, *The Enquiring Classroom*, Falmer Press)

Understanding Classroom Effectiveness
(From Mortimore, P. *et al.*, 1988, *School Matters*, Open Books)

Young Children's Attainment and Progress in School
(From Tizard, B. *et al.*, 1988, *Young Children at School in the Inner City*, Lawrence Erlbaum Associates)

The Effects of Streaming in the Primary School
(From Barker-Lunn, J., 1970, *Streaming in the Primary School*, NFER)

Health and Stress in the Classroom
(From Pollard, A., 1985, *The Social World of the Primary School*, Holt)

Developing Teaching
(From Calkins, L.M., 1983, *Lessons from a Child*, Heinemann)

Teachers' Problems with Children's Problems
(From Desforges, C. and Cockburn, A., 1987, *Understanding the Mathematics Teacher*, Falmer Press)

Craftsmanship and Artistry in Teaching
(From Nias, D.J., 1989, *Primary Teachers Talking: A Study of Teaching as Work*, Routledge)

3 Teachers as Researchers

Research as a Basis for Teaching
(From Stenhouse, L., 1985, 'Research as a basis for teaching', in Rudduck, J. and Hopkins, D. (Eds) *Research as a Basis for Teaching: Readings from the Work of Lawrence Stenhouse*, Heinemann)

Action Research: A Definition
(From Elliott, J., 1981, *Action Research: A Framework for Self-Evaluation in Schools*, Cambridge Institute of Education)

Action Research in Action
(From Bassey, M., 1986, 'Does action research require sophisticated research methods?', in Hustler, D. *et al.*, *Action Research in Classrooms and Schools*, Allen and Unwin)

Teaching as Finding Out
(From Armstrong, M., 1981, 'The case of Louise and the painting of the landscape', in Nixon, J. *A Teachers Guide to Action Research*, Grant MaIntyre)

Learning About the Classroom Through Diary Keeping
(From Enright, L., 1981, 'The diary of a classroom', in Nixon, J. *A Teacher's Guide to Action Research*, Grant MaIntyre)

Discovering About Discovery Learning Through Classroom Enquiry
(From Hulse, Y., 1988, 'Discovering discovery learning', in Conner, C. *Topic and Thematic Work in the Primary and Middle Years*, Cambridge Institute of Education)

Responsibility in Learning
(From Fraser, A., 1987, 'Sometimes they know themselves better than we do maybe'. Unpublished MA thesis, University of East Anglia)

Studying Classroom Organization
(From Groarke, J. *et al.*, 1986, 'Towards a more open classroom', in Hustler, D. *et al.*, *Action Research in Classrooms and Schools*, Allen and Unwin)

Reflective Teaching in Action
(From Southworth, P., 1987, 'Happy talk', *Cambridge Journal of Education*, 17,3)

The Effect of Teacher Enquiry on the Child
(From Pickover, D., 1984, 'Recognising individual needs', in Thompson, A. and L. (Eds) *What Learning Looks Like*, Longman for the Schools Council)

Classroom Enquiry as a Way of Understanding Learning
(From Rowland, S., 1986, 'An approach to understanding children', in Hustler, D. *et al.*, *Action Research in Classrooms and Schools*, Allen and Unwin)

Using Observation to Learn about the Classroom
(From Siegan-Smith, N., 1984, 'Talking counts', in Thompson, A. and L. (Eds) *What Learning Looks Like*, Longman for the Schools Council)

Teachers Working Together in School Through Action Research
(From Day, C., 1986, 'Sharing practice through consultancy: Individual and whole school staff development in the primary school', in Holly, P. and Whitehead, D., *Classroom Action Research Bulletin*, 7, Cambridge Institute of Education)

The Meaning of Reflective Teaching
(From Pollard, A. and Tann, S., 1987, *Relective Teaching in the Primary School*, Cassell)

What is Appealing about Action Research?
(From Cummings, C. and Hustler, D., 1986, 'Issues in action research', in Hustler, D. *et al.*, *Action Research in Classrooms and Schools*, Allen and Unwin)

A Teacher's Learning
(From Waterson, M., 1984, 'However do they do it?', in Thompson, A. and L. (Eds) *What Learning Looks Like*, Longman for the Schools Council)

Index

The Study of Primary Education — A Source Book: Contents of Volumes 1, 2 and 3